Impossible Persons

Linguistic Inquiry Monographs
Samuel Jay Keyser, general editor

A complete list of titles printed in the Linguistic Inquiry Monograph series appears at the back of this book.

Impossible Persons

Daniel Harbour

The MIT Press
Cambridge, Massachusetts
London, England

© 2016 Massachusetts Institute of Technology

All rights reserved. No part of this book may be reproduced in any form by any electronic or mechanical means (including photocopying, recording, or information storage and retrieval) without permission in writing from the publisher.

This book was set in Times Roman and Syntax-Roman by the author.

Library of Congress Cataloging-in-Publication Data
Names: Harbour, Daniel, author.
Title: Impossible persons / Daniel Harbour.
Description: Cambridge, MA : The MIT Press, [2016] | Series: Linguistic
  Inquiry Monographs | Includes bibliographical references and index.
Identifiers: LCCN 2016007201 | ISBN 9780262034739 (hardcover : alk. paper) |
  ISBN 9780262529297 (pbk. : alk. paper)
Subjects: LCSH: Grammar, Comparative and general—Person. | Grammar,
  Comparative and general—Number. | Grammar, Comparative and
  general—Pronoun. | Grammar, Comparative and general—Morphosyntax. |
  Semantics. | Universal grammar.
Classification: LCC P240.85 .H37 2016 | DDC 415/.5—dc23 LC record available at
https://lccn.loc.gov/2016007201

Why be difficult, when, with just a little more effort, you can be downright impossible?
—Sidney Harbour, my grandfather

Contents

Series Foreword   xi
Acknowledgments   xiii
Abbreviations and Notation   xv

1   **In a Nutshell**   **1**
     1.1   Three Theses   1
     1.2   Methods   5

2   **The Path to Partition**   **7**
     2.1   Introduction   7
     2.2   A Problematic Problem   8
     2.3   A Problem with Promise   17
     2.4   Alternatives   30
     2.5   Conclusion   38

3   **The Partition Problem**   **39**
     3.1   Introduction   39
     3.2   The Full Problem   40
     3.3   Empirical Domain   44
     3.4   Partitions Illustrated   50
     3.5   Conclusion   64

4   **The Partition Problem Solved**   **65**
     4.1   Introduction   65
     4.2   Elements of the Solution   67
     4.3   Solution of the Partition Problem   78
     4.4   ∅   95
     4.5   The Partition Element Problem   97
     4.6   Conclusion   98

5 Morphological Composition 101
- 5.1 Introduction 101
- 5.2 Clusivity 103
- 5.3 Second and General First Person 113
- 5.4 Limits and Constraints 121
- 5.5 Conclusion 128

6 Number and the Functional Sequence 129
- 6.1 Introduction 129
- 6.2 Lattice Diagrams 130
- 6.3 Partitions with Number 133
- 6.4 Two Semantic Asides 146
- 6.5 Interfaces 153
- 6.6 Conclusion 168

7 Spaces, Objects, Paths 169
- 7.1 Introduction 169
- 7.2 Empirical Case 170
- 7.3 Theoretical Underpinnings 178
- 7.4 Conclusion 185

8 Oldfangled *and* 187
- 8.1 Introduction 187
- 8.2 Interlinguistic Adequacy 188
- 8.3 Intralinguistic Adequacy 199
- 8.4 The Challenge of Mixed Partitions 210
- 8.5 Conclusion 216

9 The Form of the Phi Kernel 217
- 9.1 Introduction 217
- 9.2 Operations 217
- 9.3 Order 219
- 9.4 Combinatorics 220
- 9.5 Valence 222
- 9.6 Cognition and Evolution 228
- 9.7 Conclusion 232

10 Conclusion 233

A Empirical Appendices 235
- A.1 Preponderant Syncretism in Georgian 235
- A.2 Nonstandard Tripartitions? 237

B	**Formal Appendices**		**249**
	B.1	Zero Bottoming	252
	B.2	π-Internal Composition	257
	B.3	Larger Ontologies	259
	B.4	Privative Features	259
	B.5	Number: Formal Details	262

Notes 265
References 287
Index 307

Series Foreword

We are pleased to present the seventy-fourth volume in the series *Linguistic Inquiry Monographs*. These monographs present new and original research beyond the scope of the article. We hope they will benefit our field by bringing to it perspectives that will stimulate further research and insight.

Originally published in limited edition, the *Linguistic Inquiry Monographs* are now more widely available. This change is due to the great interest engendered by the series and by the needs of a growing readership. The editors thank the readers for their support and welcome suggestions about future directions for the series.

Samuel Jay Keyser
for the Editorial Board

Acknowledgments

This book happened by accident.

In 2011, I was a visiting fellow at New York University. To round off the lecture series I was giving on phi features, I had two talks planned on person. The first, which I had just given, catalogued problems. The second, due the next day, would show why past solutions, my own included, were wanting. But my plan to push the field backward went into reverse, as, over coffee and goading from David Adger and Stephanie Harves, a solution took up residence on my napkin.

My thanks, therefore, go first and foremost to David and Stephanie for their midwifery, to Stephanie and Alec Marantz for arranging the fellowship, and to the British Arts and Humanities Research Council for funding the research and trip. (The napkin, spruced up, appears on pages 98–99.)

Either side of that coffee, the ideas reported below had slow gestation, then long development. I started thinking about person in 2004 and first attempted a solution in 2006, at a conference in Leipzig. An initial write-up of the current ideas emerged in 2012, but, at 60 pages, it was a little dense and I resolved to spell out the specifics in more detail. This book is the result.

Since 2004, I have doubtless come to owe thanks to many more people than I will remember to name here. To those I fail to list, I offer not only thanks, but apologies.

Earlier versions of this book received extremely helpful attention from Jonathan Bobaljik, Elizabeth Cowper, Daniel Currie-Hall, Terje Lohndal, three reviewers, and, at the 60-page stage, from David Adger and Linnaea Stockall. I also thank two research assistants, Kyle Helke and Itamar Kastner, for very valuable input.

For data and related discussion, I am indebted to the foregoing as well as to David Aaron, Klaus Abels, Rusiko Amirejibi, Sylvia Blaho, Pavel Caha, Wallace Chafe, María-Cristina Cuervo, Roberta D'Alessandro, Noriko Davidson, Mark Donohue, Helder Ferreira, Bettina Gruber, Heidi Harley, Léa

Nash, Andrew Nevins, Justin Nuger, Roumyana Pancheva, ʻŌiwi Parker Jones, Isabella Pederneira, David Pesetsky, Alexander Popiel, Ian Roberts, Peter Svenonius, Dániel Szeredi, Tuệ Trịnh, Jochen Trommer, Alex Trueman, Kevin Tuite, Bert Vaux, and Tom Weir.

Preliminary versions of this work were presented at New York University, as already mentioned, and at the University of Cambridge, University of Toronto, Universitetet i Tromsø, and the 2013 LOT Summer School in Groningen.

The work was funded by the Arts and Humanities Research Council under grant AH/G019274/1, Project א (Atomic Linguistic Elements of Phi), Subproject ק (Questions Of Person).

Finally, if, at any point, visual aspects of the presentation fail to excite your displeasure, then, like me, you may owe thanks to members of tex.stackexchange.com.

Abbreviations and Notation

The following abbreviations are used in the text and examples. For the most part, I adopt the descriptive terminology that is conventional for a particular language or family (and some semantic overlap results, between aorist, past, and preterite for instance). Some terms (e.g., *minimal*) have two abbreviations, a longer one (MIN) when the term makes a passing appearance, and a shorter form (M) when it is used repeatedly and the longer form would be intrusive. Two abbreviations, C and M, are ambiguous, but one or both meanings are confined to particular languages.

¯	set-theoretic complement; negation of gloss (see also H̄, Q̄, S̄)
′	other authors' features (F′ versus my F)
∃3	affix registering presence of a third person argument
¬∃3	affix registering absence of a third person argument
1	first person
2	second person
3	third person
α, β	variables over values + and −
γ	gender head
π	person head
φ	root phi node, base of extended projection
χ	spatial head
Ψ	pseudo
Ψs	pseudosingular
ω	number head
A	agent
A	augmented (Kunwinjku; otherwise AUG)

ABS	absolutive
ACC	accusative
AFF	affirmative
AGT	agent marker
AN	animate
AOR	aorist
APPL	applicative
ART	article
ASP	aspect
ASSOC	associative
AUG	augmented (see also A)
AUX	auxiliary
BAS	noninverse (see also INV)
BEN	benefactive
C	common (mixed masculine and feminine) gender (!Ora)
C	conjunct
CAUS	causative
CL	clitic
CNT	continuous
COP	copula
D	dative argument
D	dual
DAT	dative
DEF	definite
DEFOC	defocused
DEIC	deictic
DEM	demonstrative
DIM	diminutive
DIR	directional
DIST	distal
EL	the linker *el* (Palauan)
EMPH	emphatic
EN	the suffix *en* (Yiddish)
ERG	ergative

EX	exclusive (generally, 1EX first person exclusive)
F	feminine (see also FP, FS)
FP	feminine plural
FS	feminine singular
FUT	future
GEN	genitive
Ħ	nonhuman
HAB	habitual
HON	honorific
HORT	hortative
ĦS	nonhuman singular
IMP	imperative
IMPF	imperfective
IMPRS	impersonal
IN	inclusive (generally, 1IN first person inclusive)
INAN	inanimate
INTNS	intensifier
INTR	intransitive
INV	Kiowa-Tanoan inverse (S, D, or P, depending on noun class)
IRR	irrealis
ITER	iterative
LOC	locative
M	masculine (see also, MP, MS)
M	minimal (Kunwinjku; otherwise MIN)
MIN	minimal (see also M)
MOD	modal
MP	masculine plural
MS	masculine singular
N	neuter (see also NP, NS)
NEG	negative
NMLZ	nominalizer
NOM	nominative
NP	neuter plural
NRPST	near past

NS	neuter singular
O	object
OBL	oblique
OBV	obviative
P	plural
PART	participle
PASS	passive
PAT	patient
PC	paucal
PF	perfective
POSS	possessive
PRES	present
PRET	preterite
PROG	progressive
PST	past
PV	preverb
Q	question, or interrogative, marker
Q̄	nonquestion, or affirmative, marker
REFL	reflexive
REL	relative
REM	remote past
S	subject
s	singular
s̄	nonsingular (P or D/P or other, depending on the language)
STAT	stative
SUB	subordinate
SUBJ	subjunctive
TERM	terminative
THM	theme
TR	transitive
U	unit augmented

1 In a Nutshell

1.1 Three Theses

Person seems quite innocuous, semantically. There's me and there's you, and sometimes we get together and sometimes we're joined by others. And that's about it. However, Zwicky, in a famous paper of 1977, asked why languages with three persons always treat 'you and us' as a form of *us*, not a form of *you*. And since then, proposed inventories of person features have uniformly failed to generate all and only the attested person systems, consistently invoking ad hoc devices, such as filters or geometries, to trim the generative excess. But to override generative capacity is to undercut explanatory power. So, in a deep sense, Zwicky's problem remains unsolved almost forty years after it was first posed.

This failure has arisen, I believe, because the enterprise has been largely misconceived. It has relied on the view, inherited perhaps from formal logic, that features denote first-order predicates, their combinations, conjunctions, and their values, one-place truth functors (negation and assertion). However, if we accept that there are *wh* features (Chomsky 1977) and that questions have the semantics of partitions (Higginbotham 1993), then it has been clear for a long time that some features are not predicates, but operators that induce partitions of—in this case Boolean or closely related—lattices or their atoms.

I contend that previous accounts of person have overgenerated because their feature inventories have been too large, and that their inventories have been too large because they have not appreciated that person features denote actions by sets on other sets (see Link 1983 and subsequent work on plurals, in which spirit, I will talk of actions by lattices on other lattices).

The current study aims to reframe the field's empirical perspective on person and to reshape its theoretical understanding of what features are and how they work. Central to this project are three core theses concerning the data that should be subsumed under the rubric of "person," the features that a theory of person should posit, and the broader metatheory in which such posits should be embedded.

The data and principles of the investigation are laid out in chapters 2 and 3. These center on the following empirical thesis:

Empirical thesis

The primary objects of study for person are partitions, not syncretisms. The relevant partitions are manifested in pronouns, clitics, agreement, spatial deictics, object deictics, directionals, and verbs of motion.

More fully, I take the core explicandum of a theory of person features to be a generalized version of Zwicky's problem, asking in how many ways languages could configure their person systems, in how many they do, and, if there is shortfall, why.

Chapter 2 argues that paradigms, though a frequent focus of studies of person, especially language-particular ones, ought, in fact, to be relegated to second place. The fundamental object of study should be the partition: the total set of distinctions that a language makes within its pronouns, its spatial deictics, or the other domains listed in the empirical thesis. Insofar as paradigms are useful, it is as a means of restituting underlying partitions from observables.

Using partitions, chapter 3 formulates Zwicky's problem in its most general form and presents its full empirical foundations. Zwicky focused on two particular tripartitions, that is, partitions with three elements. These differed with regard to whether the meaning 'you and us' was covered by *us* or *you*. A more general approach should consider, first, the other possible tripartitions, of which there are five, and, second, partitions of other sizes, such as the seven possible bipartitions and the unique monopartition, in which no difference between persons is made. In its general form, then, the core explicandum of the theory of person is:

Core explicandum

Of the fifteen possible partitions of four persons (exclusive, inclusive, second, third), which are attested, and why?

In formulating this problem, the breadth of data highlighted in the empirical thesis is crucial, as partitions of different sizes vary markedly in frequency across grammatical domains. Bipartitions, for instance, are more common as systems of spatial deixis than as systems of pronouns. However, the same theory could be developed on the basis of more conventional person data alone.

Chapter 4, the heart of the study, solves this generalized partition problem by defending the second core thesis:

Theoretical thesis
There are two person features (±author, ±participant). These, and their host head (π), denote lattices based on power sets of the underlying ontology. Their values denote complementary operations by which lattices act on one another.

As their names suggest, the two features reference the author and the author-cum-hearer. In contrast to previous accounts, there is no feature that references the hearer alone. The analysis therefore embeds a core asymmetry between the grammatical representation of author and hearer, and this will prove pivotal in solving Zwicky's problem, in both its original and its generalized forms.

Equally absent are bans and requirements on cooccurrences between features. There are no geometric dependencies or filters on particular feature–value pairs. Instead, occurrence of each feature is reified as an independent parameter, as is the order of semantic composition between them. As a result, the two features generate five possible systems: four subsets of features, with the full subset itself counted twice, according to the order in which the features compose. As per the core explicandum above, five is the number of partitions attested, and we will see that the account derives these and no others.

The economy of the proposal bears emphasis. The theory is built on a greater range of data than is traditionally considered by generative accounts of person. In consequence, it faces a greater risk of falsification. Instead, however, once it reifies in features a basic asymmetry between author and hearer, the results follow almost from an absence of assumptions. The features simply denote power sets that interact with each other and the power set of the ontology by basic lattice-theoretic operations, and, if unfettered by further constraints, the system derives all and only what it should.

Notwithstanding this minimality, the theory has substantial empirical coverage, as chapters 5–8 show.

Chapter 5 examines the morphology of person, focusing on compositional relations in which one person is apparently built off or shares a common basis with another. Although sporadic instances of this phenomenon have been noted previously—and in part motivated Zwicky's inquiry—the phenomenon has not received any systematic attention. The wide range of patterns that emerges includes some startling ones. Not only may inclusives subsume exclusives (a commonsense configuration, as inclusives subsume the referents of exclusives), but the reverse relations also hold: there are exclusives that are, morphologically, extensions of inclusives. And alongside the intuitive situation of inclusives built by crosscutting exclusive and second person (inclusives pool the referents of both), there are second persons built by crosscutting first person with third. Some of these patterns even cooccur in single languages. With bivalence central to its representations, the proposed two-feature inventory captures this empirical range with ease.

Chapter 6 turns to the interaction between person and number. Most basically, it shows that the proposed person features interact cleanly and neatly with number features to yield the full range of pronoun and agreement systems attested crosslinguistically. However, it also draws out a range of other consequences concerning syntactic interfaces. On the semantic side, these include defense of a phrase structure in which number dominates person and presentation of novel arguments addressing whether the denotation of plurals subsumes or excludes that of singulars. On the morphological side is an account of the tendencies for person exponents to precede number exponents and for person to be prefixal and number, suffixal.

Reprising a theme from the setting up of the core explicandum, chapter 7 articulates in more detail the connection between person and space. In addition to the semantic parity between person partitions (as traditionally understood) and (a subset of) spatial partitions, the chapter surveys a range of languages in which person and space show morphological nexuses, diachronically or synchronically. A sketch of the morphosemantics and morphosyntax of such deixes is presented, paralleling and supporting that of the preceding chapter.

Concluding the empirical portion of the study, chapter 8 compares the current proposal with previous accounts. The most straightforward argument for the present approach is that it is more parsimonious, less stipulative, and yet more explanatory: because it posits fewer features and fully exploits their combinatorial possibilities, it can eschew the additional posits and constraints that other accounts require and is free of the empirical and conceptual problems that they entrain. Nonetheless, alternative accounts frequently present language-specific arguments for their extra posits. The chapter examines the strongest of these. Whether morphological, supporting an inventory of more than two features, or semantic, supporting a feature that is hearer-based or otherwise defined, the case studies can all be reanalyzed and accommodated within the current approach.

Moving to a higher level, chapter 9 considers how the structure of the theory of person developed here should impact research into language and thought at a broader level. The discussion is based on the strong formal parallelisms between person and the theory of number explored in chapter 6. These are summarized under the third core thesis:

Metatheoretical thesis
Feature–value combinations represent actions on and by lattices. So understood, features are combinatorially free and lead the way to a general, category-independent conception of the atoms of linguistic representation.

Specifically, there are five formal commonalities between person and number at the featural level. First, the features that represent them are crucially bivalent. Second, they and their values denote lattices and actions on them: their logic is richer than the predicate calculus (first-order logic). Third and fourth, neither order of semantic composition nor cooccurrence between features or between features and values is extrinsically constrained: language optimally exploits the resources at its disposal. Fifth, "person features" do more than categorize persons (as pretheoretically understood): they are also the formal basis of the deixis of spaces, objects, and paths. Similarly, "number features" are not confined to grammatical number (as pretheoretically understood), but, are connected, at the featural level, with aspect and the integers.

These common characteristics suggest a template for future research. Where a predicate-based approach leads to problems of overgeneration, the remedy should not be to add extrinsic stipulations. Rather, on the one hand, we should seek a richer empirical base, broadening the semantics of the features themselves to move beyond pretheoretic categorical contrasts like person versus space, or number versus aspect, to more expansive, and hence parsimonious, ones. On the other hand, we should reexamine the mathematical underlay of the features we posit. If collections of features denote, not commutative conjunctions of predicates, but noncommutative applications of operations, then their generative capacity increases, leading, again, potentially, to a more parsimonious but more expressive theory.

With a smaller inventory of primitives at hand, we might begin to investigate the evolution of language from a different angle, asking what concepts a recursive syntactic system was primed to combine—hence, what language was originally, in some sense, for.

1.2 Methods

As described in the acknowledgments, this book has had a decade's gestation. Over that period, I spent many hours leafing through diverse and dusty tomes in public libraries and private collections (when more mannerly guests might have conversed with their hosts). These searches had two opposite aims: to falsify the generalizations that I believed to hold and to find examples that illustrate them with particular clarity. Further examples often arose serendipitously, on safari for other typological game. The ideas reported here thus grew organically and, although I kept track of monsters and models, I did not maintain records of the far greater numbers of languages that simply affirmed my generalizations.

As a result, this study is not a typology in the typologists' sense. Even if, like a typologist, I have surveyed a wide range of grammatical descriptions and, on occasion, sought additional data from speakers and fieldworkers, my aim has not been to produce fine-grained quantification of frequencies across a balanced sample of languages. Rather, building off such balanced typologies, I have aimed to develop a heterospective that transforms gradient rates of attestation into a categorical problem of the attested versus the unattested.

Against that backdrop, I have deliberately cherry-picked model examples. I have afforded monsters more attention than they might warrant in more statistical studies, as lone counterexamples can scupper theories that aim not to generate them. For models, I have placed the bar numerically higher, but not where a typologist might set it. Specifically, I take patterns that favor my theory seriously only when they are robust in the sense of occurring across a geographical, genetic, and grammatical range (where grammatical range encompasses metasyncretism across independent exponents and attestation in verbs and pronouns, or pronouns and spatial deictics, or other such pairs). I have not, however, sought to tie robustness to any numerical measure.

In other words, this investigation attempts to balance typology and theory, but it is, at heart, a typologically informed work of theory, rather than a theory of typological variation. Nonetheless, I hope that it will be of interest to both communities of researchers, and to others.

2 The Path to Partition

2.1 Introduction

The central problem of person, as I conceive it, makes two significant departures from much past work. On the one hand, paradigms and syncretisms, prime fare for many, are relegated to a secondary position. On the other, neglected data from deixis of spaces, objects, and paths play a central role. These two departures are addressed in this chapter and the next, respectively, setting up the problem that is then solved in chapter 4. The specific aim of this chapter is to define the concept of a partition and to argue for it as the central object of inquiry.

As a first step, section 2.2 shows that the kinds of data frequently adduced to motivate natural classes and, hence, features—namely, syncretisms and paradigms—are problematic. The nub of the problem is that every paradigm and every combination of syncretisms is attested. So, these data yield no obvious constraints on what is possible and which features are motivated. Though this does not entail that paradigms and syncretisms are evidentially nugatory, it does reveal that we need a means of marshaling the data productively.

Section 2.3 provides this marshaling by formalizing the notion of partition that is implicit in Zwicky's problem and in other work. Partitions are paradigms without accidents, that is, without the loss of distinctions that homophonous exponents or the action of morphological and phonological processes can cause. I propose that underlying partitions can be restituted from superficial paradigms by superposition. Adopting this approach, one can calculate the expected rates at which tripartitions, or three-person systems, should occur. (For ease of exposition, I confine calculations to tripartitions. Other partitions are reintroduced in the next chapter.)

Reality departs radically from expectations, however: with just a few exceptions, which, on inspection, prove unproblematic, all tripartitions but one are unattested. Moreover, the disparity between expected and actual attestation of tripartitions is demonstrably not an artifact of calculations nor attributable to historical chance or functional pressure (section 2.4). Therefore, focusing on partitions through the lens of superposition reveals a categorical property of person that demands explanation.

2.2 A Problematic Problem

2.2.1 First Steps

In the early days of generative grammar, person and other phi features had names that simply recapitulated labels of traditional grammatical taxonomy, like $\pm$I′, $\pm$II′, $\pm$III′ for first, second, and third persons.[1] However, by the 1970s, a variety of syntactic and morphological facts (e.g., Hale 1973, Silverstein 1976) had led to the appreciation that traditional labels were, in all likelihood, not primitive grammatical entities, but, to borrow chemical terminology, molecules built from the true atoms of morphosyntax. The morphologist's quest for atoms had begun.

Silverstein, for instance, posited $\pm$ego′ and $\pm$tu′, in order to capture the natural classes of persons with respect to ergative case marking. His facts are rather involved, but the utility of his features can be appreciated in relation to the person system of Tok Pisin, an English-lexified creole of Papua New Guinea (Foley 1986). In the dual, Tok Pisin pronouns make four distinctions, lexified from English, 'you', 'me', 'them', 'two', and 'fellow':

(1) *mitupela*   me and someone other than you
    yumitupela me and you
    yutupela   you and someone other than me
    emtupela   two people who are neither you nor me

These persons are traditionally called, respectively, first person exclusive, first person inclusive, second person, and third person, but, for brevity, I will often call them simply *exclusive*, *inclusive*, *second*, and *third*. The notion of exclusion (and inclusion) inherent in the terminology refers to whether the first person excludes (or includes) the person addressed. For instance, in *We earthlings are not like you aliens, but can't we all just get along?*, the first *we* is exclusive—it contrasts the earthling speaker(s) and the alien hearer(s)— but the second is inclusive—it calls for earthling–alien, or speaker–hearer, coexistence.

With Silverstein's features, these persons correspond to the following specifications:

(2) exclusive   *mi-tupela*   +ego′ −tu′
     inclusive   *yu-mi-tupela*   +ego′ +tu′
     second   *yu-tupela*   −ego′ +tu′
     third   *em-tupela*   −ego′ −tu′

The semantics of the feature combinations is straightforward. Exclusive is plus–minus because it includes the speaker (+ego′) but excludes the hearer (−tu′). Inclusive, by contrast, includes both (+ego′ +tu′). Similarly, second person refers to the hearer (+tu′) without the speaker (−ego′), and third person excludes both (−ego′ −tu′).

Additionally, this array of features captures two facets of the morphological composition of Tok Pisin pronouns. Exclusive and inclusive share the feature +ego′; correspondingly, their forms, *mitupela* and *yumitupela*, share the morpheme *mi*. Similarly, inclusive and second person share the feature +tu′, and their forms, *yumitupela* and *yutupela*, share the morpheme *yu*. Thus, Silverstein's features do dual service to the category of person, capturing the way in which semantics and morphology dovetail.

Contrastive features like Silverstein's had entered linguistic theory via phonology (Jakobson, Karcevsky, and Trubetzkoy 1958 [1971]), and among their earliest application to morphosyntactic categories were treatments of syncretism. In Jakobson's (1958 [1971]) analysis of Russian nominal case, for example, the collapse of two otherwise distinct cases in a given context was taken to show that these fall within the natural class defined by the value of some feature. True to this precedent, much work on phi features, including the seminal Hale 1973 and Silverstein 1976, has taken natural classes in morphology, and especially syncretism, as central sources of evidence (see, more recently, Noyer 1992, Kerstens 1993, Harley and Ritter 2002a, Benincà and Poletto 2005, Ackema and Neeleman 2013, among many others).

As a means of assessing the initial plausibility of a feature set, this is a reasonable procedure. However, if natural classes and syncretism count as evidence, then, at some point, it becomes incumbent on the field to ask two related questions about the general theoretical and empirical terrain.

First, once the field had more or less settled on a stock of features, it ought to have been asked whether that feature set represented a unique solution to the motivating empirical concerns or whether alternatives existed. That watershed moment was reached, I believe, with Noyer's (1992) dissertation, which provided feature theory with a foundation in broad typology complemented by language- and family-specific case studies. Thereafter, the field began to focus on questions subsidiary to the actual inventory, like the features' internal properties (valence) and their organization (hierarchy); see in particular Harley and Ritter 2002a.

Noyer's inventory of three features, ±author′, ±hearer′, ±participant′, essentially upheld Silverstein's proposals. The first two features were renamings of ±ego′ and ±tu′, illustrated above; and ±participant′, meaning 'does (not) include at least one of author and hearer', was also present in Silverstein's study, though more marginally. Noyer used ±participant′ in conjunction with ±author′ to capture the person distinctions of languages like English: third person is −author′ −participant′; second is −author′ +participant′, the nonauthor participant; and first person is +author′ +participant′, which subsumes both exclusive and inclusive because it must include the author, by dint of +author′, but merely may include the hearer, by dint of +participant′. (The combination +author′ −participant′ picks out no persons, as it specifies both presence and absence of the author.)

In purely logical terms, this inventory raises the issue of expressive adequacy, namely, whether any other sets of (three) features generate the person systems for which ±author′, ±hearer′, and ±participant′ are posited. In other words, had the field hit on *the* solution, or merely on one within a larger solution space? An uncomfortable redundancy gives this question extra edge: ±participant′ is not logically independent, but can be defined Booleanly in terms of the first two. To paraphrase the definitions in semiformal notation, +participant′ = +author′ +hearer′. Common considerations would favor an inventory without this redundancy. To my knowledge, neither the broad question nor the redundancy was ever addressed.

Suppose that alternative sets of descriptively adequate features do exist (which is correct; see chapter 8). The empirical worry would then arise that proponents of these alternatives might find different syncretisms in their favor. Which leads to the second general question that ought to have been asked, namely, what range of person syncretisms is attested worldwide.

The field might have been rather disquieted by the anarchic result, because, in the realm of person syncretism and paradigm shapes, anything goes. Indeed, among languages with three persons, there are some that display every possible syncretism. In Girawa (Gasaway, Lillie, and Sims 1977; figure 2.1), for example, singular object agreement differentiates all three persons (top row, *or–ot–ok*). However (middle row, left to right), agreement distinctions collapse for first and second person present continuous singular subjects (*ram–ram–ra*), as they do also for first and third singular benefactives (*mur–mus–mur*), and for second and third plural benefactives (*muk–mar–mar*). And present continuous

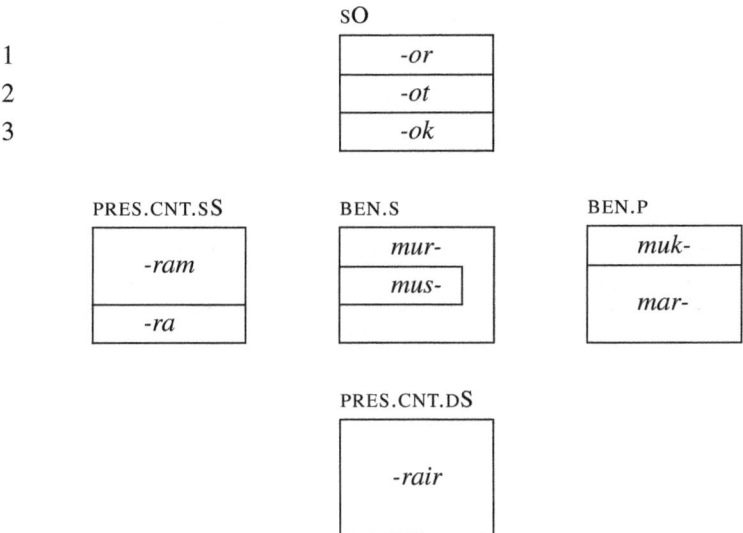

Figure 2.1
Three-person syncretisms (Girawa)

dual subject agreement loses person distinctions altogether (bottom row, *rair–rair–rair*). (Also in the Trans–New Guinea family, see Binumarien; Oatridge and Oatridge 1965.)

One finds the same variety at the familial level in Romance, allowing a broader range of grammatical phenomena (figure 2.2). At the two extremes, among numerous examples, we have the singular present indicative (top row) and subjunctive (bottom row) of the Italian for 'say': where the indicative has different forms for each person (*dic-o* 'I say', *dic-i* 'you say', *dic-e* 'he/she/it says'), the subjunctive collapses all of these into a single form (*dic-a* 'I say, you say, he/she/it says').

The middle row of the figure shows that every pairwise syncretism is also attested. Leftmost, French presents an instance of first and second patterning against third: in the present indicative of 'go', first and second person plural take one form of the root (*all-ons*, go-1P; *all-ez*, go-2P), whereas third person plural takes another (*v-ont*, go-3P). Singular imperfective desinences in Spanish present a different pattern: first and third consist simply of *a* (*tení-a* 'I/he/she/it was holding'), as against second person *as* (*tení-as* 'you.S were holding'). And, remaining with this verb but returning to suppletion in the present, first person shows one form of the root (*teng-o* 'I hold'), but second and third, patterning together, show another (*tien-es* 'you.S hold', *tien-e* 'he/she/it holds').

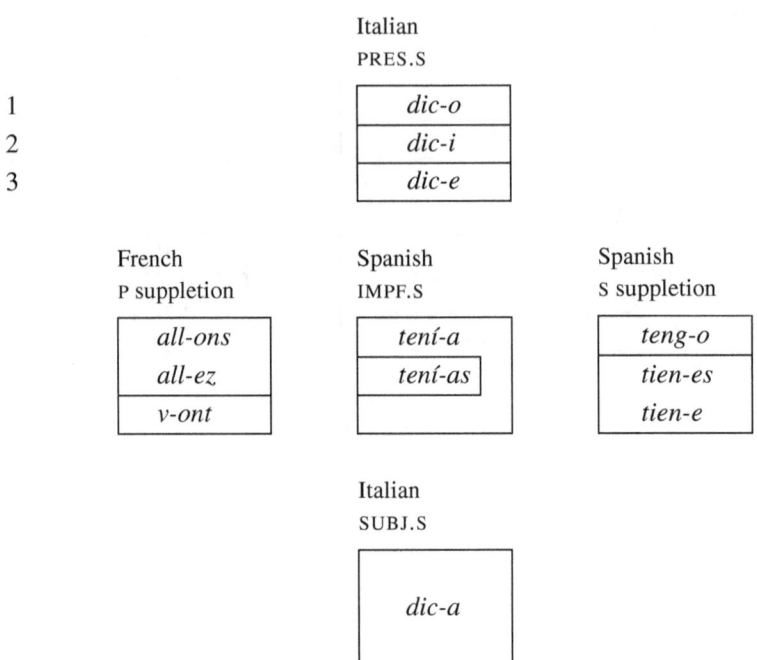

Figure 2.2
Three-person syncretisms (Romance)

Two methodological clarifications are needed at this point. First, when seeking syncretisms, I am interested in morphemes, not words. (If identity of words were the criterion, the Spanish imperfective would count as syncretism, but the present tense would not, leaving the distribution of root forms as a non-phenomenon, though it has been the subject of productive debate.) The utility of the morpheme has been recognized in so many frameworks that its legitimacy is not in doubt (e.g., Bloomfield 1933, Hockett 1947, Matthews 1972, Lieber 1980, Zwicky 1985, Halle and Marantz 1993, not to mention much descriptive work; see Anderson 2015 for an overview). That said, the exact location of morpheme boundaries can be debated, just as word boundaries can. So, throughout this study, I avoid examples reliant on obviously contentious decompositions and ensure that none of my generalizations are hostage to the reanalysis of single morphemes.

Second, several of the morphemes discussed in this chapter in particular have wider distributions than the discussion portrays. For instance, both *all* and *v* in the French example occur beyond the three forms just cited: *v* in all singular present indicatives, 1s *v-ais*, 2s *v-as*, 3s *v-a*; *all* in the infinitive *all-er* and all imperfectives, including 1s/2s *all-ais*, which repeat the syncretism of figure 2.2, and 3s *all-ait*. Such expansion and contraction of distribution does not speak against a person-based account of the forms that illustrate a particular syncretism. Rather, they show that person interacts with other factors. Even if one claims that person affects, say, the realization of tense, which, in turn, affects the placement of stress, which is the factor that immediately conditions the *v–all* alternation, this does not undermine the claim that the illustrative forms reflect a sensitivity to person, which, in consequence, show two persons patterning against a third. Like considerations apply to several of the examples in figures 2.2–2.3.

Syncretic saturation holds analogously for languages with more complex person systems. With exclusive, inclusive, second, and third at play, the range of possible syncretisms increases, as there are six ways of collapsing four persons down to a three-way distinction, and seven of collapsing to two.[2] Nonetheless, all are attested, as figure 2.3 shows.[3]

Given the potential range of person features (again, see chapter 8) and the saturated space of syncretisms, person—once seemingly innocuous—begins to present a significant analytic challenge. If order is to be found amid this profusion of data, then we need some means of marshaling the facts, that is, an anabasis from the peripheral phenomenon of syncretic classes to the generative core of person.

2.2.2 A Predictable Mess

Before proceeding, though, it is important to understand why the richness of the data should not leave us, like Moses's spies, daunted at the border. One might, after all, respond to the data by denying that there are features at all, or by accepting features but denying their universality. However, some standard generative views about the structure of the grammar and of learnability make this reaction unwarranted.

Consider, for concreteness, a model of the grammar in which syntax manipulates features and the output of those manipulations is then mapped onto phonetic signals, as in the Y-model of Chomsky 1981 together with the late insertion of Halle and Marantz 1993. On this approach, many accidents can befall the set of distinctions that a given feature inventory generates. First, there are postsyntactic operations on features, which might alter specifications, making feature sets identical though they were distinct in the syntax and remain so in the semantics. Second, distinct feature sets might be mapped onto nondistinct phonemic strings, either because their exponents are phonetically

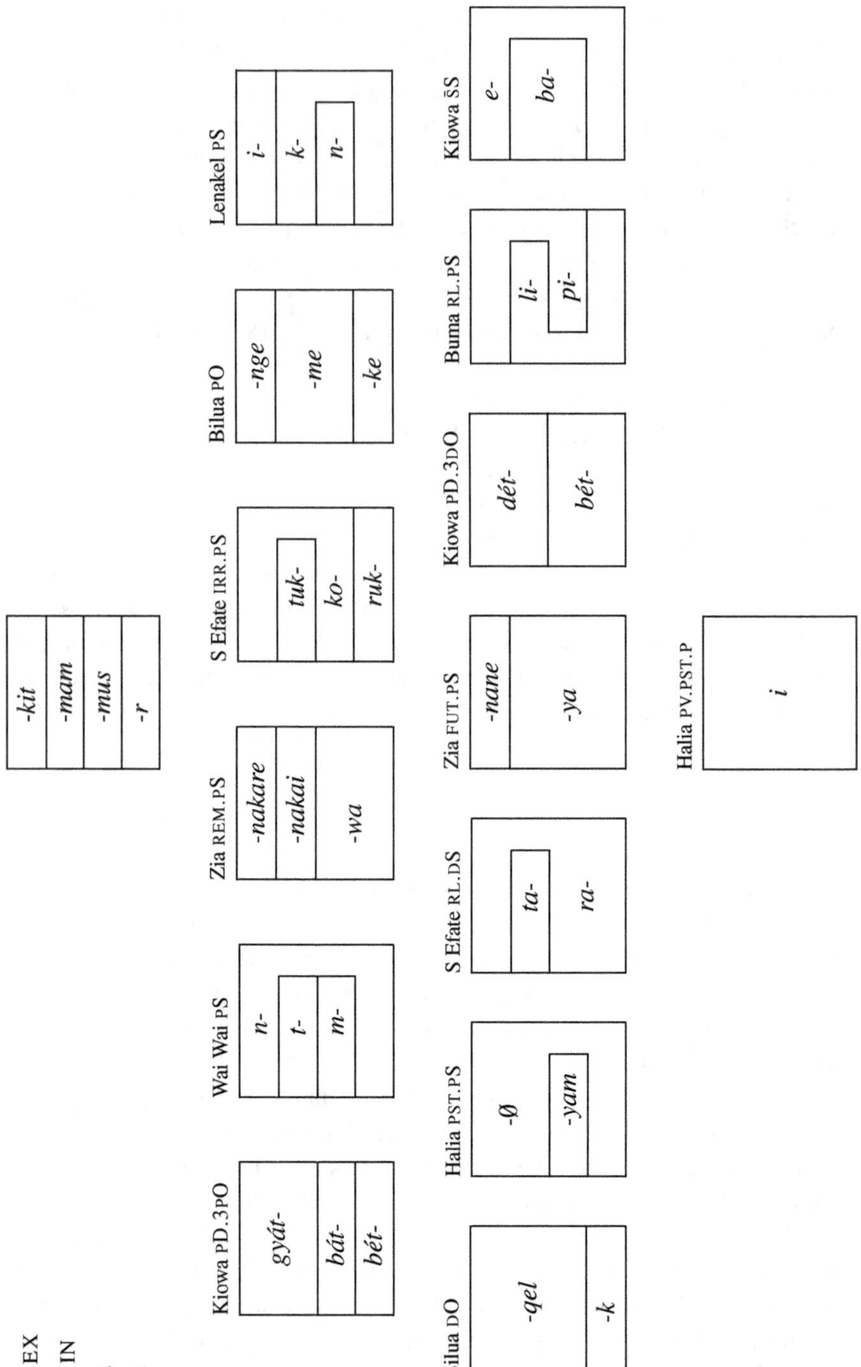

1EX
1IN
2
3

S Efate PO

| -kit |
| -mam |
| -mus |
| -r |

Kiowa pD.3pO

| gyát- |
| bát- |
| bét- |

Wai Wai pS

| n- |
| t- |
| m- |

Zia REM.PS

| -nakare |
| -nakai |
| -wa |

S Efate IRR.PS

| tuk- |
| ko- |
| ruk- |

Bilua PO

| -nge |
| -me |
| -ke |

Lenakel pS

| i- |
| k- |
| n- |

Kiowa šS

| e- |
| ba- |

Buma RL.PS

| li- |
| pi- |

Kiowa pD.3DO

| dét- |
| bét- |

Zia FUT.PS

| -nane |
| -ya |

S Efate RL.DS

| ta- |
| ra- |

Halia PST.PS

| -ø |
| -yam |

Bilua DO

| -qel |
| -k |

Halia PV.PST.P

| i |

Figure 2.3
Four-person syncretisms

identical (exponential homophony) or because they fail to find exact individual exponents and are swept up by a general one (default exponence). Third, even when the mapping to exponence preserves distinctness, the operations of phonology may efface differences (by deletion, devoicing, tone spreading, and so on). A theory of grammar set up in this way has no means of forcing outputs to preserve every instance of an underlying distinction. So, no syncretism is expected to be impossible.

A simple learnability consideration underlines this. Arguments from poverty of the stimulus (as in Socrates's dialogue with Meno or, for language, Chomsky 1980) hinge on the acquisition of knowledge that stretches beyond what the holder of that knowledge has been exposed to. In learning the forms of a person paradigm, poverty of the stimulus hardly, if ever, applies—unless a paradigm is itself exceedingly rare, as, say, a distributive remote past negative subjunctive might be. In all other circumstances, learners are likely to encounter a surfeit of the stimulus. So, no matter how odd a syncretic pairing, there is little reason to question its learnability.

Looking at individual paradigms, then, is to repeat the error that Socrates observes in Meno's struggle to define the concept of virtue by listing individual characteristics that are virtuous: it is like trying to understand what a plate is by looking at broken shards. Or, returning to our earlier metaphor (and swapping ancient Greeks), paradigms are phenomena at the periphery and what we need is an anabasis to lead us into the heart of the terrain.

2.2.3 Number Crunching

Admirers of the big-data blunderbuss may think that all that is needed at this point is a good dose of statistics to sort out real universal patterns from parochial quirks, or possibly (again) to blast the enterprise out of the water. However, a number of careful statistical studies tell against either extreme.

Baerman, Brown, and Corbett (2005) and Baerman and Brown (2013), for instance, present the results of broad typological studies of syncretism. They find that first-cum-second and second-cum-third syncretisms substantially outnumber first-cum-third. But the facts surrounding these tendencies are subtle, showing effects both for grammatical number and for language-internal systematicity (metasyncretism, in the sense of Williams 1994, Bobaljik 2002, Harley 2008). For singular, second-cum-third is the most common syncretism and the few cases of metasyncretic singulars are of this type. Metasyncretism is more frequent beyond the singular, however, where first-cum-third and second-cum-third are more common. Thus, rather than revealing that some patterns are more fundamental than others, the study concludes that syncretic frequency is context-dependent.

However, one must handle these results with care, as the studies from which they come were not designed to detect the statistical signature of an underlying feature inventory in the distribution of syncretic patterns. Two factors in particular affect the tallies in Baerman, Brown, and Corbett 2005 and Baerman and Brown 2013.

First, they do not disaggregate syncretisms of three-person systems from those of four-person systems. The generalizations, therefore, potentially combine patterns that feature-based accounts would take to be distinct.

Second, the studies restrict themselves to data in which whole forms are identical, not morphemes. This conservative method is intended to make the results neutral with respect to the debates about morphemes in general and language-specific decompositions in particular. It means, however, that many syncretic morphemes are not included because they happen always to occur within words in which a different morpheme shows a greater range of distinctions. This excludes much data from languages where multiple morphemes within a single word display different sensitivities. The Spanish suppletion of figure 2.2 illustrates this: though they share the root *tien*, second and third singular *tien-es* and *tien-e* are distinct at the word level.

Georgian (appendix A.1) presents this problem very pointedly via an elaborate array of participant- versus nonparticipant-sensitive morphemes. It is of particular note that the language's first–second metasyncretism occurs, not only in the plural, but also in the singular, where Baerman and colleagues found metasyncretism only for second and third person.

In consequence, theoreticians disposed to treat morphemes and metasyncretisms seriously must handle Baerman and colleagues' results with care. It would be a substantial undertaking to rerun these studies at the morphemic level while avoiding the methodological pitfalls that motivated the criterion of whole-word identity. So, as matters stand, these careful typologies do not threaten the notion of features, because they approach the data so differently.

Work by Michael Cysouw points to a different problem. His wide-ranging typological studies of person paradigms (2003, 2011; see also Cysouw 2005a) show that there is no strict cutoff between common systems and rare ones. If there were such a distinction, sorting the universal from the parochial would be easy. But, instead, Cysouw demonstrates a steady cline from the reasonably common to the very rare. Given these statistical properties, one might cock the big-data blunderbuss at features themselves, asking, again, whether they are the right thing to posit at all.

However, the frequency clines of Cysouw 2003, 2011 are also not immediately problematic for the commitment to features. The studies count whole paradigms of person and number. These are factors that most generative work would disaggregate, and Cysouw's criteria for distinguishing person from number, especially as concerns the speaker–hearer dyad, are quite different from those of most feature-based work. If paradigms are epiphenomena generated by features, then the quantitative procedure demanded from a generative standpoint examines the likelihood of syncretisms relative to an array of underlying feature inventories. This is not something that can be simply extracted from Cysouw's findings.

Importantly, however, proof in principle of such an approach is given in Sauerland and Bobaljik 2013 (for a different approach, see Pertsova 2011). Applying standard probabilistic techniques to Cysouw's (2003) database, Sauerland and Bobaljik offer a pilot study of syncretisms within four first persons: exclusive minimal 'me', inclusive minimal 'me and you', and their nonminimal counterparts, 'me and others' and 'me, you, and others'. The conclusion reached is useful, yet relatively weak. The null hypothesis—treating each first person as sui generis and wholly distinct from the others—is rejected in favor of feature-based approaches, which divide exclusive, inclusive, minimal, and nonminimal into natural classes.

In terms of positive findings, Sauerland and Bobaljik are cautious: "[S]ome analyses that combine a parameter space restricted by universal grammar and some accidental homophony are consistent with Cysouw's dataset" (2013, 50). That is, despite the cline in Cysouw's frequency of paradigms, his findings are not necessarily incompatible with a model that assumes a feature inventory ("parameter space") given ("restricted") by Universal Grammar, the realization of which can be partially masked in individual languages by postsyntactic operations, exponential homophony, and phonological processes ("accidental homophony").

The tentativity arises in part because the pilot study concerns just exclusive and inclusive minimal and nonminimal. The authors note that expanding the distribution modeling to second and third person goes beyond their computational resources. This difficulty would magnify if further number distinctions (dual, paucal, greater plural) were introduced.

In consequence, we return to the original issue of marshaling the data so as to abstract away from the noise of individual paradigms in specific languages and reveal the features at the generative core of person.

2.3 A Problem with Promise

The key to a tractable anabasis lies, I suggest, in the notion fundamental to Zwicky's problem, which is not the paradigm, but the partition. When Zwicky asked why languages with three persons treat the inclusive as a form of first person, not of second, he was not asking about the existence of paradigms. One can, of course, find languages in which some paradigms group inclusive and second person together to the exclusion of exclusive (and third). Figure 2.3 illustrates this for Bilua object plurals; see also the discussion of Tiwi below and chapter 5 on Nishnaabemwin, which belongs to the Algonquian family on which Zwicky focused. However, none of these languages treats inclusive and second person identically under all circumstances: each has one or more paradigms in which the two diverge. In this, they differ from the three-person systems of languages like English, in which first person subsumes exclusive and inclusive, not in some paradigms, but in all.[4]

The central insight of Zwicky 1977, then, is that there is a divide between possible paradigms and possible partitions. Similar distinctions are made in other work, including in Sauerland and Bobaljik 2013, where the paradigm with homophony is referred to as a d-partition and a paradigm without, as an m-partition. McGinnis (2005), in particular, draws attention to the analytic significance of the distinction between syncretism as a property of paradigms and conflation, as she calls it, as a property of partitions in a very enlightening discussion of the Algonquian facts that occupied Zwicky and many others besides.[5] Calabrese (2008) and Arregi and Nevins (2012) discuss similar phenomena under the rubric of absolute versus contextual neutralization.

Methodologically, then, we need a means of identifying partitions as opposed to mere paradigm. The method I propose is a simple one: superposition. Imagine drawing each of the paradigms of a language on separate slips of translucent paper and then overlaying them. In this way, distinctions that have been effaced from one paradigm will be restored in combination with others. The result is the maximally distinct paradigm for that language, and this can emerge even if no individual paradigm makes all distinctions.

This graphic approach can be made more rigorous as follows. One can define a language as exhibiting quadripartition if, for each pair of persons (exclusive/inclusive, exclusive/second, ..., second/third), there is a paradigm in which that pair is morphologically distinct. Similarly, a language exhibits tripartition if there is exactly one pair of persons that is not distinguished by any paradigm (but where every other pair of persons is distinguished by at least one paradigm). Notice that these more rigorous definitions do not assume any ordering between the persons, in contrast to the graphic representation, which uses the order exclusive–inclusive–second–third. Readers may, therefore, translate the graphic representations that follow into more formal language, if desired.

To illustate, Kiowa has a preponderant paradigm contrasting only exclusive-cum-third with inclusive-cum-second, and a rarer one contrasting general first with second-cum-third. (These are graphically represented in (24) along with a second preponderant pattern.) The first paradigm renders four person pairs morphologically distinct: exclusive/inclusive, exclusive/second, inclusive/third, and second/third. The second does so for exclusive/third, inclusive/second, and, again, exclusive/second and inclusive/third. So, all six ($^4C_3$) pairs of persons of the quadripartition are distinguished. As a result, Kiowa exhibits a quadripartition, even though none of the three paradigms described individually distinguish all four persons.

Naturally, it is a matter for investigation whether superposition reveals anything of worth. I argue that it emphatically does. It reduces the Wild West of paradigms to a nearly categorical problem of the attested versus the unattested. The full presentation of this problem, together with its empirical foundations, is deferred until the next chapter. The remainder of this chapter concentrates on the validity of superposition as a method for identifying partitions.

First, section 2.3.1 offers a simple count of how many tripartitions, that is, partitions with three persons, one should expect superposition to produce given that every possible paradigm is attested. Section 2.3.2 shows, however, that all but one is absent and that if a paradigm exhibits syncretism that splits exclusive from inclusive, then, at the level of the partition, the language distinguishes four persons, not three.

Naturally, superposition has its limits. It is only applicable in languages with multiple paradigms to superpose. Just as nothing forces an individual paradigm to reflect all underlying distinctions of a language, so nothing forces a language to have a particular number of paradigms, nor every underlying distinction to be present in at least one paradigm. One should not be surprised, then, if some language with few or no paradigms to superpose converges on an otherwise unattested partition. However, one ought, I think, to be surprised at how few and how weak such cases are (appendix A.2).

Finally, section 2.4 discounts several obvious alternative accounts of the disparity in expected versus attested partitions. These cover which paradigms should be counted, and how, as well as historical and functional factors that might impinge on attestation. Even taken together, these alternatives are insufficient to explain the shortfall. In fact, in some cases, they make it more remarkable.

2.3.1 Probable Partitions

Consider *Robinson Crusoe*. After Crusoe rescues hapless Friday, the two need a language to communicate in. The more intellectually flexible of the two sets to work, and Friday soon discovers Crusoe's scant array of pronouns (an oddity that he puts down to too much time spent with a talking parrot): search where he might in the paradigms of Crusoe's language, Friday cannot find any distinction between exclusive and inclusive. Praise be to the mountain god Benamuckee, his own language abounds in paradigms. Maybe peoples far from the divine mountain have more primitive forms of speech (ones that parrots can learn). What are the chances, he wonders, that other far-flung peoples might only have, in total, three persons, conflating two of his four as Crusoe does with his bland *we*?

Answering Friday's question sets the stage for showing that the patterns that languages ought, naively, to display substantially mismatch the patterns that they do exhibit. More formally, the question is: what are the chances that a selection of paradigms will not converge on quadripartition when superimposed?

This amounts to a counting problem concerning the number of ways of choosing appropriately from the 14 three-, two-, and one-cell paradigms that make up the bottom three rows of figure 2.3. Two observations make this a simple calculation. Subject to some straightforward assumptions, we expect 371 languages in 1000 to show tripartition, with the six tripartitions accounting evenly for about 62 cases each. (Readers not interested in the details may jump to the next section.)

First, if a language chooses more than one paradigm with three distinctions, then superposition will converge on quadripartition. This follows because every three-cell paradigm collapses two persons and distinguishes all others. Consider the two paradigmatic carapaces below:

(3)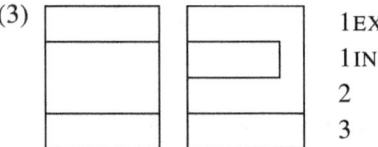
1EX
1IN
2
3

The one on the left collapses second person and inclusive, the one on the right, second and exclusive. So, conversely, each distinguishes what the other conjoins: the first, inclusive versus second person, the second, exclusive versus second. Superposition, then, renders all four persons distinct, as is apparent in the middle section of the composite paradigm in (4):

(4)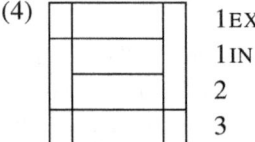
1EX
1IN
2
3

For the second observation, define a *subparadigm* as the result of removing zero or more distinctions from a given paradigm or partition. This makes superposition a means of restituting a partition from a selection of its subparadigms. For superposition to converge on a tripartition, then, once the lone three-cell paradigm permitted by the previous paragraph has been chosen, all subsequent choices must be subparadigms of the three-cell choice. (This follows because superposing subparadigms of P converges on nothing more distinct than P, but a "foreign" subparadigm introduces a distinction that P does not make and is equivalent, in essence, to superposing two three-cell paradigms.)

We can now state which sets of paradigms will converge on tripartition. Each three-cell paradigm has three subparadigms with two cells and one with one.[6]

Two examples are shown below:

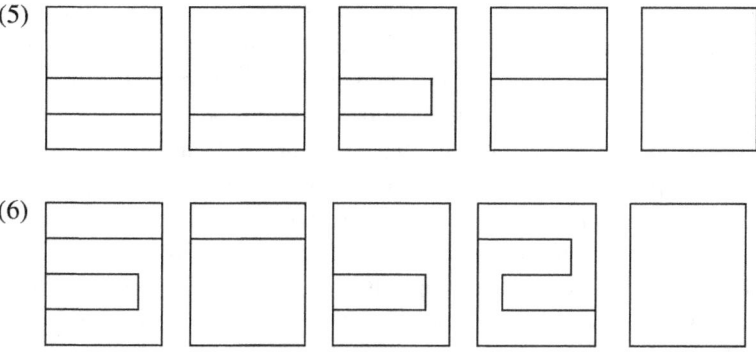

So, a necessary condition for superposition to converge on a tripartition in some language is that all choices be subparadigms of one of the six tripartitions. This restricts choices to one of six sets of five paradigms. (These sets of paradigms are nondisjoint, as a consequence of note 6; for instance, (5) and (6) share their middle paradigm.)

The next question is: what is the probability of finding languages that converge on tripartitions by dint of drawing paradigms from only one of these sets? At this point, we must assume that every paradigm is as likely to occur as any other (assigning some paradigms weighted or interdependent chances of occurrence would skew the distribution and beg the question of what the basis for such weightings is).

Suppose, for the moment, that languages choose a stock of paradigms, each of which can be instantiated several times. In morphological terms, this amounts to the assumption that paradigms repeat not by chance but by design, as instances of more abstract metaparadigms (Williams 1994, Bobaljik 2002, Harley 2008). This conception entails that each choice of (meta)paradigm that a language makes diminishes the supply available for the next choice. As a result, we quickly hit zero, making this a convenient first-case scenario (for some alternatives, see section 2.4).

So conceived, the first choice of paradigm is drawn from 14 possibilities, the second from 13, and so on. The number of ways of making k such choices is given by the binomial coefficient $^{14}C_k$. The fraction of these that converge on a given tripartition is 5 for the initial choice, 4 for the second, and so on; that is, ^5C_k for k choices. Given that there are 6 tripartitions and so 6 such sets of 5 choices, the chance of picking paradigms that do not converge on quadripartition is:

(7) $\quad 6 \times \dfrac{^5C_k}{^{14}C_k} \quad$ for $\quad 1 < k \le 5$

For $k = 1$, where (7) is greater than 1, the probability is of course 1, as a single paradigm gives us nothing to superpose and so no way of reaching more than three distinctions. And for $k > 5$, where ^5C_k is undefined, the probability is 0, as, once 5 choices have exhausted the subparadigms of one tripartition, later choices must come from subparadigms of other tripartitions.

Concretely, we can apply (7) to an imagined, balanced sample of 1000 languages. The expected rates of attestation are shown in (8). These report that, in a sample of 1000 languages with just one metaparadigm, which has three or fewer person distinctions, superposition will avoid quadripartition in all 1000 cases (which is obviously correct); and that, in a sample of 1000 languages with two distinct metaparadigms, both with three or fewer person distinctions, superposition will avoid quadripartition in $1000 \times 6 \times \frac{5}{14} = 659$ cases. This number falls to $1000 \times 6 \times \frac{5 \times 4}{14 \times 13} = 165$ when three such metaparadigms are chosen, and so on, down to 0, when the number of distinct metaparadigms exceeds five:

(8)

Metaparadigms	Languages
1	1000
2	659
3	165
4	30
5	3
≥ 6	0

The average value over languages with one to five metaparadigms is 371. That is, in languages with up to five distinct paradigm shapes for person, we would expect superposition to reveal tripartition rather than quadripartition in 37% of cases. Moreover, we would expect these to converge uniformly on all six tripartitions. That is, any one partition should only account for about 62 cases (17%).

The Path to Partition

A more sophisticated approach might consider the weighted average of (8), with weightings given by the proportion of languages within an actual representative sample that have one, two, three, four, or five metaparadigms. However, as observed in section 2.3.3, tripartitions are more common than the unweighted average predicts. So, use of weighted averages would make it even more surprising that only one tripartition is attested. For simplicity, then, I continue with unweighted averages and show that the weaker problem that arises is still severe enough to demand a solution.

2.3.2 Superposition

Reality departs radically from these figures. One tripartition, subsuming exclusive and inclusive under a general first person, as in English, is overwhelmingly common in all parts of the world. I call this the *standard tripartition*. The other five range from utterly marginal to wholly unattested. For the five unattested tripartitions, we expect attestation at a level of 309 (31%), averaged over numbers of metaparadigms. These numbers are so far from the real rate of 0% that something else must be at work in the design of person deixis. Before we consider what this might be, it is important to show superposition in action in a range of paradigmatic terrains.

In seeking tripartitions, one might first look for languages with three-cell paradigms unlike that of English. Such paradigms are easy to find. However, they have a habit of not occurring alone. In Tiwi (Osborne 1974), for instance, one finds the following variety among the verbal paradigms.[7]

Leftmost is augmented subject agreement in the nonpast (for any object other than third minimal); augmented direct object agreement is shown in the middle; and rightmost is minimal indirect object agreement. These syncretize exclusive and second, inclusive and second, and exclusive and third, respectively.

(9)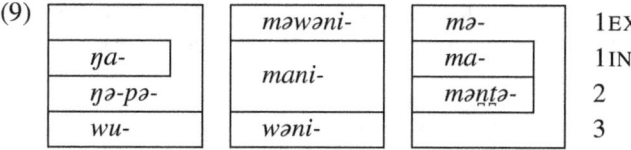

As presented, the minimal indirect object agreement paradigm (rightmost) assumes that third person *mə* is genderless and so shared between masculine, which is unmarked, and feminine, which is marked by an additional *rə*. (So, default 'masculine' is *mə* and feminine is *mə-rə*.) Homing in on gender reveals two further syncretic patterns: for third person singular objects, feminine *tə* is common to all minimal nonthird person agents in the past tense (below left), whereas feminine *pə* occurs in the nonpast, irrespective of agent number (right):

(10)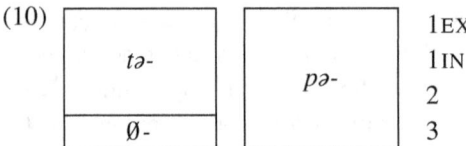

Given this exuberant variation, superposition will obviously reveal quadripartition. There is, after all, more than one three-cell paradigm in (9). So, by the first argument of section 2.3.1, quadripartition must emerge. (Equally, there are more than five paradigms. This exceeds the maximum allowed by the text following (6). So, again, the system must be quadripartite.)

To illustrate, we can remove lexical content from the paradigms shown in (9) and (10) and partially superpose the carapaces. This is shown below (left), and, as augmented indirect object agreement on the (right) reveals, the full partition is instantiated within a single paradigm:

(11)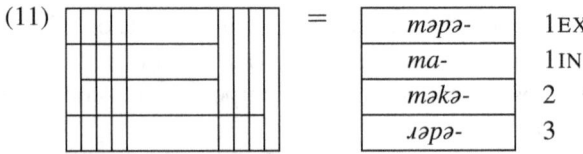

Within Tiwi, this result may not seem too surprising. Roughly half the paradigms of the language are free of syncretism and therefore exhibit the full partition (the precise proportion depends on how far one decomposes the paradigms that Osborne gives).

This is by far the most common situation that one encounters when examining in full the paradigmatic array of a language with a potentially interesting three-cell paradigm. To drive the point home, a similar situation is found in Anejom̃ (Lynch 2002), which also presents a substantial inventory of person-sensitive paradigms. For instance, in person–number–tense combinations, any person can syncretize with third, as exclusive does in the intentional trial (below left), inclusive, in the past plural (middle), and second person, in the aorist dual (right):

(12)

etiji	ekris	ekrau	1EX
tiji	eris	tau	1IN
atiji	aris		2
		erau	3

Indeed, exclusive and second syncretize with third at the same time, in the aorist trial (below left). And all persons can sometimes syncretize optionally, as in the aorist nonsingular (right):

(13)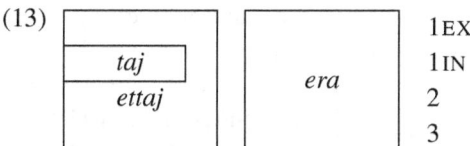

However, in superposition, quadripartition—the dominant paradigmatic pattern in Anejom̃—again emerges. It is illustrated below with the intentional dual:

(14)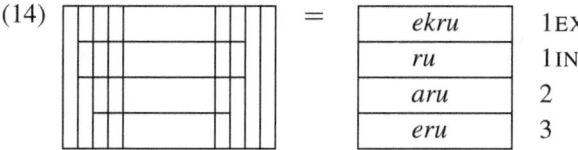

However, the characteristic that Tiwi and Anejom̃ share, that an overall minority of their paradigms monopolize the majority of the syncretic wealth, is not universal. In other languages, the proportion of four-cell paradigms drops much further, in some cases even to zero. So, we can incrementally attenuate the grip that the majority pattern has on the language and that the minority has on syncretism. Still, superposition almost always reveals quadripartition.

Initially, consider Walmatjari (Hudson 1978). Among the elements that compose its second-position auxiliary are agreement markers for subject, applicative, and/or direct object, with person and number generally expressed separately. The number markers display a range of person-sensitive syncretisms, some of them recurrently. For instance, left to right below are the number markers for plural subjects, dual objects, and plural high applicatives:

(15)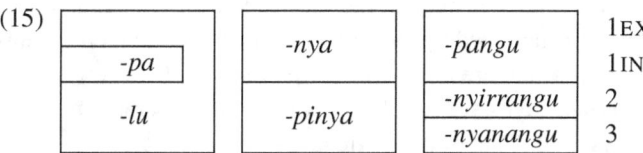

In superposition, quadripartition emerges, and is instantiated by person markers (shown below for subject markers). However, in contrast to Tiwi, this paradigm is in a minority.

(16)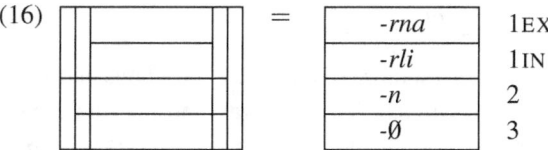

The Walmatjari situation, with person but not number markers distinguishing all persons, is perhaps relatively unsurprising. However, in Bilua (Obata 2003), this unconcern spreads to person itself. Bilua has three sets of clitics (subject proclitics, subject enclitics, and object clitics), all of which follow the same pattern: in the plural, second and inclusive collapse, and in the dual, only third person is distinct. This shown below for the subject proclitics (plural left and dual right):

(17)

nge		qe	1EX
me			1IN
			2
ke		qo	3

These clitics also form part of the full pronouns. For instance, the plural pronouns are exclusive *ani-nge*, inclusive *ani-me*, second *me*, and third *se* (the similarity of which to the paradigm above left suggests that, in some cases, the clitics are just number markers with sensitivity to person, rather than person markers per se). Concentrating on the person portion of these pronouns reveals another pattern, in (18). (Full third person pronouns are identical to deictics and, in some cases, to various clitics as well. Distal third persons are shown below.)

(18)

ani-	1EX
	1IN
∅-	2
se-	3

We therefore have two three-cell paradigms. So, superposition again yields quadripartition. This is instantiated by the person component of dual pronouns (the complete forms of which are *e-qe, ani-qe, qe, nio-qa*). However, unlike what happens in the languages seen so far, this is the only paradigm of the language that displays the full set of distinctions:

(19)

	=	e-	1EX
		ani-	1IN
		∅-	2
		nio-	3

In Suena (Wilson 1974), matters are more striking still. Pronouns and verbs are morphologically constituted in much the same way and no single morpheme distinguishes all four persons. Illustrating with verbal affixes, person may be more or less finegrained but does not distinguish clusivity, as shown below for the dual/plural of past/future (left) and remote past (right):

(20)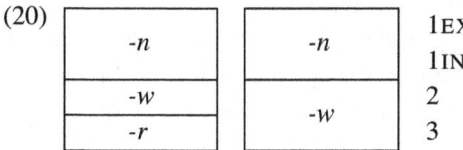
	1EX
	1IN
	2
	3

Person-sensitive number suffixes, on the other hand, do discriminate between clusives. Yet they are largely syncretic for other persons, as shown for the dual (left) and plural suffixes (right) below:

(21)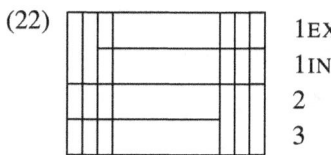
	1EX
	1IN
	2
	3

Nonetheless, when all these paradigms are superposed, the quadripartition again emerges:

(22)
	1EX
	1IN
	2
	3

Jabêm and Kiowa are more spartan still. Whereas Suena has at least some morphemes specific to either exclusive or inclusive, as in (21), Jabêm and Kiowa lack even that.

Jabêm (Dempwolff 1939 [2005], Ross 2002) has relatively few (nonsingular) person paradigms: only four or five, depending on how one treats the rather regular relationship between dual and plural in the independent pronouns (Ross, for instance, subsumes them under a single paradigm). These show three patterns, each collapsing exclusive with another person. Independent pronouns and possessor suffixes do not distinguish the clusives from one another (left). The subject prefixes collapse exclusive with second person (middle), and possessor pronouns collapse it with third person (right):

(23)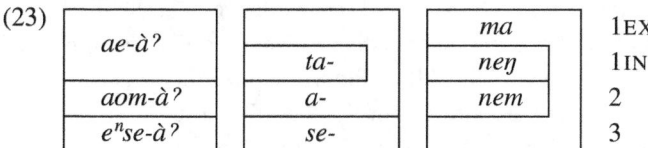
	1EX
	1IN
	2
	3

Obviously, with multiple three-cell paradigms, superposition will reveal quadripartition. However, as stated, no paradigm of the language has exponents both for exclusive alone and for inclusive alone.

Kiowa presents a yet more startling system (Watkins 1984, Harbour 2007b), in two ways. First, the language is far richer in agreement than Jabêm. Indeed, it is quite notoriously complex. And yet, second, it does not even have a single morpheme used solely for exclusive or for inclusive. In this regard, it differs from Jabêm, in which the subject prefix *ta-* and the possessor pronoun *neŋ* are used only for the inclusive. In Kiowa, both exclusive and inclusive always syncretize and no morpheme is used for either of them alone.

Specifically, dative agreement distinguishes only a general first person, so the clusives syncretize with each other. This is shown below for first, second, and third person plural possessors of plural objects (left). Usually, datives maintain a distinction between second and third person, but this is not always the case. Sometimes, these two collapse, leading to a first–nonfirst pattern, as with plural possessors of dual objects (middle). Beyond the datives, that is, for all (di)transitive agents and for unaccusative subjects, exclusive syncretizes with third person, and inclusive with second, as shown for intransitive agreement (right):

(24)

gyát-	1EX
bát-	1IN
bét-	2

dét-	
bét-	

e-	1EX
ba-	1IN, 2
	3

And yet, in superposition, the standard quadripartition reemerges:

(25)

	1EX
	1IN
	2
	3

As with Jabêm, not even addition of pronouns helps here, as these distinguish only first and second person, without clusivity or number (or third person). That is, they are defective versions of the (leftmost) dative pattern.

Finally, to lead us back to the core question that is the focus below, it is instructive to compare Kiowa with one of its Tanoan relatives that has abandoned clusivity. The well-described agreement system of Southern Tiwa (summarized in Rosen 1990, drawing on work by Allen, Frantz, and Gardiner) is one such.

All two-way syncretisms are attested in Southern Tiwa. Leftmost in (26), agreement prefixes for plural agents acting on third singular objects show syncretism of nonsecond persons, *i*, as against second person, *ma*. Syncretism between first and second person arises for nonsingular agents acting for a third person possessor of a nonplural object (other object numbers behave likewise; third person agents with third person applicatives trigger passivization). Finally, first–nonfirst syncretism arises for singular agents acting on inverse objects:[8]

(26)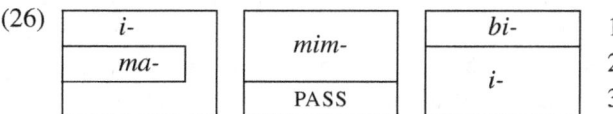

The first of these patterns is particularly interesting in relation to Kiowa, as the agreement prefixes seem obviously cognate: Southern Tiwa *i* corresponds to Kiowa *e*, and Southern Tiwa *ma* to Kiowa *ba*. Where the Kiowa syncretism distinguishes exclusive (*e*, shared with third) from inclusive (*ba*, shared with second), the Southern Tiwa syncretism collapses the clusives with each other and with third. The result is a simple second–nonsecond syncretism (*i–ma–i*).

The contrast between Kiowa and Tiwa is not a parochial quirk. As stressed at the outset, when languages move away from quadripartition to tripartition, the reduction in complexity all but always involves the replacement of clusivity with a general first person. The range of examples above shows that this result is invariant over a wide range of syncretisms and holds even when no morpheme or paradigm of the language distinguishes all four persons.

2.3.3 Limits of the Method

Readers will have noticed several qualifications above to the effect that, when superposition converges on a tripartition, it is "almost always," rather than simply "always," the partition that conflates clusives. The reason is that there are indeed exceptions: Sanuma appears to conflate inclusive with second person, and Teanu and Caddo conflate inclusive with third. (For a functionalist perspective on this pattern, see section 2.4.4.)

My treatment of these exceptions is primarily qualitative. Analysis brings language-specific and crosslinguistic facts to light that suggest that morphological operations, scant exponence, historical and geographic contingencies, and possibly even descriptive error, are responsible for these apparent instances of nonstandard tripartitions. Instead, there are linguistic arguments for proposing underlying quadripartitions for these languages.

So as not to slow the flow of the argument, I defer these language-specific analyses to appendices A.2.1–A.2.3. For now, I address these and other potential exceptions at a more general level, emphasizing that they must be understood in theoretical and qualitative context.

Nonabsolute generalizations have been misinterpreted by some as the death knell of generative linguistics. Evans and Levinson 2009 peddles this error. It is the intellectual equivalent, however, of standing by a swimming pool and complaining that the tilers have been slack because the grouting looks wavy. Language is rarely limpid, and surface generalizations in linguistics, like the surface of a pool, are subject to perturbations that prevent one from appreciating the structure that lies beneath. The job of the linguist, like that of any thinker, is to perceive the order that underlies the perturbation, not to funk dejectedly at the size of the Philistines' grapes.

In the current case, exceptions are expected on methodological grounds. Superposition as a means of undoing the perturbations that yield individual paradigms has limited effect when the paradigms themselves are few. Nothing prevents a language from having an underlying quadripartition of person, but populating only few (meta)paradigms and subjecting these to morphological processes general enough and/or exponents scant enough that superposition acts nearly or wholly trivially. In such cases, superposition may converge on a three-element system, but that will be a subparadigm of an underlying quadripartition, not a tripartition in its own right.

Consequently, we can tolerate desultory exceptions to the generalization that superposed paradigms converge on only one three-person system. Provided the number of exceptional languages is low, we can regard the robustly attested systems alone as true tripartitions, treating the others as quadripartitions subject to swingeing syncretisms. It is hard to say a priori how many exceptions is too many, but three is surely not.

In fact, tripartition is more common than forecast in the previous section (31%): 132 of 200 languages in Cysouw's (2013) WALS sample (66%) display the standard tripartition. If we interpret this as a bias against quadripartition and toward tripartitions as a class, then we would expect greater rates of attestation of nonstandard tripartitions too. This makes the three exceptions an even poorer showing.

Thus, qualitative, quantitative, and theoretical factors speak against rejecting superposition in light of the apparent counterexamples of appendices A.2.1–A.2.3.

2.4 Alternatives

The foregoing shows that results of superposing paradigms are robust, yet unexpected. They reveal a clear disparity among tripartitions, only one of which is attested. In this, partitions differ from paradigms, where everything

The Path to Partition   31

is possible. Only one task remains before we can declare that (non)attestation of partitions is a solid enough problem to demand further investigation and explanation: we must show that it is not an obvious artifact of alternative factors.

Four seem to be self-evident contenders. Two aim to lessen the numbers of expected tripartitions, by questioning how paradigms are counted (section 2.4.1) and which types of paradigms should be included (section 2.4.2). The other two seek an alternative explanation for the distributional skew in diachrony (section 2.4.3) and functionalism (section 2.4.4). All are inadequate, even taken jointly. In fact, some only heighten the problem.

2.4.1 How to Count
In calculating the expected number of tripartitions, each choice of paradigm was taken to reduce the stock available for subsequent choices. This mathematical assumption that corresponds to the linguistic view that languages do not have just paradigms, but metaparadigms, larger abstract paradigmatic shapes of which individual paradigms are instantiations. However, a linguistically viable alternative is to regard each paradigm as arising autonomously from the underlying partition, by its own set of morphological operations, exponents, and phonological processes. In reality, neither position is likely to be absolutely correct for all languages. So, if we have produced a bound corresponding to the assumption that languages choose only metaparadigms, it makes sense to calculate the complementary bound, corresponding to the assumption that each paradigm represents a separate choice. The actual expectations, then, are likely to be in the middle. However, this alternative does not improve matters empirically.

This calculation is simpler than the earlier one. If the stock of choices is constant, then the probability of picking one of the 5 subparadigms of a given tripartition from the 14 available also remains constant, at $\frac{5}{14}$. For k choices, we raise this fraction to the power of k. So, taking all 6 tripartitions into account, the probability that k paradigms will not converge on quadripartition is:

(27) $6 \times \dfrac{5^k}{14^k}$ for $k > 1$

(For $k = 1$, when (27) is greater than 1, the probability is of course 1, as a single paradigm gives us nothing to superpose and so no way of reaching more than three distinctions.)

Unlike the previous count, (27) tends to 0 without ever reaching it. However, within the same imagined, balanced sample of 1000 languages, it ceases to be distinct from 0 for $k > 10$. So, we have:

(28)

Paradigms	Languages
1	1000
2	765
3	273
4	98
5	35
6	12
7	4
8	2
9	1
≥ 10	0

Comparing this with the earlier count in (8), we see that the expectation of avoiding quadripartition is higher than before, for each $1 < k < 10$. Averaging over the first five values, as before, we consequently expect increased frequency of languages with one to five paradigms (some possibly identical in structure) that do not converge on quadripartition under superposition: 434 (43%) as opposed to the earlier figure of 371 (37%).

Furthermore, this change does not address why one of the 6 tripartitions should be so much more frequently attested than the others. Thus, in like-for-like comparison, this method of counting makes the absence of nonstandard tripartitions a more significant problem than before.

2.4.2 What to Count

A more successful way of reducing expectations is to question which paradigms ought to be counted, or, more precisely, whether the one-cell paradigm counts. There is a clear linguistic reason for raising this point. Take the English past tense, which is impervious to changes in person. One might claim that this is a one-cell paradigm with respect to person. However, it is at least as reasonable to say that past tense is insensitive to person because it lacks person features and so is not a person paradigm at all.

Compelling as this thinking may be for English, there are two reasons not to take this line in all cases. First, the exponent that inhabits a one-cell paradigm might recur in a richer paradigm elsewhere in the language. For example, Damin *n!aa* covers all spatial deictics but is restricted to nonfirst persons when used as a pronoun (see the next chapter for more detail). If *n!aa* is a person exponent when used for person deixis, then, barring homophony, it is also a person exponent when used for spatial deixis. In consequence, this one-cell

The Path to Partition 33

paradigm does count as a person paradigm. (See Harley 2008 for several examples along such lines, especially in Nubian; analogously, compare the expanding range of Suena *w* from second person to nonfirst in (20).)

Second, if a language with an otherwise rich system of person marking lacks person distinctions in one specific context, then it is reasonable to entertain that the lack of distinction is a morphological quirk, rather than an ad hoc absence of person from the morphosyntax. The nonsingular aorist and feminine marking for minimal agents present examples of this in Anejoñ (13) and Tiwi (10), respectively.

Nonetheless, even if one finds such considerations underwhelming and recalculates the distributions accordingly, one does not come significantly closer to the actual distributions. Excluding one-cell paradigms means that each tripartition has only $5 - 1 = 4$ subparadigms and that there are only a total of $14 - 1 = 13$ to choose from. So, for the paradigm-wise count, we have (29):

(29) $\quad 6 \times \dfrac{4^k}{13^k} \quad$ for $k > 1$

For $1 \leq k \leq 8$, this equals 1000, 568, 175, 54, 17, 5, 2, and 0. The average of these values is 363 (36%) over the first five values. Similarly, for the metaparadigm count, we have (30):

(30) $\quad 6 \times \dfrac{^4C_k}{^{13}C_k} \quad$ for $1 < k \leq 4$

For $1 \leq k \leq 4$, we have 1000, 462, 84, 8, and 0 for $k \geq 5$. These average to 311 (32%).

Clearly, these percentages are lower than their respective alternatives (36% as against 43% for individual paradigms, and 32% as against 37% for metaparadigms). However, these numbers are still far from actual ones and do nothing to explain the disparity between tripartitions. Moreover, they lessen the expected rates of all tripartitions, where we want to lessen only those of the nonstandard tripartitions. As Cysouw shows, standard tripartition is much more prevalent than predicted.

2.4.3 Diachronic Residue

A different tack is to grant that any partition is linguistically possible but to suppose that historical accidents explain why nonstandard tripartitions have not developed. On this view, quadripartition and standard tripartition hold near-universal sway today because they were, by coincidence, present at the dawn of the major human migrations and have, by and large, been passed down to subsequent generations. It goes without saying that diachrony affects synchrony and can straightforwardly account for a skewed distribution of tripartitions. However, relative to that skew, these same factors in fact increase the likelihood of nonstandard tripartitions. So, historical accident does not obviate the need for more fundamental explanation.

Bickel and Nichols (2005) present a historical-cum-typological survey of clusivity that advocates of a diachronic approach to partitional disparities would find appealing. They argue that the distribution of clusivity contrasts corresponds to the footprint primarily of two ancient migrations into what they call the Circum-Pacific area, encompassing the Ancient Sunda area, defined as the near Pacific islands, New Guinea and Australia, and the Pacific Rim, defined as Melanesia, coastal New Guinea, and the western Americas. Of the Circum-Pacific languages sampled, 47% exhibit clusivity, as opposed to 21% elsewhere.

Moreover, clusivity is shown to remain most robust in regions where it is bolstered by concentration or buffered from outside influence by geographic isolation. This highlights the impact of diachronic transmission and areal influence on the distribution of systems of person deixis.

Real as these factors are, they do not seem sufficient to account for the sharp absence of all but one tripartition from the world's languages. Consider Africa, Europe, and north Asia, areas beyond the Circum-Pacific. Though less frequent than in the Circum-Pacific, clusivity does occur here. It is present in 17% of languages in Europe and north Asia as an aggregate area and in 20% of languages in Africa, according to Bickel and Nichols's sample (though they suggest that the African figure might be higher, given the larger sampling in Cysouw 2003). These figures imply that languages' destinies can be decoupled from their pasts and that they may innovate (or lose) distinctions that their ancestors bore.

The profusion of paradigms, which saturate the range of what is possible, bears witness to language's capacity for innovation. And this returns us to the original question: if languages may innovate and proliferate at the paradigmatic level, why does that innovation not filter up to the level of language-wide systems?

Honing that question, we do not know what inventory of paradigms early human migrants bore with them. Nothing dictates that migration occurred in an era of paradigmatic uniformity. Rather, it is possible that, in at least one early migrant language, some nonstandard three-cell paradigm—that is, one with three forms not conflating exclusive and inclusive—was also prominent. (To argue that it was not, based on posterior distributions, would be circular when we are trying to account for absence from that posterior distribution.) We must then suppose that, by additional accidents, that paradigm failed to flourish at the expense of its four-cell, or nonclusive three-cell (English-like), kin in each descendant language. Moreover, the same accident must have befallen all other clusive three-cell paradigms that arose at later dates. These scenarios, though possible, are not obviously compelling.

Nonetheless, if one wished to accommodate the impact of history on the likely distribution of tripartitions, one would heavily weight the standard tripartition and lessen the others. This would, of course, account for the observed skew. However, a historical approach would perhaps surprisingly also increase the likelihood of encountering nonstandard tripartitions in the remaining portion of languages, for two reasons.

First, recall that superposition reveals quadripartition whenever it encounters two three-cell paradigms. However, if clusive three-cell paradigms are created and preserved by historical accident, then each is constrained to specific genetic and geographic localities. So, the likelihood of encountering two in any one language decreases. Accordingly, languages that lack a four-cell paradigm—and have no historic reason for exhibiting a nonclusive three-cell paradigm—become more likely to converge on a nonstandard tripartition. (Loss of quadripartition is a plausible setting for this scenario, and, even if this loss occurs under areal pressure from languages with standard tripartitions, nothing forces adoption of the neighbors' tripartition, rather than one that accommodates a clusive contrast.)

Second, a plausible corollary of these historical contingencies is that two-cell paradigms are likely to arise, not out of the blue, but from etiolation of a three-cell paradigm already present in the language. That is, two-cell paradigms are not randomly distributed with respect to three-cell paradigms, but are likely to be related as subparadigms. But recall that superposition reveals quadripartition whenever a three-cell paradigm occurs with a two-cell paradigm that is not its subparadigm. (Similar observations hold for pairs of two-cell paradigms.) So, historical considerations decrease the likelihood of finding paradigms that are not related as subparadigms and, consequently, increase the likelihood of finding nonstandard tripartitions.

In sum, diachrony indubitably accounts for some skew in the distribution of tripartitions. However, it is implausible that it accounts for the all-but-total absence of nonstandard tripartitions. If anything, it makes the matter less explicable.

2.4.4 Functional Pressure

A final factor to which one might appeal in accounting for the shortfall between the possible and the actual is functional pressure. That is, the absence of nonstandard tripartitions might reflect the pressures of use to which humans are subject in daily social interactions.

At first glance, such an account can be plausibly given in terms close to what I posit in chapter 4. First, we are egotistical creatures, conceiving of the world in terms of our experience of and action on it (a position that Dixon 1994 articulates well in relation to ergativity). Second, our earliest social interactions occur in one-on-one settings, which affords us an awareness of *you*. With *me* and *you* as fundamental concepts, ones that continue to be central to later life, languages might be constrained to distinguish at least first and second person. And if first and second person are distinguished not only from each other but also from everything else, then we arrive at third person, too.

However, such thinking is hard to make more than superficially plausible. When considered more closely, it emerges as too lax, failing to constrain the class of usable languages appropriately.

First, if a purported Principle of Egotism leads to any grammatical concept, it is first singular, not first person. First person is inherently numberless, covering all groups that include the author. Our experiences and actions occur overwhelmingly in the first singular and so a grammatical correlate of that fact should be first singular. Similarly, the numberless notion of second person is not what emerges from the one-on-one structure of early interactions. Rather, given first singular, the speaker–hearer dyad furnishes second singular, a lone hearer. So, these functional pressures, if real, are satisfied by any partition that permits reference to the speaker alone and to the hearer alone, when allied with an appropriate number system.

In that light, consider Zwicky's imaginary partition of exclusive, inclusive-cum-second, and third. The singulars of these are first singular, second singular (as the singular of inclusive-cum-second is the singular of inclusive, which is nonexistent, and the singular of second person), and third singular. As a result, the purported functionalist principles admit the very system that we have been trying from the outset to exclude.

In fact, the apparent tripartition of Teanu and Caddo verbs (exclusive, second person, and inclusive-cum-third; appendices A.2.2–A.2.3) also permits reference to first and second singular. This is prominent as a syncretism in Tupinambá, and, in "You and I = Neither You nor I," Rodrigues (1990) proposes that the pattern has a principled source: the language treats identically all sets of referents that themselves treat *you* and *I* identically. This leads to amalgamation of inclusive and third person because one includes both *you* and *I* and the other excludes them both.

As an engine of functionalist explanation, the Principle of Participant Parity, as we might call Rodrigues's proposal, seems plausible. Again, we might root it in our early experience of the speaker–hearer dyad. However, this highlights a second problem for functionalist approaches to the Tupinambá data. In his typology of clusive syncretisms, Cysouw (2005a) rightly asks why the

Tupinambá syncretism is not more widely attested if it derives from a design feature of human language. This question applies with equal force to partitions. The case study of Teanu (appendix A.2.2) shows that the emergence of this syncretism, at least in that instance, is highly contingent. Consequently, this raises the broader challenge of how we sort of out principled principles from ad hoc principles of functionalism in anything other than a post hoc fashion that appeals to the data they are supposed to explain.

In a similar vein, properly circumscribing the application of apparently genuine principles is difficult. Consider the tripartition consisting of exclusive, inclusive, and second-cum-third in light of the more plausible Principle of Egotism. In truly egotistical fashion, this system is maximally distinct regarding groups containing the author but shows scant interest in others. The Principle of Egotism ought, then, to justify it. Its nonattestation cannot be attributed to the failure to distinguish second person from third, as conflation of these two is a recurrent feature of the Enlhet-Enenlhet family (Unruh and Kalisch 2003) discussed in chapter 3. This makes the proper application of functionalist principles appear opaque.

Nonetheless, we must recognize that a dedicated functionalist might devise answers to the questions. Even if so, a larger challenge would remain, concerning the categorical nature of the data under discussion.

To set the problem up, consider a different type of categoricality, namely, the character of some grammaticality judgments. Concretely, take the effects of person on argument structure, which are evident both in alternations (like the obligatory use of passive, or similar devices, when third persons act on nonthird in some languages) and in outright bans (like the Strong Person Case Constraint, the requirement that, when both indirect and direct objects control agreement, the latter must be third person) (Hale 1972, Rosen 1990, Dixon 1994, Haspelmath 2002). As pointed out by the authors just cited and other authors, such effects look like grammatical reification of the functional tendency for argument hierarchies (agent over experiencer over patient) to correspond to animacy hierarchies (participants over other animates over inanimates): it is more likely for me to do something to a ball than vice versa.

However, functional infrequency alone does not account for categorical ungrammaticality, as Jelinek (1993) and Adger and Harbour (2007) argue for voice alternations and the Person-Case Constraint, respectively. If it did, then, for example, tonic-pronouned *They sold him us*, with *us* as (a possibly focused) direct object, would be identical in acceptability to weak-pronouned **They sold im əs*. However, the version with tonic pronouns is fully grammatical, whereas its weak-pronoun counterpart is, for me at least, barely even parsable.

Such cases limit legitimate invocation of functionalism. Functionalism may offer insight into statistical skews—why, that is, some grammatical characteristics are common and others, rare. However, something additional is required to account for why some constructions in some languages move from rare to impossible.

The same issue arises here. It strikes me as plausible to appeal in part to functional pressures when considering the rarity of languages that use person pronouns but have fewer than four (Harbour 2014b, 2016), or of languages that have four or more numbers but lack the dual (Harbour 2014a). However, attestation of tripartitions is not merely skewed. It borders on, or indeed is, categorical. The distribution of syncretisms shows that a language can contextually dispense with any given person distinction. We require an explanation for why this should be possible at the level of the morpheme but impossible at the level of the partition. After all, speakers can resort to circumlocution to specify a person distinction that is not formally part of their grammar. So, notions like popularity do not seem adequate to account for the categorical absence of nonstandard tripartitions.

2.5 Conclusion

Early theories of features took an innocent approach to the identification of featurally natural classes, particularly in the guise of syncretism and paradigms. I have offered both a fuller survey of the data, highlighting the danger of that innocence, and an alternative articulation of the challenge that a theory of person faces. Making partitions the primary object of explanation, and relegating paradigms to a secondary status, I have proposed superposition as a means of restituting the explicandum from the data that comprise several major typological studies and my own reading. With attention temporarily narrowed just to tripartitions and nothing smaller, this has led to appreciation of a categorical disparity between the standard tripartition, which conflates exclusive and inclusive, and the five other possible tripartitions.

This disparity is robust in several senses. Simple calculation leads one to expect that tripartition as a whole will not be particularly rare and that there will be parity between all tripartitions. The degree of divergence between expectation and actuality is demonstrably not an artifact of how one counts paradigmatic frequency, nor of which paradigms one counts, nor, plausibly, of historical accident or functional pressure. On the contrary, most of these increase expectations of finding nonstandard tripartitions.

Superposition is, therefore, the anabasis that leads from the peripheral plethora of paradigms, with their apparent profusion of natural classes, to the categorical problem of partitions on which we can found a theory of features for partitions of all sizes.

3 The Partition Problem

3.1 Introduction

From a formal point of view, the question of why only one of six tripartitions is attested is sufficient to warrant investigation. It constitutes a classic problem of the kind formulated by Jakobson (1958 [1971]) with his unsaturated feature matrices. Moreover, it already challenges some conceptions of linguistic theory. Construction Grammar (Goldberg 1995, 2009, Booij 2010), for instance, is committed to the claim that any learnable grammar is a possible grammar. Given that every paradigm is attested, and therefore learnable, it is a mystery why languages should exhibit the higher-level order that superposition reveals, why the freedom of the paradigm does not percolate up to be enjoyed by partitions.

However, as thus far formulated, the problem does disservice both to empirical properties of natural language and to the solution that follows, depriving them of their full generality. One way of seeing this is to recall that the problem of syncretisms was set up with regard one-, two-, and three-cell paradigms, yet, in considering partitions, attention was confined to tripartitions. The obvious parallel question is whether the monopartition or any bipartitions are attested and, if so, which. This chapter sets about generalizing the problem in this way.

Section 3.2 introduces a formal notation for describing partitions and uses it to state which partitions are attested. The set comprises the quadripartition and standard tripartition, as discussed in the previous chapter, as well as two bipartitions and the monopartition. Interestingly, these form a chain of subpartitions (defined below), which further suggests that there is an underlying order to the attested systems.

Bipartitions and monopartition are rather thinly attested in relation to joint systems of pronouns and agreement. However, section 3.3 argues that the data considered in the last chapter are at once too narrow and too coarse. Instead, it lays out two theses about the range of data to which a theory of person has access and obligations. One concerns the relationship of person deixis to that of spaces, objects, and paths. The other claims that languages can operate distinct partitions in these different deictic domains, including, in some languages, for pronouns and for agreement, which were mostly lumped together in the previous chapter. Although these positions are relatively uncontroversial, potential qualms are quelled by explaining that no element of the solution relies on them crucially.

Finally, section 3.4 illustrates all 5 attested partitions over the deictic domains just mentioned. The robustness of their attestation contrasts sharply with the (near to) nonattestation of other partitions and so hones the questions that form the cornerstone on which the theory of person is based: why are only 5 of 15 possible partitions to be found? and why do we find those 5 in particular?

3.2 The Full Problem

Zwicky's problem, as he originally formulated it in 1977, was restricted to two tripartitions. It asked simply why the standard tripartition was attested and one other, conflating inclusive with second person instead of exclusive, was not. By considering all tripartitions, the previous chapter generalized this question somewhat. Full generalization, however, needs to move beyond tripartition.

A fully general version of the partition problem should investigate partitions of all sizes. Just as we asked which of the possible tripartitions is attested, so we should ask which of the possible bipartitions are. And just as we showed that quadripartition is attested, so we should ask whether monopartition is.

The answers to these questions are presented graphically in figure 3.1. This lays out all possible partitions of the person space (using a notation explained two paragraphs below). In distribution and shape, the lattice of partitions on four persons is, of course, identical to the lattice of syncretisms possible within a quadripartite person system (figure 2.3). However, the difference in terms of attestation is striking. Whereas every possible syncretism can be found in various languages, only 5 of the possible 15 partitions are attested: the quadripartition, 1 tripartition, 2 bipartitions, and the monopartition. These are highlighted by boxes in the figure. Five tripartitions and 5 bipartitions are unattested.

The partition problem thus consists of two questions, concerning what is attested and why:

(1) *Partition problem*
   a. Why are only 5 of 15 partitions attested?
   b. What distinguishes the attested partitions from the unattested ones?

The Partition Problem

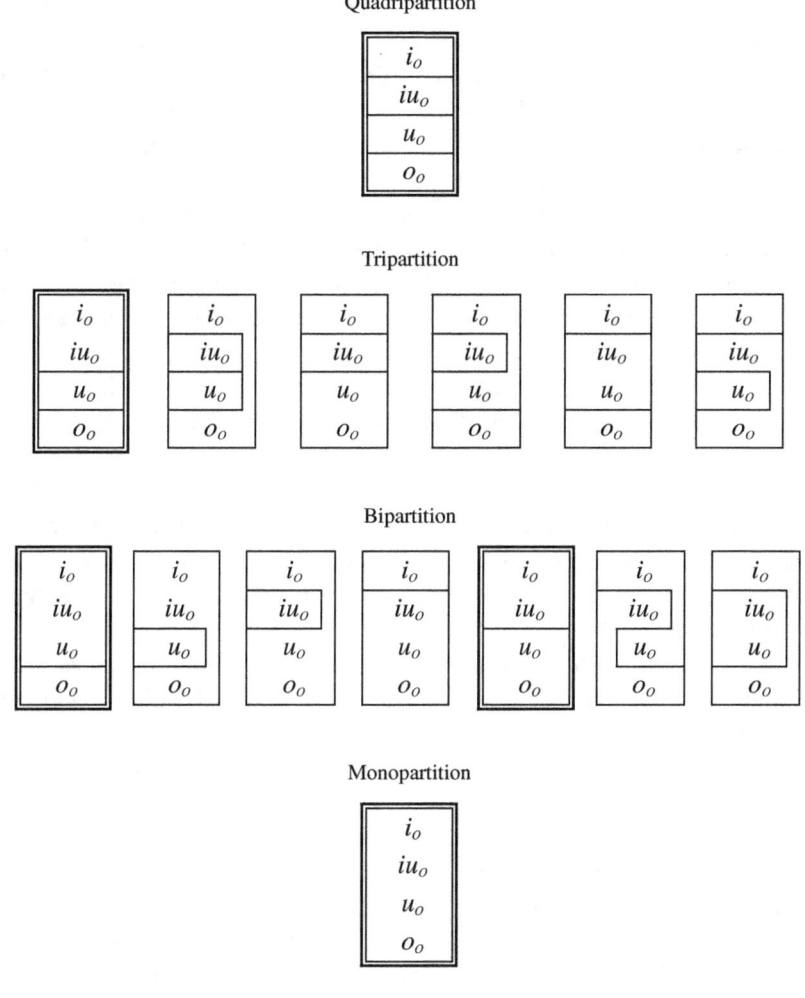

Figure 3.1
Partitions of the person space

To make these questions more precise, I use the following terminology and notation. The *author* (or speaker, signer, ego, etc.) is represented as i, and the *hearer* (or listener, audience, tu, etc.), as u. Both are assumed to be unique, though this assumption is not crucial (see section 4.2.1 for further discussion of ontological commitments). Alongside the author and the hearer, which are jointly called the *participants*, are an unspecified number of *others*, represented as o, o', o'', and so on (though prime marks are omitted where it is simpler to do so).[1]

The purpose of this notation is to capture the fundamental difference between partitions and paradigms. Partitions are divisions of semantic spaces; paradigms, their sometimes partial reflection in the morphology. To avoid confusion between the objects that are partitioned on the one hand and their morphological reflection on the other, I will talk about partitions in terms of author, hearer, participants, and others, representing them with $i, u, o, o', o'', \ldots$. The previously introduced terms *first person exclusive*, *first person inclusive*, *second person*, and *third person*—or, more concisely, *exclusive*, *inclusive*, *second*, and *third*—are used only for the morphosyntactic categories that result from partition, notated as 1EX, 1IN, 2, and 3, with plain 1 for the conflation of 1EX and 1IN.

In this notation, *first exclusive*, for example, may refer to the singleton set of the speaker alone $\{i\}$, to dyadic sets of the speaker and one third person other $\{i, o\}, \{i, o'\}, \{i, o''\}, \ldots$, to triadic sets of the speaker and two others, $\{i, o, o'\}, \{i, o, o''\}, \{i, o', o''\}, \ldots$, and so on through larger sets of referents. For convenience, I abbreviate this large list of sets as i_o. The normal size of i indicates that the speaker is an element of every one of these sets whereas the subscripted o indicates that others may occur in any arrangement or number, including none.

Similarly, *second person* ranges over the set u_o, which abbreviates the singleton $\{u\}$, the dyads $\{u, o\}, \{u, o'\}, \{u, o''\}, \ldots$, the triads $\{u, o, o'\}$, $\{u, o, o''\}, \{u, o', o''\}, \ldots$, and so on.

Inclusive ranges over iu_o, that is, the dyad $\{i, u\}$, the triads $\{i, u, o\}$, $\{i, u, o'\}, \{i, u, o''\}, \ldots$, the tetrads $\{i, u, o, o'\}, \{i, u, o, o''\}, \{i, u, o', o''\}$, $\ldots$, and so on. (So, inclusive differs from the previous two persons in having a dyad rather than a singleton as its minimum element.)

Last, *third person* ranges over o_o, that is, the singletons $\{o\}, \{o'\}, \{o''\}, \ldots$, the dyads $\{o, o'\}, \{o, o''\}, \{o', o''\}, \ldots$, the triad $\{o, o', o''\}$, and so on. (Third person thus differs from the others in lacking a unique minimum.)

For the moment, I take it as given that i_o, u_o, iu_o, and o_o are natural elements for the semantics to partition. However, this too is to be explained, given that the ontology is simply the unorganized set $\{i, u, o, o', o'', \ldots\}$. Therefore, parallel to questions (1a–b) about the inventory of partitions, we can ask two questions about the inventory of partition elements:

(2) *Partition element problem*
   a. Why are maximally four partition elements generated from the ontology?
   b. What distinguishes attested elements from unattested ones?

The Partition Problem   43

Answers to these questions emerge naturally in the course of the next chapter. For now, though, I simply continue to work only with i_o, u_o, iu_o, and o_o, as in the previous chapter.

It is important to emphasize, though, that the partition problem becomes a more onerous if we do not restrict attention to i_o, u_o, iu_o, and o_o. For instance, chapter 4 shows that, if one alters (complicates) its minimal assumptions about how persons are derived, then aberrant partition elements emerge, one placing first person singular with the inclusives, another comprising all exclusives except first singular. Naturally, there are 15 possible partitions of these four elements and 10 are new when compared with figure 3.1.[2] With these, one must ask why only 5 of 25 systems are attested. Clearly, other arrays of partition elements increase the shortfall. So, if 5 out of 15 seems modest, it is not.

With the notation just introduced, figure 3.1 can now be read as follows. The sole element of the top row is the partition present in Tok Pisin. The person exponents *mi*, *yumi*, *yu*, and *em* denote i_o (exclusive), iu_o (inclusive), u_o (second), and o_o (third).[3] In running text, I use "|" to indicate that all four elements are distinguished. Hence, the quadripartition is represented as $i_o \mid iu_o \mid u_o \mid o_o$.

The highlighted element of the second row is the standard tripartition. Like the quadripartition, it distinguishes u_o and o_o, that is, second and third person, from each other and from the clusives. However, it conflates the clusives into a general first person, $i_o iu_o$, which are, consequently, shown without a dividing line, $i_o iu_o \mid u_o \mid o_o$.

With the notation now illustrated with respect to familiar systems, we can turn to the novel ones. In the third row, the highlighted system on the left is the *partition bipartition*, $i_o iu_o u_o \mid o_o$, so called because it distinguishes sets containing the participants, that is, author and/or hearer, from those containing none.

Third from the right in the same row is the *author bipartition*, $i_o iu_o \mid u_o o_o$. This distinguishes sets that contain the author from those that do not.

Finally, in the bottom row is the monopartition, $i_o iu_o u_o o_o$, in which no person distinctions are made.

Returning, then, to the partition problem, we can phrase (1) more precisely as:

(3) *Partition problem—more precisely*

Why, of the 15 partitions available, are quadripartition, monopartition, the standard tripartition, and the author and participant bipartitions the ones that are attested?

This collection is suggestively coherent in that the partitions highlighted in each row of figure 3.1 are subpartitions of those highlighted in higher rows (where *subpartition* is defined analogously to *subparadigm*, as a partition arrived at by removing zero or more distinctions from a given partition). The monopartition is, of course, a subpartition of all bipartitions and, so, of the author and participant bipartitions in particular. These in turn are subpartitions of the standard tripartition. Last, the tripartition is a subpartition of the quadripartition.

This last relationship may seem trivial, because the discussion so far has made everything that is not the quadripartition look like an etiolated version of the quadripartition. There are, though, many quadripartitions other than that in figure 3.1, as the problem of partition elements highlights. For instance, the Sanapaná system of section 3.4.3 is a quadripartition, consisting of the author bipartition plus singular–plural number, but, because it does not distinguish second person from third, it does not have the standard tripartition as a subpartition.

Chapter 4 derives this chain by proving a stronger result: that once one has the (right) resources for deriving the bipartitions, the other partitions, and the correct partition elements, follow and nothing besides. Before that, though, and for the rest of the chapter, we will see what each of the partitions looks like in concrete terms.

3.3 Empirical Domain

The range of partitions presented in the next section is drawn from a broader range of data than is typical of treatments of person in generative frameworks. In particular, I make two assumptions about what data to consider and how to consider them.

The first assumption is that systems of spatial deixis are pertinent to theories of person partitions (section 3.3.1). This leads to the claim that language may operate different partitions of the same semantic objects (i, u, o) in different semantic domains (person versus space). I capture this modularity by means of *domains*, a concept that can be explicated in terms of uninterpretable features, to use Minimalist terminology (that is, features present in the syntax and possibly pronounced in the morphology, but ignored by the semantics). Building on this, the second assumption is that pronouns and agreement are to be treated in some languages as independent domains that may, in consequence, be differently partitioned (section 3.3.2).

Neither assumption is especially novel, except in the current context. Nonetheless, the key elements of the theory developed and applied in the subsequent chapters is independent of them (section 3.3.3). So, readers are not obliged to accept them, even if I believe them to be correct.

3.3.1 Person and Space

Generative work on person normally confines itself to what Siewierska (2004) more analysis-independently calls "person markers," that is, pronouns, clitics, and agreement. However, since at least Humboldt 1830, it has been recognized that there is a close connection between deixis of persons and deixis of spaces, paths, and objects.

Generative work has shown a significant appreciation of Humboldt's (1836 [1999]) contributions to the philosophy of linguistics and the study of polysynthesis (see, e.g., respectively Chomsky 1966 and Baker 1996). Yet generative theories of person features have paid little, if any, attention to the rich seam of data that spatial deixis provides. In this regard, generative thinking is at odds with numerous functionalist and typological studies, such as Weissenborn and Klein 1982, Anderson and Keenan 1985, and Imai 2003.

A broad empirical and theoretical case for using spatial data in studies of person is presented in chapter 7. Anticipating that justification, however, the data adduced for partitions below include not only pronouns, clitics, and agreement, but also spatial deixis (like English *here–there*), object deixis (*this–that*), directionals (*hither–thither*, *hence–thence*), and verbs of person-directed motion (of which English *come–go* is an inaccurate but indicative example).

Crosslinguistically, bipartition is much more frequent for deixis of spaces, paths, and objects than it is for persons. Including spatial data therefore opens up a richer array of partitions than would otherwise be available. Increased data may lubricate a problem, but they also threaten potential solutions. So, the solution that emerges is both more general and more robust than would otherwise be the case.

The English examples two paragraphs higher illustrate an important point. Whereas the pronouns show a tripartition, deixis of spaces, objects, and the like uses only a bipartition. If one posited that tripartition holds across the language as a whole, then one would have to treat nonperson deixis as collapsing some of these distinctions. This amounts to systematic syncretism, rather than partition, and so predicts that there should be no constraint on the structure of two-term systems of spatial deixis. The data do not support this view, however. So, we must allow for partitional polyploidy, that is, for languages to pick one partition for personal pronouns and another, or others, for spaces and the like.

I will refer to person and space as constituting separate *domains*. That is, though I will analyze them as using the same features and as sharing elements of functional structure, I envisage them as hermetically sealed in terms of syntactic operations. For instance, the features on pronouns do not enter into agreement relations with those on spatial deictics. Rather, however much pronouns enter into case and agreement relations and propagate their feature content throughout the clause, they do not determine the feature content of spatial deictics.

A simple, though not incontrovertible, case for this position comes from the acceptability of the kinds of things one encounters on the phone (4), on answering machines (5), and on postcards (6):

(4) I'm there now.

(5) I'm not here now.

(6) Don't you wish you were here?

If spatial deictics copied features from pronouns, then (4) should be unacceptable, as it would assert, in essence, that the author is where the author is not. Mechanically, this would be exactly like the agreement mismatch *I are there now*, in which *are* fails to match its subject in person/number features. Plainly, this problem does not arise if the person content of the pronoun and the person content of the locative do not interact in the syntax. This separateness is what the notion of domain is intended to capture.

3.3.2 Pronouns and Agreement

Pronouns and agreement raise special questions about domains. For languages in which agreement is nearly always a reflection of overt elements elsewhere in the sentence (e.g., Dutch, English, French, German), it is natural to treat pronouns and agreement as belonging to the same domain. After all, if verbs copy their person features from pronouns, then the features underlying agreement are simply those underlying pronouns, and divergences between the two will count as mere syncretism, which this chapter systematically ignores.

However, returning to Humboldt's legacy, there is a long tradition of regarding person markers bound to the verb as saturating any requirements that the verb or sentence may place on arguments. A striking case of this is Yimas (Foley 1991). The language permits agreement for all arguments of intransitives, transitives, and ditransitives, encoding three persons and four numbers. In addition, the language has independent pronouns that can be used in isolation from verbs, or with them, when verbal morphology fails to disambiguate certain person–number combinations. Yet it would be wrongheaded, for several reasons, to regard pronouns as the source from which Yimas verbs copy their person and number content.

Most obviously, pronouns are relatively infrequent, occurring, as just implied, for emphasis or disambiguation. In a sense, then, they are peripheral to Yimas grammar, rather as temporal adjuncts like *today* and *yesterday* are peripheral to the English past tense. An analysis in which the English verb copies its value of ±past from such sporadic elements is not obviously appealing. So, assigning that exact role to pronouns in languages where they are just as infrequent is dubious.

The case for not doing so is particularly strong for Yimas. Foley (1991) explains that bound person forms are themselves not obligatory. Rather, under certain discourse conditions, such as familiarity or old information, they may be omitted. Thus, they function rather like subject noun phrases in languages like Italian and Spanish. This, again, makes the bound person forms of Yimas seem analogous to full argumental noun phrases in more familiar languages, that is, central, rather than peripheral, to the organization of the grammar.

Other languages manifest the relative unimportance of pronouns in other ways. Some languages fail to lexicalize all person–number combinations. This is well-attested in Southeast Asian languages, at least in some registers, where epithets like 'mother', 'servant', 'body' systematically replace pronouns tied to specific persons (see, e.g., Cooke 1968). Others simply leave lexical gaps, forcing the functional load onto verbs (as in Caddo; appendix A.2.3) or context and circumlocution (as in Kawésqar, Aguilera 2011).

Indeed, in Wichita (Rood 1976), a relation of Caddo, verbs assume this load entirely, as the nearest equivalent to pronouns are relative clauses, such as these (my glossing):

(7) *na- c- ʔi- h*
    PART-1-be-SUB
    'I' [lit., 'who am']

(8) *na- s- á:k-ʔi- h*
    PART-2-P- be-SUB
    'you.P' [lit., 'who are']

Given the weight of this evidence, I take the free pronouns versus bound person forms of, say, German to bear fundamentally different relationships to one another than is the case in languages like Yimas, Caddo, and Wichita.

In sum, where argumental nouns and pronouns are obligatory, one can reasonably take the verbs to copy all person and number features from nominals, thus making pronouns and verbs a single domain in the sense of containing only a single set of interpreted features, propagated through the syntax by copying.

In Yimas, where argumental nouns and pronouns are significantly less central than bound forms, these last are themselves loci of interpreted features, as are the independently usable pronouns. When they cooccur, the information from both sources is, I suggest, pooled to arrive at a more specific referent than either the free or bound person forms alone may allow.

By way of precedent, one can think of information pooling as governing nonthird person gender in French. Consider:

(9) *Je suis français-e.*
    1S am   French- F
    'I am French.'

Je 'I', like other nonthird pronouns in French, does not distinguish gender, but adjectives like *français(e)* 'French(F)' do. One can, of course, imagine that *je* bears gender features, but leaves them unpronounced. However, the absence of gender from nonthird, and especially first, person pronouns is a robust pattern both in French and crosslinguistically. A simple conspiracy of silence is too haphazard to constitute an explanation of this common pattern. It is more reasonable to regard gender as absent from the pronoun, with first person feminine readings of *je* in (9) arising from the same pooling of information envisaged above.[4]

Of course, the degree of centrality or peripherality of a language's pronouns to the operation of its grammar forms something of a cline. So, case-by-case analysis is required to decide how the partitions of a given language should be counted. By way of illustration, consider Brazilian Portuguese. Its verbs distinguish only between first and nonfirst person in both singular and plural, as shown for the present tense of 'hit' in table 3.1 (right). This has the appearance of the bipartition. However, Brazilian Portuguese requires overt pronouns under a good range of circumstances (e.g., Duarte 1995), and these distinguish three persons in both numbers (table 3.1 left). So, on the above criteria, Brazilian Portuguese agreement is not an instance of bipartition.

Table 3.1

Brazilian Portuguese pronouns and agreement

	Pronouns		Agreement	
	Singular	Plural	Singular	Plural
1	eu	nós	bat-o	bat-emos
2	vôce	vôces	bat-e	bat-em
3	ele	eles		

The Partition Problem

There are, though, two ways to account for the simplicity of verb agreement in Brazilian Portuguese. The verb might copy all features but pronounce only some. If so, morphological operations or an attenuated lexicon cause agreement to be an impoverished reflection of pronominal person, even though the two use identical features syntactically. Alternatively, however, one might claim that Brazilian Portuguese verbs are sensitive only to the contrast between first and nonfirst. This entails that verbs differ featurally from pronouns. So, notwithstanding the feature-copying relationship between the two, the verbal paradigms instantiate a different partition.

For current purposes, it is not necessary to determine how to handle cases like Brazilian Portuguese. Instead, though it would be straightforward, and tempting, to include such cases, I leave them aside, in order to minimize reliance on examples that cease to be if analyzed via obvious alternatives. These considerations do not apply toward the extreme ends of the cline, however. So, as a broad brush measure, I take pronouns to constitute a separate domain from the verb in languages where agreement is rich and arguments are often absent.

3.3.3 Empirical Alternatives

Although the positions just outlined reflect my actual views about how one ought to regard the data relevant to this study, I do not require that readers accept either that theories of the morphosemantics of person have rights and responsibilities to data from spatial deixis, nor that it is wrong to regard pronouns as the central locus of person in all languages. The theory of features that follows can be motivated from a subset of its data. It is our understanding, not the solution, that suffers if the theses above are rejected.

Repudiating the two assumptions makes examples of the bipartitions and monopartition extremely rare. This reflects the fact that most languages make at least three person distinctions by some grammatical means or other. Poor pronoun systems are frequently supplemented by rich agreement systems, as in Hocąk and Kiowa, discussed below; and poor agreement systems generally cooccur with richer inventories of pronouns, as in English and Brazilian Portuguese.

Yet, even on this narrow view, one still requires an answer to Zwicky's problem and to its generalization to all six tripartitions. The proposal of the next chapter meets this challenge better than past proposals do. As detailed in chapter 8, it requires fewer features and fewer constraints on features. Thus, even an exiguous construal of the problem favors the theory proposed here.

If the rarity of bipartitions and the monopartition—that is, of one- and no-feature systems—were felt to be a concern relative to this narrowed view, one could reasonably appeal to functional pressures. It is only when freed from substantial practical load that the pronoun system of language etiolates to a mere bipartition. Thoroughgoing two-person languages, as in the Enlhet-Enenlhet family (section 3.4.3), are exceedingly rare. It seems to be a psychological fact about humans that we like a minimum level of richness to our pronominal systems. Indeed, this holds not only for person, but for number as well (Harbour 2014b, 2016). So, insofar as the rarity of small feature systems poses a problem, it concerns the class of probable grammars, not the space of the possible. In consequence, it is not something that a theory of features is obliged to derive directly.

In other words, the exiguated problem does not materially alter the solution. Given that theories with more data stand a greater chance of falsification, good methodology commends the broader view. Moreover, if, as argued below, parallel problems and solutions emerge both for person and for spatial deixis, then we have reasons for regarding this move as having been justified a posteriori. Consequently, I proceed to the generative core of person by relying on data from diverse deictic domains: spaces, paths, objects, and persons, with the latter divided into pronouns and agreement in some cases.

3.4 Partitions Illustrated

We are now ready to survey the range of data. The empirical cases of this section are presented in figure 3.2. Each row illustrates a range of instantiations of, from top to bottom, quadripartition, standard tripartition, author bipartition, participant bipartition, and monopartition. Sections 3.4.1–3.4.5 treat these in turn.

The tables making up figure 3.2 omit variants and allomorphs irrelevant to the point at hand. References for the featured languages are given in the discussion that follows. As a general policy, wherever possible, examples eschew number. That is, although the languages may well use number elsewhere, the cited phenomena happen to be number-neutral. The purpose of this decision is to highlight that we are dealing with pure person partitions, rather than the interaction of person with number. (Further number-neutral partitions are to be found in the pure person probes of Béjar 2008, but I do not discuss these here, to avoid additional theoretical exposition.)

3.4.1 Quadripartition

A range of quadripartitions is presented in the top row of figure 3.2.

Leftmost are the pronouns of Imonda (Seiler 1985): exclusive *ka*, inclusive *pəl*, second person *ne*, and third person *ehe*. Clearly, these are the same person

Quadripartition

Imonda Pronouns		Canela-Krahô Agreement		Waray-Waray Spatial deixis		Cebuano Directional verbs	
1EX	ka	1EX	i-	1EX	adi	1EX	ngari
1IN	pəl	1IN	pa-	1IN	ini	1IN	nganhi
2	ne	2	a-	2	itu	2	nganha
3	ehe	3	ih-	3	adtu	3	ngadto

Standard tripartition

Jarawa Pronouns		Washo Subject agreement		Palauan Spatial deixis (AN)		Abruzzese Object deixis (FS)	
1	mi	1	le-	1	tia	1	šta
2	ŋi	2	m-	2	tilecha	2	ssa
3	əhi	3	-a-	3	se	3	chela

Author bipartition

Damin Pronouns		English Spatial deixis		Kiowa Object deixis (BAS)		Laz, Directionals (AFF-<u>DIR</u>-come-3S)	
1	n!aa	1	here	1	éyde	1	ko-<u>mo</u>-xt-u
2/3	n!uu	2/3	there	2/3	óyde	2/3	ko-<u>me</u>-xt-u

Participant bipartition

Winnebago Pronouns		Bulgarian Spatial deixis		Catalan Object deixis (FS)		Georgian, Direc. (<u>DIR</u>-1/2/3-gave-3S)	
1/2	nee	1/2	tuk	1/2	aquesta	1/2	<u>mo</u>-m/g-c-a
3	'ee	3	tam	3	aquella	3	<u>mi</u>-s-c-a

Monopartition

Spanish Obj. marker (AN)		Tewa Agent marker		Russian Acc. case (AN)		Damin Object deixis	
1/2/3	a	1/2/3	<u>di</u>	1/2/3	ACC = GEN	1/2/3	n!uu

Figure 3.2
Examples of partitions

distinctions found in Tok Pisin, but without the complication of a singular–dual–plural number system. Numberless pronouns are, in fact, characteristic of the whole Waris family (e.g., Nimboran, Anceaux 1965; Waris, Brown 1990; and Daonda, Punda, Simog, and Sowanda, discussed in the appendix to Seiler 1985).

Second from left is the subject agreement system of Canela-Krahô (Popjes and Popjes 1986). Again, this system distinguishes four persons (exclusive *i-*, inclusive *pa-*, second *a-*, third *ih-*) but no number. Canela-Krahô indicates nonsingularity in pronouns by means of separate plural words. So, if one treats number words (Dryer 1989) as being phrase-structurally distinct from pronominal number and more akin to nominal modifiers (hence, more like *two* than like dual, say), then the language counts as having a numberless quadripartition in its pronouns as well as its verb agreement.

Second from right are the spatial deictics of Waray-Waray (Wolf and Wolf 1967). A quadripartition of spatial deictics is one that differentiates between spaces in the vicinity of the speaker but not of the hearer (exclusive *adi*), those in the vicinity of speaker and hearer alike (inclusive *ini*), those in the vicinity of the hearer alone (second person *itu*), and those beyond the vicinities of both (third person *adtu*).[5] (For convenience, I write as though speaker and hearer were singular. However, exclusive *adi*, say, can refer to an object in the vicinity of a first person exclusive, as in 'This is our table, that is yours'. This simplification applies throughout the discussion below.)

Finally, rightmost are the directional verbs of motion in Cebuano (Bunye and Yap 1971). By directional verbs, I mean words somewhat like *come* and *go*, but with stricter requirements on where the endpoints are in relation to speaker, hearer, and others. Hence, Cebuano distinguishes between motion toward the speaker but not the hearer (exclusive *ngari*), motion toward speaker and hearer (inclusive *nganhi*), motion toward hearer but not speaker (second person *nganha*), and motion directed elsewhere (third person *ngadto*).

Thus, it is clear that (numberless) pronouns, (numberless) agreement, spatial deictics, and directional verbs of motion can all exhibit quadripartition of person.

3.4.2 Standard Tripartition

Tripartition too is attested across a range of domains.

Leftmost, again, are numberless pronouns, in this case, of Jarawa (Kumar 2012). These distinguish first person (*mi*, covering English 'I, we'), second person (*ŋi*), and third person (*əhi*, covering English 'he, she, it, they'). The same system occurs in Pirahã (Everett 1986), despite some controversy (see Harbour 2014b for discussion), as well as in Panare pidgin Spanish (Riley

The Partition Problem   53

1952) and Samoan Plantation pidgin English (Mühlhäusler 1987) during their early stages.[6]

Second from left is the agreement system of Washo (Kroeber 1907). It too is numberless, comprising just first person (*le-*), second (*m-*), and third (*-a-*). Bengali, too, presents a three-person agreement system in which, according to Milne (1913 [1993], 144), "plural and singular forms of inflection are identical." Commenting on the fate of what once were number markers, Milne admonishes that "[i]t should never be forgotten that the correct use of the verbal inflections does not depend on the *number* of the noun or pronoun but on the *rank* of the person referred to" (p. 144).

Second from right, Palauan (Josephs 1975) shows that spatial deixis can be tripartite as well as quadripartite, as in Waray-Waray. In fact, this partition extends to the directionals, which are, in this case, fully independent verbs of motion, 'come' and 'go' (table 3.2).[7] Two question–answer pairs illustrate the contrast (my glosses, based on Josephs's grammar and dictionary). Both involve the speaker asking, and the hearer agreeing, to go to the speaker's house. They differ as to whether the speaker implies an intention to be at home at the time.

In the first case, where there is no such implication, both speaker and hearer use *mo* 'go$_3$' (subscripts 1, 2, 3 indicate first, second, and third person loci):

(10)   Ng   sebechem el   mo   er a blik er a klukuk?
       IMPF   can.2S   EL   go$_3$ at home   tomorrow
       'Can you go to my house tomorrow?'

(11)   Chochoi. Ng   sebechek el   mo   er a blik er a klukuk.
       yes   IMPF can.1S   EL   go$_3$ at home   tomorrow
       'Yes, I can go to your house tomorrow.'

If, by contrast, the speaker intends to be home, then the hearer's going terminates where the speaker will be. As a result, the appropriate verb is *me* 'go$_1$ (to

Table 3.2

Demonstratives, locatives, and directional verbs in Palauan

Deictic	Speaker	Hearer	Other
'this', 'that' (AN)	ng(i)ka	ngilecha	ng(i)ke
'this', 'that' (INAN)	tia	tilecha	se
'here', 'there'	er tia	er tilecha	er se
'come', 'go'	me	eko	mo

speaker)' (i.e., 'come'). Conversely, because replies swap the roles of speaker and hearer, the reply uses *eko* 'go$_2$ (to hearer)':

(12) *Ng   sebechem   el   me   er a blik   er a klukuk?*
     IMPF can.2S   EL   go$_1$ at home   tomorrow
     'Can you come to my house tomorrow?'

(13) *Chochoi. Ng   sebechek el   eko   er a blik   er a klukuk.*
     yes   IMPF can.1S   EL   go$_2$ at home   tomorrow
     'Yes, I can come to your house tomorrow.'

Finally, rightmost, complementing spatial deixis, are the Abruzzese (feminine singular) object deictics, that is, words like *this* and *that* (Verratti 1968): *šta* is used to refer to a feminine singular object in the speaker's, or speaker-and-hearer's, vicinity; *ssa*, to one in the hearer's (but not speaker's) vicinity; and *chela*, to one removed from both. Thus, these deictics show the same sensitivities as the partition elements of Jarawa, Washo, and Palauan.

Two points are worth noting about the Abruzzese system. First, although reports of such person-based systems are common (see chapter 8), descriptions often state only that the first two terms are used for objects near the speaker and those near the hearer, respectively. Strictly speaking, this underdetermines which of these is used for objects near to both. Whenever explicit statements are available or can be inferred from examples (e.g., Roberta D'Alessandro, pers. comm., on Abruzzese, Josephs 1975 on Palauan, Eaton 2010 on Sandawe, Meira 1999 on Tiriyó), first plurals pattern with first singular, as per this partition.

Second, it is important to differentiate between, say, the Abruzzese and Scots systems of object deixis. Scots is also a three-term system, consisting of *this*, *that*, and *yon* (ignoring plurals), and, as in Abruzzese, the first of these terms picks out objects in the speaker's vicinity. However, the systems differ with regard to the deictic extents of the second and third terms: covering objects in the middle distance, *that* can pick out objects at a greater remove from the hearer than *ssa* can. Accordingly, *yon*, unlike *chela*, excludes mid-distant objects. It is used only for things at a substantial remove. Whenever I exemplify a partition within a system of object deixis (or spatial deixis, directional verbs, etc.), the systems in question are person-based, like Abruzzese, and not, unless otherwise stated, distance-based, like Scots. (The two types of system are further discussed in chapter 7.)

3.4.3 Author Bipartition
When we turn to bipartitions of either kind, pronoun systems become much scarcer. Nonetheless, some are attested, and other domains provide more ample instances. We begin with the bipartition contrasting just first with nonfirst (second and third).

Leftmost, Damin makes just this distinction in its pronoun system, with *n!aa* denoting "any set which includes the speaker, including the set which includes only the speaker," and *n!uu*, "any set which does not include the speaker" (Hale 1998, 207; see also Hale and Nash 1997). However, as Hale makes plain, Damin is a ritual language, mastery of which was facilitated by its spartan vocabulary. Its Lardil-speaking users also had a pronoun system distinguishing four persons and three numbers at their disposal. So, one might question whether it is a language in the sense relevant to generative work, even if it is hard to see what would prevent its acquisition as a sole first language.

However, first–nonfirst systems are attested elsewhere. A scantily documented case arises in what Laycock (1977) calls Morwap and Burung (2000) terms Elseng (with equivocal references to Morwap). Both present incomplete pictures, but each suspects that the language has just two pronouns, numberless first person *ka* and numberless nonfirst *sou* (Burung's orthography). As explained in Harbour 2014b, Burung's documentation completely covers the first person, where Laycock registers uncertainty, and Laycock's completely covers the second person, where Burung's account is incomplete. Moreover, where they overlap (parts of first person, parts of second, and all of third), the accounts are in agreement. Thus, the case for this being an author bipartition appears strong.

A complication, though, is that Mark Donohue has conducted fieldwork on Elseng (as footnoted in his 2004 grammar of Skou), and his unpublished notes record a four-person system with third person identical to deictics (pers. comm.). This calls Laycock's and Burung's accounts into question. However, it is remarkable for two well-trained linguists independently to converge on so unusual a system if it is not the actual one. Given the alternyms listed in Lewis, Simons, and Fennig 2014—Djanggu, Janggu, Morwap ("pej.," "vigorously rejected as a language name by speakers and government officials"), Sawa, Tabu—it is possible that Laycock and Burung documented a distinct dialect from Donohue. Nonetheless, some doubt must remain.

If we relax the self-imposed abstention from partitions with number, then another set of cases becomes available, from the Enlhet-Enenlhet family (Unruh and Kalisch 2003). For instance, examples from Sanapaná (Gomes 2013) show that the singular pronoun *ko'o* is first person (14) but *hlejap* covers second (15) and third person masculine (16):

(14) *Hawe ko'o as- melaja.*
    NEG   1S   1S-slow
    'I am not slow.'

(15) *Ta'asek akjehlna ap- ta- o hlejap?*
    which   fruit   2/3-eat-Q 2s/3s
    'Which fruit did you eat?'

(16) *Hlejap metko patakon ap- angok.*
    2s/3s   NEG   money   2/3-POSS
    'He doesn't have money.'

Similarly, in the plural, first person is *enenko'o* (17) but second and third (masculine) are both served by *hlengap* (18)–(19):

(17) *E-   hl-mame-kama enenko'o.*
    DEIC-P- work- CAUS   1P
    'We are working.'

(18) *Taehlnatemo ap- ke-len-mote-mo na'ak hlengap?*
    why   2/3-M- P- sit-   Q   LOC   2P/3P
    'Why are you seated?'

(19) *Taehlnatemo hlengap ap- ke-len-tep- ma?*
    why   2P/3P   2/3-M- P- leave-NOM
    'Why did they leave?'[8]

(Adelaar with Muysken (2014) cites Sušnik 1977 as documenting the same bipartition with singular–plural number in Lengua-Maskoy.)

Beyond the domain of pronouns, the first–nonfirst bipartition is more frequent. It is at its most abundant for object and space deixis. In English, for instance, *here* refers to spaces in the speaker's, or speaker and hearer's, vicinity, and *there*, to spaces beyond, whether in the hearer's vicinity or not. Similarly, in Kiowa (ignoring number; Watkins 1984, Harbour 2007b), *éyde* refers to objects in the speaker's vicinity, and *óyde* to objects beyond.

The same partition is found also in directionals. These are closely analogous to directional verbs of motion (as in Cebuano above; see also chapter 7), but instead of being bundled in with other lexical content, they are affixes that specify directionality of lexically independent verbs. An example of such a system is Laz, for which Rostovtsev-Popiel (2012) provides a neat triplet of examples, the question (20) 'Did he come to you / go to him?', and two possible answers, (21) 'Yes, he went to him' and (22) 'Yes, he came to me'.

The verb of motion is the same in all three cases, *xt*. To the extent that Laz offers a formal distinction between coming and going here, it is by means of these directionals, and they are partitioned into first and nonfirst. That is, (20)–(21) share *me*, for motion to second or third persons, whereas (22) uses *mo* for motion to the speaker:

(20) Ko-   me-   xt-   u-   i?
     AFF-DIR$_{2/3}$-come.PRET-3S.PRET-Q
     'Did he come to you?', 'Did he go to him?'

(21) Ho ko-   me-   xt-   u.
     yes AFF-DIR$_{2/3}$-come.PRET-3S.PRET
     'Yes, he went to him.'

(22) Ho ko-   mo-   xt-   u.
     yes AFF-DIR$_1$-come.PRET-3S.PRET
     'Yes, he came to me.'

When this range of data is taken into account, the author bipartition is well-attested.

3.4.4 Participant Bipartition

The second bipartition differentiates participants, that is, first and second person, from third.

Its seemingly unique occurrence as a pronoun system is found in Hocąk (leftmost in the penultimate row of figure 3.2; Hartmann and Marschke 2010, Helmbrecht and Lehmann 2010; also called Winnebago, Lipkind 1945). The two pronouns are participant *nee* and nonparticipant *'ee*. Both are undifferentiated for number. The following examples show that *nee* occurs for (23) exclusive and (24) inclusive and second person:[9]

(23) Biik ha- šac- wi-   ra   nee ⟨p⟩- hiwenį.
     cards 1EX-play-AUG-when   1/2 1EX-dealt
     'When we played cards, I dealt.'

(24) Tee nee woore-ra   nee hį- hanį, nee ⟨šį⟩-hanį.
     this 1/2 work- DEF   1/2 1IN-have   1/2 2- have
     'This is our job, it is yours.'

Both examples are interesting. In (23), *nee* is used contrastively, singling out me from exclusive us, even though exactly the same pronoun would be used to emphasize the agent of 'we played'. And in (24), *nee* is used emphatically but for two different referents within the same sentence, first for the inclusive, then for second person.

Examples of *nee* with augmented reference are exceedingly rare, to judge by the examples that Hartmann and Marschke, Helmbrecht and Lehmann, and Lipkind give: (25) is apparently unique. Suffixed with *wi* 'AUG', the verb shows that the pronoun has inclusive augmented reference (me, you, and others), as opposed to (24), where its inclusive use, in *nee hį-hanį* 'we have', is for minimal number:

(25) *Ne- šən ha- ji- wi.*
 1/2-only 1EX-come-AUG
 'We only came.'

Similarly, *'ee*, the nonparticipant pronoun, ranges over both minimal (26) and augmented (27), and readings of both are well-attested:

(26) *'Ee-xjį nąącge-ra teek.*
 3- INTNS heart- DEF ache
 'He was heartsore himself.'

(27) *Nee nį-š'ak 'ee šaak-ire.*
 1/2 2- old 3 old- 3AUG
 'They are older than you.'

Moving away from pronouns, this bipartition is again better-attested—though, it seems, not as richly as the author bipartition. Second from left in figure 3.2 are examples of Bulgarian spatial deixis. These distinguish between spaces in the vicinity of the speaker and/or hearer, *tuk*, and those beyond their vicinity, *tam*. As an example using object deictics, of how these differ from, say, English *this* and *that*, if you and I are standing at either end of a table (so, reasonably far apart), next to our beer bottles, and if there is a third bottle on the windowsill, then only the bottle on the windowsill would be designated as *onazi*, whereas both the bottle near you and that near me would be designated as *tazi* (Roumyana Pancheva, pers. comm.). (In English, it is likely that only the last of these would be *this*, both of the others counting as *that*.)

Second from right are examples of Catalan object deixis, in this case, for feminine singular objects. Again, one is used for objects in the speaker and/or hearer's vicinity, *aquesta*, and another for objects at a greater remove, *aquella*. Both are discussed further in chapter 7.

Finally, rightmost is another example of directionals, from Georgian (Hewitt 1995). Its directionals are obviously cognate with those of Laz in section 3.4.3 (both are Kartvelian languages). However, they are differently aligned in Georgian. The examples below use the aorist of 'give'. Aorists in Georgian are formed with, among other things, directional preverbs. While for many verbs, the directional semantics has been attenuated or lost, directionality is retained for many verbs of motion and transfer. The pertinent point here is the encoding of giving to a participant versus a nonparticipant. Whereas the second person in Laz is classed with third, in Georgian, it is classed with first. As a result, Laz *mo* is restricted to first person (20), but Georgian *mo* covers (28) first and

(29) second. By contrast, Georgian *mi* is confined to third person (30), whereas Laz *me* has a wider range (21)–(22). (More Georgian examples of this kind are given in appendix A.1.)

(28) Mo- m- c- a.
 DIR$_{1/2}$-1S-give-3S.AOR
 'He gave it to me.'

(29) Mo- g- c- a.
 DIR$_{1/2}$-2-give-3S.AOR
 'He gave it to you.'

(30) Mi- s- c- a.
 DIR$_3$-3-give-3S.AOR
 'He gave it to him.'

The following minimal pair from Rostovtsev-Popiel 2012 highlights the different treatment that second person receives in Georgian (31), where it shares *mo* with first person, and Migrelian (32), where (in common with Laz) it shares *me* with third:

(31) Me shen-tan mo- v- di- var.
 I you- ASSOC DIR$_{1/2}$-1S-go-am
 'I am coming to you.'

(32) Ma sk'an-da me- [v]-wl-k.
 I you- TERM DIR$_{2/3}$-1S-go-1S.PRES
 'I am coming to you.'

3.4.5 Monopartition

Finally, we come to monopartition. This is a somewhat trickier phenomenon to identify, as the criteria are more obviously theory-dependent than in the foregoing cases. For instance, consider verbs of motion. In Waray-Waray, these are quadripartite, as already shown. In other languages, they show no person sensitivity and rely on external means, such as clitics or oblique case, to indicate direction or terminus (e.g., Hiaki, Dedrick and Casad 1999; Warlpiri, Simpson 2002; and, more generally, Wilkins and Hill 1995).

The analytic problem such languages pose is most readily seen relative to some semitheoretic notation. Suppose that a telic verb of motion contains a terminus somewhere in its representation, terminus(x), and that, when termini discriminate between persons, they do so by means of a person head, π, that hosts one or more person features. Concretely, Laz, a simpler system than Waray-Waray, would represent *mo*, motion toward speaker, as terminus(x) $\wedge$ $\pi_{+\text{author}}(x)$, and *me*, motion not toward speaker, as terminus(x) $\wedge$ $\pi_{-\text{author}}(x)$.

Consequently, one might think that languages without speaker-sensitive directionality would simply dispense with the feature content of the person head, using just terminus$(x) \wedge \pi(x)$. If so, then languages like Hiaki and Warlpiri exhibit monopartition of the person space in the domain of verbs of motion. But this begs the question of why one would suppose that $\pi(x)$, and hence π, is present at all.

In other words, the challenge is to determine when the person space is syntactically represented but undivided and when it is undivided because unrepresented. That is, we must discriminate between monopartition and absence of partition. Languages without pronouns, like Wichita, are challenging precisely in this way: do they have an undifferentiated pronominal space, or do they dispense with the category entirely?

These concerns notwithstanding, monopartition is strictly distinct from absence of partition in the context of the theory developed below. This is because not only person features, but also π, the person head, have concrete semantics. It is responsible for introducing a variable and restricting it to the domain of animates. As a result, an animacy distinction that is sensitive to person as a whole but insensitive to particular values of person counts as a monopartition.[10]

A well-known and morphologically simple example is Spanish *a*, which is used before animate direct objects, including emphatic pronouns, proper names, humans, and animals, as in (33), but not before biological inanimates, as in (34):

(33) ¿*Viste   a/*Ø   me / Cristina / unos chicos / los cuervos?*
     saw.2S   ACC   1S   Chris   some boys   the ravens
     'Did you see me / Chris / some boys / the ravens?'

(34) ¿*Viste   Ø/*a los coches / los libros / un puerto?*
     saw.2S   ACC   the cars   the books   a harbor
     'Did you see the cars / the books / a harbor?'

This is the leftmost example in the bottom row of figure 3.2. (Use of *a* has some implications concerning specificity, but specificity is neither necessary nor sufficient for its use.)

In a similar vein, moving along the bottom row of figure 3.2, animate direct objects in Tewa behave as a class, irrespective of person and in distinction to inanimates (Harbour 2013). This sensitivity to animacy affects agreement, argument structure, and incorporation, all of which are rather involved. However, one effect of object animacy is straightforward and morphologically uniform, even if, oddly, it plays out on agents.

Tewa has an (optional) agentive marker *di* (or *d̲i* after a vowel). Typical examples of its use are:[11]

(35) Tsé- ḏi- bo wên senä?- di dí- khen- má?.
    seven-REL/AGT-EMPH one.INV man.INV-AGT 3:1-chase-PROG
    'Seven guys are chasing us.'

(36) Naa-ḏi wí- yą̂ą-i.
    1- AGT 1:2S-grab.FUT
    'I will grab you.' (The hyphen in yą̂ą-i is orthographic.)

(37) Naa-ḏi wí?bo dó- kéyí.
    1- AGT alone 1S:3S-get.FUT
    'I will get him myself.'

(38) I pu- ?ay óe- yoe- ?an i P'óséwhâa Sedó- ḏi.
    DEF rabbit-DIM 3S:3S.AN-leave-PST the coyote old.man-AGT
    'Old Man Coyote left the little rabbit.'

These examples have been chosen to show a variety of persons in agent and object roles. Their common point is that all have animate objects, first nonsingular in (35), second singular in (36), and third singular in (37)–(38), whether represented only by agreement (35)–(37) or by agreement and a noun phrase (38). In all four cases, the agents bear explicit agentive marking, tsédibo wên senä?di 'seven men' in (35), naaḏi 'I' in (36)–(37), and i P'óséwhâa Sedóḏi 'Old Man Coyote' in (38).

Agentive marking is robustly absent from transitives with inanimate objects. Typical examples are given below, with the direct objects múu 'sack', nan 'dust', both incorporated, and in yán t'ún 'the willow basket', unincorporated:

(39) Naa dó- múu-pa?.
    1 1S:3S-sack-make.PROG
    'I am making a sack.'

(40) Síphêe Sedó i- nan- athątha- ?an.
    bat old.man 3S:3-dust-shake.off-PST
    'Old Man Bat shook the dust off.'

(41) Heḏiho i- kê? i tųųyó i- n yán t'ún.
    and.so 3S:3-get.PST the chief the-INV willow basket
    'And so the chief took the willow basket.'

Observe that the unsuffixed agent naa 'I' of (39) contrasts with naaḏi of (36)–(37), as does Sedó 'Old Man' of (40) with Sedóḏi of (38).

Some basic facts about agreement support this. In the case of first person acting on third, absence of agent marking is the only morphological change: (36), (37), and (39) all share the agreement prefix dó. For other argument combinations, this prefix too is sensitive to the change in animacy, as in the third-singular-on-third-person examples (38), which uses óe, and (40)–(41), which use *i*. This evidence underlines that agentive <u>d</u>i is sensitive to object animacy in its own right, not simply as a reflex of the agreement prefix.

Russian, second from the right in figure 3.2, provides a different form of evidence for animates behaving as an otherwise undiscriminated class. As is widely discussed (e.g., Jakobson 1958 [1971], Bobaljik 2002, Corbett 2007, Caha 2009), in particular declension classes, the Russian accusative is curious in always being syncretic with another case. For inanimate nouns and their adjectives, that case is the nominative. For animates, it is the genitive.

For instance, nominative *každ-yj student* 'every student' contrasts with the syncretic accusative–genitive *každ-ogo student-a*. Morphologically, these clearly resemble the inanimate nominative–accusative *každ-yj moment* 'every moment' and genitive *každ-ogo moment-a*. Yet, here, the accusative shifts its syncretic allegiance to the nominative, leaving the genitive now unambiguous.

The syncretisms also affect pronouns. Inanimate *èt-o* 'this' is nominative–accusative, contrasting with genitive *èt-ogo*, whereas animate *on* 'he' is only nominative, contrasting with accusative–genitive *ego*.[12] Similarly, first and second person pronouns show a unique form for nominative (e.g., *my* 'we') and a shared one for accusative–genitive (*nas*).

Clearly, exponence of this syncretism is not uniform across adjectives, nouns, and pronouns nor across persons, numbers, and genders. However, one requires a means of representing animacy so as to trigger assimilation of accusative with genitive. Assigning π to all animate nouns in the syntax and having the case system be sensitive to its presence, not content, accomplishes this. That said, this example is like that of Brazilian Portuguese, in that case and agreement are often taken to be concomitant processes. So, this is a genuine example only to the extent that one divorces case assignment from person agreement in Russian. Given that objects do not agree in Russian, this is at least plausible, and, even if rejected, the example still usefully illustrates how one might detect monopartition of person.

Sensitivity to animacy without sensitivity to particular persons is not the only criterion for identifying a monopartition. A language can present internal reasons for regarding spatial or object deixis as involving π even when these do not differentiate between persons.

A suggestive case again comes from Damin. For deixis beyond person, the language has only a single term, *n!uu*, covering spaces and objects at any remove from the speaker, hearer, or others. Interestingly, though, this term is already familiar from the earlier discussion of bipartition: it is used as a second and third person pronoun, contrasting with first person *n!aa*. If we take *n!aa* as realizing $\pi_{+\text{author}}$, then we can capture the distribution of *n!uu* by supposing that it realizes π in the absence of specific content. This allows it to occur both for second and third person pronouns, $\pi_{-\text{author}}$, and for the spatial deictic structure, $\chi—\pi$ (chapter 7), in the absence of person features. If so analyzed, then spatial *n!uu* reflects a monopartition of person.

Colloquial German, rightmost in figure 3.2, presents slightly different reasons for regarding some undiscriminated deixis as involving π. Where higher registers of German have both proximal and distal demonstratives *dieser/diese/dieses* and *jener/jene/jenes*, the latter have fallen from colloquial use. Despite this, the *dies* group has not expanded to fill the gap. Rather, it has ossified as part of a now defective paradigm and, instead, in many dialects, including my spouse's (from the Ruhr Valley, represented below), one finds stressed definite articles used to cover objects both near and far:

(42) *Du nimmst den   Koffer   und ich nehm' den.*
you take.2S "the.MS" suitcase and I   take.1S "the.MS"
'You take that suitcase and I'll take this/that one.'

(43) *Die   ess'   ich jetzt und die   lass'   ich für*
"the.P/FS" eat.1S I   now and "the.P/FS" leave.1S I   for

nachher.
after

'I'm going to eat those ones / that one now and I'll leave those ones / that one for later.' (e.g., one or more potatoes)

(44) *Das   ist mein Hemd und das   ist deins.*
"the.NS" is my   shirt and "the.NS" is yours
'This/that is my shirt and that is yours.'

To disambiguate linguistically, spatial deictics are coopted, as in *den hier* 'this', *das da* 'that' (lit.: the.MS here, the.NS there). Structurally, these phrases have at least two properties relevant here. First, their order is not reversible:

(45) *Nimm   das   da   / *da   das.*
take.IMP "the.NS" there   there "the.NS"
'Take that one.'

Second, the "definite article" cannot be replaced by other determiners, like 'one' or 'all', though *dieses* is permitted:

(46) **Nimm   eins   da   / alle da.*
take.IMP one.NS there   all there
'Take one [that is] there / all [that are] there.'

(47) *Nimm   dieses hier.*
take.IMP this   here
'Take this one.'

I take these properties as indicating that the demonstratives, both proximal *dieses* and undifferentiated *der, die, das*, form part of the same functional sequence as the spatial deictics *hier* and *da*. If the functional sequence is $\chi\!-\!\pi$ (chapter 7), and if *hier* and *da* occupy the spatial head χ, then it is plausible to treat *der* and the like as exponents of π that are insensitive to feature content.[13]

So, although the criteria for identifying monopartitions are more theory-dependent and, therefore, weaker, the criterion used—animacy that is not discriminated for persons—is a natural one within the current theory and enjoys a good enough range of examples for the monopartition of person to appear soundly attested.

3.5   Conclusion

Five partitions, of a possible 15, are systematically attested across a range of deictic data, from persons to paths and from objects to spaces. This uniformity of attestation suggests that these constitute an empirically natural class and that it is legitimate, if not incumbent, to allow them to shape our understanding of what is a possible person.

Formulated as the partition problem, the question that these data pose is why only certain partitions are attested across languages and across domains: the quadripartition; its subpartition, the standard tripartition; its subpartitions, the author and participant bipartitions; and their subpartition, the monopartition.

Empirically general and robust, the partition problem provides a suitably solid basis on which to build a theory of person.

4 The Partition Problem Solved

4.1 Introduction

My solution to the partition problem is minimal: its posits are modest (section 4.2) and their use, unfettered (section 4.3). I argue for the smallest possible ontology for persons (section 4.2.1), proposing that it is organized into substructures that generate power sets, or lattices (section 4.2.2). These lattices are the denotations of the syntactic entities that the account posits: two person features and their host head, π. These occur above a root node, φ, that, syntactically, anchors the phi structure and, semantically, introduces a variable (section 4.2.3).

Organization and lattices may sound novel, but here I am merely being explicit about things that all or most theories assume, usually tacitly. Consonant with this connection to past work, the features I posit have familiar names, ±author and ±participant. The innovations of the account lie in two places.

The first is parsimony. The account requires less manipulation of the ontology than most approaches, and this is reflected in the smaller feature inventory: I eschew the hearer-based feature (and others) that alternative accounts require for descriptive adequacy (chapter 8).

Moreover, I afford the features unfettered freedom. There are no combinatorial constraints on cooccurrence of the features themselves ("geometries") nor on specific feature–value combinations ("filters"). Instead, every combination of features is regarded as grammatically legitimate, and every choice that the account permits is taken to be a point of genuine grammatical variation.

These points of variation are reified as parameters: two syntactic (1a), one per feature, and one semantic, excrescent when both features are active (1b):

(1) *Structure of parameters*
    a. Syntactic: Is each feature present?
    b. Semantic: How do multiple features compose?

(A further excrescent parameter concerns the representation of third person within one partition.) These are spelled out more precisely in section 4.3.

The semantic parameter (1b) is the most significant, as it stems from the second, and more substantial, innovation, rooted in the semantics afforded to the feature values (section 4.2.3). These are defined as operations by which the lattices that organize the ontology act on each other. The operations are complementary and closely resemble Cartesian product formation and complementation in set theory. Because the latter is noncommutative, semantic composition of the features is also noncommutative. As a result, different orders of composition allow one feature set to produce two partitions. This is crucial for deriving five partitions from two features (four feature sets).

Values have been viewed differently in previous work. The accounts mentioned in earlier chapters operationalize the lattices that their features denote as predicates of a variable. The values then assert or deny whether the variable ranges over the lattice. For instance, +author′, interpreted as 'contains the speaker' or, more explicitly, 'x contains the speaker', is a predicate of the implicit variable x and, by asserting it via "+", we confine x to the lattice (power set) of sets that contain i. (Equivalent mechanisms hold even when values are absent, as in privative accounts.)

The consequent difference between my account and previous ones amounts to function application versus function modification. When handling multiple features, traditional accounts use function modification to arrive at predication over a single variable. For instance, this mechanism takes +author′ 'x contains the speaker' and −hearer′ 'x does not include the hearer' and creates exclusive 'x contains the speaker *and* does not include the hearer', guaranteeing that the two x's are the same. Because it relies on conjunction as just illustrated, function modification makes the composition of multiple features inherently commutative. Below, however, features compose successively, by function application, which is not generally commutative. As a result, the account has greater generative capacity from a two-feature inventory.

The derivations of the partitions are presented in section 4.3. This begins by laying out the parameter space sketched in (1). It also highlights some technical points concerning the empty set and a Gricean principle eliminating overlap when the features denote nondisjoint sets. The derivations begin with the most parametrically and computationally simple system, monopartition (section 4.3.1) and build the most complex, quadripartition (section 4.3.5). Together, these show that the account can generate all attested partitions and nothing more.

Finally, section 4.4 (and appendix B.1.1) ties together the role that the empty set plays in the account, building on sections 4.2.2 and 4.3.4–4.3.5.

4.2 Elements of the Solution

Whether it says so or not, every account of person requires a mental ontology and a means by which the grammar accesses that ontology. Implicit in the features that most, if not all, accounts posit as the means of access is, additionally, an organization of the ontology into, for instance, the participants alone. In this, my account is no different from others, though it may be more explicit.

The ontology I adopt was presented in section 3.2 (where the partition element notation i_o, iu_o, u_o, o_o was introduced). Its minimality is defended in section 4.2.1.

Section 4.2.2 proposes that the ontology is organized into three lattices, or, technically, atomic join-complete semilattices, based on power sets. The sets that generate these power sets are egocentrically nested subsets of the ontology, which therefore incorporate an inherent asymmetry between speaker and hearer. Although other accounts organize the ontology similarly, they do so symmetrically. The asymmetry I presuppose connects fundamentally to Zwicky's (1977) observation about impossible partitions.

Finally, section 4.2.3 presents the means by which the grammar accesses the organized ontology. These are an author and a participant feature plus a functional sequence that begins with a root node, φ, and proceeds to a head, π, where features reside. The features are bivalent and—in the chief innovation of this account—their values denote, not truth functors, which would reduce the features to first-order predicates, but actions by and on the person lattices.[1]

4.2.1 Ontology

The mental ontology of section 3.2 assumes a unique speaker, i, a unique hearer, u, and multiple others, o, o', o'', and so on. The others are animates in a loose, culturally determined sense, covering, maximally, humans, animals, supernatural entities, and biological inanimates that display properties of animates (like dolls, the sun, the wind, etc.).

These ontological distinctions are taken for granted in all accounts of person that I am aware of and in much other work besides, and the existence of multiple others is similarly uncontroversial. The uniqueness of the i and u, however, is neither obvious nor uncontested. As a result, there are three rival ontologies to mine (figure 4.1).

The features and operations I posit below are numberless. So, they yield essentially the same partitions irrespective of the population of authors and hearers (appendix B.3). This makes the choice between populations in part a matter of convenience: the smaller the ontology, the neater the calculations. However, there are several arguments for favoring the smallest ontology, some

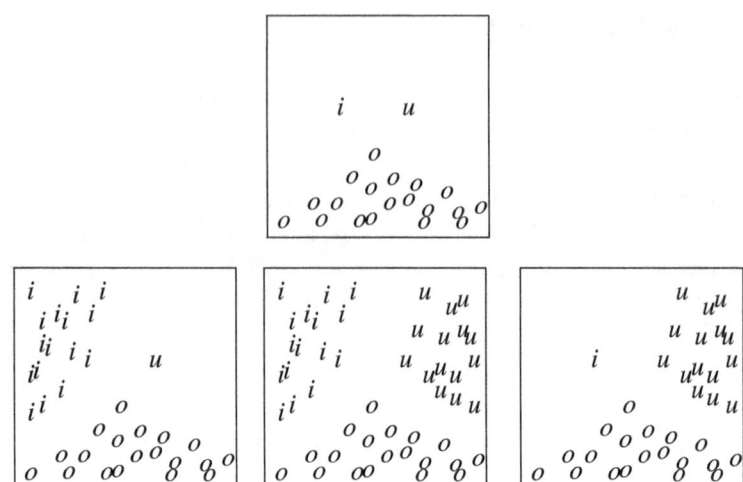

Figure 4.1
Ontology (top) and three alternatives

inconclusive. Failure to address these might leave readers in doubt as to the foundations of the account.

4.2.1.1 Inconclusive Arguments Conceptual arguments for the uniqueness of *i* tend to run along two mutually incompatible lines. Some observe, as in Corbett 2000, that *we* is not the plural of *I* in the same way that *cats* is the plural of *cat*: *three cats* is a cat plus two more cats, but *we three* is not me plus two more me's. Others claim that "we never speak in choruses" (Harley and Ritter 2002b, 31) and, hence, that the linguistic settings for multiauthor *we* are extremely marked (Cysouw 2003). Neither case convinces.

A basic objection to the argument from plurality is that it does not formally define the notion of plurality. If plurality in English means nonsingleton, then the notion of plurality in *we* and *cats* is indeed the same, as neither refers to singletons. The heterogeneity of *we*-pluralities is determined, not by the plural, but by the nature of the first person itself, which is different from the nature of *cat*. This position is discussed in chapter 6.

A second objection is that the argument from plurality does not define its tacit notion of equivalence. Clearly, if I own three cats, I do not own the same cat three times. Rather, *cat* is an equivalence class for a set of entities, and I claim to own three of members of that class. For the argument from plurality to work, it must be explained why there is no plausible equivalence relation between my ego and others'.

A candidate for the relation is that of shared or joint intentionality, so-called "*we*-intentions." *We're making hollandaise*, where *we* means Dierk and I, can be true in two ways. Either Dierk and I cooperate—say, with me pouring and him stirring. Or I am at my hob and he is at his, both making hollandaise in our own ways for our own ends. Shared intentionality is the subject of a substantial philosophical and psychological literature, and some have gone so far as to suggest that it is "biologically primitive" (Searle 1995; see Gold and Harbour 2012 for further references and discussion in light of linguistic theory). Certainly, shared intentions are fundamental to human nature and society, and one could use them as the criterion of equivalence—cooperation is action by multiple i's, independence is action by i plus o's—making an ontology with multiple i's licit.

The second argument against multiple i's is that they would be restricted to choric behaviors, which humans do not engage in. Interestingly, this tacitly assumes the second counterargument to the previous position: that the equivalence relation for the different i's is not identity, but being joint and equal actors in a special kind of activity. Here, though, the joint activity is restricted to speaking. Again, the argument is unconvincing.

First, functional pressures rarely, if ever, amount to vetoes or compulsion on grammars (section 2.4.4). So, rarity of choric speech does not entail its ungrammaticality, let alone its ontological impossibility.

Second, the claimed rarity of use seems simply false. Jewish liturgy, for example, includes numerous instances in which a first person plural thanks, pleads, remonstrates, or otherwise communicates with the tribal deity. Given that everyone says the same thing at once and does so, frequently, not for selfish but for communal ends, this seems precisely to be a choric first person act. I suspect that Jews are not the only group to have addressed deities in this fashion. (In a more modern vein, see List 2014 on aggregate, common, and corporate attitudes.)

Establishment of group identity is, like shared intentionality, a fundamental of human nature and society, and the role of language in achieving this is a whole discipline in its own right: sociolinguistics. So, contrary to assertion, choric *we* seems both plausible and useful.

Similarly "sociolinguistic" reasoning carries over into conceptual arguments for multiple u's. Being able to refer to 'you who are present', as opposed to 'you and absent others', would effectively establish or reinforce group identity (a use to which paucals are sometimes put; Corbett 2000). Complementarily, it might be flattering or respectful to refer to one's addressees with a form meaning u's plus o's, implying social distance between speaker and addressees via a buffer of others (as is achieved by honorific plurality for a single addressee in French *vous*, Russian *vy*, Georgian *tkven*, etc.).

Thus, contrary to most writers, I believe that purportedly anomalous first and second plurals are not only readily conceivable, but potentially useful.

4.2.1.2 Arguments for a Minimal Ontology However, ontological traction is possible here. A unique i is certainly plausible, given the brute psychological fact that we have access only to our own consciousness and that our conception of the world is naturally centered around the only perceptions to which we have direct access.

Moreover, it is highly suggestive that wide-ranging typological studies, including some designed with these questions in mind (Noyer 1992, Cysouw 2003, Simon 2005, Bobaljik 2008), have not found languages that differentiate choric *we* or mass *you* from other *we*'s and *you*'s. These would falsify the smallest ontology. So, their absence is telling.

Ultimately, basic properties of pronominal reference tell against an ontology with multiple i's. Assuming that the ontology is available to all languages and not subject to parameterization, we need look no further than English. Consider (2), where the choric *we* is, referentially, $I \sqcup he$, with I denoting i and *he*, i':

(2) We$_{ii'}$ beseech you for forgiveness for he$_{i'}$ has made hollandaise and I$_i$ have eaten it.

Given the ontological parity of i and i', they should be represented by the same pronoun, just as, gender aside, every o can be referenced by *he*, making (3) felicitous:

(3) They$_{oo'}$ beseech you for forgiveness for he$_o$ has made hollandaise and he$_{o'}$ has eaten it.

So, if the plurality of i's and the plurality of o's are ontological analogues, one ought to be able to replace *he* in (2) with I, as in (4):

(4) *We$_{ii'}$ beseech you for forgiveness for I$_{i'}$ have made hollandaise and I$_i$ have eaten it.

However, choric enunciation of the entirety of (4) is impossible with the disjoint reference indicated. Instead, as in (2), one of i and i' must be referenced by *he*. This means that, in denotations like ii', a distinction must be maintained between the speaker's i and others'. But this contradicts the notion that the i's form the required equivalence class and so presents a sound reason for rejecting multiple i's.[2]

One can mount a simple argument for uniqueness of u, if cognitive representations are assumed to develop, phylogenetically and/or ontogenetically, according to general principles of economy. We granted at the outset that at least one u and multiple o's are ineliminable. Suppose further that u and the o's are added to our mental ontology in separate events—possibly reflecting discrete maturational stages: emergence of u marking our earliest social interactions, emergence of o's marking our awareness of others. If so, then awareness of second person pluralities comes later than both of these. (This is plausible if activities with multiple interactants require sophistication.) The question is whether the representation of second person pluralities requires additions to the mental ontology. If it does not, then principles of economy confine us to a unique u.

In fact, one can represent pluralities of hearers with a single u and multiple o's, if we suppose that hearers are egocentric. So, when an addressed group hears a second person plural, each hearer egoistically interprets u as referring to themselves and conceives of the others as o's. This exactly parallels the manner in which, in replying with a first person plural, that audience member would consider themselves the unique i and the other group members, o's. The uniqueness of u then parallels that of i: u is the i-like version of an o, properties of the ego invested in an other.

Thus, despite problems with previous arguments, the most minimal ontology, with one i and one u, can be justified by appeal to typology and basic considerations of economy and uniqueness of the speaker.

4.2.2 Organization

I propose that the grammar of person does not have direct access to the ontology of person. Rather, access is mediated by an organization of the ontology into three structures that I posit as the denotations of two features and their hosting functional head. The structures result from taking three subsets of the ontology and performing two actions on them. The subsets are (5a) the speaker alone, (5b) the speaker plus the hearer, and (5c) the entire ontology:

(5) a. $\{i\}$
  b. $\{i, u\}$
  c. $\{i, u, o, o', o'', \ldots\}$

From these, we first form the power sets, that is, each set of all subsets, of (5a–c), giving (6a–c).

(6) a. $\{\{i\}, \{\}\}$
  b. $\{\{i\}, \{i, u\}, \{u\}, \{\}\}$
  c. $\{\{i\}, \{i, o\}, \{i, o'\}, \{i, o''\}, \ldots, \{i, o, o'\}, \{i, o, o''\}, \ldots,$
  $\{i, o, o', o''\}, \ldots,$
  $\{i, u\}, \{i, u, o\}, \{i, u, o'\}, \{i, u, o''\}, \ldots, \{i, u, o, o'\}, \{i, u, o, o''\}, \ldots,$
  $\{i, u, o, o'o''\}, \ldots,$
  $\{u\}, \{u, o\}, \{u, o'\}, \{u, o''\}, \ldots, \{u, o, o'\}, \{u, o, o''\}, \ldots,$
  $\{u, o, o', o''\}, \ldots,$
  $\{o\}, \{o'\}, \{o''\}, \ldots, \{o, o'\}, \{o, o''\}, \ldots, \{o, o', o''\}, \ldots,$
  $\{\}\}$

Clearly, the set-theoretic notation makes for hard reading. So, I will switch from talking of these objects set-theoretically, as sets of sets, to regarding them lattice-theoretically, as lattices of sets, and I accompany this with the following change of notation. An element of a power set written as, say, $\{x, y, z\}$ will now be represented as an element of a lattice simply as xyz. For example, $\{i\}$ becomes i; $\{u, o\}$, uo; and $\{o, o'o''\}$, $oo'o''$. To further differentiate the two modes of representation, I reserve $\varnothing$ for lattice-theoretic structures (rather than the more usual $\bot$) and write the empty set as a literally empty set, $\{\}$, when talking set-theoretically. With this, we can rewrite (6) more transparently as (7):

(7) a. $\{i, \varnothing\}$
   b. $\{i, iu, u, \varnothing\}$
   c. $\{i, io, io', io'', \ldots, ioo', ioo'', \ldots, ioo'o'', \ldots,$
      $iu, iuo, iuo', iuo'', \ldots, iuoo', iuoo'', \ldots, iuoo'o'', \ldots,$
      $u, uo, uo', uo'', \ldots, uoo', uoo'', \ldots, uoo'o'', \ldots,$
      $o, o', o'', \ldots, oo', oo'', \ldots, oo'o'', \ldots, \varnothing\}$

Although this change is largely a matter of presentation, it has two further advantages, enabling the discussion to avail itself of standard lattice-theoretic operations in the current chapter and of clear and conventional graphic representations when we combine person features with number (chapter 6). (Readers who prefer power sets to lattices may rephrase everything that follows in terms of traditional sets with all their concomitant swirls and curlicues.)

The representation of these structures can be further simplified by using the subscript notation introduced in chapter 3:

(8) x_y is the list of sets of the form $\{x\} \cup y$, for $x \in X$, $y \in \mathcal{P}(Y)$.

For instance, i_o abbreviates lattice elements that contain i and any number of o's, including possibly none; that is, i_o is the list of i alone, as well as with any one o ($io, io', io'', \ldots$), with any two ($ioo', ioo'', io'o'', \ldots$), with any three ($ioo'o'', \ldots$), and so on. Likewise, iu_o is $iu, iuo, iuoo', iuoo'o'', \ldots$; and u_o is $u, uo, uoo', uoo'o'', \ldots$. Finally, o_o is the list of any o alone ($o, o', o'', \ldots$), any pair ($oo', oo'', o'o'', \ldots$), any triple ($oo'o'', \ldots$), or any larger collection. In consequence, we can write the three structures of interest simply as:

(9) a. $\{i, \varnothing\}$
   b. $\{i, iu, u, \varnothing\}$
   c. $\{i_o, iu_o, u_o, o_o, \varnothing\}$

The final step in producing the organization of the ontology relevant below is to remove the empty sets from each of these:

(10) a. $\{i\}$ author lattice ($\mathscr{L}_{au}$)
 b. $\{i, iu, u\}$ participant lattice ($\mathscr{L}_{pt}$)
 c. $\{i_o, iu_o, u_o, o_o\}$ π lattice ($\mathscr{L}_\pi$)

As (10) indicates, I call these the *author lattice*, the *participant lattice*, and the *π lattice*, respectively, and notate them $\mathscr{L}_{au}$, $\mathscr{L}_{pt}$, and $\mathscr{L}_\pi$. Although I call these "lattices", absence of the empty set (a bottom element, $\bot$) makes them technically atomic join-complete semilattices. The power sets in (9) are true lattices, but this distinction is irrelevant to my purposes.

Both of the moves in (6) and (10) are innocent. Power set lattices have an established history within linguistics, beginning with Link 1983, and even theories that do not rely on them directly still have devices that create them or their elements (e.g., the PL operator of Chierchia 1998 or the reticulator of Borer 2005). And exclusion of the empty set raises no questions, as its presence or absence does not affect the partitional yield of the account (appendix B.1.1). Its removal makes the calculations cleaner.

Even before we turn to solving the partition problem, two properties of the structures in (10) already count in their favor: nonnovelty and asymmetry.

As mentioned in chapter 2, traditional accounts of person posit three features, ±author′, ±participant′, and ±hearer′ (e.g., Silverstein 1976, Noyer 1992). These are interpreted as predicates and so, in standard predicate calculus, they must predicate of some variable. The domain of this variable is precisely the π lattice: it ranges over all combinations, of any size, of author, hearer, and others, until the features constrain it more precisely. For instance, +author′ +participant′(x), 'x contains the author and contains the author and/or hearer', confines x to sets that contain the author and permits, but does not force, inclusion of the hearer and others. So, the π lattice corresponds to an object posited on other accounts.

Moreover, the two features just mentioned correspond in essence to the author and participant lattices. By forcing x to contain i, u, or iu, +participant′ requires x to have a subset that is an element of the participant lattice. Similarly, +author′ forces x to have a subset that is an—or rather, the—element of the author lattice. Thus, all three lattices of the current theory have correlates within traditional approaches to person.

My theory posits no lattice equivalent of +hearer′. That is, there is no hearer lattice consisting only of $\{u\}$. This structure would create symmetry between i and u: there is one structure containing only the latter, one containing only the former, one containing both but nothing else, and one containing both and everything else. Consequently, my account creates an essential asymmetry between i and u. One way of appreciating this asymmetry is to note that the subsets of the ontology that generate the three lattices form a chain (as, therefore, do the lattices themselves):

(11) $\{i\} \subset \{i, u\} \subset \{i, u, o, o', o'', \ldots\}$

That is, these organize the ontology into a series of egocentrically nested sets.

This asymmetry lies at the heart of Zwicky's problem. In current notation, Zwicky's observation was that $i_o i u_o \,|\, u_o \,|\, o_o$, the standard tripartition, is attested, but $i_o \,|\, i u_o u_o \,|\, o_o$, conflating inclusive with second person, is not. Another way of expressing this is that i and u cannot be permuted:

(12) $\overset{\text{attested}}{i_o i u_o \,|\, u_o \,|\, o_o} \xrightarrow{i \leftrightarrow u} \overset{\text{unattested}}{u_o u i_o \,|\, i_o \,|\, o_o}$
$= i_o \,|\, i u_o u_o \,|\, o_o$

The same asymmetry holds of the author bipartition. Author–nonauthor is attested, but hearer–nonhearer, that is, second-cum-inclusive versus exclusive-cum-third, is not:

(13) $\overset{\text{attested}}{i_o i u_o \,|\, u_o o_o} \xrightarrow{i \leftrightarrow u} \overset{\text{unattested}}{u_o u i_o \,|\, i_o o_o}$
$= i_o o_o \,|\, i u_o u_o$

This disparity is clearly reflected in (11), which affords author a more central position than hearer.

4.2.3 Operation

If the ontology and its organization are largely uncontroversial and unoriginal, the substance of my theory lies in how grammar accesses these. To this end, I posit two features, two values, and a categorial head that hosts them within a larger a functional sequence, but the values are the chief innovation of the account.

The categorial head is labeled π and its denotation is the π lattice:

(14) $[\![\pi]\!] = \mathscr{L}_\pi$

Similarly, the two features also denote lattices:

(15) $[\![\text{author}]\!] = \mathscr{L}_{au}$

(16) $[\![\text{participant}]\!] = \mathscr{L}_{pt}$

That is, there is an author feature that denotes the author lattice and a participant feature that denotes the participant lattice. (The feature names are chosen to emphasize the connection with past work. As previously stated, I write my features without prime marks and others' with.) Just as there was no hearer lattice in the previous section, so there is no hearer feature, like Noyer's (1992) ±hearer′ or Silverstein's (1976) ±tu′.

These lattices do not sit inertly. Rather, they interact by means of the values + and −. Only the features take values, distinguishing them from the categorial head that is their host. The values denote the complementary lattice operations of disjoint, or pairwise, addition and joint, or cumulative, subtraction. More specifically, suppose F and G denote sets $\mathscr{L}_F$ and $\mathscr{L}_G$. Then + takes every possible pairing of elements in $\mathscr{L}_F$ in $\mathscr{L}_G$ and joins them together ($\sqcup$):

(17) $[\![+F(G)]\!] = \{g \sqcup f : f \in \mathscr{L}_F, g \in \mathscr{L}_G\}$

I refer to this either as the *positive action* of F on G, or as the *action* of +F on G.

Conversely, in the *negative action* of F on G, that is, when −F acts on G, every element of $\mathscr{L}_F$ is subtracted from every element of $\mathscr{L}_G$. However, in contrast to addition, which is pairwise and distributive, subtraction takes place cumulatively: all f_i in $\mathscr{L}_F$ are subtracted simultaneously from each g in $\mathscr{L}_G$:

(18) $[\![-F(G)]\!] = \{(((g\backslash f_1)\backslash f_2)\backslash \ldots \backslash f_n) : g \in \mathscr{L}_G\}$ for $\mathscr{L}_F = \{f_1, \ldots, f_n\}$

This cumbersome expression can be simplified because all the sets relevant here have a unique maximal element. Once the maximum has been subtracted, subtraction of all other elements is redundant. (To illustrate with the participant lattice, once one has subtracted $f_3 = iu$ from $g = iuo$, leaving just $iuo\backslash iu = o$, subtraction of the remaining elements, $f_1 = i$ and $f_2 = u$, has no effect: $o\backslash i = o\backslash u = o$.) Thus, we can write:

(19) $[\![-F(G)]\!] = \{g\backslash \max(\mathscr{L}_F) : g \in \mathscr{L}_G\}$

For clarity, the symbols + and − are used only in morphosyntactic representation. Their semantic denotations are $\oplus$ and $\ominus$, respectively:

(20) $[\![+F(G)]\!] = \mathscr{L}_G \oplus \mathscr{L}_F$

(21) $[\![-F(G)]\!] = \mathscr{L}_G \ominus \mathscr{L}_F$

Like union and complementation in set theory, and like addition and subtraction in standard arithmetic, $\oplus$ is commutative but $\ominus$ is not. An illustration of the latter is: $\mathscr{L}_{au} \ominus \mathscr{L}_{pt} = \{i\backslash iu\} = \{\varnothing\}$ but $\mathscr{L}_{pt} \ominus \mathscr{L}_{au} = \{i\backslash i, iu\backslash i, u\backslash i\} = \{u, \varnothing\}$. This noncommutativity will be crucial below in deriving five partitions from the four feature sets that the inventory {±author, ±participant} allows.

The example of noncommutativity just given, though valid, is not a true representation of the account, because the author and participant lattices never act on each other directly (though nothing untoward would result if they did; appendix B.2). Instead, they act on the π lattice or on the output of action on the π lattice. Thus, when π has feature content F, its denotation is:

(22) $[\![\pi_F]\!] = [\![F]\!]([\![\pi]\!])$
$= [\![F]\!](\mathscr{L}_\pi)$

As detailed in the derivations, F may contain two features, or one, or none, and, when it contains two features, the order in which they act is of major import.

The final element to the proposal is a variable. A numberless first person pronoun, say (like Jarawa *mi*), does not denote the whole of $i_o i u_o$. Rather, the pronoun can assume any of the values in that set. In technical terms, the first person pronoun denotes a variable over $i_o i u_o$, the range of meanings of the general first person. It would be possible to build this variable directly into the denotation of π. However, on purely technical grounds, I prefer an account in which the π head and its contents are semantically uniform and the variable comes from elsewhere.

To that end, I posit a head φ that introduces a variable over a set (23). (Naturally, both λ-terms have types, but only that of x is shown, because only it will be relevant below.)

(23) $[\![\varphi]\!] = \lambda S . \lambda x . x \in S$
$\quad\quad\quad\quad\quad\quad\quad{\scriptstyle x \in D_e}$

Syntactically, φ is the root of the functional sequence to which π belongs:

(24) $\pi\,(\pm\mathrm{au})\,(\pm\mathrm{pt})$
$\quad\quad\quad\diagdown$
$\quad\quad\quad\quad\varphi$

The nature of the syntactic representation is explained four paragraphs below.

I will refer to φ as the *root node* of this functional sequence, because it occupies a position analogous to the lexical roots that anchor the extended projections of nouns and verbs. (This is the opposite of traditional usage, according to which the root node is the highest in the tree, rather than, as here, the most embedded; but, given the prominence that roots and extended projections occupy in current thinking, the reversal should be easily assimilated.)

Putting these pieces together, function application captures the desired property that pronouns denote variables over specific sets:

(25) $[\![\pi_F \text{—} \varphi]\!]$
$= [\![\varphi]\!]([\![\pi_F]\!])$
$= \lambda S . \lambda x . x \in S([\![F]\!](\mathscr{L}_\pi))$
$= \lambda x . x \in [\![F]\!](\mathscr{L}_\pi)$

The Partition Problem Solved 77

The last line characterizes the elements x that are in the result of applying the feature content of π to the π lattice.

Advocates of presuppositional accounts of person (e.g., Cooper 1983, Heim and Kratzer 1998, Sauerland 2005) can, of course, represent φ as introducing a variable that is subject to as yet unspecified presuppositions:[3]

(26) $[\![\varphi]\!] = \lambda S . \lambda x \in S . x$

This approach does not necessarily differ from my own, provided that I can posit that some higher head, like D, "presuppositionalizes" expressions like $\lambda x . x \in S$, turning them into $\lambda x \in S . x$. Nothing I say about person per se bears or depends on this issue, but the account of number in chapter 6 (and Harbour 2014a) might require a rather hefty calculus for handling interaction between presuppositions if one wishes all phi features to be purely presuppositional.

The syntactic structure (24) is also flexible with regard to readers' interpretation. As shown, it consists purely of functional spine. Readers who prefer standard X′ Theory may read (24) as a statement of the functional hierarchy before the rules of projection have taken effect. If so, the real syntactic structure would be:

(27)
```
        πP
       /  \
      π    φ
```

This traditional representation makes the analogy between φ and other roots plain to see. Compare this to the simplified DP structure below with its nominal root:

(28)
```
        DP
       /  \
      D    N
```

Given my past joint work (Adger et al., 2009), I think of (24) in terms of Mirror Theory, depicting all there is to the syntax (Brody 2000, Brody and Szabolcsi 2003; on the generation of nonbranching structures using standard Merge, see Adger 2012). However, everything in this chapter is neutral between these and several other interpretations. What matters here is the semantics of φ, π, and its feature content, all of which is unaffected by the representational issues just touched on. (The same neutrality holds true when we turn to number in chapter 6. Only when it comes to linear precedence, in the final third of that chapter, does the choice between these representations become contentful. Details about Mirror Theory are deferred until then.)

Leaving aside some assumptions about derivations, the foregoing is all there is to the proposal. A root node, φ, introduces a variable. A head, π, constrains that variable to the domain of speaker, hearer, and animate others. And the feature content of π, ±author and ±participant, acts on the domain to constrain the variable further. Along with the ontology and its organization, reassuringly little of the account is novel. Its main innovation lies in the semantics it affords to feature values, in virtue of which the features denote, not predicates, but actions by lattices. Other than that, its novelty lies chiefly in what it eschews. There is no third feature, based on the hearer or anything else. Nor are there "geometries," stipulating that certain features must, or must not, cooccur. Nor are there "filters" on specific feature–value combinations. On the contrary, as we will now see, the account achieves generative adequacy precisely because it is free of these extras.

4.3 Solution of the Partition Problem

We can now solve the partition problem. That is, we can show that the feature system so far defined delivers all and only monopartition, author and participant bipartition, standard tripartition, and quadripartition. The derivational details are presented in sections 4.3.1–4.3.5, respectively, building from the simplest to the most complex. Before that, I lay out the solution and its parameters and note some formalities relevant to the derivations.

It should be evident that the generative capacity of the account is in the right order of magnitude with regard to its motivating problem. It posits two features. Two features generate four feature sets. This falls one short of the number of partitions. However, once two features are activated, they must be composed in a particular order. Given that feature composition is noncommutative (section 4.2.3), it is possible that composing two-feature systems in different orders yields different partitions. If so, then the account maximally generates five partitions, as desired.

In fact, order of composition is material below. So, π is parameterized by an activation parameter for each feature (29a–b) and by a parameter affecting order of composition (29c). Languages, or rather, their deictic domains, are characterized by, as it were, deleting one feature in (29c) and keeping or removing 'not' in (29a–b):

(29) *Parameters of π*
 a. The author feature is (not) present.
 b. The participant feature is (not) present.
 c. The author/participant feature composes with π first.

Moreover, for tripartition, there are two ways, both exploited, of representing third person, using opposite values of ±author:

The Partition Problem Solved

(30) *Subsidiary parameter*
    Tripartite o_o uses +author/−author.

Because this parameter does not affect the inventory of partitions but instead affects only some internal workings, I list it separately and label it as subsidiary.

In affecting presence or absence of features from heads, (29a–b) are parameters as conceived in Borer 1983. By contrast, (29c) and (30) are semantic parameters, along the lines of Chierchia 1998.[4] The semantic parameters apply nonvacuously only when the syntactic parameters are both active, and (30) applies only when the setting of (29c) yields a tripartition.

Languages can operate different partitions in different deictic domains, as already discussed under the rubric of polyploidy. Repeating an earlier example, English in most of its modern varieties illustrates this: it has tripartition for person deixis, but bipartition for all forms of spatial deixis (*we–you–they* versus *here–there*). Consequently, (30) is not a language-wide parameter, but varies according to the context in which π occurs.[5]

The space of possible parameter settings is shown in table 4.1, along with the space of attested partitions. As the table implies, there is an exact match between these. The correlation shown is natural in that complex partitions, those with more partition elements, are attributed to greater feature sets: monopartition requires no features; the bipartitions, one; and the tri- and quadripartition, two. The task ahead is to prove what the table asserts.

The partitions are derived in the order shown in the table, reflecting their scandent complexity (sections 4.3.1–4.3.5). Each derivation offers two distinct modes of presentation to illustrate how the system works. The first is rote application of the definitions of π, the features, and their values. To increase understandability, these are accompanied by diagrams that depict how specific feature–value pairs act on their inputs to produce the various partition elements.

Table 4.1
The parameter space and its yield

Parameters		Partition	
Features	Order	Size	Elements
{ }		monopartition	$i_o\ iu_o\ u_o\ o_o$
{±author}		bipartition	$i_o\ iu_o\|u_o\ o_o$
{±participant}		bipartition	$i_o\ iu_o\ u_o\|o_o$
{±author, ±participant}	±pt(±au(...))	tripartition	$i_o\ iu_o\|u_o\|o_o$
{±author, ±participant}	±au(±pt(...))	quadripartition	$i_o\|iu_o\|u_o\|o_o$

Before we proceed, attention must be drawn to one convention and two formal points. The first formal point concerns the emergence, effect, and elimination of empty sets. As already explained, the three person lattices are power sets with the bottom element, ∅, removed. It may therefore surprise some to see the empty set resurface, through the action of negative features. To a certain extent, this surprise is artificial, because person lattices with zeroes have the same partitional yield as those without (appendix B.1) and if these had been used instead, no comment would be necessary. Yet, even so, we require a means of winnowing empty sets from the final yield, because, as explained below, there are no empty persons. I attribute this winnowing to the domain restriction introduced by φ (section 4.3.2).

That said, the (re)appearance of the empty set and its subsequent disappearance is not an embarrassment. The empty set plays a crucial role in the account. If it did not arise through the action of negative values, derivation of the tripartition and the quadripartition would flounder and founder, respectively.

Other than winnowing zeroes away, the semantic effect of φ is limited. Ultimately, it merely supplies the variable that ranges over the partition elements. Unlike π and its features, then, it does not affect the structure of the partitions themselves. Its omission therefore makes for simpler equations. So, I adopt the convention of ignoring it except when zeroes are directly discussed.

The second formal point is the principle of *Lexical Complementarity*, invoked to induce a partition when the denotations of two feature combinations are not disjoint but exist in a subset–superset relation. Informally, it states that the feature combination with the larger denotation is used only when the smaller one is inappropriate. Formally:

(31) *Lexical Complementarity*
Let F, G be feature specifications where $[\![F(\pi)]\!] \subset [\![G(\pi)]\!]$. Then use of $[\![G(\pi)]\!]$ is confined to $[\![G(\pi)]\!] \setminus [\![F(\pi)]\!]$.

That is, if G subsumes F, then G is used to "catch F's semantic slack." Honing semantic denotations in this way is not novel. It will be familiar to readers from the literature on scales and implicatures, and, in the field of phi features, equivalent principles are explicitly incorporated into McGinnis's (2005) reworking of Harley and Ritter 2002a (where the same mechanism is, McGinnis argues, implicit) and into Krifka's (2007) analysis of Tok Pisin pronouns. The principle is required only when multiple features are activated (sections 4.3.4–4.3.5).[6]

In feature systems based on first-order predicates, Lexical Complementarity is usually a concomitant of privativity, playing a role similar to that of minus values. As a result, one might wonder whether bivalence and complementarity are both strictly necessary. They are. On the one hand, bivalence is an important part of the current account, both semantically (this chapter) and morphologically (chapter 5). Privative rewrites of my features raise problems in both domains (section 9.5, appendix B.4). On the other hand, Lexical Complementarity is independently required for number features (chapter 6) and these, too, are crucially bivalent (section 9.5).

With these resources now in place, we are ready to proceed.

4.3.1 Monopartition

Derivation of the monopartition is trivial, because monopartition is simply the π lattice, the denotation of π:

(32) $[\![\pi]\!] = \mathscr{L}_\pi$
$= \{i_o, iu_o, u_o, o_o\}$

or, in partition notation, $i_o iu_o u_o o_o$. This corresponds to the parameter setting below:

(33) *Parameters of the monopartition*
    a. The author feature is not present.
    b. The participant feature is not present.

Because the parameter affecting order of composition is vacuous, I have omitted it. The same holds for the representation of third person.

4.3.2 Author Bipartition

Because it involves the smaller of the feature lattices, the author bipartition offers the simplest start for illustrating the operations by which the lattices interact. It corresponds to the parameter setting below (though, given that it applies trivially, one could omit the order parameter, as was done for the monopartition):

(34) *Parameters of the author bipartition*
    a. The author feature is present.
    b. The participant feature is not present.
    c. The author feature composes with π first.

These settings generate two expressions, $+\text{author}(\pi)$ and $-\text{author}(\pi)$, the denotations of which we now calculate.

For the plus value, we begin by applying the semantic values and definitions given above:

(35) $[\![+\text{author}(\pi)]\!]$
$= \mathscr{L}_\pi \oplus \mathscr{L}_{au}$
$= \{i_o, iu_o, u_o, o_o\} \oplus \{i\}$
$= \{i_o \sqcup i, iu_o \sqcup i, u_o \sqcup i, o_o \sqcup i\}$

In the last step of (35), we have moved i into the larger set and shown that it is to be joined to each of i_o, iu_o, u_o, and o_o. The symbol $\sqcup$ represents the lattice-theoretic join of two elements. Returning to set-theoretic terms, it equates to the union of the sets in question. To unpack this, recall, from (8), that u_o abbreviates a list of elements:

(36) $u_o = u,\ uo,\ uo',\ uo'',\ \ldots,\ uoo',\ uoo'',\ uo'o'',\ \ldots,\ uoo'o'',\ \ldots$

So, $u_o \sqcup i$ is shorthand for the join of i with each of these lattice points:

(37) $u_o \sqcup i$
$= u \sqcup i,\ uo \sqcup i,\ uo' \sqcup i,\ uo'' \sqcup i,\ \ldots,\ uoo' \sqcup i,\ uoo'' \sqcup i,\ uo'o'' \sqcup i,\ \ldots,$
$uoo'o'' \sqcup i,\ \ldots$
$= iu,\ iuo,\ iuo',\ iuo'',\ \ldots,\ iuoo',\ iuoo'',\ iuo'o'',\ \ldots,\ iuoo'o'',\ \ldots$
$= iu_o$

Concerning the step between the two long lines, recall that u and i stand for the sets $\{u\}$ and $\{i\}$, respectively. So, the join $u \sqcup i$ is the union $\{u\} \cup \{i\} = \{i, u\}$, which is iu in the lattice notation. Likewise, $uo \sqcup i$ is $\{u, o\} \cup \{i\} = \{i, u, o\}$, or iuo, and so on. The transition from the second long line to the last line involves just the notational convention in (8).

Similarly, o_o abbreviates:

(38) $o_o = o,\ o',\ o'',\ \ldots,\ oo',\ oo'',\ o'o'',\ \ldots,\ oo'o''\ \ldots$

So, adding i to each of these yields:

(39) $o_o \sqcup i$
$= o \sqcup i,\ o' \sqcup i,\ o'' \sqcup i,\ \ldots,\ oo' \sqcup i,\ oo'' \sqcup i,\ o'o'' \sqcup i,\ \ldots,\ oo'o'' \sqcup i,\ \ldots$
$= io,\ io',\ io'',\ \ldots,\ ioo',\ ioo'',\ io'o'',\ \ldots,\ ioo'o'',\ \ldots$
$= io_o$

This is the set of elements containing i and at least one o. That is, io_o is i_o with i itself removed, as $\{i_o\} = \{i, io_o\}$.

For i_o and iu_o, the operation $\sqcup i$ is redundant. For instance:

(40) $i_o \sqcup i$
$= i \sqcup i,\ io \sqcup i,\ io' \sqcup i,\ io'' \sqcup i,\ \ldots,\ ioo' \sqcup i,\ ioo'' \sqcup i,\ io'o'' \sqcup i,\ \ldots,$
$ioo'o'' \sqcup i,\ \ldots$
$= ii,\ iio,\ iio',\ iio'',\ \ldots,\ iioo',\ iioo'',\ iio'o'',\ \ldots,\ iioo'o'',\ \ldots$
$= i,\ io,\ io',\ io''',\ \ldots,\ ioo',\ ioo'',\ io'o'',\ \ldots,\ ioo'o'',\ \ldots$
$= i_o$

The crucial step, "eliminating" the double i's, follows from basic set theory. Again, iio is shorthand for the set $\{i, i, o\}$. The axiom of extension, one of the axioms of Zermelo-Fraenkel set theory, entails that $\{a,a\} = \{a\}$. So, $\{i,i,x\} = \{i,x\}$. In the more abbreviated notation, then, when there are double i's, iix, one is redundant and we can just write ix. Hence, $i_o \sqcup i = i_o$, and, similarly, $iu_o \sqcup i = iu_o$.

So, returning to (35), we have:

(41) $[\![+\text{author}(\pi)]\!]$
$= \mathscr{L}_\pi \oplus \mathscr{L}_{au}$
$= \{i_o, iu_o, u_o, o_o\} \oplus \{i\}$
$= \{i_o \sqcup i, iu_o \sqcup i, u_o \sqcup i, o_o \sqcup i\}$
$= \{i_o, iu_o, iu_o, io_o\}$
$= \{i_o, iu_o\}$

where the last step follows, again, from the axiom of extension, as $\{iu_o, iu_o, x\} = \{iu_o, x\}$ and $\{i_o, io_o, x\} = \{i, io_o, io_o, x\} = \{i, io_o, x\} = \{i_o, x\}$. This completes calculation of the plus value, delivering a general first person, covering both exclusive and inclusive. In short, +author picks out not just i, the first person singular, but every first person, regardless of clusivity and number.

The preceding derivation also shows that disjoint addition, $\oplus$, is distinct from set-theoretic union. Union would just return $\mathscr{L}_\pi$, as $\mathscr{L}_{au} = \{i\}$ is a proper subset of $\mathscr{L}_\pi = \{i_o, iu_o, u_o, o_o\}$. Rather, $\oplus$ is like forming the Cartesian product of two sets and then taking the union of each subproduct. That is, $\mathscr{L}_\pi \times \mathscr{L}_{au} = \{(x, y) : x \in \mathscr{L}_\pi, y \in \mathscr{L}_{au}\} = \{(x, i) : x \in \mathscr{L}_\pi\}$. Taking the union $\{x\} \cup \{i\}$, that is, $x \sqcup i$, of each (x, i) gives the last three lines of (41).

Turning now to the minus value of the author feature, we have:

(42) $[\![-\text{author}(\pi)]\!]$
$= \mathscr{L}_\pi \ominus \mathscr{L}_{au}$
$= \{i_o, iu_o, u_o, o_o\} \ominus \{i\}$
$= \{i_o \backslash i, iu_o \backslash i, u_o \backslash i, o_o \backslash i\}$

As before, we have moved i into the larger set and shown that it is to be subtracted from the elements abbreviated by i_o, iu_o, u_o, and o_o.

For u_o and o_o, this subtraction is redundant. For instance, if we take oo' as a representative member of o_o and subtract i, then we have, in set-theoretic terms, $\{o, o'\} \backslash \{i\} = \{o, o'\}$, or, in the more concise notation, $oo' \backslash i = oo'$. The redundancy of this subtraction holds for all members of o_o. So, we have:

(43) $o_o \backslash i$
$= o \backslash i, o' \backslash i, o'' \backslash i, \ldots, oo' \backslash i, oo'' \backslash i, o'o'' \backslash i, \ldots, oo'o'' \backslash i, \ldots$
$= o, o', o'', \ldots, oo', oo'', o'o'', \ldots, oo'o'', \ldots$
$= o_o$

Hence, $o_o \backslash i = o_o$ and, similarly, $u_o \backslash i = u_o$.

By contrast, for i_o and iu_o, the subtraction is contentful. For the latter, we have the converse of (37):

(44) $iu_o \backslash i$
$= iu \backslash i, iuo \backslash i, iuo' \backslash i, iuo'' \backslash i, \ldots, iuoo' \backslash i, iuoo'' \backslash i, iuo'o'' \backslash i, \ldots,$
$\qquad\qquad\qquad\qquad\qquad\qquad\qquad\qquad\qquad iuoo'o'' \backslash i, \ldots$
$= u, uo, uo', uo'', \ldots, uoo', uoo'', uo'o'', \ldots, uoo'o'', \ldots$
$= u_o$

(Rephrasing a representative subexample in set-theoretic notation, we have $\{i, u, o\} \backslash \{i\} = \{u, o\}$, hence $iuo \backslash i = uo$.)

Matters are very similar for i_o, but, just as $o_o \sqcup i$ is io_o (that is, a little less than i_o (39)), so, conversely, $i_o \ominus i$ yields a little more than o_o. This is where the empty set enters the computation:

(45) $i_o \ominus i$
$= i \backslash i, io \backslash i, io' \backslash i, io'' \backslash i, \ldots, ioo' \backslash i, ioo'' \backslash i, io'o'' \backslash i, \ldots, ioo'o'' \backslash i, \ldots$
$= \varnothing, o, o', o'', \ldots, oo', oo'', o'o'', \ldots, oo'o'', \ldots$
$= \varnothing, o_o$

The crucial difference between this subtraction and the previous ones is that i_o contains i, which is what we are subtracting. We therefore have $\{i\} \backslash \{i\} = \{\}$, or $i \backslash i = \varnothing$.

So, returning to (42), we have:

(46) $[\![-\text{author}(\pi)]\!]$
$= \mathscr{L}_\pi \ominus \mathscr{L}_{au}$
$= \{i_o, iu_o, u_o, o_o\} \ominus \{i\}$
$= \{i_o \backslash i, iu_o \backslash i, u_o \backslash i, o_o \backslash i\}$
$= \{\varnothing, o_o, u_o, u_o, o_o\}$
$= \{\varnothing, u_o, o_o\}$

where, again, the last step follows from the axiom of extension. The result is second-cum-third person plus the empty set.

Before discussing the empty set, it may be helpful to visualize the computations and their outputs. One means of doing so is presented in figure 4.2. This represents (41) and (46) by placing the elements of the π lattice (i_o, iu_o, u_o, o_o) vertically on the left, beneath the underlined label $\mathscr{L}_\pi$. On the same line as this label, in the middle, is the name of the action performed in each case: in the upper figure, $\oplus \mathscr{L}_{au}$, and in the lower figure, $\ominus \mathscr{L}_{au}$. On the right is the outcome: $\mathscr{L}_\pi \oplus \mathscr{L}_{au}$ in the upper figure, with i_o and iu_o beneath it, and $\mathscr{L}_\pi \ominus \mathscr{L}_{au}$ in the lower figure, with $\varnothing$, u_o, and o_o.

The Partition Problem Solved

The actions themselves are depicted by arrows, showing what is mapped to what. In the upper figure, $\oplus \mathscr{L}_{au}$ maps both i_o and o_o to i_o, and both iu_o and u_o to iu_o. In the lower figure, $\mathscr{L}_\pi \ominus \mathscr{L}_{au}$ splits i_o between $\varnothing$ and o_o, and maps o_o to itself and both iu_o and u_o to u_o. The arrows are labeled with the name of the action they depict—namely, $\sqcup i$ or $\setminus i$—which may seem like overkill in the current example, but will be useful in 4.3.3.

Figure 4.2 may enlighten the calculations, but it is slightly less informative. For instance, the upper figure does not indicate that $\mathscr{L}_\pi \oplus \mathscr{L}_{au}$ maps i_o onto the whole of i_o but that it maps o_o only into a subpart of i_o. And the lower figure does not indicate which parts of i_o are mapped onto $\varnothing$ and which onto o_o. So, these figures should be treated as aids, not substitutes, for the calculations.

We have now all but derived the author bipartition. The only lingering difference is that we have $i_o iu_o \mid u_o o_o \varnothing$, instead of $i_o iu_o \mid u_o o_o$. Although the empty set in (46) will be crucial to correctly deriving the tri- and quadripartition, we do not want $\varnothing$ in our actual partition. In general, the reason for excluding empty sets from lattice-theoretic denotations of, say, *cat* is twofold. First, if the empty set is a cat, then it is also a dog, and circle, and square—a troublingly Meinongian position—and, second, and more simply, there are no empty cats—even the Cheshire cat, once his smile vanished, was taken to be elsewhere, not empty. The same points hold for second and third person.

Positive action: $+author(\pi)$

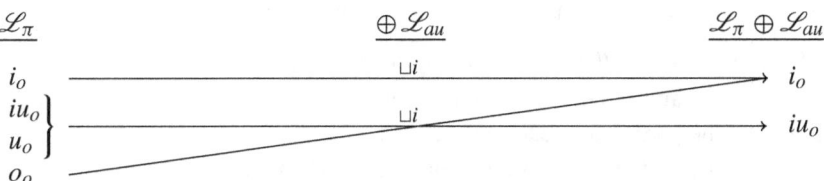

Negative action: $-author(\pi)$

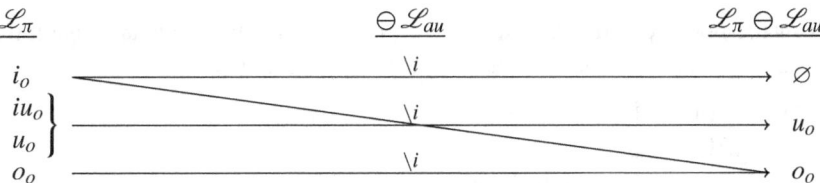

Figure 4.2
Actions on the π lattice by the author lattice

Typological studies are consonant with this. If it existed, an "empty" person would have to mean something like 'none of you' or 'no one', but no such meaning is recorded in any of the typologies of basic pronouns or agreement that I have seen. Rather, expressions meaning 'none of you' or 'no one' are complex and involve negation.

To avoid these problems, I suggest that domains of variables always exclude the empty set. So, if we momentarily lift our focus from π and its content and return to the full φ structure, the entities already posited suffice to winnow out the empty set. In this fuller structure, we have:

(47) $[\![\pi_{-\text{author}} - \varphi]\!] = \lambda x \,.\, x \in \mathscr{L}_\pi \ominus \mathscr{L}_{au}$
$\phantom{(47) [\![\pi_{-\text{author}} - \varphi]\!] = \lambda x \,.\,} x \in D_e$

So, although the nuclear part of (47) would permit x to be the empty set, the domain restriction in the preamble does not. Or, in slightly informal notation, despite (48), we have (49):

(48) $\varnothing \in \mathscr{L}_\pi \ominus \mathscr{L}_{au}$

(49) $\varnothing \notin \lambda x \,.\, x \in \mathscr{L}_\pi \ominus \mathscr{L}_{au}$
$ x \in D_e$

Taking this into account, we arrive at the author bipartition: ±author partitions $i_o i u_o u_o o_o$ into first person $i_o i u_o$ (+author) and nonfirst $u_o o_o$ (−author), yielding $i_o i u_o \mid u_o o_o$.

4.3.3 Participant Bipartition

The second bipartition corresponds to the opposite settings of all three parameters (though, again, the last is trivial in its application):

(50) *Parameters of the participant bipartition*
    a. The author feature is not present.
    b. The participant feature is present.
    c. The participant feature composes with π first.

Derivationally, matters are largely as for the author bipartition, though with some minor increase in complexity owing to the larger size of the participant lattice.

In the positive action of the feature, three distinct elements are disjointly added, i, iu, and u, to each of the elements of the π lattice:

(51) $[\![+\text{participant}(\pi)]\!]$
$= \mathscr{L}_\pi \oplus \mathscr{L}_{pt}$
$= \{i_o, iu_o, u_o, o_o\} \oplus \{i, iu, u\}$
$= \{i_o \sqcup i,\ iu_o \sqcup i,\ u_o \sqcup i,\ o_o \sqcup i,$
$\phantom{= \{}i_o \sqcup iu,\ iu_o \sqcup iu,\ u_o \sqcup iu,\ o_o \sqcup iu,$
$\phantom{= \{}i_o \sqcup u,\ iu_o \sqcup u,\ u_o \sqcup u,\ o_o \sqcup u\}$

The Partition Problem Solved 87

In the last step, each element of the participant lattice has been moved into the larger set. The top row shows that i is to be added to each element of the π lattice, just as for +author (41). The middle row shows the corresponding additions for iu, and the bottom row, for u. This leads to several redundancies: two full or partial copies of i_o and u_o, and eight of iu_o. So, the axiom of extension of applies as before, to give, ultimately, the π lattice with o_o removed:

(52) $[\![+\text{participant}(\pi)]\!]$
$= \mathscr{L}_\pi \oplus \mathscr{L}_{pt}$
$= \{i_o, iu_o, u_o, o_o\} \oplus \{i, iu, u\}$
$= \{i_o \sqcup i,\ iu_o \sqcup i,\ u_o \sqcup i,\ o_o \sqcup i,$
$\quad i_o \sqcup iu,\ iu_o \sqcup iu,\ u_o \sqcup iu,\ o_o \sqcup iu,$
$\quad i_o \sqcup u,\ iu_o \sqcup u,\ u_o \sqcup u,\ o_o \sqcup u\}$
$= \{i_o, iu_o, iu_o, io_o,$
$\quad iu_o, iu_o, iu_o, iuo_o,$
$\quad iu_o, iu_o, u_o, uo_o\}$
$= \{i_o, iu_o, u_o\}$

In the depiction of this action in figure 4.3, the elements that make up the π lattice are repeated three times, beneath the underlined $\mathscr{L}_\pi$ label. The repetitions correspond to the three rows of (51) and (52) and, as there, the top four are those to which i is added (shown by "$\sqcup i$" on the top three arrows); the middle four are those to which iu are added (shown by "$\sqcup iu$" on the arrow beside the large brace), and the bottom four are those to which u is added (shown by "$\sqcup u$" on the bottom two arrows).

For the negative action, we begin as follows:

(53) $[\![-\text{participant}(\pi)]\!]$
$= \mathscr{L}_\pi \ominus \mathscr{L}_{pt}$
$= \{i_o, iu_o, u_o, o_o\} \ominus \{i, iu, u\}$
$= \{(((i_o \backslash i) \backslash iu) \backslash u),\ (((iu_o \backslash i) \backslash iu) \backslash u),\ (((u_o \backslash i) \backslash iu) \backslash u),\ (((o_o \backslash i) \backslash iu) \backslash u)\}$

The cumbersome expressions of the last line show joint subtraction of i, iu, and u from elements of the π lattice. However, as was noted when these operations were defined, subtraction of i and u is redundant if the maximum of the lattice, iu, is also subtracted: $\{i_o \backslash iu\} = \{iu_o \backslash iu\} = \{u_o \backslash iu\} = \{\varnothing, o_o\}$ and, so, subtracting i and u either before or after subtraction of iu still returns only $\varnothing$ and o_o. More compactly, then, we can write:

(54) $[\![-\text{participant}(\pi)]\!]$
$= \mathscr{L}_\pi \ominus \mathscr{L}_{pt}$
$= \{i_o, iu_o, u_o, o_o\} \ominus \{\max(\mathscr{L}_{pt})\}$
$= \{i_o, iu_o, u_o, o_o\} \ominus \{iu\}$

$$= \{i_o \backslash iu, iu_o \backslash iu, u_o \backslash iu, o_o \backslash iu\}$$
$$= \{\varnothing, o_o, \varnothing, o_o, \varnothing, o_o, o_o\}$$
$$= \{\varnothing, o_o\}$$

The details of this calculation are as in previous examples: iu moves inside the brackets and is to be subtracted from each of the four expressions that make up the π lattice; multiple copies are removed by the axiom of extension. The negative action is depicted in figure 4.3.

When we combine (52) and (54) into a partition, we again discard $\varnothing$ as an effect of the domain of the variable. The result is the participant partition, $i_o iu_o u_o \mid o_o$. That is, we have shown that ±participant partitions $i_o iu_o u_o o_o$ into elements that contain one or both participants, $i_o iu_o u_o$ (+participant), and those that do not, o_o (−participant).

Positive action: $+participant(\pi)$

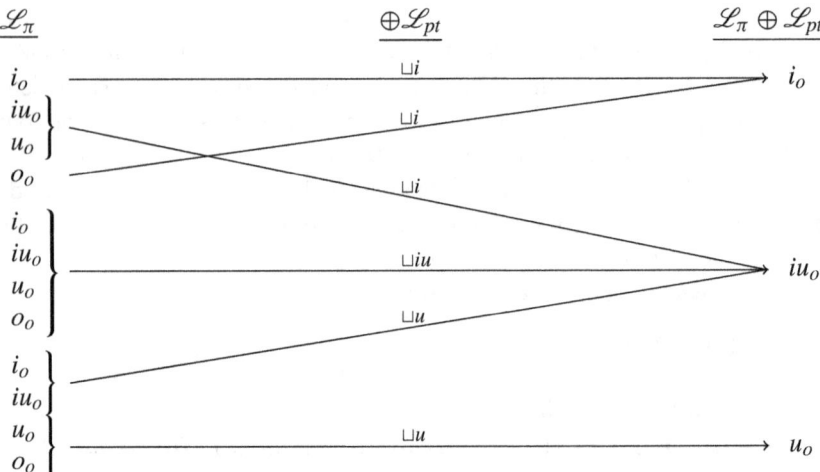

Negative action: $-participant(\pi)$

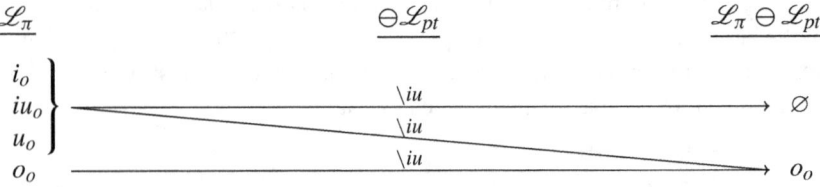

Figure 4.3
Actions on the π lattice by the participant lattice

4.3.4 Standard Tripartition

With only two features, the current theory can derive only two bipartitions. So, not only have we generated the two that are attested, but we have failed to derive any that are not. This derives both how many bipartitions are attested and which of the seven they are.

For more complex partitions, like the standard tripartition, both features must be activated. This entails that the setting of the third parameter, affecting order of composition, is no longer vacuous or trivial. For the tripartition, the author feature composes first, as shown below:

(55) *Parameters of the standard tripartition*
 a. The author feature is present.
 b. The participant feature is present.
 c. The author feature composes with π first.

Preempting the calculations slightly, the crucial point about this setting is that it forces the participant feature to compose last. Because −participant strips out all participants, this neutralizes the contrast that prior action of +author versus −author induces. As a result, the four feature–value combinations yield only three partition elements (as desired), but with two modes of representing the third person. This variation is a central aspect of the language-specific analyses in chapter 8 and is formalized below as a subsidiary parameter.

We begin with positive specification of the participant feature. The plus–plus specification is straightforward and yields the conflation of first person inclusive and first person exclusive. The calculation begins by translating features into lattices and then substituting the value for +author(π) that was derived in section 4.3.2. Thereafter, it proceeds as before, moving from $\oplus$ between two sets to $\sqcup$ within one set and removing redundant copies of the same element:

(56) $[\![+\text{participant}(+\text{author}(\pi))]\!]$
$= (\mathscr{L}_\pi \oplus \mathscr{L}_{au}) \oplus \mathscr{L}_{pt}$
$= \{i_o, iu_o\} \oplus \{i, iu, u\}$ by (41)
$= \{i_o \sqcup i, i_o \sqcup iu, i_o \sqcup u,$
$\quad iu_o \sqcup i, iu_o \sqcup iu, iu_o \sqcup u\}$
$= \{i_o, iu_o, iu_o,$
$\quad iu_o, iu_o, iu_o\}$
$= \{i_o, iu_o\}$

In essence, then, +participant acts redundantly here, mapping the denotation of +author(π) to itself.

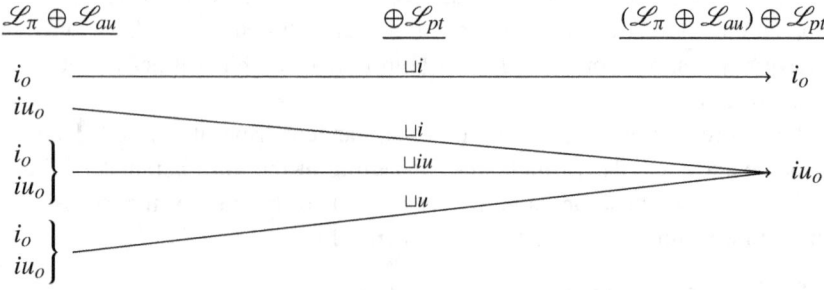

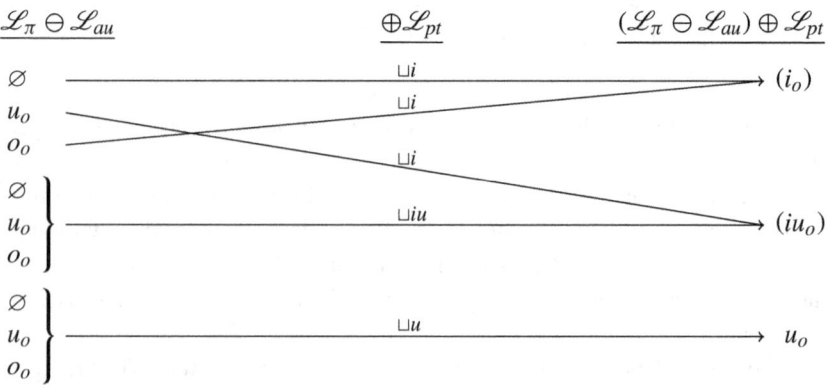

Figure 4.4
Positive actions, on $\mathscr{L}_\pi \oplus \mathscr{L}_{au}$, by the participant lattice

Derivation of the second person is more interesting, as it applies Lexical Complementarity. As (57) shows, rote computation of the plus–minus denotation yields $\{i_o, iu_o, u_o\}$. One would expect this feature combination to denote any set containing at least one participant. However, $\{i_o, iu_o\}$, the denotation of the plus–plus combination in (56), is a proper subset of $\{i_o, iu_o, u_o\}$. Consequently, Lexical Complementarity restricts the plus–minus combination in (57) to $\{i_o, iu_o, u_o\} \setminus \{i_o, iu_o\} = \{u_o\}$. (In the derivations, "≡" shows where Lexical Complementarity applies.)

(57) $[\![+\text{participant}(-\text{author}(\pi))]\!]$
   $= (\mathscr{L}_\pi \ominus \mathscr{L}_{au}) \oplus \mathscr{L}_{pt}$
   $= \{\varnothing, u_o, o_o\} \oplus \{i, iu, u\}$ by (46)

$$\begin{aligned}
&= \{\varnothing \sqcup i,\, \varnothing \sqcup iu,\, \varnothing \sqcup u,\\
&\quad u_o \sqcup i,\, u_o \sqcup iu,\, u_o \sqcup u,\\
&\quad o_o \sqcup i,\, o_o \sqcup iu,\, o_o \sqcup u\}\\
&= \{i,\, iu,\, u,\\
&\quad iu_o,\, iu_o,\, u_o,\\
&\quad io_o,\, iuo_o,\, uo_o\}\\
&= \{i_o,\, iu_o, u_o\}\\
&\equiv \{u_o\} \hspace{5cm} \text{by (31), (56)}
\end{aligned}$$

Thus, by Lexical Complementarity and (56), we have the second person. Figure 4.4 depicts the effects of +participant on ±author(π). The restrictive effect of Lexical Complementarity is shown by parentheses. In the lower depiction, corresponding to (57), i_o and iu_o are parenthesized, as these are the only outputs of the upper depiction.

The empty set plays an important role here. For Lexical Complementarity to apply between them, (56) must be a subset of (57). So, in particular, i must be present in both. Working backward, one sees that i arises in (57) via $\varnothing \sqcup i$. This in turn requires the presence of $\varnothing$ in what +participant applies to. If $\mathscr{L}_\pi \ominus \mathscr{L}_{au}$ lacked that zero, (57) would yield $\{io_o, iu_o, u_o\}$, with io_o in place of i_o. With this, the subset relationship, Lexical Complementarity, and the division between first and second person would break down. Section 4.4 presents fuller discussion, including possible alternatives, and a parallel, but more critical, case from the quadripartition.

The two remaining feature specifications, shown in figure 4.5, both characterize third person. In the first, we add i in (via +author) before stripping both i and u out (via −participant):

(58) $[\![-\text{participant}(+\text{author}(\pi))]\!]$
$$\begin{aligned}
&= (\mathscr{L}_\pi \oplus \mathscr{L}_{au}) \ominus \mathscr{L}_{pt}\\
&= \{i_o, iu_o\} \ominus \{\max(\mathscr{L}_{pt})\} \hspace{3cm} \text{by (41)}\\
&= \{i_o, iu_o\} \ominus \{iu\}\\
&= \{i_o \backslash iu, iu_o \backslash iu\}\\
&= \{\varnothing, o_o\}
\end{aligned}$$

In the second, which one might regard as more "harmonic," we anticipate the stripping out of both i and u by negatively specifying ±author, thereby stripping i out preemptively:

(59) $[\![-\text{participant}(-\text{author}(\pi))]\!]$
$$\begin{aligned}
&= (\mathscr{L}_\pi \ominus \mathscr{L}_{au}) \ominus \mathscr{L}_{pt}\\
&= \{\varnothing, u_o, o_o\} \ominus \{\max(\mathscr{L}_{pt})\} \hspace{3cm} \text{by (46)}
\end{aligned}$$

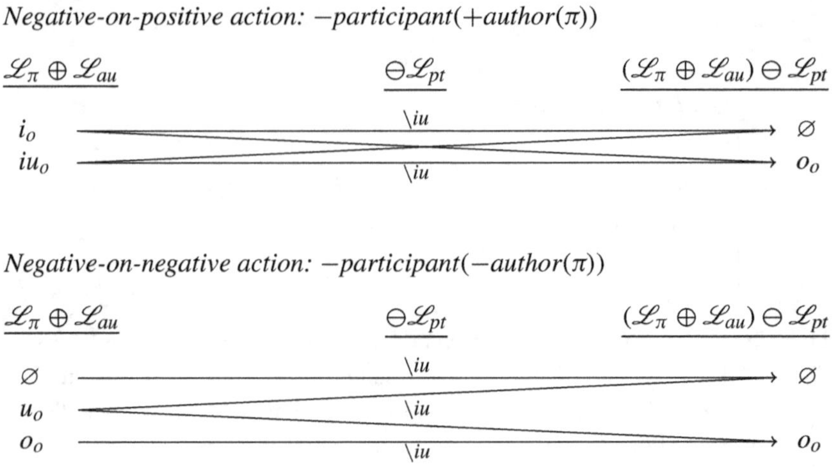

Negative-on-positive action: $-participant(+author(\pi))$

$\mathscr{L}_\pi \oplus \mathscr{L}_{au}$	$\ominus \mathscr{L}_{pt}$	$(\mathscr{L}_\pi \oplus \mathscr{L}_{au}) \ominus \mathscr{L}_{pt}$
i_o	$\setminus iu$	$\emptyset$
iu_o	$\setminus iu$	o_o

Negative-on-negative action: $-participant(-author(\pi))$

$\mathscr{L}_\pi \oplus \mathscr{L}_{au}$	$\ominus \mathscr{L}_{pt}$	$(\mathscr{L}_\pi \oplus \mathscr{L}_{au}) \ominus \mathscr{L}_{pt}$
$\emptyset$	$\setminus iu$	$\emptyset$
u_o	$\setminus iu$	
o_o	$\setminus iu$	o_o

Figure 4.5
Negative actions, on $\mathscr{L}_\pi \oplus \mathscr{L}_{au}$, by the participant lattice

$$= \{\emptyset, u_o, o_o\} \ominus \{iu\}$$
$$= \{\emptyset, o_o\}$$

One might regard the availability of two representations with identical denotations as a flaw. Or one might try to argue that learners disfavor the minus–plus specification (58): it serves no obvious purpose to add the author in if one is only to undo the action at the very next step. The minus–minus specification, by contrast, is "monotone": if one's aim is to create a third person by ridding the π lattice of all instances of i and u, then removing i is a reasonable first step and, so, $-author$ is a reasonable specification.

Although I think the nonmonotone third person is more marked in a semantic sense, this does not justify imposition of a complete ban. On the contrary, a point emphasized in the exposition above and the comparison with other accounts below (chapter 8) is that the current proposals posit no extrinsic constraints on feature combinations. So, I am committed to permitting both options and, consequently, to viewing the choice between them as another excrescent parameter:

(60) *Subsidiary parameter*
    Tripartite o_o uses $+author/-author$.

Crucially, there is evidence supporting alternative representations of third person. The different settings of (60) create distinct natural classes of persons. If third uses $+author$, then it forms a natural class with first, whereas $-author$

The Partition Problem Solved

Table 4.2

Tripartition

Category	Denotation	Features
1	i_o, iu_o	+author +participant
2	u_o	−author +participant
3	o_o	±author −participant

groups third with second. So, when a language consistently favors one of these classes over the other in the (meta)syncretisms it exhibits, then, plausibly, it clearly signals to learners how to represent third person. One way to capture the structure of agreement in Brazilian Portuguese (section 3.3.2) is as a metasyncretism of second and third and, hence, a setting of (60) to minus. By contrast, German and its relations (section 8.3.1) present good reasons for believing that languages can exploit the plus setting too.

Leaving the representation of third person aside, the key point is that activating both person features and composing ±author with π first results in tripartition. The feature specifications are summarized in table 4.2. Assuming, once again, that the domain restriction on φ winnows out $\varnothing$ from the effect of −participant, we arrive at the standard tripartition, $i_o iu_o | u_o | o_o$.

4.3.5 Quadripartiton

The remaining partition corresponds to the last available parameter setting: both features are present and ±participant composes first:

(61) *Parameters of the quadripartition*
  a. The author feature is present.
  b. The participant feature is present.
  c. The participant feature composes with π first.

With this order, ±participant does not neutralize one of the value settings of ±author and so four distinct partition elements can result.

In this partition, third person is uniquely characterized by minus–minus:

(62) $[\![-\text{author}(-\text{participant}(\pi))]\!]$
  $= (\mathscr{L}_\pi \ominus \mathscr{L}_{pt}) \ominus \mathscr{L}_{au}$
  $= \{\varnothing, o_o\} \ominus i$ by (54)
  $= \{\varnothing \backslash i, o_o \backslash i\}$
  $= \{\varnothing, o_o\}$

The minus–plus specification yields second person, given Lexical Complementarity and the specification of third:

(63) $[\![-\text{author}(+\text{participant}(\pi))]\!]$
$= (\mathscr{L}_\pi \oplus \mathscr{L}_{pt}) \ominus \mathscr{L}_{au}$
$= \{i_o, iu_o, u_o\} \ominus \{i\}$ by (51)
$= \{i_o\backslash i, iu_o\backslash i, u_o\backslash i\}$
$= \{\varnothing, o_o, u_o, u_o\}$
$= \{\varnothing, u_o, o_o\}$
$\equiv \{u_o\}$ by (31), (62)

These actions are depicted in figure 4.6. The restrictive effect of Lexical Complementarity is shown by parentheses in the upper depiction. The parenthetic outputs are those of the lower depiction.

Next, consider positive action by the author lattice. This leads to two different first persons, according to the value of ±participant. Naturally, if we rid the π lattice of all participants, using −participant, and then add in just the author, with +author, we generate the exclusive:

(64) $[\![+\text{author}(-\text{participant}(\pi))]\!]$
$= (\mathscr{L}_\pi \ominus \mathscr{L}_{pt}) \oplus \mathscr{L}_{au}$
$= \{\varnothing, o_o\} \oplus \{i\}$ by (54)
$= \{\varnothing \sqcup i, o_o \sqcup i\}$
$= \{i, io_o\}$
$= \{i_o\}$

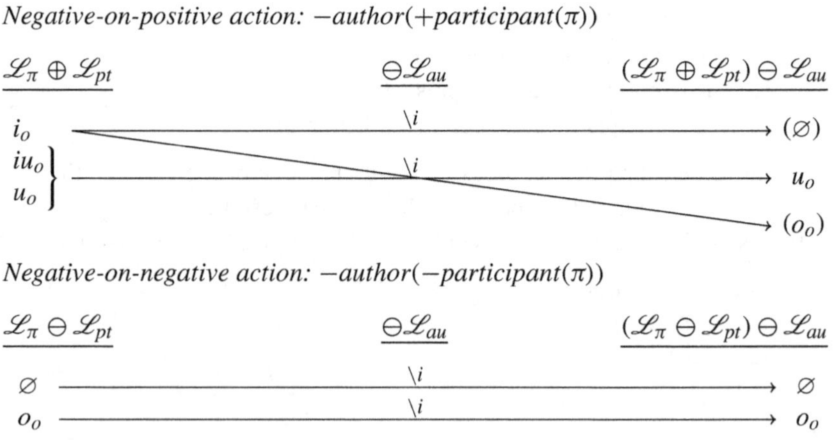

Negative-on-positive action: $-\text{author}(+\text{participant}(\pi))$

$\mathscr{L}_\pi \oplus \mathscr{L}_{pt}$	$\ominus \mathscr{L}_{au}$	$(\mathscr{L}_\pi \oplus \mathscr{L}_{pt}) \ominus \mathscr{L}_{au}$
i_o	$\backslash i$	$(\varnothing)$
$\left.\begin{array}{l}iu_o\\u_o\end{array}\right\}$	$\backslash i$	u_o
		(o_o)

Negative-on-negative action: $-\text{author}(-\text{participant}(\pi))$

$\mathscr{L}_\pi \ominus \mathscr{L}_{pt}$	$\ominus \mathscr{L}_{au}$	$(\mathscr{L}_\pi \ominus \mathscr{L}_{pt}) \ominus \mathscr{L}_{au}$
$\varnothing$	$\backslash i$	$\varnothing$
o_o	$\backslash i$	o_o

Figure 4.6
Negative actions, on $\mathscr{L}_\pi \oplus \mathscr{L}_{pt}$, by the author lattice

The Partition Problem Solved

The inclusive arises in a way that parallels second person. By having specified +participant, we have kept u in the denotation. If we then add i to everything, using +author, and apply Lexical Complementarity, every element of the result will contain both i and u:

(65) $[\![+\text{author}(+\text{participant}(\pi))]\!]$
$= (\mathscr{L}_\pi \oplus \mathscr{L}_{pt}) \oplus \mathscr{L}_{au}$
$= \{i_o, iu_o\} \oplus \{i\}$ by (51)
$= \{i_o \sqcup i, iu_o \sqcup i\}$
$= \{i_o, iu_o\}$
$\equiv \{iu_o\}$ by (31), (64)

These actions are depicted in figure 4.7. The effect of Lexical Complementarity is again shown with parentheses, removing the output of the lower depiction from the upper depiction.

Thus, the four feature specifications yield the four elements of the quadripartition $i_o|iu_o|u_o|o_o$ (once again, removing $\varnothing$, owing to the semantic effect of φ). The feature specifications are summarized in table 4.3.

4.4 $\varnothing$

The very last derivation provides the right moment for returning to the role of the empty set. The crucial point is that, if $[\![-\text{participant}(\pi)]\!] = \mathscr{L}_\pi \ominus \mathscr{L}_{pt}$ did not include $\varnothing$, then $[\![+\text{author}(-\text{participant}(\pi))]\!] = (\mathscr{L}_\pi \ominus \mathscr{L}_{pt}) \oplus \mathscr{L}_{au}$ in (64)

Positive-on-positive action: $+\text{author}(+\text{participant}(\pi))$

$\mathscr{L}_\pi \oplus \mathscr{L}_{pt}$	$\oplus \mathscr{L}_{au}$	$(\mathscr{L}_\pi \oplus \mathscr{L}_{pt}) \oplus \mathscr{L}_{au}$
i_o	$\xrightarrow{\sqcup i}$	(i_o)
$\left.\begin{array}{l}iu_o\\u_o\end{array}\right\}$	$\xrightarrow{\sqcup i}$	iu_o

Positive-on-negative action: $+\text{author}(-\text{participant}(\pi))$

$\mathscr{L}_\pi \ominus \mathscr{L}_{pt}$	$\oplus \mathscr{L}_{au}$	$(\mathscr{L}_\pi \ominus \mathscr{L}_{pt}) \oplus \mathscr{L}_{au}$
$\varnothing$	$\xrightarrow{\sqcup i}$	$\left.\begin{array}{l}i\\io_o\end{array}\right\} i_o$
o_o	$\xrightarrow{\sqcup i}$	

Figure 4.7
Positive actions, on $\mathscr{L}_\pi \oplus \mathscr{L}_{pt}$, by the author lattice

Table 4.3

Quadripartition

Category	Denotation	Features
1EX	i_o	+author −participant
1IN	iu_o	+author +participant
2	u_o	−author +participant
3	o_o	−author −participant

would not include i. In other words, the first person exclusive would exclude the first person singular. With $\varnothing$, we have $\{\varnothing, o_o\} \oplus \{i\} = \{i, io_o\} = \{i_o\}$, as shown in the positive-on-negative action of figure 4.7. Without $\varnothing$, we have just $\{o_o\} \oplus \{i\} = \{io_o\}$, which excludes i itself.

The consequent problem is not that we cannot refer to first singular i, but that i skews the partition. It is lumped in with the wrong partition element. If $[\![+\text{author}(-\text{participant}(\pi))]\!] = \{io_o\}$, then Lexical Complementarity restricts $[\![+\text{author}(+\text{participant}(\pi))]\!] = \{i_o, iu_o\}$ to $\{i, iu_o\}$. The resulting partition would be $io_o|iu_oi|u_o|o_o$. In a numberless pronominal system, then, we would expect one form to cover all exclusive persons other than the first singular itself, and a second form to cover both first singular and all inclusives. It would, therefore, be impossible to characterize the numberless, quadripartite pronominal system ($i_o|iu_o|u_o|o_o$) of languages like Imonda or agreement systems like that of Canela-Krahô or the directional verbs of motion of Cebuano (figure 3.2; the 'only inclusive' pattern of Cysouw 2003, Siewierska 2004, Siewierska and Bakker 2005). Conversely, the partition $io_o|iu_oi|u_o|o_o$ is not encountered in any typological survey or grammar I am aware of. Thus, the empty set plays an indispensable role in assigning i to the correct partition element of the quadripartition.

In fact, although I did not draw full attention to it earlier, zeroes also play a role in the derivation of the tripartition. There, second person arises because (57) $+\text{participant}(-\text{author}(\pi)) = \{i_o, iu_o, u_o\}$, while (56) $+\text{participant}(+\text{author}(\pi)) = \{i_o, iu_o\}$. Lexical complementarity confines (57) to $\{u_o\}$. This is only possible because $+\text{participant}(-\text{author}(\pi))$ contains i, which, in turn, arises because $-\text{author}(\pi)$ contains $\varnothing$; see lines 4 and 7 of (57). Without $\varnothing$, the denotation would be $\{io_o, iu_o, u_o\}$, with io_o in place of i_o. This does not have (56) $\{i_o, iu_o\}$ as a subset. Given that Lexical Complementarity is phrased in terms of subsets, it no longer induces a partition.

This particular problem could be fixed by rephrasing Lexical Complementarity in terms of nondisjoint denotations and relative size. Suppose that two feature sets, F and G, have overlapping denotations, $[\![F]\!] \cap [\![G]\!] \neq \varnothing$, with $[\![F]\!]$

The Partition Problem Solved   97

smaller than $[\![G]\!]$.[7] Then we could claim that G is used only for elements not shared with F, that is, for $[\![G]\!] \setminus ([\![F]\!] \cap [\![G]\!])$. This is in the spirit of Lexical Complementarity as it reduces to (31) in the special case where F denotes a subset of the denotation of G and, hence, where $[\![F]\!] \cap [\![G]\!] = [\![F]\!]$.

In the absence of zeroes, this revised principle would yield the standard tripartition. Specifically, it would restrict $\{io_o, iu_o, u_o\}$ to:

(66) $\{io_o, iu_o, u_o\} \setminus (\{io_o, iu_o, u_o\} \cap \{io_o, iu_o\})$
     $= \{io_o, iu_o, u_o\} \setminus \{io_o, iu_o\}$
     $= \{u_o\}$

As desired, this yields second person, just as (57) does.

For the quadripartition, however, matters remain problematic. Given the subset relation between $[\![+\text{author}(-\text{participant}(\pi))]\!] = \{io_o\}$ and $[\![+\text{author}(+\text{participant}(\pi))]\!] = \{i_o, iu_o\}$, the latter would be restricted to:

(67) $\{i_o, iu_o\} \setminus (\{io_o\} \cap \{i_o, iu_o\})$
     $= \{i_o, iu_o\} \setminus \{io_o\}$
     $= \{i, iu_o\}$

So, the revised system would still generate the unattested quadripartition $io_o|iu_oi|u_o|o_o$ while failing to generate the attested $i_o|iu_o|u_o|o_o$.

Truly numberless quadripartitions may be infrequent, in relative terms, for pronouns and agreement. Yet they are a distribution that an adequate account must derive, just as it must derive the nonattestation of $io_o|iu_oi|u_o|o_o$. This may be the only place where zeroes affect partitions, not as an artifact, but as an essential component. Yet their role is crucial. So, I conclude that there is support for the current approach both in how it allows zeroes to arise naturally in the course of computations internal to the π head and in the role that it attributes to the domain of variables in winnowing them out of the partitional yield of the whole phi structure.

4.5 The Partition Element Problem

Finally, we should return briefly to the partition element problem. Stated at the start of chapter 3, it asks why maximally four partition elements are generated from the ontology, and what distinguishes attested from unattested ones.

My answer is simply observational: given the means posited, the maximally distinct partition derivable consists of elements i_o, iu_o, u_o, and o_o. All other partition elements are unions of these. Alternative elements, like io_o and $iu_o i$ of section 4.4, are simply not generated.

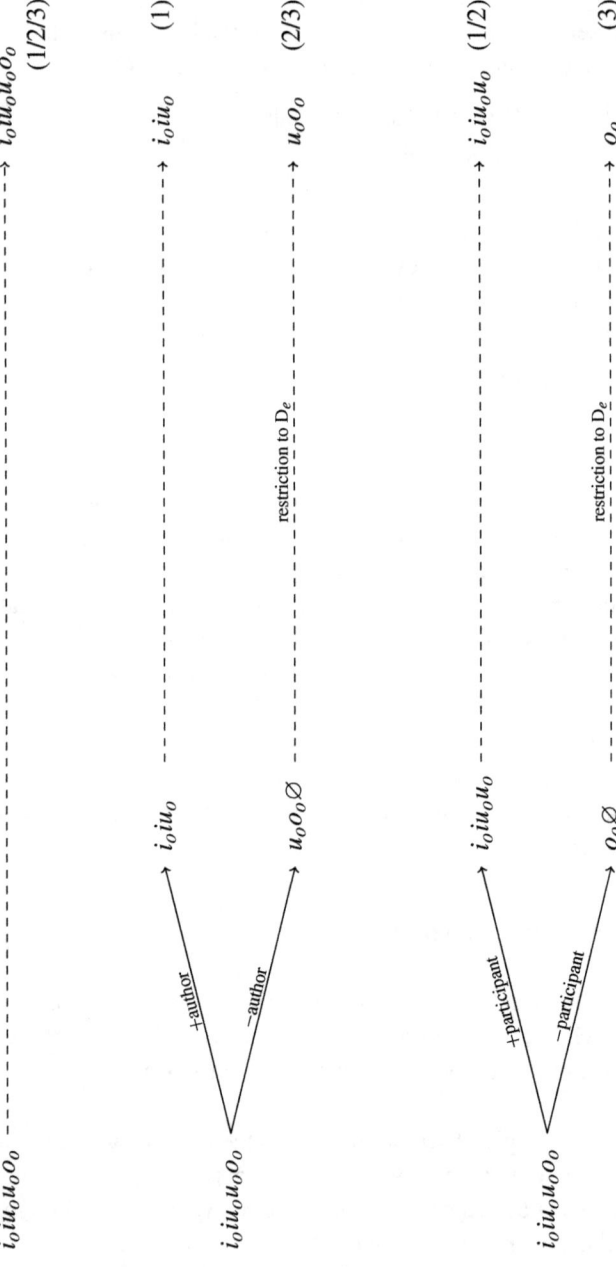

The Partition Problem Solved

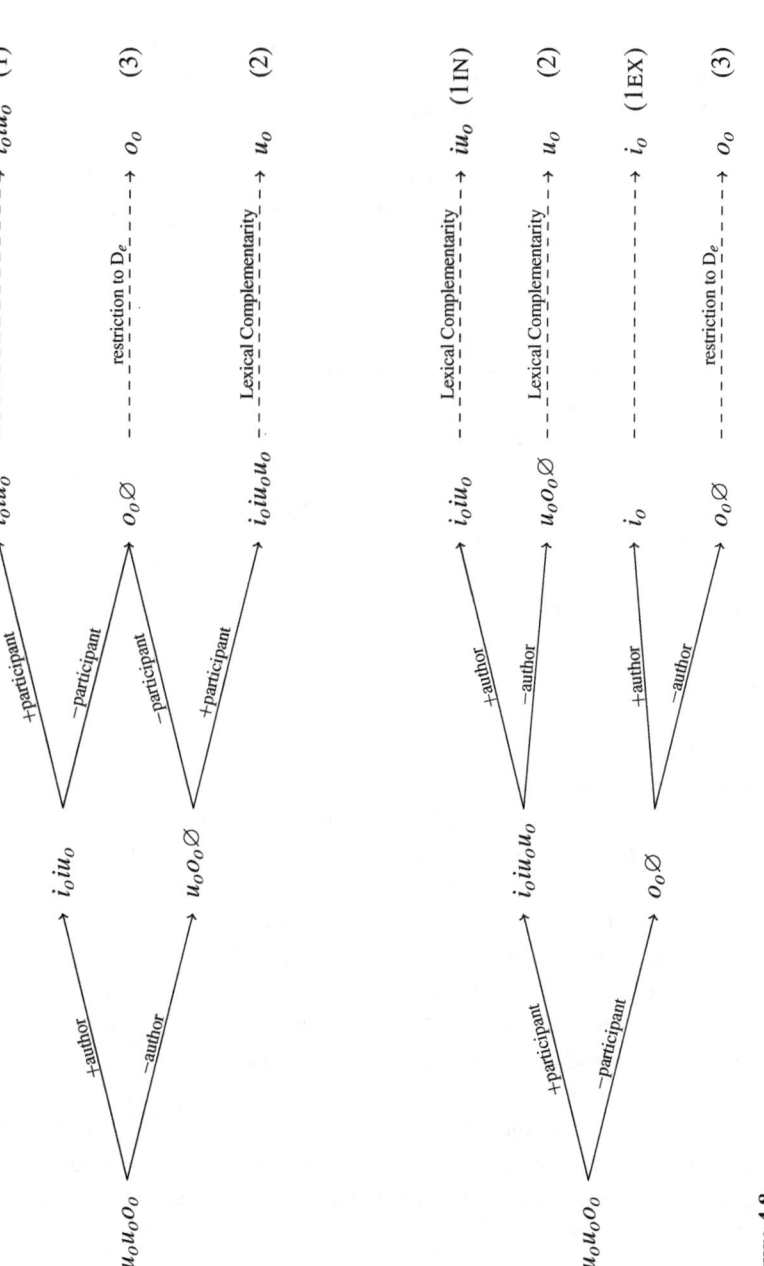

Figure 4.8
Derivations of the five attested partitions: Monopartition (top), author bipartition, participant bipartition, tripartition, quadripartition (bottom)

One further observation is due here, as it may address a question at the back of some readers' minds. The denotation $\mathscr{L}_\pi$ was written as $i_o i u_o u_o o_o$. Because this representation concatenates the four partition elements that are to be derived, it might seem to assume something that it should not. However, this is purely a matter of notation. One could equally have written $\mathscr{L}_\pi$ as the concatenation of io_o, $iu_o i$, u_o, and o_o, the elements of the aberrant partition above, without adversely affecting any of the derivations that followed.

As a result, the previous two chapters are justified in assuming i_o, iu_o, u_o, and o_o as the elements to be manipulated in formulating the partition problem.

4.6 Conclusion

Against the background of a standard mental ontology organized into lattices that are implicit in much past work, I have proposed that person consists of two features and a host head. The parameters governing these are whether each feature occurs and, if both do, how they compose (plus, in one case, which specification of the same partition element is used). These parameters are the bare necessities: they are the natural choice points that the account forces on us, and each corresponds to actual differences in the data. To remove them would incur the double cost of extrinsic stipulativity and diminished empirical coverage. As the system stands, it does exactly what it should, deriving all and only the partitions attested in the languages of the world.

Readers may have noticed an affinity between my features' division of the semantic space and the Successive Division Algorithm of Dresher 2009 in phonology. Methodological convergence from two such different domains is interesting and so, to conclude, I present the derivations in a form drawn from phonology (figure 4.8). Presenting (from top to bottom) the monopartition, author bipartition, participant bipartition, standard tripartition, and quadripartition, this explicit centerfold shows how each feature acts in turn on the whole person space ($i_o i u_o u_o o_o$, far left), producing outputs that may be acted on by other features, or trimmed by Lexical Complementarity, or winnowed of zeroes by the domain of the variable to yield the partition elements that are the grammatical persons of traditional descriptions (far right).

With this solution in hand, we now turn to its properties and consequences. The chapters that follow show that it captures much more than the crosslinguistic inventory of partitions on which we have concentrated until now. These include core morphological, semantic, and syntactic properties of person and related deictic systems.

5 Morphological Composition

5.1 Introduction

Pronunciation, like denotation, is compositional. Just as the meaning of complex wholes systematically derives from the meanings of their simplex parts (leaving idioms aside), so the pronunciation of complex structures depends on the pronunciations of their substructures (leaving blocking aside: the plural of *it* is *they*, not *its*).

Morphological compositionality ought to be as fundamental to the study of features as semantic compositionality is. If we adopt a Y-like model of the grammar, in which syntax manipulates features that are then sent for interpretation and pronunciation, then we naively expect exponence to evince evidence of the minimal units of meaning. Naturally, such correspondences will not be universal or thoroughgoing, as the mapping of syntax to sound is far from transparent. However, if correspondences are systematic and robust enough within and across language families, then they provide vital evidence of the atoms of linguistic representation.

One area in which morphological compositionality has played a fundamental role is number, and especially the dual. Most famously, the dual in Hopi is formed by crosscutting what one would otherwise describe as a "singular" verb, like *wari* in (1), with a "plural" determiner or pronoun, like *'itam* in (3) (Hale, Jeanne, and Pranka 1990, Hale 1997):

(1) *Nu' wari.*
    1S   ran.S/D
    'I ran.'

(2) *'Itam wari.*
    1D/P ran.S/D
    'We (two) ran.'

(3) 'Itam yu'tu.
    1D/P ran.P
    'We (more than two) ran.'

These and similar facts have led to the view that dual is featurally complex and that it shares part of its specification with the singular and part with the plural (Noyer 1992, Harley and Ritter 2002a, Cowper 2005, Harbour 2007b, Nevins 2011, Sadler 2011). (Number features are discussed at length in the next chapter.)

Compositionality has been less discussed for numbers other than dual (but see Harbour 2011a on unit augmented and 2014a on trial, paucal, greater paucal, and greater plural, among others).

For person, morphological compositionality has been neglected even further. Although individual cases have been discussed (e.g., Noyer 1992 on Mam and McGinnis 2005 on Algonquian), I am not aware of any attempts to map out a substantial range of patterns and to test a theory of person features against them.

The current chapter aims to redress this imbalance—and to complement the previous chapter's focus on semantic compositionality. I confine attention here to "robust" patterns. Robustness is not a measure of numerical frequency, such as purely typological studies might use. Rather, I regard a pattern as robust if it is well-embedded within an individual language or language family, affecting a range of exponents, across pronominal or verbal domains, and/or if it is attested across a geographically and genetically diverse spread of languages.

Empirically, this chapter shows that morphological compositionality affects all persons: inclusives and exclusives (section 5.2), and general first, second, and third (section 5.3). Some of the patterns are surprising at first sight: exclusives built from inclusives (section 5.2.2); second persons subsuming first persons (section 5.3.1); and crosscutting second persons, reminiscent of the Hopi dual, assembled from parts of first person and parts of third (section 5.3.2).

The analytical challenge is to show that the feature compositions of the previous chapter capture all of these. That is, the featural identities of, say, the clusives must be shown to permit exponence of the inclusive to result in a substring of the exclusive; and exponence of second person must be able to share elements with both first person and third. I will argue in chapter 8 that other theories, especially privative ones, face significant difficulties here. But in this chapter, I content myself with showing that the current theory acquits itself adequately.

Finally, a note of caution. Although important, morphological compositionality is not the sole arbiter of morphological naturalness. There are featurally possible patterns of composition that I have not found attested, and there are morphologically natural classes that cannot be accounted for in terms of single or paired feature specifications, like −F or −F +G. I do not regard this as particularly damaging. Section 5.4 examines one case of overgeneration (third person subsuming second; section 5.4.1), and one of a natural class not defined by shared feature–value pairs (exclusive, inclusive, and second; section 5.4.2). I argue that, just as functional pressures impinge on the frequency with which the partitions are attested (section 3.3.3), so there appear to be forces affecting the range of morphological compositions one encounters. Precisely what the forces are remains to be investigated, but, for the cases examined in section 5.4, underspecification of third person appears to be crucial.

5.2 Clusivity

The most obvious examples of morphologically compositional person arise with inclusives. Inclusives, which pool the referents of exclusive and second person, may reflect this morphologically (section 5.2.1). This leads, in some cases, to inclusives that wholly subsume the exclusive, which is a quite intuitive state of affairs: one increases the number of morphemes to increase the number of referents.

Interestingly, converse relations also obtain. There are languages in which exclusive subsumes inclusive (section 5.2.2). In these cases, perhaps counterintuitively, numbers of referents decrease as numbers of morphemes rise. There may even be languages in which both patterns of compositionality occur at once (section 5.2.3).

The demands placed on the inventory of person features are therefore quite stringent. Nonetheless, the current theory meets them.

5.2.1 Composed Inclusives

When introduced in section 2.2.1, the inclusive–exclusive distinction was illustrated with pronominal forms from Tok Pisin because this English-lexified creole makes the you-and-me meaning of the inclusive, *yumi*, particularly clear to English speakers. In virtue of that very aspect of the system, it is also an example of morphological compositionality in person. Table 5.1 presents the same phenomenon in the slightly richer system of Bislama (Crowley (2004) suggests that Bislama is the Vanuatuan dialect of a broader language, Melanesian Pidgin, that also includes Tok Pisin and the Solomon Islands' Pijin).

The table presents the singular, dual, trial, and plural pronouns of the language. These are mostly straightforwardly decomposable (*fala* is nonsingular, *tu* dual, *tri* trial), but with some restrictions (third person is *hem* in the singular, null in the dual and trial, and fused with number in plural *ol, olgeta*;

Table 5.1

Bislama pronouns

Person	Singular	Dual	Trial	Plural
1EX	<u>mi</u>	<u>mi</u>-tufala	<u>mi</u>-trifala	<u>mi</u>-fala
1IN		<u>yu</u>-<u>mi</u>-tu(fala)	<u>yu</u>-<u>mi</u>-trifala	<u>yu</u>-<u>mi</u>
2	<u>yu</u>	<u>yu</u>-tufala	<u>yu</u>-trifala	<u>yu</u>-fala
3	hem	tufala	trifala	ol(geta)

nonsingular *fala* is absent from some inclusives, obligatorily from plural *yumi*, optionally from dual *yumitu, yumitufala*). Putting these slight wrinkles in the exponence of number and third person aside, the important point lies in the exponence of person in the inclusive and its relationship to exclusive and second. As shown by the underlining, in all numbers, inclusive *yumi-* is composed of exclusive *mi* (single-underlined) and second person *yu* (double-underlined).

The featural explanation of this system is straightforward. In the quadripartition, inclusive is +author +participant. This shares +author with exclusive +author −participant. So, we can capture shared *mi* by claiming that it realizes +author. Similarly, inclusive shares +participant with second person −author +participant. So, we can capture shared *yu* by claiming that it realizes +participant. (Third person shares neither +author nor +participant, so we correctly derive the absence of *yu* and *mi* here.)

A different instantiation of the same compositionality arises in Kiowa (Watkins 1984, Harbour 2007b), but straddling two distinct partitions. The pronouns of the language are tripartititoned (with demonstratives for third person) but bear no indication of number for first and second person. So, *náw* means 'I', 'we.EX', or 'we.IN', and *ám* means 'you', with all the numerical ambiguity of its English counterpart. Agreement, by contrast, is very rich in person and number information, with the agreement prefix registering phi features of as many as three arguments at once. Nonetheless, inclusive agreement is always subject to one of two swingeing syncretisms, one merging it with exclusive, the other with second person (figure 2.3).

In consequence, neither pronouns alone nor agreement alone can indicate when a first person is inclusive. Instead, unambiguous signaling of inclusivity requires a pronoun, which is shared with other first persons (single underlining), and agreement, which is shared with second (double underlining):

(4) <u>Náw</u> <u>ét</u>-   p'et.

    1   1EX.P:3P-drop.P
    'We (EX) dropped them.'

(5) *Náw bát-   p'et.*
   1   1IN.P:3P-drop.P
   'We (IN) dropped them.'

(6) *Ám bát-   p'et.*
   2   2P:3P-drop.P
   'You dropped them.'

This compositionality is reminiscent of the Hopi dual in being crosscategorial: part pronominal, part verbal. Nonetheless, the feature-sharing relations are similar to those of Bislama, despite the tripartite–quadripartite difference between pronouns and agreement. The pronoun *náw* is specified for +author, which is also part of the specification of inclusive agreement, +author +participant. Additionally, the latter shares +participant with second person, facilitating syncretism with the inclusive. (The verbal prefixes encode both person and number. However, one can disaggregate these and isolate *b-* as the exponent of inclusive/second, making the Kiowa system an instance of pure person compositionality, like Bislama. See Harbour 2007b for details of the decomposition and fuller derivation of the syncretisms discussed.)

Having illustrated the same pattern wholly within pronouns, and between pronouns and verbs, I now give a purely verb-based example in which inclusive is composed from morphemes shared between exclusive and second person. Instances of this are frequent within Algonquian and were central to how Zwicky (1977) formulated and answered his question of possible partitions, as well as to Harley and Ritter's (2002a) and McGinnis's (2005) views of markedness and feature dominance. The pattern is exemplified in table 5.2 with Nishnaabemwin (Valentine 2001): inclusive shares with exclusive the +author plural suffix *min* (single-underlined), and with second person, the +participant prefix *g* (double-underlined).

This example differs from the others in not pertaining purely to person. Instead, the morpheme shared between first persons is amalgamated with

Table 5.2

Nishnaabemwin independent indicative ('make a fire')

Person	Singular	Plural
1EX	*n-boodwe*	*n-boodwe-min*
1IN		*g-boodwe-min*
2	*g-boodwe*	*g-boodwe-m*
3	*boodwe*	*boodwe-wag*

number. Naturally, pure person exponence is the most revealing means of uncovering the features that underlie person. However, number can be almost as revealing given the intimacy of its relationship to person; and, whether we regard *min* as the exponent of plural in the context of +author, or as the simultaneous exponent of plural and +author, we still need to refer to a feature shared by both persons, just as in Bislama and Kiowa.

The Khoisan language !Ora (Güldemann 2002, citing Meinhof 1930) shows the same pattern of inclusive compositionality in its pronouns, with one set of exponents fused with number and, in this case, gender; see table 5.3. (!Ora gender distinguishes masculine and feminine from mixed-gender groups. This common gender, as it is called, consequently does not exist in the singular.) Again, exponents shared with exclusive are single-underlined, and those shared with second, double-underlined. The shared first person exponents come in two sets, one triplet of genders for dual (*kham*, *sam*, *m*) in the middle column, and another for plural (*tjē*, *sē*, *da*) in the rightmost.

5.2.2 Composed Exclusives

Inclusives that include the exclusive make a certain intuitive sense, as morphology mirrors reference in these cases. Each exclusive is a proper subset of some inclusive, and we can readily appreciate that extra exponents might correspond to extra referents—a case of iconicity, in the sense of Downing and Stiebels 2012. However, conflicting patterns of containment can also obtain, in which inclusive is a substring of exclusive. Two examples of this, in pronominal systems, are given in table 5.4. The current proposal

Table 5.3

!Ora pronouns

Person/Gender		Singular	Dual	Plural
1EX	M	*ti-re*	*si-kham*	*si-tjē*
	F	*ti-ta*	*si-sam*	*si-sē*
	C		*si-m*	*si-da*
1IN	M		*sa-kham*	*sa-tjē*
	F		*sa-sam*	*sa-sē*
	C		*sa-m*	*sa-da*
2	M	*sa-ts*	*sa-kharo*	*sa-kao*
	F	*sa-s*	*sa-saro*	*sa-sao*
	C		*sa-khaoo*	*sa-du*

Table 5.4
Limbu (top) and Gumbáiŋgar pronouns

Person	Singular	Dual	Plural
1EX	<u>aŋ</u>-<u>ga</u>	an-chi-<u>ge</u>	<u>aŋ</u>-i-<u>ge</u>
1IN		an-chi	<u>aŋ</u>-i
2	khɛn-ɛʔ	khɛn-chi	khɛn-i
3	khun-ɛʔ	khun-chi	khɛŋ-haʔ
1EX	ŋaia	<u>ŋali</u>-<u>gei</u>	<u>ŋīa</u>-<u>gei</u>
1IN		<u>ŋallī</u>	<u>ŋīā</u>
2	ŋīnda	bulā	ŋudjawinj
3	gulanna	bulári	bīn

easily captures this containment relation, owing to its reliance on negative feature values. (Chapter 8 shows that such reversals of containment pose problems for theories that assume privative features.)

First, consider Limbu, a Tibeto-Burman language of Nepal and neighboring countries (van Driem 1987).[1] From the dual and plural columns, it is clear that dual is *chi* and plural, *i*. So, turning to person, we see that +author, the feature common to 1IN and 1EX, is *aŋ* (noting the place assimilation *aŋ-chi* ↦ *anchi*). First singular *aŋ-ga* 'I' corroborates this: it is +author and contains *aŋ*. To capture the occurrence of *ge* in the exclusive but not in the inclusive, we must associate it with a feature that likewise occurs in the exclusive but not in the inclusive. This is simply done: *ge* realizes −participant. This move raises two questions with respect to other pronominal forms.

First, *ge* is not surface-apparent in *aŋ-ga* 'I'. One might claim that this is concatenated, underlyingly, as +author *aŋ* and −participant *ge*, but that the vowel *e* is lowered to *a*, either idiosyncratically, or harmonically, to accord with the vowel of *aŋ*.[2] Alternatively, if one determined that singular *ga* and dual/plural *ge* were distinct morphemes, then one could engineer the nonoccurrence of −participant *ge* in the first singular by contextualizing it to −atomic, which dual and plural share but singular lacks (see chapter 6). (Consonant with this, van Driem regards *ga* and *ge* as number-sensitive allomorphs of the same person specification.)

Second, *ge* does not occur in the third person, even though exclusive and third share the feature, −participant, that *ge* realizes. There are two ways around this. The first is to claim that third person is not specified for ±participant in this context. Alternatively, one can again appeal to contextualization, by claiming that *ge* realizes −participant only in the presence of +author.

A very similar system, with some coincidental similarity of morphemes, arises in Gumbáiŋgar, a Pama-Nyungan language of northern New South Wales (Smythe 1948–49; table 5.4, bottom). Again, inclusive is, more or less, a substring of exclusive, which is formed by the addition of a final *gei* (double-underlined). The forms of the inclusive themselves (single-underlined) undergo some minor phonological changes. First, the final long vowel of dual *ŋallī* and plural *ŋīā* shortens, and the *l* of the dual degeminates, giving dual *ŋali-gei* and plural *ŋīa-gei*. Degemination arises whenever the inclusive is subject to suffixation, as exemplified in the inclusive dual accusative *ŋalī-nja* and possessive *ŋali-mbandi*. Leaving these minor phonological points aside, we can account for the distribution of *gei* by claiming that it realizes −participant, but only in the context of both +author (hence, not in the third person) and −atomic (hence, not in the singular). (Number fuses with person in *ŋallī* and *ŋīā*, making this system analogous to the mixed person–number compositionality of Nishnaabemwin and !Ora.)

This form of compositionality appears to be most robust in various Tibeto-Burman and Australian languages. However, this does not mean that it is marginal in any theoretical sense, because, when it does occur, it is a far from peripheral phenomenon. Moreover, it occurs in Mesoamerica as well.

Focusing first on Limbu, we find that exclusive compositionality is not confined to pronouns but occurs also in verbs. For instance, consider the following schema for a first person dual agent acting on a third person nonsingular object (van Driem 1987):

(7) VERB-*s*- *u*- *si*- *ge*
    VERB-D-3O-šO-1EX.š
    'he and I (VERB) them two'

(8) *a*- VERB-*s*- *u*- *si*
    1IN-VERB-D-3O-šO
    'you and I (VERB) them two'

These verbs differ from the pronouns in that there is no marker of general first person shared between inclusive and exclusive (dual *s-u* occurs also with second persons). However, there is clearly carryover from the morphemes that make up the pronouns into those that make up verbs. In particular, *ge* remains an exponent of −participant (in the presence of +author and −atomic). As a further example, consider third nonsingular acting on first. Again, *ge* is present for exclusive (9) but absent from inclusive (10):

(9) *mε*-VERB-*si*- *ge*
    šS-VERB-šO-1EX.š
    'they two (VERB) him and me'

(10) a-   m-   VERB-si
    1IN-šS-VERB-šO
    'they two (VERB) you and me'

This, therefore, supports the view taken of the morphemes, and hence the compositionality, that makeup the pronouns.

There is no such carryover to verbs in Gumbáiŋgar, because the language lacks agreement in this domain.[3] However, such carryover is attested in Wiradjuri, a language of central New South Wales (Matthews 1904). For instance, for the present tense of 'beat', we have the following for the dual:

(11) *bumurra-li*
    beat-   1D
    'you and I beat'

(12) *bumurra-li- guna*
    beat-   1D-EX
    'he and I beat'

And analogously for the plural:

(13) *bumurra-ni*
    beat-   1P
    'you all and I beat'

(14) *bumurra-ni- guna*
    beat-   1P-EX
    'they and I beat'

This is precisely the variety of exclusive compositionality evident in Limbu and Gumbáiŋgar pronouns. The shared first person exponents, fused with number, occur in both the inclusive and the exclusive. That is, dual *li* and plural *ni* are +author; and *guna*, which occurs in the exclusive, both dual and plural, realizes −participant (again, subject to restrictions affecting singular and third person).

As in Limbu, the exclusive exponent, *guna*, occurs also in the pronominal domain, with varying degrees of allomorphy. In the nominative, *guna* itself occurs:

(15) *ngulli*   we.IN.D   *ngeani*   we.IN.P
    ngulli-guna we.EX.P   *ngeani-guna* we.EX.P

In the possessive, which ends in *ng*, this shortens to *una*:

(16) *ngulliging*   ours.IN.D   *ngeaniging*   ours.IN.P
    ngulliging-una   ours.EX.D   *ngeaniging-una*   ours.EX.P

Further shortenings of *guna* may be identifiable in the accusative. In the dual, *gu* may be a substring, *uggu*. In the plural, which already ends in *gu*, we find *na*, which has the appearance of haplology:

(17) *ngullinya*   us.IN.D   *ngeaninyagu*   us.IN.P
    ngulliny-uggu us.EX.D   *ngeaninyagu-na*   us.EX.P

Similar patterns, with different morphemes, are given by Koch (2004), for the New South Wales languages Gundungurra, Ngunawal, Dyirringany, and Thurawal, and, citing Schmidt 1919, for South Australian. Whether these languages exhibit similar patterns as an areal trait or via inheritance does not strike me as particularly crucial. The pattern is well-embedded in these grammars, in that it affects multiple numbers and can hold for both pronouns and verbs. It is also robust enough to persist under allomorphy and, possibly, historical change of the exclusive marker itself.

As a final instance of this pattern, I observe that composed exclusives arise also in the Americas. In its possessives, Mam (England 1983) deploys both prefixes and enclitics to encode exclusivity. As shown in table 5.5, the exclusive subsumes the inclusive. Both share the prefix *q*, which is consequently +author (and −atomic), but, of the two, only the exclusive bears the enclitic *a*.

An interesting feature of Mam is that enclitic *a* occurs in four cells of table 5.5, in singular and plural of both exclusive and second. This aspect of Mam has drawn a reasonable amount of theoretical attention, and we will return to it in chapter 8. It is, however, a coincidental fact about Mam, as England emphasizes: related languages have as many as four distinct exponents corresponding to these four *a*'s. But such variety is orthogonal to the crucial point, which is that Mam, and its relatives, exhibit composed exclusives.

There is an interesting difference between inclusive and exclusive compositionality. Both involve a +author exponent. The morpheme that compositional inclusives add to this is often shared with another person (second). For

Table 5.5

Mam possessives

Possessor	Singular ('cat')	Plural ('cats')
1EX	*n-wīxh-a*	*q-wīxh-a̳*
1IN		*q-wīxh*
2	*t-wīxh-a*	*ky-wīxh-a*
3	*t-wīxh*	*ky-wīxh*

Morphological Composition 111

compositional exclusives, further sharing is rarer. Generally, morphemes like *ge*, *gei*, and *guna* are not shared with other persons. Mam and its relations are exceptional here, even if the second shared exponent does not correspond to a simplex natural class (exclusive, second).

Thus, I conclude that exclusive compositionality is a real phenomenon and that it counts in favor of the current feature inventory that it is able to capture it.

5.2.3 Both in Bahing (and Bilua)

I end this section by returning to Tibeto-Burman, and, in particular, to Bahing, which is remarkable in that there is a plausible decomposition of its pronouns according to which the language exhibits both patterns of compositionality at once. That is, it has both the compositional inclusive of Tok Pisin and the compositional exclusive of Limbu. Though I remain neutral as to whether the decomposition that yields this appearance is the correct one, one must acknowledge it as plausible. So, it is worth examining the data and showing that the current theory can accommodate simultaneous occurrence of both patterns. Adding strength to this claim is the fact that the same convergence of patterns arises in the Oceanic language Bilua.

The relevant forms are presented in table 5.6. The nonsingular first persons all share *gō* (exclusives *gōku*, *gōsūku*, inclusives *gōi*, *gōsi*). So, *gō* is the exponent of +author. I will assume that the exponent of second person, −author +participant, is *gan* (hence dual *gani*) and that its *-n* deletes before *si* in the plural (hence *gasi*, not **gansi*). First and second singular then are both truncated relative to the plural: compare first person *go* with *gō* and second person *ga* with *gan*. Formally, one can treat this as number-conditioned allomorphy. (An alternative is to take second person always to be *ga*, in which case, dual shows allomorphy, being *ni* for second person *gani* but *i* for inclusive *gōi*, **gōni*.) It is straightforward then to treat *ku* as the exponent of −participant (in the presence of +author and −atomic), giving composed exclusives, like dual *gō-ku*. This exhausts the person exponents.

Table 5.6

Bahing pronouns

Person	Singular	Dual	Plural
1EX	go	gō-ku	gō-sū-ku
1IN		gō-i	gō-si
2	ga	gan-i	ga-si
3	harem	harem-dau	harem-dau-si

The remaining exponents pertain to number. Plural is *sū* for exclusive (*gōsūku*) and *si* for inclusive and second (*gōsi, gasi*). Dual is zero for exclusive (*gōku*) and *i* for inclusive and second (*gōi, gani*; or *i* for inclusive and *ni* for second, if one takes the second person exponent to be *ga*, not *gan*). This derives all the forms shown, except for third person. These share a third person root, *harem*, with *dau* marking both nonsingulars, and *si*, shared with first and second persons, additionally marking the plural.

With this analysis in place, one can make apparent why—and, more importantly, how—Bahing seems to exhibit two distinct patterns of compositionality simultaneously.

First, if we consider only person exponents, the Limbu pattern emerges. Exclusive shares an exponent (*gō*) with inclusive but has an extra exponent too (*ku*). These are shown in table 5.7, with single versus double underlining showing which features match which exponents.

Second, if we contrast exponence of +author with the conditioning effect of +participant on number, the Tok Pisin pattern emerges. On the one hand, exclusive and inclusive share the specification +author, which second person lacks. Consequently, both first persons have the exponent *gō* (single-underlined in table 5.8). On the other hand, inclusive and second share +participant, which conditions dual *i* and plural *si* (double underlined). As a result, first person inclusive shares exponents both with exclusive (*go*) and with second person (*i, si*).

Adding grist to the mill, a configuration isomorphic to Bahing duals is found in the plural object clitics of Bilua. The forms in question are 1EX.P *ani-nge*,

Table 5.7

Bahing composed exclusive

Person	Dual	Plural
+author −participant	*gō-ku*	*gō-sū-ku*
+author +participant	*gō-i*	*gō-si*

Table 5.8

Bahing composed inclusive

Person	Number conditioner	Dual	Plural
+author	−participant	*gō-ku*	*gō-sū-ku*
+author	+participant	*gō-i*	*gō-si*
−author	+participant	*gan-i*	*ga-si*

1IN.P *ani-me*, 2P *Ø-me*, 3P.DIST *se*. The clusives, *ani-nge* and *ani-me*, share +author *ani*, just as the Bahing duals, *gō-ku* and *gō-i*, share *gō*. Similarly, inclusive and second in Bilua, *ani-me* and *Ø-me*, share *me*, just as the same persons, *gō-i* and *gan-i*, share *i* in Bahing. Thus, we have the Tok Pisin pattern again. Yet we also have a version of the Limbu pattern, though without complete subsumption: exclusive in both languages exhibits an exponent not shared with any other person, Bilua *nge*, paralleling Bahing *ku*.

Appealing as this simultaneous display of compositionality in Bahing is—and the supporting instance in Bilua notwithstanding—it obtains only relative to some specific assumptions.

The first is that the second person varies between *gan* and *ga*, with *n* absent before plural *si* (hence *gasi*, not **gansi*). If, instead, second person is taken to be invariant *ga*, then the variation in form must be attributed to the dual: *i* for the inclusive (*gōi*) and *ni* for second person (*gani*) (in addition to zero for the exclusive *gōku*). On this alternative, the dual would no longer count as an instance of the Tok Pisin pattern.

The second assumption is that the plural *sū* of the exclusive (*gōsūku*) is underlyingly distinct from the *si* of the inclusive and second plurals (*gōsi*, *gasi*). If, instead, there is one underlying form (*si*, say, from which *sū* derives by backing, rounding, and lengthening), then there is no variation at all and, so, no overlap shared by −participant forms to the exclusion of +participant. In other words, *si* and *sū* would count as instances of the same exponent and the double underlining of table 5.8 would extend through the entire plural column. On this alternative, the plural would no longer count as an instance of the Tok Pisin pattern.

Therefore, Bahing presents Limbu-style exclusive compositionality together with Tok-Pisin-style inclusive compositionality only if at least one of the preceding two alternative morphological decompositions is rejected. It is certainly plausible that, underlyingly, second person is *gan*, and *si* and *sū* are distinct, as originally suggested. Therefore an assessment of the current theory's capacity to cope with patterns of composition should entertain the possibility that Bahing displays both Limbu and Tok Pisin compositionality simultaneously; and the theory has no difficulty with this possibility.

5.3 Second and General First Person

Let us return for a moment to Mam. Table 5.5 shows that the language displays not only a compositional exclusive, but a compositional second person too. In singular and plural alike, second and third person share a prefix; but, distinguishing them, second additionally bears the enclitic *a*.[4]

This section deals with compositionality of the kind just illustrated, that is, compositionality beyond clusivity. Necessarily, in the last section, attention was confined to quadripartitions of person. So, for balance, this section focuses on tripartitions, a move that enables us to examine compositionality of general first person, too.[5]

5.3.1 Exponents Shared between First and Second

A pattern that it does not take much effort to find is one in which a first and second person mark number with an exponent that third person does not use. This is straightforwardly accommodated on the current theory because these two persons share the specification +participant but differ in their specification for ±author. Consequently, shared material can be attributed to +participant (and number, in the European examples below), and differences, to ±author. Examples of this are found in the plural pronouns of several European languages and of Oneida, in the historical development of Afroasiatic verb agreement, and, simultaneously, in the pronouns and verb agreement of Yimas.

Table 5.9 presents the plural pronouns in a variety of case or clitic guises: masculine nominative in Spanish, (gender-free) nominative in colloquial Italian, dative in Romanian, and object clitics in French.[6] In all cases, the first and second person share an ending that the third person lacks. The Spanish pronouns are particularly interesting. Spanish (along with other Romance varieties) has innovated a new plural marker, the *otros* of *nosotros*, *vosotros*. Synchronically, *otros* occurs independently as the masculine 'others' (alongside feminine *otras*, in virtue of which the language also has *nosotras*, *vosotras* and, hence, unlike most Romance languages, a gender distinction in all plurals). Significantly, the innovated marker maintains the distribution of older plural markers shared between first and second to the exclusion of third. This suggests that the distribution is not a historical reflex or a phonological quirk, but is semantically, hence featurally, real.

Table 5.9

Romance pronouns

Person/ Number	Spanish NOM(M)	Italian NOM	Romanian DAT	French CL
1P	*n-os-otros*	*n-oi*	*n-ouă*	*n-ous*
2P	*v-os-otros*	*v-oi*	*v-ouă*	*v-ous*
3P	*ellos*	*loro*	*lor*	*les*

A similar pattern is found in Slavic languages. For instance, in Polish, the nominative first and second plural pronouns, *my* and *wy*, share an ending that third plurals, masculine *oni* and feminine/neuter *one*, lack. The same pattern is found in the syncretic genitive–accusative–locative, where first person *nas* and second person *was* (in which the *w* of the nominative *wy* is discernible) share an *as* that third person *(n)ich* lacks. (In other cases, such as the dative and instrumental, all three persons share endings with each other—*nam, wam, im*, and *nami, wami, nimi*—and with common nouns, as in *psom* 'dogs.DAT' and *psami* 'dogs.LOC'.)

Icelandic (Einarsson 1945) too has developed a strong version of this pattern, outside the nominative, both in the singular and in the plural. In the singular, the accusative, dative, and genitive differ only in their initial consonant for first and second (*mig, mér, mín*; *þig, þér, þín*). These rhyming triples contrast with third singular (e.g., masculine *hann, honum, hans*). In the plural, too, first and second are again distinguished only by their onsets (*okkur, okkur, okkar*; *ykkur, ykkur, ykkar*) and differ substantially from third (masculine: *þá, þeim, þeirra*). In the last three triplets, first and second exhibit syncretism in the accusative and dative (as do the honorific plurals), in distinction to third person.

An extreme version of this pattern is found in the independent (numberless) pronouns of Oneida (Abbott 2006). Here, the first person forms are wholly subsumed by second (table 5.10). The first person varies according to whether it is sentence-initial, between the particles and the verb, or sentence-final. Second person simply suffixes *sé* to each of these. Analytically, one can posit that the first person forms realize just +participant and that, in that context, *sé* realizes −author, the feature that distinguishes second person from first. (For the reverse configuration of first and second person, see the discussion of Tarascan in section 5.4.1.)

In the domain of verbs, the history of the suffixal conjugation of Afroasiatic too suggests morphological compositionality dependent on the shared feature +participant. The conjugation has come to cover past, perfective, and stative across different members of the family and is sensitive to person, number, and,

Table 5.10
Oneida pronouns

Person	Initial	Medial	Final
1	í·	ní	niʔí
2	i·sé	ni·sé	niʔi·sé
3	né·	né·	né·

in the second and third person, gender. It is illustrated for Akkadian (Buccellati 1997, Caplice 2002), Hebrew (Sivan and Levenston 1975), and Tigrinya (fieldnotes, Zekaryas Solomon) in table 5.11. The point of interest is how Hebrew and Tigrinya (and their respective closer relatives) have come to efface a morphological distinction attested in Akkadian.

Anciently, Akkadian (and Ancient Egyptian) first singular and second had entirely distinct agreement forms, the first beginning with *k* (underlined), the second with *t* (double-underlined). This difference was reflected in the subject pronouns, *k* 'I', *t* 'you.S/P'. However, in all later languages, the different consonants were lost in the verbal suffixes (even though some pronouns retain pronominal reflexes of *k* and *t*, as in Hebrew *anoxi* 'I' and *ata* 'you.MS', *at* 'you.FS'). This morphological leveling was achieved in two ways. In some languages, like Hebrew, *t* spread from second person into first singular. In others, like Tigrinya, *k* spread from first singular into second.

That all members of the family heterogeneously arrived at, and kept, the same distribution (≡) suggests that they were under strong internal pressure to reinterpret the person-specific markers as general +participant suffixes. This, therefore, constitutes a plausible instance of morphological compositionality

Table 5.11

Afroasiatic suffixal conjugation: Akkadian 'decide' (top), Hebrew 'declare' (middle), Tigrinya 'judge' (bottom)

Person	Singular	Plural
1	*parsā-ku*	*parsā-nu*
2M	*parsā-ta*	*parsā-tunu*
F	*parsā-ti*	*parsā-tina*
3M	*paris*	*pars-ū*
F	*pars-at*	*pars-ā*
1	*paras-ti*	*paras-nu*
2M	*paras-ta*	*pras-tem*
F	*paras-t*	*pras-ten*
3M	*paras*	*pars-u*
F	*pars-a*	*pars-u*
1	*färäd-ku*	*färäd-na*
2M	*färäd-ka*	*färäd-kum*
F	*färäd-ki*	*färäd-ken*
3M	*färäd-ä*	*färäd-u*
F	*färäd-ät*	*färäd-a*

Morphological Composition

between first and second person: Tigrinya/Hebrew *k/t* realize +participant, and the remaining parts of the suffixes realize ±author together with gender and/or number. These cases differ neatly from the Romance and Slavic ones discussed above in that here the exponents of +participant are pure, that is, not coupled with number.

The case of Afroasiatic involves divergence of the morphemes that make up agreement from those that make up pronouns. In Yimas (Foley 1991), by contrast, some +participant exponents evidence a closer relationship between pronouns and agreement.[7]

Although the pronominal decomposition suggested below directly affects only a rather limited number of forms, and so might be taken as a rather marginal case, its significance lies precisely in the fact that it straddles both the pronominal and the verbal domains.

Yimas has a tripartition of person agreement and possession (table 5.12), as well as pronouns, though the third person forms are identical to demonstratives. Within these categories, first and second person are wholly distinct for the singular (*ama*, *mi*) and wholly identical for paucals (*paŋkt* for pronouns, *paŋkra* for prefixes). However, for the other nonsingulars—namely, dual and plural—there is a clear relationship between first and second. Second person (*kapwa*, *ipwa*) is first person (*kapa*, *ipa*) with extra rounding. Yimas has a number of such floating segments, as Foley describes at length.

We can capture the exponents for these last pronouns as in (18). According to this decomposition, *kapa* and *ipa* are not specifically first person, but express +participant in general.

(18) +participant D ↔ *kapa*
      +participant P ↔ *ipa*
      −author ↔ ^{w} / [+participant ___]

Table 5.12

Yimas pronouns (top) and possessor/intransitive prefixes

Person	Singular	Dual	Paucal	Plural
1	*ama*	*kapa*	*pa[ŋ]-ŋkt*	*ipa*
2	*mi*	*kapwa*		*ipwa*
1	*ama-*	*kapa-*	*paŋ-kra-*	*ipa-*
2	*ma-*	*kapwa-*		*ipwa-*
3	*m-, na-*	*mpɨ-*	*kra-*	*mpu-*

(I assume that ^{w} is blocked from singular and paucal by more highly specified exponents.)

The case for +participant exponents receives support from the paucal pronoun *paŋkt*, which realizes both first and second person, to the exclusion of any other difference between them. As indicated in table 5.12, it is composed of two exponents, *paŋ* and *ŋkt* (subject to deletion of one *ŋ*). This *paŋ* further occurs as part of verbal agreement for first and second paucal: *paŋkra* consists of +participant *paŋ* and a paucal exponent, *kra*, shared with third person:

(19) *paŋ-kra- wa-t ~ paŋ-kra- wa-r- ŋkt*
   1/2-PCS-go- PF ~ 1/2-PCS-go- PF-PC
   'we few / you few went'

(20) *kra- wa-t*
   PCS-go- PF
   'they few went'

Pursuing paucal +participant *paŋ* further into the verbal domain yields another instance of morphological compositionality. *Paŋ* occurs on transitive verbs in the following participant-on-participant scenarios:

(21) *pa[ŋ]-ŋa- tpul-c- ŋkt*
   1/2- 1SO-hit- PF-PC
   'you few hit me'

(22) *pa[ŋ]-ŋkra- tpul-c- ŋkt*
   1/2- 1DO-hit- PF-PC
   'you few hit us two'

(23) (*kapa/paŋkt/ipa*) *paŋ-kul- cpul-c- ŋkt*
   1D/ 1PC/ 1P 1/2-2PO-hit- PF-PC
   'I (or we two/few/all) hit you few'

Of these, (23) presents further second person compositionality, of the type seen in Afroasiatic. Second paucal consists of something shared between first and second person, *paŋ*, on the one hand, and something unique to second person, the object marker *kul*, on the other.[8]

Thus, Yimas presents composed second persons both in the pronominal domain, for dual and plural, and in the verbal domain, for paucal, with the paucal +participant exponent *paŋ* spanning both of these.

5.3.2 1 + 3 = 2

We have just seen several cases in which first and second person share exponents, in virtue of +participant. We also saw, in Mam, that second person may share exponents with third person (viz. singular *t* and plural *ky*; table 5.5).

This is possible in virtue of −author, and one finds similar patterns in tripartitions. For example, the nominative pronouns of Afrikaans (table 5.13) suggest a decomposition in which second person is *j*-, third person is *h*-, and these share the number exponents -*y* for singular and -*ulle* for plural.

Given the existence of both patterns (and the fact that second bears the same relationship to third in Mam as it does to first in Oneida), we predict the possibility of a second person composed by crosscutting first and third—hence the odd equation that is the title to this section. Such systems are indeed attested (though I have yet to find an instance of this in the singular).

The most robust examples come from the Eastern Highland languages of Papua New Guinea. For instance, in Yagaria (Renck 1975), a variety of forms, both verbal and pronominal, display the pattern. Table 5.14 presents the neutral conjugation of the verb 'put' and of the basic pronouns. Yagaria verbs frequently undergo vowel mutations in second and third nonsingular. For 'put', there is a nonsingular first–nonfirst contrast between *bolo* and *bele*. At the same, there is a third–nonthird contrast in person–number suffixes, between *da* and *ta*. These two patterns meet in the second person, which shares *bele* with third and *ta* with first. There is no uniquely second person exponent in the nonsingular, making its expression purely compositional.

Table 5.13

Afrikaans nominative pronouns

Person	Singular	Plural
1	*ek*	*ons*
2	*j-y*	*j-ulle*
3	*h-y*	*h-ulle*

Table 5.14

Yagaria neutral conjugation (top) and pronouns

Person	Singular	Dual	Plural
1	*bolo-da*	*bolo-ta-'a*	*bolo-ta*
2	*bolo-ka*	*bele-ta-'a*	*bele-ta*
3	*bolo-na*	*bele-da-'a*	*bele-da*
1	*da-gaea*	*la-'a-gaea*	*la-gaea*
2	*ka-gaea*	*la-ta-gaea*	*la-pa-gaea*
3	*a-gaea*	*ta-gaea*	*pa-gaea*

The same pattern arises more strikingly in pronouns. Second person is composed of *la*, which is shared with the first person nonsingular (and so is a +participant form), and dual *ta* or plural *pa*, both of which are shared with third person (and so, presumably, express number fused with, or in the context of, −author). Here, second person has two exponents where third and sometimes first have just one, thus making the compositionality more transparent.

It is significant that the Yagaria compositionality is not confined to a single set of exponents and characterizes both verbal and pronominal exponence. Together, these make it unlikely that we are dealing with a coincidental conspiracy of homophones. Data from related languages underscore this.

In a short comparative grammar, Deibler (1976a; see also Deibler 1976b) shows that the same pattern arises in Gahuku and Yaweyuha. In Yaweyuha, it has been lost in subject agreement (and in pronouns) but is retained in benefactives. Gahuku retains it in both places (table 5.15). The salient observation is that, although all three languages retain basically the same +participant exponent, *l*~*la*~*li*, the −author exponents have undergone what appears to be wholesale replacement: Yagaria *pa* and Yaweyuha *bi* may be related, but there is no obvious connection between these and Yagaria *ta* or Gahuku *ki*. (Certainly, comparison of forms in the 34 pages of Deibler 1976a gives no basis for positing historical correspondence between Yaweyuha *b* and Gahuku *k*.) If the pattern has been preserved despite thoroughgoing replacement of the exponents involved, then this speaks strongly for its reflecting the underlying featural reality.

Interestingly, a largely identical pattern arises in Paumarí (Chapman and Derbyshire 1991), an Arauan language of Brazil. The second plural prefixes

Table 5.15

Gahuku and Yaweyuha subject prefixes (top) and benefactive suffixes

Person	Gahuku		Yaweyuha	
	Singular	Plural	Singular	Plural
1	*n-*	*l-*	*n-*	*l-*
2	*g-*	*l-k-*	*Ø-*	*d-*
3	*a-*	*k-*	*Ø-*	*d-*
1	*-ni*	*-li*	*-ni*	*-li*
2	*-gi*	*-li-ki*	*-Ø*	*-li-bi*
3	*-Ø*	*-ki*	*-Ø*	*-bi*

Morphological Composition

Table 5.16

Paumarí possessives and imperatives

Person	Possessive ('arm')		Nonimperative
	Singular	Plural	Plural
1	o-vadi-Ø	a̱-vadi-Ø	a̱(ri)-
2	i-vadi-ni	a̱-va̳-vadi-ni	a̱-va̳- / a̱-vi̳-
3	vadi-Ø (M) vadi-ni (F)	va̳-vadi-Ø	va̳- / vi̳-

combine first person *a* and third person *va∼vi*, both in possessives and in verbs (table 5.16; though, in verbs, first plural is sometimes *ari*, which the second person does not share). A further complication concerns the suffix *ni* of the possessives. In the plurals, *ni* occurs only in second person, suggesting that first and third form a natural class to the exclusion of second. Supporting this, there are nouns for which first and third plural share the nonzero suffix *na* (*a-gora-na* 'our house', *a-va-gora-ni* 'your.P house', *va-gora-na* 'their house'). However, the first–third configuration vanishes in the singular, where none of these suffixes distribute across a simple natural class: *ni* occurs for second and for third feminine, and Ø∼*na*, for first and for third masculine. We can, therefore, tentatively disregard these suffixes qua indicators of featurally natural classes and focus on the prefixes, providing a further instance of second person composed by cross cutting first and third.

5.4 Limits and Constraints

The foregoing sections have explored how the theory of the previous chapter captures cases that are attested. There is, however, some mismatch between what the theory permits and what one finds, with overgeneration in some cases, and undergeneration in others. These mismatches do not endanger the theory, however. Section 5.4.1 focuses on one case of overgeneration and what initially looks like its attestation in Vietnamese. Section 5.4.2 focuses on one case of undergeneration and its attestation in Svan. Together, these sections show that a variety of forces shape the exponents that a language may have and that these are both a source of the shortfall and an alternative means of capturing natural classes.

5.4.1 Incomplete Attestation: Subsumption by Third

Not every compositional relation made possible by the current theory has been exemplified above. For instance, data already discussed illustrate the general phenomenon of composed third persons (in Yagaria verbs, table 5.14, third person nonsingular shares a root allomorph, *bele*, with second person, but bears a unique person–number suffix, *da*). However, given the feature specifications, it ought to be possible for a second person to be wholly subsumed by third person. That is, we can imagine there being exponents α for −author and β for −participant, yielding a second person, α, that is a substring of third person, $\alpha\beta$.

I argue in this section that incomplete attestation of compositional patterns is not particularly problematic for the current theory. The theory makes a range of possible exponential relations available, but other forces (both I-linguistic and E-linguistic, in the sense of Chomsky 1986) may make some of these rare to vanishing.

Let me begin with what looks like a subsumptive third person in Vietnamese (Ngô 1999).[9] The language displays a quadripartition of person. Formal *tôi* and informal *mình* 'I' pluralize to give the formal and informal exclusives *chúng tôi* and *chúng mình*. Inclusive is *chúng ta*, exploiting the same number marker. For second person, there are various forms of address, registering age, gender, and social status, such as *ông* and *bà*, used, respectively, for a middle-aged male or female, and *anh* and *cô*, used, respectively, for a young male or female.

Interestingly, there is a third person form related to each of the second persons. For example, *ông ấy*, *bà ấy*, *anh ấy*, and *cô ấy* are used to refer to (rather than address) a middle-aged or young male or female. Moreover, the second person forms and their third person analogues all pluralize with *các*, as opposed to the plural for first persons, *chúng*: *các ông* 'you.P (middle-aged males)' and *các ông ấy* 'they (middle-aged males)', and *các cô* 'you.P (young females)' and *các cô ấy* 'they (young females)'.[10]

The result is that third person appears to be morphologically compositional: *ông*, *bà*, *anh*, and the like realize −author, the feature shared by second and third person in a quadripartition, and *ấy* realizes −participant, the feature that differentiates second and third.[11]

However, Ngô does not regard the second person forms as pronouns. (In fact, he lists as pronouns only the first persons above and the third persons of note 10.) This is because all the terms of address are kinship terms: *ông* 'grandfather', *bà* 'grandmother', *anh* 'elder brother', *cô* 'aunt (father's or mother's younger sister)'. Other kinship terms also have this range of uses, like *bác* 'uncle, aunt (father's or mother's elder brother or sister)', 'you (addressee of parents' age)', *bác ấy* 'he, she (of parents' age)'. The word *ấy* itself is a demonstrative.

This makes it likely that these items are epithets, rather than pronouns. That is, they are not pronunciations of the features ±author and ±participant. Instead, they contain implicit variables (e.g., Higginbotham 1997) that can be bound by entities in the discourse. In the case of second person, the binder is phonologically null. For third persons, the binder can be the demonstrative *áy*.[12]

Would it matter for my account of person if third person were never expressed as second person plus an extra morpheme? In short, no. The featural identities derived in the last chapter define the maximal space of possible morphological relations between persons. Other formal pressures on I-languages or functional pressures on E-languages may constrain which relations may come into existence easily or at all. To underline this point, I offer two observations on relative or absolute infrequency of other exponential relations.

First, in their study of Basque dialects, Arregi and Nevins (2012) observe that morphological composition of person and number is more frequent in second and third person than in first. That is, for second person, one frequently encounters separate exponence of person and number, but for first person these tend to be fused.

No typological study that I am aware of enables one to check whether this holds crosslinguistically. However, one certainly finds other places in which it is true. For instance, in the prefixal conjugation of Afroasiatic, exemplified by Modern Hebrew in table 5.17, first plural is realized by the simplex exponent *n*, whereas second and third express person prefixally, as *t* or *y*, and number suffixally, as *u*. Similarly, in the Svan present perfect (Tuite 1998), inclusive and exclusive are both monomorphemic, *n* and *xw*, but second and third person are realized by a combination of prefixes, *ž* and *x*, and a shared plural suffix, *x*.

Consonant with Arregi and Nevins's observation is the fact that, in both Oneida (table 5.10) and Yimas (table 5.12), it is second person that subsumes first, not the reverse. That is, in the relevant parts of both these languages, the

Table 5.17
Svan and Hebrew simplex versus split person–number

Person	Svan (break.TR.PF)	Hebrew (break.TR.FUT)
1EX	*n-ik'wīša*	*n-šaber*
1IN	*gw-ik'wīša*	
2	*ž-ik'wīša-x*	*t-šabr-u*
3	*x-ok'wīša-x*	*y-šabr-u*

form used for first person is just +participant, to which second person adds an extra exponent, for −author.

The reverse pattern of subsumption does occur, but apparently much less frequently. The sole convincing example I have found, serendipitously, comes from the pronouns of Tarascan (Wares 1956). This is plainest in the possessives: 1S *hučíti* subsumes 2S *čiti* and 1P *hučári* subsumes 2P *čári*. Evidently, first person prefixes *hu* to second, making first person bimorphemic, but second person, monomorphemic.[13]

If there is a genuine skew in frequencies, favoring split and subsumptive second persons over first, then it shows that independent factors shape the inventory of person and number exponents. So, one should not naively expect all exponential relations between persons to be instantiated.

Morphological compositionality in number reinforces this position, in that there is a disparity between how singular behaves in comparison to other numbers. As said at the outset, the Hopi dual suggests a feature identity in which dual shares something with singular and something with plural. Reflecting this, one finds languages in which, morphologically, plural subsumes dual, and others in which dual subsumes plural. This is shown for Mokilese and Sursurunga pronouns in table 5.18. By contrast, I have not been able to find a language in which singular subsumes dual (or any other number)—that is, in which singular is constructed from dual, as the Mokilese plural is. This aligns with the typological observation that singular is a morphological default (some languages, like English, have unaffixed singulars and affixed plurals, but the reverse is not found on a language-wide scale; Corbett 2000). Again, then, this suggests that featurally possible morphological exponence relations are not instantiated with equal frequency.

I conclude, therefore, that although it is important for a theory to capture robustly attested patterns of morphological compositionality, it does not necessarily detract if the theory permits patterns of compositionality that are not

Table 5.18

Mokilese and Sursurunga: Converse subsumption

Person	Mokilese		Sursurunga		
	Dual ⊂	Plural	Dual ⊃		Plural
1EX	kama	kama-i	gi-ur		gim
1IN	kisa	kisa-i	git-ar		git
2	kamwa	kamwa-i	ga-ur		gam
3	ara	ara-i	di-ar		di

(frequently) attested. There are other forces at work here and, until further studies elucidate them, we will not know which patterns we ought, or ought not, to expect.

5.4.2 Nonfeaturally Natural Classes

Morphological compositionality is about natural classes: shared exponence is taken as an indicator of shared features. However, shared features are not the only means of capturing natural classes. Systematic underspecification can do so too. And, on the current approach, shared features cannot be used to capture one particular exponentially common class, the quadripartite nonthird persons (1EX, 1IN, 2). Evidence from the Person Case Constraint suggests that underspecification is a possible alternative for capturing the contrast.

To see that the nonthird persons of a quadripartition may have uniform exponence, again consider Svan. Table 5.19 presents two paradigms. In the imperfective (exemplified by the subdialect Becho, of Lower Bal; Topuria 1965 via Tuite 1998), the exclusive and second singulars indicate number with the suffix *sgw*, to the exclusion of third singular, which has no ending; and exclusive, inclusive, and second indicate plurality with the suffix *d*, in contrast to third person, which takes *x*. The present perfect shows the same pattern in a different location. The perfect uses dative prefixes (one can think of them as meaning not 'I have broken it' but 'it is broken to me'). Concomitant with the dative is an applicative (which was not parsed out when the same facts were presented in table 5.17). This takes the form *i* for exclusive, inclusive, and second, and *o* for third, in both numbers.

It is easy to understand the development of such a system in E-linguistic terms. As Svan (unlike its relatives Georgian, Laz, and Migrelian) expanded the very restricted clusivity contrast of Old Georgian into the domains shown in table 5.19, it expanded the range of the plural *d* and applicative *i*. In so doing, the new clusives continued to use exponents that the erstwhile general

Table 5.19

Svan third–nonthird marking

Person	'was/were preparing it'		'has/have broken it'	
	Singular	Plural	Singular	Plural
1EX	*xw-amara-sgw*	*xw-amara-d*	*m-i-k'wīša*	*n-i-k'wīša*
1IN		*l-amara-d*		*gw-i-k'wīša*
2	*x-amara-sgw*	*x-amara-d*	*ž-i-k'wīša*	*ž-i-k'wīša-x*
3	*amara*	*amara-x*	*x-o-k'wīša*	*x-o-k'wīša-x*

first person had used, thus minimizing superficial disruption to the language. The question is, however, what ramifications this had on the I-languages of people who had then to acquire this expanded system.

In the tripartition, first and second share +participant to the exclusion of third. So, plural *d* and applicative *i* can be characterized as being sensitive to that feature–value pair. In the quadripartition, however, exclusive, inclusive, and second do not share any feature: the first two, but not the last, are +author; the last two, but not the first, are +participant. So, it is a challenge to capture the distribution of these morphemes in purely featural terms.[14]

A plausible alternative is to regard third person as being underspecified. The range of possible underspecifications that the current approach might entertain deserves systematic investigation in its own right (something that has not been seriously undertaken for any nonprivative feature system that I am aware of). However, there is a long tradition of regarding at least third person as wholly or partly underspecified with respect to person features (beginning with Benveniste 1966). In particular, several accounts of the Strong Person Case Constraint (e.g., Anagnostopoulou 2003, Béjar and Řezáč 2003, Adger and Harbour 2007, Řezáč 2008 others) treat (some) third persons in this way, and Svan is a language that obeys the Strong Person Case Constraint: in any verb that encodes an indirect object, the direct object must be third person (Kevin Tuite, pers. comm.).

Two ways in which one might underspecify third person within the current system, without having to reevaluate the semantics, are as follows. First, as noted in section 4.3.4, −author is redundant when applied before −participant: if the latter strips out author and hearer, then the effect of −author is achieved whether −author is there or not. So, one might derive third person purely from −participant(φ).[15] Alternatively, one might suppose that the lattice of others is accessible directly via a root denoting o_o, rather than by invoking the whole phi structure and then removing the speaker and hearer. (This is a reasonable move, as o_o is semantically uniform and hence plausibly primitive, in contrast to i_o, iu_o, and u_o, which are nonuniform in mixing the speaker and/or hearer with others.)

On both these approaches, there are features, and, in the latter case, heads, that are present for exclusive, inclusive, and second, but absent for third. On the latter approach, for instance, one can treat *d* as the realization of plural, and *i* as the realization of the applicative head, in the context of the root φ node; or one could regard the conditioning factor as the presence (of either value) of the feature ±participant (or, alternatively, ±author, given note 15).

Georgian, a relative of Svan, lends support to the idea that exponents can care about the presence of a feature but not its value (or of a head in the same functional sequence as the feature). In subject agreement, Georgian *t*, like its Svan cognate *d*, is confined to nonthird persons, that is, to first and second (as Georgian lacks a clusivity contrast). Table 5.20 illustrates this for 'write': *v/Ø-c'er-t* 'we/you write' have *t*, and *c'er-en* 'they write' does not. This fact in isolation suggests that *t* is sensitive to the presence of +participant, the feature that first and second share in a tripartition.

However, *t* spreads into the third person in the dative. Like the Svan perfect in table 5.19, Georgian 'love' encodes its experiencer through dative agreement and an applicative head (*i–u*, which displays nonthird–third sensitivity, like the Svan cognates *i–o*). The presence of a fused exponent, *gv*, for first person and plural bleeds the occurrence of plural *t* in the first person *gv-i-qvar-s* 'we love it' (see the discussion of table 5.17; *s* is controlled by the third singular object). In second person, there is no fusion of person and number, and so *t* occurs as expected, *g-i-qvar-t*. The surprise, if one thinks of *t* as sensitive to +participant, is *u-qvar-t* 'they love it', where *t* registers the plurality of the third person dative ('he loves it', *u-qvar-s*, lacks *t*).

Adger and Harbour (2007), though they do not treat Georgian directly, provide a natural account of this disparity. They argue that third person indirect objects bear −participant (*pace* note 15; this distinguishes such objects from other third persons, which are unspecified for the feature, and causes them, but not third person direct objects, to engage in person case effects). If we adopt this position, then we can capture the correct distribution of *t* by claiming that it "cares" about the presence of ±participant, but not its specific value. This non-value-specific sensitivity entails that *t* is available for first and second person, which are always specified for ±participant, whether agents or experiencers (or objects), but that it is available for third persons only when they are indirect objects.[16]

Georgian therefore suggests that we may need exponents sensitive to features but not their values, quite independently of the problem of how to create a natural class of nonthird persons in quadripartite systems (cf. Béjar and Hall 1999). Thus, both mechanisms suggested above are independently motivated:

Table 5.20

Georgian *t* in agents and experiencers

Person	'write'	'love (it)'
1P	*v-c'er-ṯ*	*gv-i-qvar-s*
2P	*Ø-c'er-ṯ*	*g-i-qvar-ṯ*
3P	*c'er-en*	*u-qvar-ṯ*

a common and much-discussed mode of underrepresentation for third person, and exponents that are sensitive to a feature but blind to its values. So, though exclusive, inclusive, and second share no feature–value pair, the theory still has the means to treat these as a natural class.

5.5 Conclusion

This chapter has achieved several goals. Empirically, it has shown that morphological composition is just as important for person as it is for number and that the range of compositional patterns attested is wide, robust, and intriguing. Analytically, it has shown that the theory of the previous chapter is able to capture these, including some particularly complex cases, in which distinct patterns cooccur in the same language, as in Bahing and Mam. And theoretically, it has clarified how one should treat the shortfall between what the theory permits and what languages attest.

On this last point, this chapter has shown that there is some mismatch between possible and actual patterns of composition, in contrast to the previous chapter about possible partitions, where the generable and the actual align perfectly. There is overgeneration in the sense that there are unattested possibles, like third persons that subsume second. And there is undergeneration in the sense that languages show recurrent natural classes that cannot be captured by a single feature–value pair. Neither case is overly problematic, however, as there are, plausibly, other forces at play in shaping shared exponence and other mechanisms at work in creating classes of persons. In fact, the mechanism of third person underspecification, invoked for the latter case, may be one of the forces that makes subsumptive third persons rare: each occasion on which third person is underspecified is an occasion on which it fails to share features with, and hence cannot subsume, second person.

I conclude that the current theory adequately meets the challenge that morphological compositionality sets. When we come to consider other theories of person in chapter 8, I will argue that these same facts are quite detrimental, in particular to privative ones, which will have difficulty with the reciprocal subsumption of exclusive by inclusive and inclusive by exclusive.

6 Number and the Functional Sequence

6.1 Introduction

A very basic demand on any theory of person is that it interact with a theory of number to yield familiar inventories of pronouns and agreement in a straightforward fashion. This chapter shows that the current theory does so.

The theory of number adopted below is that of Harbour 2014a (though many other accounts, if extended to the full variety of numbers attested crosslinguistically, would work just as well; e.g., Noyer 1992, Harley and Ritter 2002a, Cowper 2005). It posits three features, ±atomic, ±minimal, and ±additive, as well as a parameter, *value recursion*, permitting cooccurrence of opposing values, +F −F, on a single head. The feature names make their interpretations, I hope, intuitive: +atomic picks out atoms, +minimal picks out elements that are minimal with respect to some property, +additive picks out a set of elements that is closed under addition; and the minus values do the opposite. These informal definitions will become clearer when used below (see appendix B.5 for formal details).

Beginning with tripartitions (section 6.3.1), then moving to quadripartitions (6.3.2) and, briefly, to bipartitions (6.3.3), this chapter shows that a compositional account of number readily interfaces with the features and structures of chapter 4.[1] The lattice diagrams used in this exposition (in lieu of full semantic formalism) are explained in the preliminary section 6.2.

In addition to these core questions, the chapter addresses matters surrounding the morphological and semantic interpretation of number and the interface of these domains with syntax. Section 6.4 focuses on the common semantic and morphological basis of number in personal pronouns and common nouns (section 6.4.1) and the issue of whether the denotation of plurals includes that of singulars (section 6.4.2).

Section 6.5 is concerned with interfaces. First, section 6.5.1 addresses the syntax–semantics interface and justifies the phrase structure implicit in sections 6.3.1–6.3.3, which places person below number:

(1)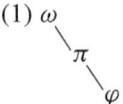

Section 6.5.2 draws out the consequences of this phrase structure for linear order while explaining and exploiting aspects of its Mirror Theory–style representation. Following Trommer 2002 and Harbour 2008, it illustrates that the propensity for person to precede number linearly holds across pronouns and verbs in both head-initial and head-final languages. Moreover, focusing on Classical Arabic, Walmatjari, and Yimas, it shows that verbs in particular are subject to a range of further generalizations about person–number linearization, some of which have escaped previous notice.

Finally, in a more tentative vein, section 6.5.3 extends the mechanisms of section 6.5.2 to sketch an account of why agreement might alternate on a paradigm-wide scale between being purely suffixal and predominantly prefixal in languages like Classical Arabic. The results of these conjectures are shown to derive the internal structure of the notoriously knotty Kiowa-Tanoan agreement prefix.

Thus, the current theory facilitates analysis of a rich range of phenomena in the interaction of person and number.

6.2 Lattice Diagrams

An advantage of approaching person and number via lattices is that the structures in question can be conveniently visualized via Hasse diagrams, allowing one to sidestep some otherwise rather hefty semantic formalism (appendix B.5). This section provides a quick introduction to the diagrams and their use.

As a basic illustration, let us begin with the three structures that organize the underlying ontology of persons. First, and most simply, there is the author lattice (figure 6.1). This consists of a single element, i, and so illustrates just one notational convention: that each element of the lattice is represented as a point in the corresponding Hasse diagram.

The participant lattice (figure 6.2), being more complex, illustrates two further conventions. First, its elements are organized into two rows. The singletons i and u are rowmates and the dyad iu is one row higher. This convention

Figure 6.1
Author lattice

Figure 6.2
Participant lattice

is followed in all diagrams below: elements of the same cardinality are placed on the same row and cardinality increases on each higher row.

Second, *iu* is linked to *i* and to *u* by lines. These lines show which elements are in a subelement/superelement relationship (or subset/superset, to revert to set-theoretic terminology). That is, we link the points corresponding to *i* and *iu* because $i \sqsubset iu$ (set-theoretically, $\{i\} \subset \{i, u\}$); and likewise for *u* and *iu*. Conversely, we do not link the points corresponding to *i* and *u* because neither is a subelement of the other (elements of equal cardinality never are).

With these pointers, the π lattice is also legible (figure 6.3). It has an atomic row comprising *i*, *u*, *o*, *o′*, and *o″*. Above this is a row of dyads showing one value each of exclusive (*io*), inclusive (*iu*), second (*uo′*), and third (*o′o″*). Above the dyadic line come, in succession, the triads, tetrads, and so on. For reasons of space, some atoms and many joins are omitted: there are more than three others (*o‴*, *o⁗*, ...); some of the dyads (e.g., *io′*, *uo*, and *oo″*) are absent, as are many triads, tetrads, and so on; and the lattice does not stop with pentads but continues on with hexads, heptads, and the like. These are omitted for tractability and clarity: as figure 6.4 illustrates, proper Hasse diagrams quickly become unruly even for modest sizes of power sets.

To reflect this incompleteness, figure 6.3 adopts the representational convention that its lines do not stop at the (two left, two right, and five top) edge points, but continue slightly beyond them. This is intended to show that the diagram is not complete but leaves part of the lattice (power set) unrepresented. This contrasts with figures 6.2 and 6.4: with all joins represented, these diagrams are exhaustive and, so, lines stop at the edge points. Readers should imagine depictions of larger lattices like figure 6.3 as extending leftward, rightward, and upward.

In discussing the interaction of number with person, the primary focus will be on tripartition and quadripartition, where number is at its most elaborate.

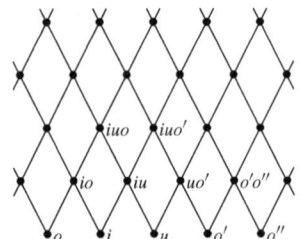

Figure 6.3
π lattice

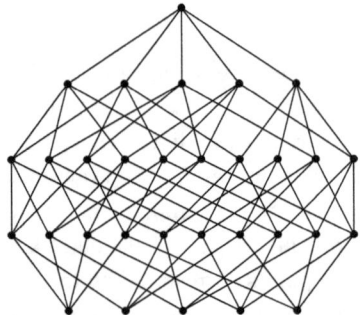

Figure 6.4
Full Hasse diagram of a five-member power set (minus bottom element)

As a preliminary, I illustrate the relevant structures here, leaving those of the two bipartitions until section 6.3.3.

For both the tri- and the quadripartition, the structures of second and third person are the same (figure 6.5). There is a salient difference between these two persons. As in the π lattice (figure 6.3), the lowest row of third person consists of multiple singleton o's, and every element on higher rows is the meet (set-theoretically, union) of these atoms. The second person, by contrast, has only a single atom, u. The dyadic row of this lattice consists of u joined with each possible o, and elements on higher rows are joins of these dyads. This difference in structure simply reflects the ontological assumption that u is unique whereas the o's are not. (In lattice-theoretic terms, then, second person has a bottom element and is a true lattice, but third person lacks this and is an atomic join-complete semilattice.)

The three types of first person are shown in figure 6.6. Like second person, all contain a bottom element. For the general first person of the standard tripartition, the bottom element is i. Moreover, as shown by the labeling, its larger

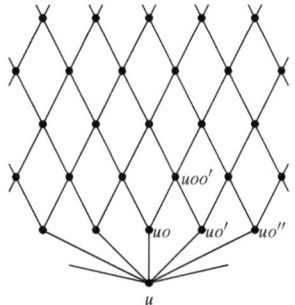 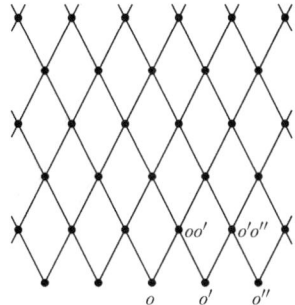

Figure 6.5
Second and third person

elements consist both of those containing i and o's, such as io, io', ioo', and others containing i, u, and o's, such as iu and iuo; that is, it subsumes exclusive and inclusive. By contrast, the lattice in the lower left of the figure shows the exclusive proper. This shares the same bottom element as the general first, but its higher elements lack u and consist instead only of additional o's, as in io, io', io'', ioo', and $io'o''$. The inclusive lattice is shown in the lower right. Unlike in the previous structures, the bottom element here is a dyad, iu, rather than a singleton, and elements on all higher rows have greater cardinality than before. That difference aside, however, the lattice is built in the same way as the exclusive, with the second row introducing single o's, as in iuo and iuo', and higher rows representing joins of these elements, like $iuoo'$.

With these structures in place, we are ready to proceed to number.

6.3 Partitions with Number

6.3.1 Tripartition

In a numberless tripartition, the person structures are simply those discussed in chapter 4. These are shown in figure 6.7. The pronominal systems of Jarawa (Kumar 2012) and of Pirahã (Everett 1986) provide examples. For instance, Jarawa *mi*, which covers the meanings of English *I* and *we*, binds a variable that ranges over the leftmost structure of figure 6.7. Similarly, *ŋi*, which is number-ambiguous in exactly the same way as English *you*, binds a variable that ranges over the central structure of figure 6.7. And *əhi*, which covers the meanings of English *he*, *she*, *it*, and *they*, binds a variable that ranges over the rightmost structure of figure 6.7. The same is true, respectively, for Pirahã first person *ti*, second person *gíxai*, and third person *hi*.

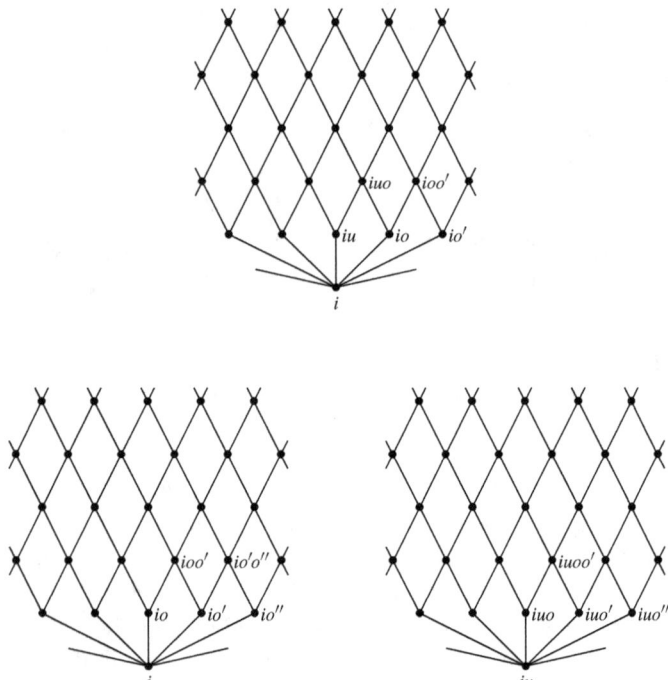

Figure 6.6
First person lattices: General (top), exclusive (left), and inclusive

A minimal increase to the complexity of these systems is to introduce a sole number contrast, singular–plural. This is achieved via the feature ±atomic, which partitions the person structures into atoms versus nonatoms, that is, into singularities versus pluralities (figure 6.8). (On whether the denotation of plurals ought to exclude atoms, see section 6.4.2.) A morphologically transparent example of such a system is (Modern) Mandarin. The singulars are *wŏ* 'I', *nĭ* 'you', and *tā* 'he, she, it'. Semantically, these are the result of applying +atomic to any of the three person specifications. Hence, these pronouns bind elements below the atomic line, which cuts across the three lattices of figure 6.8. For example, *wŏ* 'I' binds $i = +\text{atomic}(+\text{participant}(+\text{author}(\pi)))$, the unique atomic element of the general first person lattice.

The plural pronouns of Mandarin are the same as the singulars, but with *men* attached: *wŏmen* 'we', *nĭmen* 'you', and *tāmen* 'they'. Semantically, these are the result of applying −atomic to the three persons of the tripartition. Illustrating again with first person, *wŏmen* 'we', $-\text{atomic}(+\text{participant}(+\text{author}(\pi)))$, binds a variable that ranges over the portion of the general first person lattice that lies above the atomic line of figure 6.8.

Number and the Functional Sequence 135

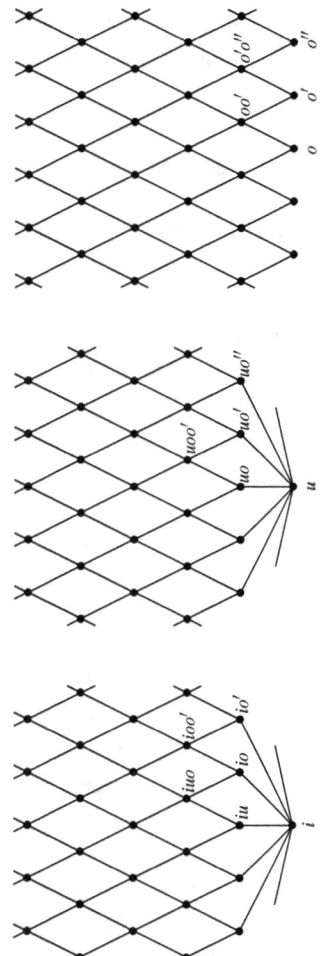

Figure 6.7
Tripartition without number oppositions

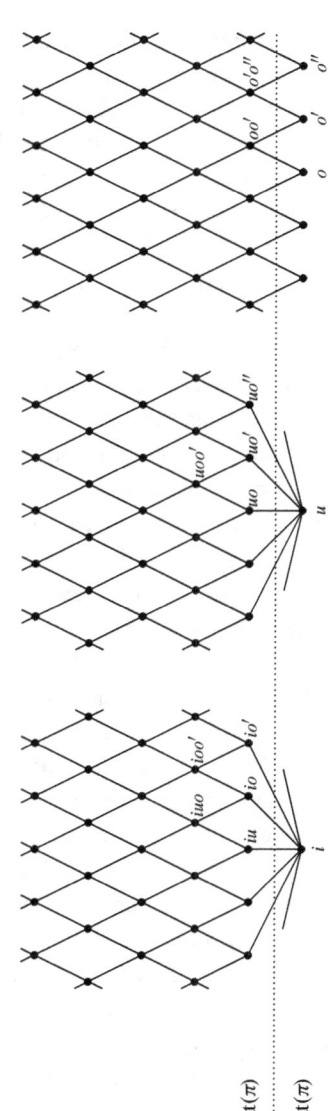

Figure 6.8
Tripartition with singular–plural opposition

Further features can be added to the number system, resulting in finer partitions of the person lattices and, so, in further number distinctions among the pronouns. For instance, using ±minimal, one can partition plurals into those of the most minimal kind versus everything else. This yields a distinction between dyads (the most minimal pluralities) and things triadic and larger (nonminimal pluralities), that is, between dual and plural.

This system is exploited by Sanskrit, for instance, where the nominative singular (masculine) pronouns are *ayam* 'I', *tvam* 'you', *sas* 'he'; the dual, *āvām* 'we two', *yuvām* 'you two', *tau* 'they two'; and the plural, *vayam* 'we', *yūyam* 'you', *te* 'they'. Without entering into formal details, one can readily appreciate that, for the second person for instance, +minimal(−atomic(+participant (−author(π)))) takes the second person, +participant (−author(π)), focuses on the nonatoms via −atomic, and then, via +minimal, picks out the most minimal of these, resulting in dyads containing the hearer *u* (*yuvām*); these are the elements sandwiched between the two horizontal cuts of figure 6.9. Changing +minimal to −minimal instead picks out nonminimal pluralities, those second persons (*yūyam*) larger than dyads, and hence above the higher cut of figure 6.9.

Naturally, other number distinctions may occur. Kiwai (Ray 1933) differentiates singular, dual, trial, and plural. I defer treatment of the trial until we reach quadripartite systems, where it is more common (in Cysouw's (2003) survey, Kiwai is unique in exhibiting trial in the absence of a clusivity contrast). A more common number is the paucal. It occurs in the system singular, dual, paucal, and plural for Yimas where, as already discussed in chapter 5, it is present in first and second person pronouns and in all three persons on verbs. Paucal also occurs without dual: for instance, in some or all persons of Choctaw (Broadwell 2006), Tukang Besi (Donohue 1999), and Walapai (Redden 1966). Figure 6.10 shows the number divisions for first and second person pronouns in Yimas.

The feature responsible for differentiating paucal from plural is ±additive. It takes a lattice region and divides it into additively complete (unbounded) versus additively incomplete (bounded) subregions. The cut that this feature induces is not numerically specific and may vary from speech act to speech act, not to mention from speech community to speech community. If the cut is low, then the bounded subregion is a paucal and its complement is the plural; if it is high, then the bounded subregion is the plural and its complement, the greater plural (see Harbour 2014a for details). Figure 6.10 shows a low cut of five, meaning that, in this case, triads, tetrads, and pentads would be covered by a paucal, and anything larger by a plural.

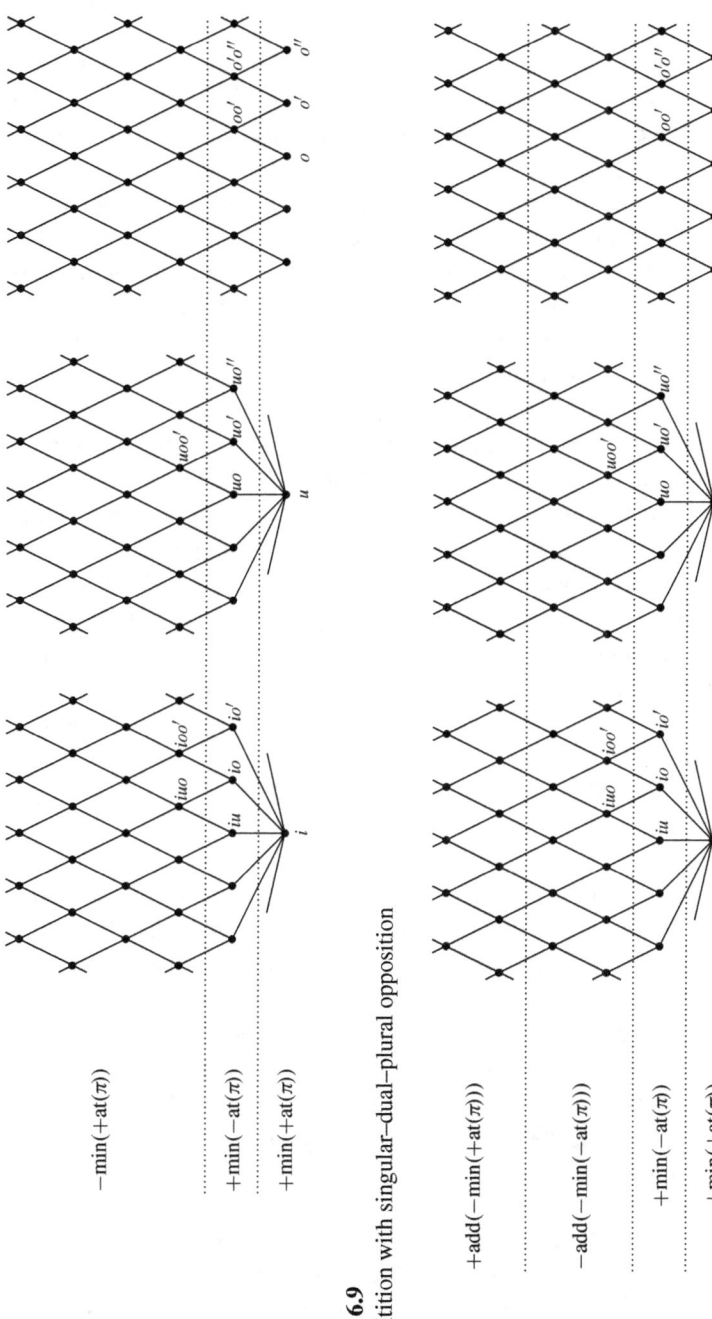

Figure 6.9
Tripartitition with singular–dual–plural opposition

Figure 6.10
Tripartitition with singular–dual–paucal–plural opposition

6.3.2 Quadripartition

A large part of the discussion of number for tripartitions carries over directly to quadripartitions. However, owing to their clusivity distinction, they also display a further range of systems, stemming from the distinction between minimality and atomicity.

As with tripartitions, the simplest systems are those without number. The pronouns of Nimboran (Anceaux 1965) present this pattern: 1EX *ŋo* ('I, we.EX'), 1IN *ió*, 2 *ko*, 3 *no*. The same sets of referents are available in Central Aymara (Hardman 2001): 1EX *naya*, 1IN *jiwasa*, 2 *juma*, 3 *jupa* (though these also admit optional number marking). These pronouns bind variables that range over the structures in figure 6.11.

And, again as with tripartitions, quadripartitions can display a singular–plural contrast. Returning to Chinese, we find such a system both in northern Mandarin (Norman 1988) and in Min Nan Taiwanese (Maryknoll Language Service Center 2013). The former simply has inclusive *zánmen* alongside the pronouns described in the previous section. Min Nan has singular–plural pairs for the exclusive, *góa* 'I', *góan* 'we.EX'; second person, *lí* 'you.S', *lín* 'you.P'; and third person, *i* 'he, she, it', *in* 'they'. Alongside these sits the inclusive *lán*, which lacks a number distinction. The structures these pronouns range over are shown in the top part of figure 6.12. As before, these differences are attributable to the feature ±atomic, and it will be noticed that the −atomic forms are morphologically uniform in both languages, ending in *n* in Min Nan and in *men* in Mandarin (in both varieties with and those without a clusivity contrast).

Instead of contrasting atomicity with nonatomicity, languages may contrast minimality with nonminimality. The resulting system differs from singular–plural only in its treatment of the speaker–hearer dyad. Whereas languages like Min Nan treat this dyad on a par with all other plurals, languages sensitive to minimality do not. The speaker–hearer dyad is the most minimal of the inclusives and so is placed on a semantic par with 'I' (the minimal exclusive), 'you.S' (the minimal second person), and 'he, she, it' (the minimal third persons). A transparent example of such a system comes from the pronouns of Timbira (de Castro Alves 2004): alongside the pairs *wa / wa=mɛ̃* 'I / we.EX', *ka / ka=mɛ̃* 'you.S/P', and *ke / ke=mɛ̃* 'he, she, it / they' sits the pair *ku / ku=mɛ̃* 'we.IN.D/P'.

The structures that these pronouns range over are shown in the lower row of figure 6.13. The point of contrast to note between figures 6.12 and 6.13 is that, where the cut cast by ±minimal kinks around to include the speaker–hearer dyad, that cast by ±atomic cuts uniformly across the bottom of all the lattices.[2]

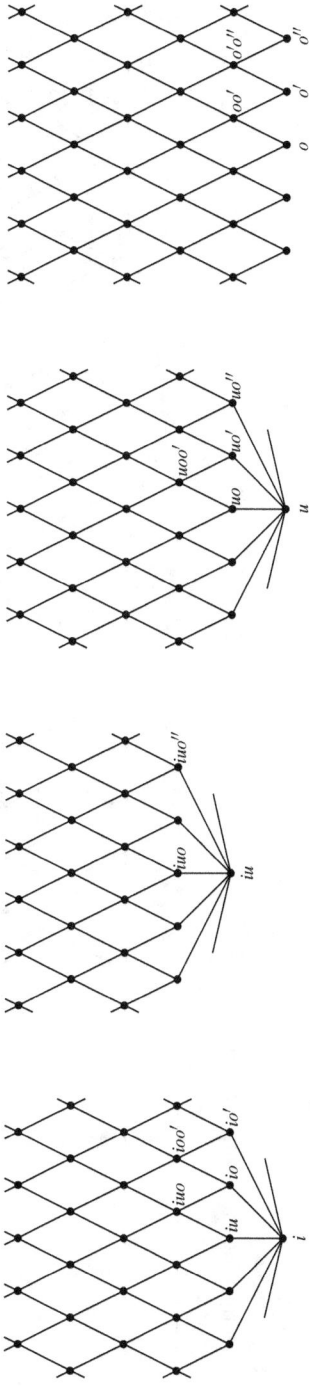

Figure 6.11
Quadripartition without number oppositions

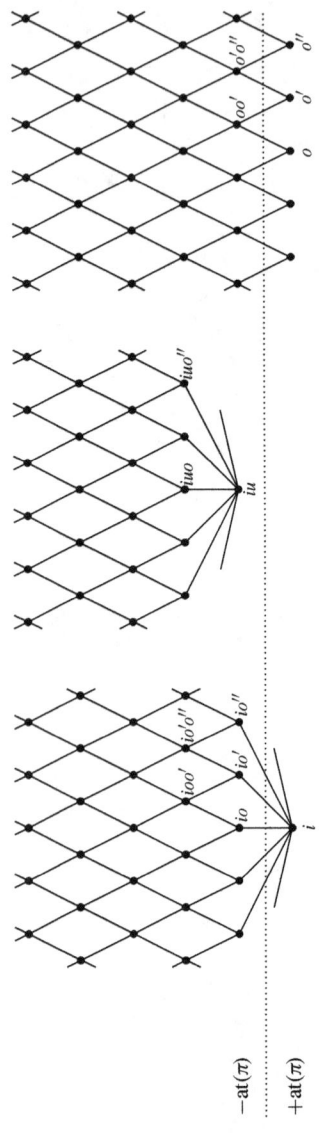

Figure 6.12
Quadripartition with singular–plural opposition

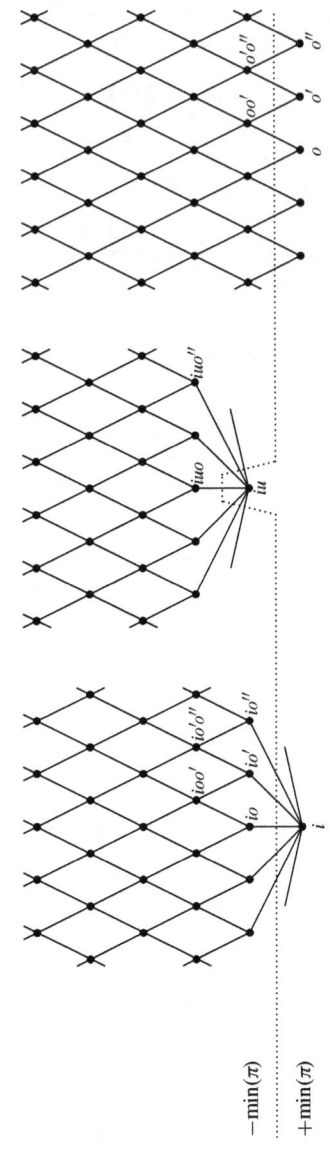

Figure 6.13
Quadripartition with minimal–augmented opposition

Returning momentarily to tripartitions, the previous section implied that singular–plural contrasts in tripartite systems are always attributable to ±atomic. However, minimal–augmented contrasts call this into question. Without a clusivity contrast, ±minimal partitions the lattices of the tripartition exactly as ±atomic does. In Harbour 2011a, I concluded, therefore, that extensionally equivalent grammars with tripartitions for person might differ with respect to which feature each speaker deploys in their I-language. Interestingly, however, Onambélé (2012) (see also Schadeberg 1977) shows that this conclusion was too hasty, as a contrast emerges, in Ewondo just in the hortative, between the speaker–hearer dyad (2) and other inclusives (3):

(2) Ń- dí- íg.
    HORT-eat-MIN
    'Let's (both) eat.'

(3) Ń- dí- àn.
    HORT-eat-AUG
    'Let's (all) eat.'

Everywhere else, Ewondo, like English, lacks clusivity or any hint of the dual. In the present, for instance, first plural agreement covers dual and nondual, inclusive and exclusive:

(4) By-ă- sye.
    1P-PRES-work
    'We work.'

(5) Bǐ wǎ by-ă- sye.
    we you.S 1P-PRES-work
    'You and I work.'

(6) Bǐ mínínga by-ă- sye.
    we woman 1P-PRES-work
    'The woman and I work.'

Onambélé suggests that pronominal reference in Ewondo uniformly uses ±minimal, but because, like English, it confines the inclusive to its hortatives, it is only in this one corner of the language that the choice of feature becomes apparent. The emergence of a number distinction in inclusives is a recurrent feature also of Turkic (Nevskaya 2005). So, use of ±minimal within a tripartition is not isolated to Ewondo.

The use made of ±minimal in the previous section was in cooccurrence with ±atomic to produce the number system singular–dual–plural. This feature combination has the same effect in quadripartitions, yielding systems like Comanche (Charney 1993) and Hawaiian (Elbert and Pukui 1979). I do not discuss the details, however, as, to the trivial extent that they differ from the tripartition, they are subsumed by the trial, which was deferred to the current section and to which I now turn.

Exact trials, as opposed to approximative plurals, are not the most common phenomenon. However, the means I will propose of accounting for them is conservative: it recycles features, rather than proposing new ones, and is not unique to the trial, but is required for other numbers and applies also to other features. Triads, the referents of the trial, are the most minimal of the nonminimal nonatoms. That is, given a lattice, −atomic picks out everything dyadic, triadic, or larger. Of these, +minimal picks out the dyads, so −minimal picks out everything triadic and larger. Consequently, +minimal, if applied after −minimal, picks out the most minimal of nondyad plurals, which is to say, the triads. Featurally, then, trial is +minimal(−minimal(−atomic(π))). Note that this procedure works for inclusive as well as for the other persons: for the inclusive, −atomic does not effect any partition, but, thereafter, ±minimal acts identically on all four person structures.

The system singular–dual–trial–plural is attested in Larike (Laidig and Laidig 1990), but, as a concrete illustration, I offer the yet more complex system of Mussau (Brownie and Brownie 2007), involving both trial and paucal (table 6.1). Featurally, the system results from the addition of ±additive to the combinations of the previous paragraph. The lattices over which Mussau pronouns range are shown in figure 6.15.[3]

The parameter by which languages may exploit cooccurrence of plus and minus versions of the same feature was termed *value recursion* in Harbour 2011a, 2014a. It was initially argued for in the treatment of Kiowa-Tanoan noun classes (Harbour 2007b, 2011c; see also Watanabe 2014), where it only affects uninterpretable instances of ±atomic and ±minimal. The trial, by contrast, exploits interpretable value recursion of ±minimal, applying the plus value to the output of the minus, as discussed two paragraphs higher.

Also on the interpretable side, value recursion may be parameterized to affect ±additive. The result is a system with two approximative numbers, reasoning as follows. First, the feature divides a region, R, into bound and open subregions, −additive(R), and +additive(R), respectively. It is possible to subdivide the open region still further, into another closed region, −additive(+additive(R)), and a smaller open region, which arises by the action of Lexical Complementarity on +additive(R). Depending on where a speech community conventionalizes the approximate cardinality of the cuts, the resulting regions, −additive(R), −additive(+additive(R)), and +additive(R), can be paucal, greater paucal, and plural as in Sursurunga (Hutchisson 1986, Corbett 2000), or paucal, plural, and greater plural as in Mele-Fila (Clark 1975), or

Number and the Functional Sequence

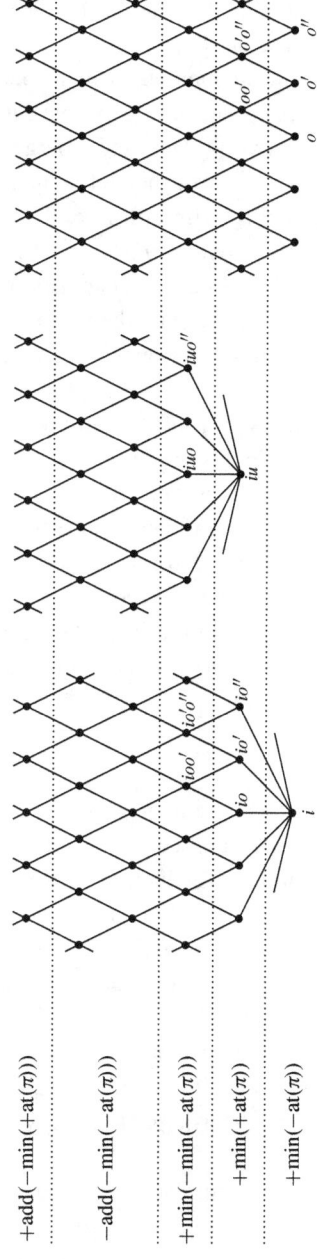

Figure 6.14
Quadripartition with singular–dual–trial–paucal–plural oppositions

Table 6.1
Mussau pronouns

Person	Singular	Dual	Trial	Paucal	Plural
1EX	*aghi*	*angalua*	*angotolu*	*angaata*	*amami*
1IN		*italua*	*itotolu*	*itaata*	*ita*
2	*io*	*amalua*	*amotolu*	*amaata*	*am*
3	*ia*	*ilalua*	*ilatolu*	*ilaata*	*ila*

143

plural, greater plural, and greatest plural as in Warekena (Aikhenvald 1998). For reasons of space, illustrations of these systems are omitted.

The final number that warrants discussion is unit augmented, which, like trial, exploits value recursion of ±minimal (but in the absence of ±atomic). It occurs, for instance, in the pronominal system of Äiwoo (Næss and Boerger 2008; figure 6.15, table 6.2). Unit augmented occurs as a further refinement of the minimal–augmented system, illustrated above by Timbira. Like Timbira, Äiwoo has a minimal category that picks out one dyad, *iuji* 'you.s and I' (the minimal inclusive), and three singletons, *iu* 'I' (the minimal exclusive), *iumu* 'you.s' (the minimal second person), and *ine* 'he, she, it' (the minimal third person). The number feature specification of these pronouns is, again, +minimal.

The elaboration of Äiwoo lies in the further subdivision of the −minimal regions of the four person structures. The language singles out the most minimal elements of these nonminimal regions. The result is one triad, *iudele* 'you.s, I, and another', and three dyads, *iungole* 'I and another', *imile* 'you two', and *ijiile* 'they two'. These are the unit augmented forms, so called because they augment the minimal by exactly one. As with the trial, this is achieved, featurally, by value recursion: +minimal(−minimal(π)). (Lexical Complementarity restricts the augmented, −minimal(π), to tetrads and larger for the inclusive and to triads and larger for other persons.)

6.3.3 Bipartition

The interaction of number with bipartitions does not differ in any significant respect from its interaction with the richer partitions discussed above, except that these smaller systems seem to support fewer number distinctions. Apparently, languages' tolerance for distinctions in person and number grows in tandem (cf, the rarity of trial number, or indeed, multiple approximative numbers, in the absence of a clusivity contrast). Consequently, I illustrate just one pronoun system for each bipartition.

The participant bipartition occurs only once as a pronoun system, in Hocąk/Winnebago, and it is numberless. So, there is no interaction to illustrate. The structures in figure 6.16 depict the range of +participant *nee* 'I, we, you' and −participant *'ee* 'he, she, it, they'.

The author bipartition occurs with singular–plural number in Sanapaná (Gomes 2013). Figure 6.17 shows the results of applying ±atomic to ±author(π). Below the dotted line are the ranges of first singular *ko'o* (left) and second-cum-third singular, masculine *hlejap* and feminine *hleja*. Above the line are their respective plurals, *enenko'o* 'we', and masculine *hlengap* and feminine *hlenga* 'you, they'.

Number and the Functional Sequence

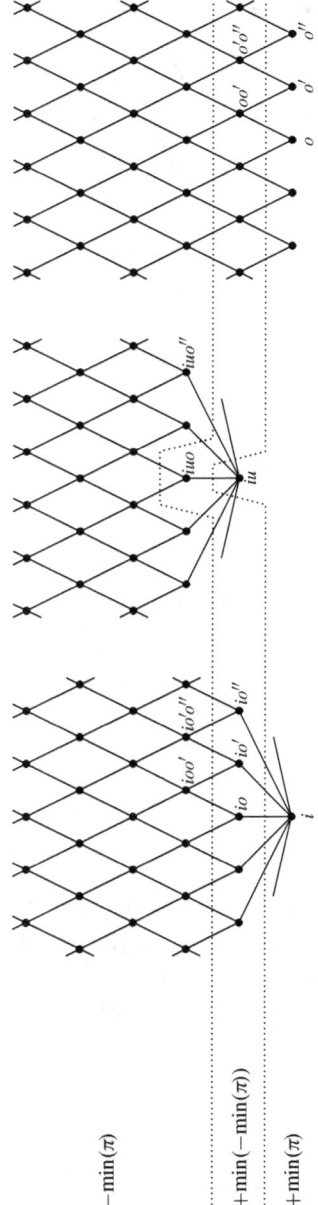

Figure 6.15
Quadripartition with minimal–unit augmented–augmented oppositions

Table 6.2
Äiwoo pronouns

Person	Minimal	Unit augmented	Augmented
1EX	iu	iungole	iungo(pu)
1IN	iuji	iudele	iude
2	iumu	imile	imi
3	ine	ijiile	ijii

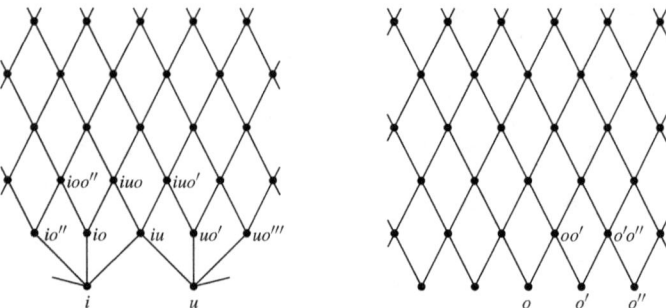

Figure 6.16
Participant bipartition without number oppositions

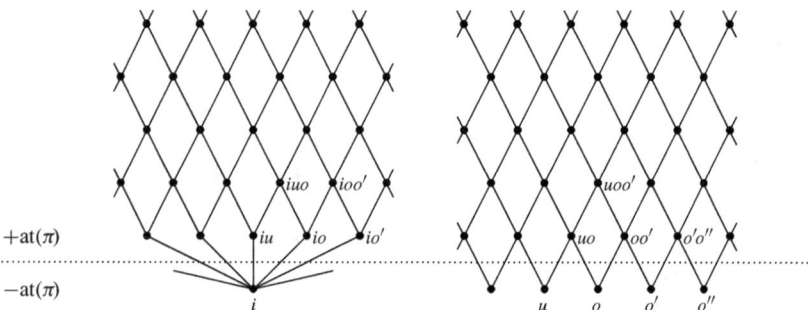

Figure 6.17
Author bipartition with singular–plural number

The foregoing sections therefore show that the person structures of the quadripartition interact straightforwardly with number features to yield a wide variety of numbers: singular, dual, trial, and plural; minimal, unit augmented, and augmented; and paucal, greater paucal, greater plural, and greatest plural.

6.4 Two Semantic Asides

6.4.1 Heterogeneous Plurals, Homogeneous Semantics

A common observation in the literature on person and number is that first person plurals differ from plurals of third persons and common nouns. Whereas a third person plural denotes a plurality every atom of which is a third person singular—*cats* is a plurality each atom of which is a cat; *they*, a plurality each atom of which is a he, she, or it—*we* does not denote a plurality each atom of which is an I. Rather, *we* denotes a plurality comprising the speaker with you and/or some other(s).

Slightly more subtly, crosslinguistically, second person plurals do not distinguish groups consisting entirely of actually present hearers and those containing a mix of hearers and absent others. For this distinction to be possible, one would need an ontology consisting of multiple *u*'s (permitting a contrast between the all-hearer plurality $uu'u''$ and the mixed plurality $uu'o$). The fact that no language makes such a distinction leads (Bobaljik 2008; see also Cysouw 2003, Siewierska 2004, Simon 2005) to conclude that *u* is unique, as assumed here (section 4.2.1). If so, then second person pluralities too are heterogeneous, like first person plurals.

This raises the question of whether the semantics of plurality is different for *us* and *you*, versus *them* and *cats*. On the current theory, the answer is that it is not. Above, the same features were used for all numbers, irrespective of person. That is, first, second, and third person have identical number specifications whether dual, trial, unit augmented, greater paucal, or other. These numbers simply arise from the action of number features on the structures that result from applying person features to the π lattice, and if the features work for homogeneous third person lattices, then they obviously work for homogeneous common noun lattices as well. First and second person pluralities differ from other ones owing to the structures on which the number features act, not because of the semantics of number itself. They inherit their heterogeneity from their number-free lattices, not from number.

If one took seriously the idea that plurality, not to mention duality, paucality, and augmentation, were semantically different for *us* versus *cats*, then one ought to suppose that distinct number features were used in each case (the difference is not obviously attributable to a special mode of semantic composition). This would be semantically and morphologically deleterious. First, there is a remarkable semantic match between the number categories available for first and second persons and those available for third persons and common nouns. So, there would need to be a complete duplication of features.

Second, many languages display morphological parity between number marking on first and second persons and that on third persons and/or common nouns. For instance, the plural suffix of Mandarin *wǒmen* 'we' and *nǐmen* 'you' occurs, as already indicated, in third person *tāmen* 'they'; moreover, it occurs in the common nouns *xuěshengmen* 'students' and *lǎoshǐmen* 'teachers' (Chappell 1996). The same pattern occurs in Pipil (Campbell 1985), where *met* occurs both in the pronouns *tehemet* 'we', *amehemet* 'you', *yehemet* 'they' and in common nouns such as *ah-alma-met* 'souls' and *tsih-tsinnanats-met* 'large-buttocked women'. A third language with this morphological property

Table 6.3
Aymara (left) and Maskelynes: Pan-personal augmented morphemes

Person	Numberless	Augmented	Minimal	Augmented
1EX	naya	naya-kana	kinau	kinami-to
1IN	xiwasu	xiwasu-naka	ki^{n}daru	ki^{n}da-to
2	xuma	xuma-naka	karu'ku	kami-to
3	xupa	xupa-naka	kai	kali-to

is Gaahmg (Stirtz 2011). The singular pronouns *ā* 'I', *ɔ̄* 'you.S', *ē̄* 'he, she, it' pluralize via the same suffix, *gg*: *ā-gg* 'we', *ɔ̄-gg* 'you.P', *ē̄-gg* 'they'. This suffix also pluralizes vowel-final nouns, like *wāā-gg* 'lakes', *mɔ̄ðɔ́-gg* 'locusts', and *rē̄ē̄-gg* 'threads'.

Patterns like this are not limited to the plural. In addition to Timbira (de Castro Alves 2004), discussed above, we find uniform marking of the augmentation in the pronouns of Aymara (Hardman 2001) and Maskelynes (Tryon 1976); see table 6.3. In Aymara, the augmented pronouns are entirely morphologically compositional, consisting of *naka* suffixed to the shorter forms.[4] In Maskelynes, though there is less compositionality between minimal and augmented forms, a suffix *to* shared among all persons is nonetheless discernible (the *ru* of the minimal inclusive *ki^{n}daru* is the vestige of an erstwhile dual, cognate with the Mussau dual *lua* of table 6.1, but reanalyzed as +minimal, on the current account).

One finds pronominal number markers similarly shared between nonthird and third for dual (*lua*), trial (*tolu*), and paucal (*ata*) in Mussau (table 6.1), and for unit augmented (*le*) in Äiwoo (table 6.2). (See also Mokilese and Sursurunga, table 5.18.)

Returning to Pipil, we find that verbs too may exhibit number marking shared among first, second, and third person. For instance, alongside the singulars *ni-panu* 'I pass', *ti-panu* 'you pass', and *panu* 'he passes' sit the plurals *ni-panu-t* 'we pass', *ti-panu-t* 'you pass', and *panu-t* 'they pass'. All the plurals, irrespective of person, are formed by the addition of *t* to the corresponding singular.

Of course, nothing in the account of person and number requires that number exponents be shared this way across all persons, let alone between pronouns and common nouns. The latter especially appears to be a minority pattern (Daniel 2013). Languages may have an identifiable plural morpheme in some of their pronouns, but fail to use this for nouns; or the plural may fuse the expression of number and person, as in English *I* and *we*; or nouns may not mark plurality at all. This is compatible with everything that has been said above. The approach provides the means for morphologically uniform number to exist, but leaves open that other factors might lead these features to be pronounced differently.[5]

Nonetheless, existence of this pattern in pronouns, in verbs, and between pronouns and nouns speaks strongly in favour of an account where number features are the same for persons and common nouns.

6.4.2 Plurals That Do Not Exclude Singulars

As presented above, the plural consists only of nonatomic elements. It excludes the singular, because ±atomic partitions the lattice into a collection of atoms versus everything else. It has been noted that plurals do not always preclude a singular interpretation, however (Hoeksema 1983, Schwarzschild 1996, Spector 2007, Sauerland, Anderssen, and Yatsuhiro 2008). For instance, (7) would normally be taken to imply that people with only one child can avail themselves of early boarding:

(7) People with children may board the plane early.

If plural *children* refers only to things dyadic or larger, then there is a puzzle about how (7) can come to include families with a singular child. The same goes for (8), which invites both single- and multiple-child families to board:

(8) If you have children, please board now.

Insofar as there is a consensus concerning what these examples show, it is that the plural does not exclude the singular, which would entail that the approach to number outlined above is incorrect.

It is not obvious, however, that the availability of singular children in the interpretation of (7) and (8) should be attributed to the semantics of number. First, the availability of the singular interpretation of the plural is context-dependent. It is, for instance, odd to say (9), if you see only one child, or (10), if you own only one car:

(9) I see children.

(10) I own cars.

Unavailability of the singular here is obviously attributable to Gricean inference (one could have said *a child*, but did not, so one must have intended something that plural conveys but singular does not). But this only serves to underline that it is the interaction of context and plural marking that makes the singular available in (7) and (8).[6] This in turn opens the possibility that the plural does not ordinarily contain the singular, but that certain contexts may act on pluralities to make their atomic constituents individually available. This position would enable one to maintain the semantics for number features given above.

The exact mechanism of atomic restitution lies beyond the scope of this inquiry (a choice function might do), but a number of observations make this avenue appealing. First, the contexts that support singular interpretations of plurals also support *any*:

(11) People/Anybody with any children may board the plane early.

(12) If you have any children, please board now.

Conversely, *any* degrades (9) and (10):

(13) ?I see any children.

(14) ?I own any cars.

It is plausible that (whatever licenses) *any*, or a covert counterpart, permits the restitution of atoms from pluralities—in which case, plurals like *children* need not, of themselves, make individual atoms available.

More compelling, and more relevant in the current context, is the behavior of plural personal pronouns in the same contexts, something that has not been considered before, I believe. Take:

(15) People who spot us will call the police.

(16) If anyone spots us, they'll call the police.

It would be inappropriate to respond to these by saying that we'd better go out individually so that people only see us one at a time. In other words, risk arises if any atom of the plurality that *us* denotes is seen.[7]

However, the claim that *us* ranges over the pluralities and the atoms of the first person lattice (the top structure of figure 6.6) is insufficient to capture the correct meanings. The speaker, i, is the only atomic element of the lattice, and so the claim would permit *us* to refer, additionally, only to the speaker, but not to the hearer or individual others. So, this fails to capture that (15)–(16) can mean that you or others should avoid being seen just as much as I should.

This problem is avoided if we regard the context as contributing something that restitutes atoms from pluralities. If the referent of *us* here is iuo, then restitution permits reference to the speaker, i, or to the hearer, u, or to one other, o, as required.

Evidence from languages with inclusives supports the idea that atomic restitution, not an alternative semantics for plural, underlies the singular interpretation of some morphological plurals.

In the 1970s, civil disobedience stymied the use of the Hawaiian island of Kahoʻolawe as a bombing range for the US Navy. This took the form of native Hawaiians prominently living and hunting on the island, as, with civilians present, bombing had to cease. Given this background, I asked a speaker,

'Ōiwi Parker Jones, to imagine that he was engaged in this resistance and was instructing his group to split up, with one member paddling north, another paddling south, third going elsewhere, and so on. In this context, he judges that (17), using the inclusive plural, would be felicitous:

(17) Inā 'ike 'ia   kākou, (e) pono ana (lākou) e   ho'opau
     if see PASS 1IN.P ASP must ASP 3P   ASP CAUS.finish
     i   ka pōkā pahū   'ana.
     ACC the shell explode NMLZ
     'If we get seen, they'll have to stop bombing.'

The relevant reading here is that it suffices for any one of *kākou* (the speaker, the hearer, or others, or their synecdochic parts) to be seen in order for the desired end to be achieved. It is not the case that the bombing will only stop if everyone, or minimally the speaker and the hearer, is seen (which would render the splitting-up strategy pointless).

The same reading is available for the dual, where it suffices for either the speaker or the hearer to be seen:

(18) Inā 'ike 'ia   kāua, ...
     if see PASS 1IN.D
     'If we two get seen, [they'll have to stop bombing].'

Thus, in this syntactic context, the dual and the plural both permit a reading that includes the atoms. This is potentially surprising because there are no free-floating atoms in the structure that the inclusives range over. All the atoms are packaged within pluralities. So, the dual and the plural cannot permit atomic reference in virtue of not having excluded the atoms, as there are no atoms not to exclude. Rather, the atoms can only be available because something permits the unpacking of pluralities and the restitution of the atoms that they contain.

This case from inclusives is made most strongly by languages with a minimal–augmented number system. Kapampangan (Forman 1971, Mirikitani 1972) is one such. The point about these languages is that the feature responsible for the minimal–augmented contrast is distinct from that responsible for the singular–plural contrast of English, on a variety of approaches (beginning with Thomas 1955 and including Noyer 1992, Harbour 2011a, 2014a; the last of these shows that Harley and Ritter's (2002a) attempt to make do with a single feature, though parsimonious, is problematic). If the availability of singular interpretations of morphological plurals depends on the semantics of "the plural feature," then we do not expect such interpretations to be available for first person augmented and certainly not for first person minimal, neither of which owes its interpretation to "pluralization" as conventionally understood.

However, both augmented and minimal inclusives permit this interpretation. To verify this, I asked a native speaker of Kapampangan (David Aaron) to translate the two sentences below, which envisage how one might try to be rescued when stranded on an island:

(19) *Nung atin manakit kekata- mu, miligtas ta- mu.*
 if AUX see 1IN.OBL-AUG save 1IN.ABS-AUG
 'If someone sees us (you, me, and others), we'll be saved.'

(20) *Nung atin manakit kekata, miligtas kata.*
 if AUX see 1IN.OBL(.MIN) save 1IN.ABS(.MIN)
 'If someone sees us (you and me), we'll be saved.'

I then asked him whether it is possible to continue these with 'So, the best thing is for us.AUG/MIN to split up' (*Kaya ing pekamasaleseng gawan mikawani tamu/kata*). He confirms that it is. The felicity of this continuation means that, in this context, augmented and minimal inclusives permit reference to individual atoms, even though they are not created by pluralization in the English sense.

Generalizing over the pronominal evidence from English, Hawaiian, and Kapampangan, the pertinent point is that it is not morphological plurals, but semantic pluralities—of diverse featural origins: minimal, augmented, dual, plural—that, in certain contexts, make their constituent atoms available. This cannot be attributed to pluralization per se, because, whatever the *ren* of *children* expresses, it is distinct from the semantic primitives that generate and distinguish between minimal and augmented. Moreover, first person structures either contain only one proper atom (*i*, if exclusive or general first) or contain none at all (if inclusive). Atoms of first person pluralities are only available if the plurals themselves are in some sense dismantled, as a choice function over their members would allow.

Thus, personal pronouns cast new light on the question of how some morphological plurals come to permit reference to singulars. In the relevant contexts, first person pronouns appear, like normally nominal plurals, to permit reference to atoms. However, owing to the nature of the structures that pronouns range over, the atoms to which they permit reference cannot arise via a semantics that makes plural the union of singular and plural (or singular, dual, and plural, or minimal and augmented) as I have defined them. I therefore conclude that these data do not force one to revise the definitions of ±atomic and ±minimal, nor the approach to number in which they are embedded.

6.5 Interfaces

The foregoing discussion has so far assumed without comment a phrase structure in which number (ω) dominates person (π):

(21)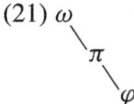

A consequence of this phrase structure is that person features act on the π lattice before number features do. In fact, this assumption is crucial to deriving only, and all, the correct inventory of person–number categories (section 6.5.1), and it provides the correct input to account for generalizations concerning linear order of person and number (sections 6.5.2 and 6.5.3). (Chapter 7 presents additional reasons for assuming that number dominates person.)

Up to this point, the discussion has been syntactically ecumenical, regarding structures like (21) as, essentially, functional hierarchy that might be subject to X′ Theory principles of projection or might, as per Mirror Theory, represent the syntax directly. This ecumenism was straightforward, given the nature of the discussion: chapter 4 was concerned primarily with the semantic interpretation of a single head, π, and its contents; chapter 5, with the morphological realization of the same; and the foregoing sections of this chapter, with the relationship between the semantic interpretations of two heads, π and ω, and their contents. These matters are all neutral with respect to principles of projection and other areas of difference among a wide range of syntactic theories. This holds also for section 6.5.

However, from section 6.5.2 on, I make use of a specifically Mirror Theory reading of (21) (consistent with my joint past work in Adger, Harbour, and Watkins 2009) and of the underlying theory. To explain these, I first lay out how a standard X′ structure is represented in Mirror Theory. In (22), there is a head X that takes a complement YP and projects up to XP, where it takes a specifier ZP:

(22)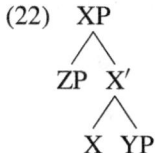

Mirror Theory does away with bar levels (like Bare Phrase Structure, Chomsky 1995), and also with the distinction between heads and phrase markers. As a result, (22) is telescoped to (23):

(23)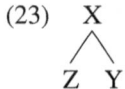

For readers used to X′ Theory and the headedness parameter, it is tempting to read (23) as stating that Y and Z are in a symmetric relation. This would be wrong. Although structure building in Mirror Theory is based on set-theoretic Merge (Adger 2012), which is symmetric and does not care about left versus right, left branches versus right branches in structures like (23) represent distinct relationships. A left branch is a specifier relationship, with Z as the specifier of X, and a right branch shows the complement line. As a result, a rightward branch as in (24) shows the functional sequence, that is, the object we have worked with up to now:

(24)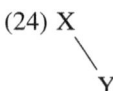

With the mode of representation thus clarified, the two principles of Mirror Theory relevant below both concern the relationship between syntax and linear order. The first is just that the linear order of affixes is the mirror order of the rightward-branching functional sequence. That is, if x is the exponent of X and y is the exponent of Y, then the pronunciation of X—Y in (24) is y-x. Second, contrasting with this, specifiers, defined as noncomplements that engage in feature sharing with the host head (cf, specifier–head agreement), are linearized on the left. So, (23) is pronounced as z y-x, where z is the exponent of Z.

In addition, I highlight now that the discussion below will make two slight additions to the theory—or, if you prefer, it will be specific about issues on which past work has been silent. The first concerns the pronunciation of heads that host features, in particular when these receive separate exponence. Second, and relatedly, I will propose what it means for a head to host uninterpretable features (of the kind that give rise to agreement) and how these features can give rise to a specifier-like configuration and, so, at times, to leftward linearization.

6.5.1 Syntax–Semantics

To see that the account of person and number offered in chapter 4 and above requires number to dominate person, consider what would happen if they were reversed:

(25) π
$\quad\diagdown \omega$
$\qquad\diagdown \varphi$

In essence, the core problem with this structure is that person, by adding and subtracting, undoes the work of number. For instance, if number, acting first, picks out all singletons and then person adds further quantities in or takes them out, then a change in cardinality will result, yielding number distinctions different from those derived above. This problem plays out in several different ways, all of them deleterious.[8]

Most simply, one loses the contrast between clusive singular–plural (Min Nan) and clusive minimal–augmented (Timbira) systems. Major calculations are not needed to see this. Consider just the simplest case, the action of +atomic and +minimal on the power set of the ontology: +atomic of course picks out just the atoms, and +minimal picks out exactly the same subset. These features yield different partitions only if the minimal element(s) of the structure they apply to are nonatomic, which only happens if person acts before number. Otherwise, as discussed for English and Ewondo, the partitions created by the features are identical, and, indeed, that is why all persons other than first inclusive make the same distinctions, numerically speaking, in Min Nan and Timbira. (These points apply with equal force to the more anonymous lattice of the domain, mooted in the previous paragraph.) Consequently, the phrase structure in (25) makes the theory expressively inadequate.

Naturally, the same problem affects the derivation of singular–dual–plural (Hawaiian) and minimal–unit augmented–augmented (Äiwoo) systems. For Hawaiian, +minimal(+atomic(φ)) picks out the atoms of the φ lattice (see note 8); +minimal(−atomic(φ)) picks out the most minimal nonatoms, that is to say, the dyads; and everything triadic or larger falls to −minimal(−atomic(φ)). Exactly the same distinctions emerge for Äiwoo: +minimal(φ) picks out the most minimal elements of the φ lattice, that is, the atoms; +minimal(−minimal(φ)) picks out the most minimal nonatoms, again, the dyads; and, given Lexical Complementarity, −minimal(φ) picks out all other nonminimal elements. In other words, once again, two featurally distinct systems, {±atomic, ±minimal} and {±minimal} with value recursion, collapse, leading to further descriptive inadequacy.

Moreover, not only does the phrase structure in (25) fail to make enough distinctions, but the distinctions it makes are the wrong ones. Consider the very simple case of attempting to derive first and second singular in a system like English. As discussed two paragraphs higher, +atomic(φ) yields the atoms of the φ lattice, that is, $\{i, u, o, o', o'', \ldots\}$. Composing in the order

±participant(±author(+atomic(π))), the minus value of ±participant strips out all participants, irrespective of the value of ±author, and leads to third person, as in chapter 4. For the other two cases, we have:

(26) +participant(+author(+atomic(π)))
$= (\{i, u, o, o', o'', \ldots\} \oplus \{i\}) \oplus \{i, iu, u\}$
$= \{i, iu, io, io', io'', \ldots\} \oplus \{i, iu, u\}$
$= \{i, iu, io, io', io'', \ldots, iu, iu, iuo, iuo', iuo'', \ldots\}$
$= \{i, io, io', io'', \ldots, iu, iuo, iuo', iuo'', \ldots\}$

(27) +participant(−author(+atomic(π)))
$= (\{i, u, o, o', o'', \ldots\} \ominus \{i\}) \oplus \{i, iu, u\}$
$= \{\varnothing, u, o, o', o'', \ldots\} \oplus \{i, iu, u\}$
$= \{i, iu, io, io', io'', \ldots,$
$\quad iu, iu, iuo, iuo', iuo'', \ldots,$
$\quad u, u, uo, uo', uo'', \ldots\}$
$= \{u, uo, uo', uo'', \ldots\}$ by Lexical Complementarity and (26)

The problem here is that, although these are first and second person, they are not singular. Rather, they are a number category that subsumes singular and dual. Although such classes arise syncretically within richer number systems (see, for instance, the discussion of Hopi at the start of chapter 5), they are not a basic number category of any language discussed in major typological studies. Consequently, we have a simple failure to derive the singular.

Thus, if anything like the current approach to person and number features is correct, then these must be embedded in a phrase structure that causes person to act before number.

6.5.2 Syntax–Morphology I

Crosslinguistically, person and number appear rather robustly to be linearized with person to the left, number to the right (Noyer 1992 especially chapter 2, Trommer 2002, Harbour 2007a, 2008, Arregi and Nevins 2012). The patterns occur both in pronouns and in verbs and are evident both in head-initial languages like Classical Arabic and in head-final ones like Walmatjari, as exemplified and analyzed below. Updating my previous account (Harbour 2007a, 2007b), I regard this pattern as arising from the interaction of the phrase structure argued for above with mechanisms of linearization.[9]

Beginning with pronouns, the segmentation in tables 6.4 and 6.5 shows that, with the exception of the Arabic first person and the Walmatjari second singular, these consist of a person portion, which is constant within each row (e.g., 3 *h* in Arabic, 1EX *nga* in Walmatjari), to which is suffixed a number marker (that shows varying degrees of constancy, dependent on the precise segmentation).

Number and the Functional Sequence   157

Table 6.4

Classical Arabic pronouns

Person	Singular	Dual	Plural
1	'anā	naḥnu	
2M	'ant-a	'ant-um-ā	'ant-um
F	'ant-i		'ant-un-na
3M	h-uwa	h-um-ā	h-um
F	h-iya		h-un-na

Table 6.5

Walmatjari pronouns

Person	Singular	Dual	Plural
1EX	nga-ju~ji	nga-jarra	nga-nimpa~nampa
1IN		ngali-jarra	ngali-mpa
2	nyuntu	nyurra-jarra	nyurra-warnti
3	nyantu	nyantu-jarra	nyantu-warnti

Within a Mirror-Theoretic approach to syntax and its interfaces (Brody 2000, Brody and Szabolcsi 2003), the chain of functional heads is assumed to correspond to the linear order of affixes, as if one were the mirrored reflection of the other (for a slightly more abstract view of the relationship, see Adger 2012). If so, then we immediately expect $[\omega_G [\pi_F [\varphi]]]$, where F and G are feature bundles, to correspond to the linear order $\varphi-\pi_F-\omega_G$. Pronouncing just the features leads to the order *person–number*, as per the pronouns. (Naturally, similar relationships can be captured in a range of frameworks.)

The verbs of Classical Arabic and Walmatjari also both show the linear pattern person-left–number-right, and they do so in two distinct ways. First, person and number morphemes for a single argument can abut. In Arabic, the details of the suffixal conjugation are as discussed for Hebrew with regard to table 5.11. So, again taking *t* to realize +participant, a form like *katab-t-um-ā* 'you.D wrote' consists of person, *t*, before number (and gender), nonsingular *um* and dual *ā*. The plurals show the same pattern: the masculine/mixed plural *katab-t-um* 'you.P wrote' is a substring of the dual, with, therefore, the same pattern of person before number; similarly, the feminine plural is identical to the masculine, but with the addition of the number-sensitive gender marker *na*, *katab-t-un-na* 'you.FP wrote'.

Table 6.6
Classical Arabic prefixal conjugation

Person	Singular	Dual	Plural
1	'-amlik		n-amlik
2M	t-amlik	t-amlik-ā	t-amlik-ū
F	t-amlik-ī		t-amlik-na
3M	y-amlik	y-amlik-ā	y-amlik-ū
F	t-amlik		y-amlik-na

Leaving gender aside (for current purposes, one can regard it as collocated with number), we can account for this just by supposing that, in verbal agreement, the structure $[\omega_G [\pi_F [\varphi]]]$ is attached to a head, such as Aspect, in the extended verbal projection [Asp [... [V]]]. This yields V–Asp–φ–π_F–ω_G, from which emerges the morphemic string *verb–person–number* (where *verb* stands for the typical Afroasiatic intercalation of the root and functional material).

Still within Classical Arabic, a more striking instance of the pattern arises in the imperfective, prefixal conjugation (table 6.6). For some combinations of phi features, person and number (and gender) straddle the verb. Again, however, person is to the left and number, to the right, as in 2-*verb*-D *t-amlik-ā* 'you.D will possess' or 3-*verb*-P *y-amlik-ū* 'they will possess'.

Leaving aside momentarily what causes agreement to be prefixal here, we can account for the discontiguous version of the pattern with the addition of a merely minor assumption about how linearization proceeds. First, suppose that we have:

(28) ω
　　＼π
　　　＼φ-*amlik*

This shows the previously linearized material, *amlik*, together with the phi structure that is the target of exponence at this point. The hyphen between the root φ node and *amlik* indicates that the phi structure is to be pronounced as a prefix to the verb.

Where the phi structure is realized by a single morpheme, as in the first-person nonsingular *n*, this linearizes unproblematically, as *n-amlik*. Where person and number are realized separately, the result is not a perfect linear string, but a structure that specifies linear precedence of *t* relative to both *ā* and *amlik*:

(29) $ā$
　　＼*t-amlik*

The hyphen between *t* and *amlik* shows, again, that *t* is a prefix of the verb. Furthermore, by the eponymous mirror of Mirror Theory, *t* is to precede *ā* linearly.

Of course, *t* can linearly precede both *amlik* and *ā*, but it can only be the linearly adjacent prefix of one of them. The question, then, is whether the previously established linear adjacency between *t*, as the base of the phi structure, and *amlik* is preserved, or whether the later one, between *t* and number, is. If linearization is about establishing, not disestablishing, linear order, then we correctly expect the previously established relation to trump, leading to the order *person–verb–number*, or, in this case, *t-amlik-ā*.[10]

Walmatjari too displays contiguous and discontiguous agreement, and, strikingly, the two may cooccur. The locus of agreement in the language is the second-position auxiliary. Focusing solely on this, (30) and (31) illustrate abutting agreement for, respectively, a second plural subject and an exclusive dual object (single underlining); and (31) and (32) illustrate discontiguous agreement for, respectively, second and exclusive subjects (double underlining):

(30) *pa-   ja- n-ta*
　　　AUX-1S-2-P
　　　'you all (VERB) me'

(31) *ma- n-tarra-nya-lu*
　　　AUX-2-1EX- D- P
　　　'you all (VERB) us two'

(32) *ma- rna- n-panya*
　　　AUX-1EX-2-P
　　　'we (VERB) you'

In all cases, the person morphemes (1EX *tarra, rna*; 2 *n*) precede number (D *nya*; P *ta, lu, panya*).

Another language, Yimas (Foley 1991), even presents cases of double straddling, with one split flanking the other. In (33), the second paucal agent agreement (double-underlined *pu-...-um*) flanks the third plural dative (single-underlined *nan-....-ŋkan*) and both straddle the verb (*ŋa-t*):

(33) *ta-   pu-nan-ŋa- t- ŋkan-um*
　　　NEG-3- 2P- give-PF-PC- P
　　　'you few did not give (it) to them'

As per Harbour 2008, such cases can be derived by cyclic, root-outward application of the mechanisms discussed for Classical Arabic (29): if the syntax yields $\varphi_{3P} - \varphi_{2PC} - verb$, and linearization first targets the head nearer the verb, then φ_{3P}–2P-*verb*-PC results, and then 3-2P-*verb*-PC-P (given that, in this context both 2PC and 3P are realized by multiple exponents, 2P–PC and 3–P).

This approach to linearization makes several predictions and is altogether more streamlined than previous treatments of similar data. First, consider the contrast between split and unsplit forms in Classical Arabic (table 6.6). If we take a form with discontiguous agreement and tinker solely with the phi features so as to produce an unsplit form, then it is always the suffix that is lost. For instance, 3FP *y-amlik-na* straddles the verb, but the corresponding singular 3FS *t-amlik* exploits just the leftmost position. In other words, the (leftmost) person position is the base position of the agreement.

The same holds for Walmatjari, in that, when a change in number means that there is only one agent agreement morpheme (double-underlined), it occupies (and indeed is) the person morpheme of the corresponding split example:[11]

(34) a. *ma- rna- ny-pinya-lu*
        AUX-1EX-2- D-   P
        'we (VERB) you two'

   b. *ma- rna- ny-pinya*
        AUX-1EX-2- D
        'I (VERB) you two'

(35) a. *pa- n-rna- panya-pila*
        AUX-2-1EX-P-   D
        'you two (VERB) us'

   b. *pa- n-rna- panya*
        AUX-2-1EX-P
        'you (VERB) us'

The same is true of Yimas. The following are not perfect minimal pairs with (33), but they nonetheless show again the retreat to the person position: when agreement is unsplit, it occupies the prefixal position of its split analogue. Thus, compare unsplit *pu-* in (36) and *nan-* in (37) with split *pu-*...*-um* and *nan-*...*-ŋkan* in (33):

(36) *pu-kay-cay-c- ŋkt*
     3P-1P- see- PF-PC
     'we few saw them'

(37) *ta- pu-nan-tpul-c- um*
     NEG-3- 2P- hit- PF-P
     'you all did not hit them'

In all such examples, flanking agreement alternates with an unsplit prefix, rather than an unsplit suffix, indicating that the prefix does indeed occupy the base position.

Like Arabic, with the examples 3FP *y-amlik-na* and 3FS *t-amlik*, Yimas also shows examples of split/unsplit pairs in which the unsplit counterpart does not merely suppress the number suffix, but instead involves a wholly different prefix in the base position. In the following examples, the negative-conditioned split *pu-...-rm* alternates with unsplit prefixal *impa-*:

(38) ta-   <u>pu</u>-wa-na-   <u>rm</u>
     NEG-3- go- NRPST-D
     'they two did not go yesterday'

(39) <u>impa</u>-wa-nan
     3D- go- NRPST
     'they two went yesterday'

The fact that the person position is the base position follows straightforwardly on the current account. The only way to produce agreement that straddles the verb (as in Arabic and Yimas) or another agreement string (as in Walmatjari) is to place a complete phi structure at the left edge of the previously linearized material. From that position, straddling agreement emerges only if there are multiple exponents for a given phi specification, in which case person is positioned on the left and number, on the right. If, however, only a single exponent is available for the whole phi set, then, like the phi structure itself, the exponent occurs at the left edge of the previously linearized material, hence, in the same position as person when there is straddling.

Furthermore, it follows from this that there is no need to stipulate that, say, in Classical Arabic agreement, 1P *n* and 3FS *t* are prefixes, but (M)P *um* and FS *ī* are suffixes, as Noyer (1992), Halle (1997), and Banksira (2000) do for various Afroasiatic languages. Instead, prefixality and suffixality in straddling configurations emerge from a phrase structure that places person below number and that translates this into linear precedence. Afroasiatic does not display the richer flanked splits of Walmatjari and Yimas. These potentially pose further problems for accounts that stipulate direction of affixation item by item, as such stipulations do not determine relative order between the prefixes, or between the suffixes. Here, flanking, and hence the relative, mirrored order of prefixes and suffixes, is derived by assuming cyclic, root-outward exponence, as illustrated with respect to (33).

The foregoing therefore shows that the phrase structure that the syntax–semantics interface forces us to posit, with number above person, is readily embedded within a straightforward approach to linearization (here, Mirror Theory with cyclic, root-outward insertion). This derives significant facts about the linear precedence of person over number across languages of different headedness, within pronouns and verbs, and in situations where person and number exponents either abut, straddle, or flank.

6.5.3 Syntax–Morphology II

Before leaving the issue of linearization, I wish to speculate on what mechanisms might lead to prefixal versus suffixal linearization of whole phi structures, that is, what establishes the base position. Though strictly speaking orthogonal to the main concern of this chapter—the semantic, syntactic, and morphological interaction between person and number—it is nonetheless at home in a treatment of linearization, so I offer some tentative thoughts.

Even accounts that attribute the bulk of affix ordering to the syntax need to recognize that, for agreement at least, there are certain cases where a syntactic analysis is implausible. A particularly dramatic case of this arises in Classical Hebrew (Kautzsch 1910), and examining it sheds light on the base placement of phi structures.

Like Classical Arabic, and most of Afroasiatic, Classical Hebrew has both a prefixal conjugation (involving straddling) and a suffixal conjugation, the imperfective and perfective, respectively:

(40) −perfective: prefixal paradigm

w-   'ēl   šadday   y-bārēk   'ōt- kā
and-Almighty God   3-bless.IMPF ACC-2MS
'And [may] God Almighty bless thee.'   (Gen. 28:3)

(41) +perfective: suffixal paradigm

hinnēh bērak-   tī   'ōt- ō
behold bless.PF-1S   ACC-3MS
'Behold, I have blessed him.'   (Gen. 17:20)

Curiously, though, the values of perfectivity are swapped when these verbs are preceded by a version of 'and' with sequential narrative, rather than purely conjunctive, force (this 'and.ASP' also triggers stress shift, which I leave aside here). In such narratives, then, the perfective is, morphologically, 'and.ASP' plus the imperfective, and the imperfective is 'and.ASP' plus the perfective. Hence, although the examples below are in the order (42) prefixal, (43) suffixal, like (40) and (41), the order of ±perfective differs between the two pairs:

(42) +perfective: 'and.ASP' prefixal paradigm
   way-   y-bārek   'ōt- ō
   and.ASP-3-bless.IMPF ACC-2MS
   'And he blessed him.' (Gen. 28:1)

(43) −perfective: 'and.ASP' suffixal paradigm
   ū-   bērak-   tī   'ōt- āh
   and.ASP-bless.PF-1S ACC-3FS
   'And I will bless her.' (Gen. 17:16)

The syntax of the conjunctive forms makes it implausible that the difference in base position of the phi structures could be due to a difference in height of verb movement (or its equivalent in other frameworks). The conjunctive forms are exceptionlessly clause-initial, in contrast to the nonconjunctive forms, which permit a variety of topics and foci to precede them, as in (40) and (41). In Harbour 2007a, I argue that this is due to movement of the verb into the C domain, rather than, say, to a truncation of the clause that removes the position for topics and foci. For instance, predicate clefts, a verbal topic/focus construction involving an uninflected copy of the verb, are possible with conjunctive verbs (44):

(44) *way-   y-bārek   bārōk 'ēt   kem*

   and.ASP-3-bless.IMPF bless ACC 2MP
   'Therefore he blessed you still.' (Josh. 24:10)

However, (44) reverses the usual order of cleft verb before inflected verb:[12]

(45) *ṣēyd-   āh   bārēk   'ă- bārēk*

   provision-3FS bless 1S-bless.IMPF
   'I will abundantly bless her provision.' (Ps. 132:15)

The reversed order of (44) is typical of examples in which, on crosslinguistic grounds, one would expect movement into the C domain. The *wh*-question below is illustrative, in that inflected *yōkīăḥ* precedes uninflected *hōkēăḥ*:

(46) *ū- mahy–y-ōkīăḥ   hōkēăḥ mik- kem*

   and-what– 3-reprove.IMPF reprove from-2MP
   'But what doth your arguing reprove?' (Job 6:25)

Thus, (42), (44), and, to a lesser extent, (46) show that agreement can remain prefixal no matter how high verbs move in the clause. Nonetheless, as exemplified by (40) and (45), the prefixes are not substantially higher than the verb when it is not in C, as they do not settle on any preverbal constituent, such as topics or clefts. So, we are justified in pursuing an account of prefixality that is external to the syntax.

The mechanism I would like to suggest relies on three things, none particularly controversial: collocation of phi structures on interpretable heads (see also Trommer's (2002), notion of anchoring), the possibility of fused exponence between a head and agreement, and a general requirement for specifiers to appear on the left (even though I do not claim that there are any true specifiers involved here).

As a first step, I represent a phi structure that is dependent on another head as in (47):

(47)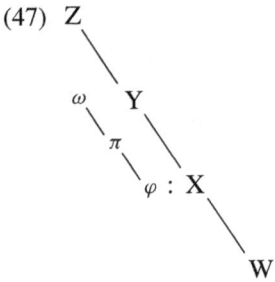

The root phi node forms a complex head with X. The normal extended projection continues from W through X and up to Y, and the extended projection of the phi sequence projects from φ.

We can now envisage three scenarios for the pronunciation of φ–X. First, a single exponent might realize X and the whole of phi structure, an example of which is the third singular preterite Italian *pens-ò* or Spanish *pens-ó* 'he, she, it thought'. There is no reason to think that *ò*~*ó* should be decomposed into separate parts for preterite, or third, or singular, given that no part of the exponent is shared with the other preterites (e.g., Italian 1s *pens-ai*, 2s *pens-asti*, 3p *pens-arono*) or third singulars (e.g., Spanish present *piens-a*, imperfective subjunctive *pens-ara*, or future *pens-ará*). Consequently, *ò*~*ó* realize the whole complex of the head, T, plus its feature content, the preterite, and the phi structure for 3s. Given this fusion, the position of T in the functional sequence anchors the position of the agreement.

Second, we can envisage an exponent that realizes the host head and some, but not all, of the phi structure, as in the Italian third plural conditional. By way of introduction, the singular, *penser-ebbe* 'he, she, it would think', is formed with a suffix, *ebbe*, that is absent from other persons, like 2s *penser-esti* and 1p *penser-emmo*. Moreover, *ebbe* occurs only in the conditional and so *ebbe* does not look like a default. This contrasts with other endings of the conditional, versions of which may be recognizable, for instance, in the 2s preterite *pens-asti* and 1p future *penser-emo*. Given that future (e.g., 1p future *penser-emo*) uses *penser*, the same extension of the root as the conditional, the locus of exponence of the conditional must lie, at least in part, in the suffixes. Thus, *ebbe* realizes both elements of the conditional and of 3s.

With this in place, consider now the plural, *penser-ebbe-ro* 'they would think'. The obvious analysis is that *ro* realizes plurality. This is reinforced by the imperfective subjunctive, for which third singular is *pens-asse* and third plural *pens-asse-ro*, using the same exponent of plural as the conditional. This then hems in the analysis of *ebbe*: it is a numberless third person conditional. So, as desired, it realizes the host head but only some of the hosted phi structure.

Still, the linear order of *penser-ebbe-ro* follows naturally. The position of the conditional is fixed by its place in the extended verbal projection. Because *ebbe* realizes both conditional and third person, it anchors the phi structure in the position of the exponent of conditional. The act of opening the phi structure up for coexponence with the conditional plausibly opens number up for exponence too. Combined with the general mapping from person-below-number to person-before-number, this suffices to ensure that plural *ro* immediately follows *penser-ebbe*.

The stages of this process are represented in (47). The root and other material, realized as *penser*, is inflected as third plural conditional. This is realized as *ebbe* for third conditional and *ro* for plural. The former is linearized directly after the previously linearized material, giving *penser-ebbe*, to which *ro* is then further suffixed, so as to follow *ebbe*, giving the full form *penser-ebbe-ro*.

(48)
$$\begin{array}{c} P \\ \diagdown \\ 3 \\ \diagdown \\ \varphi : F_{cond} \\ \diagdown \\ penser \end{array} \quad \Rightarrow \quad \begin{array}{c} C \\ ro \diagdown \\ \diagdown \\ penser\text{-}ebbe \end{array} \quad \Rightarrow \quad \begin{array}{c} C \\ \diagdown \\ penser\text{-}ebbe\text{-}ro \end{array}$$

Finally, leading back to Classical Hebrew, the most interesting case arises when the head that hosts a phi structure either goes unrealized or is realized without any of the phi features that it hosts. That is, the extended projection is realized as a sequence of suffixes to the verb, without opening phi up for exponence at the same time. Different theories, or their implementations, will have different things to say about this, but, within the framework of assumptions adopted here, the result is clear. The phi structure is not in the complement line of the extended projection, but it does, by definition, share features with the head with which it forms a complex unit (if it did not, they would be wholly separate entities). It therefore meets the structural criteria of a specifier and, so, is linearized to the left.

Two further factors impinge on this leftward placement. First, the phi structure is not a maximal projection, unlike other specifiers. So, I assume that the linearization algorithm places it to the left but as a linear dependent of other material, like a clitic. Second, there is the preference for not disrupting previously established linear relations, linearization being about establishing adjacency relations, not disestablishing them—which is behind the splitting of prefixal phi structures across verbs (*person–verb–number*, not *person–number–verb*).

Applying this principle of preservation to the schematic example in (46), we derive the previously posited prepositioning of phi relative to the whole string. Specifically, given the string W-X, the phi structure hosted by X is linearized at the left edge, as φ-W-X, not between W and X (*W-φ-X). Less abstractly, for Hebrew, we map syntactic Asp_φ—V via V–Asp_φ to φ-V.ASP, which yields verb-flanking agreement if person and number have separate exponents.

As have already seen numerous examples of this, I do not illustrate it further. Instead, I underline the plausibility of regarding prefixality as a reflex of lacking an exponent that fuses the host head with at least some of phi.

Within Afroasiatic, the groundwork for this case was laid in the discussion of table 5.11. There, I argued that the *k* in some languages, *t* in others, realizes +participant in the suffixal conjugation. Across the family, both *k* and *t* lead morphological lives beyond the suffixal conjugation, as exponents of first singular and of second person, but only here have they spread to first singular and all second persons. This suggests that they have become dependent on the particular tense or aspect that the suffixal conjugation encodes in each language. so, they can reasonably be regarded as realizing more than just person features, and this suffices, in current terms, to anchor them in the suffixal position.

More generally, we expect anchored agreement to be more sensitive to the anchoring head than prefixal agreement is. This clearly requires thorough exploration of its own, but, for the languages discussed above, it does seem to hold. In Romance, exemplified above with Italian and Spanish, agreement is suffixal and so tightly fused with tense and mood that they are not always readily morphologically dissociable. In Yimas, on the other hand, though some agreement affixes are sensitive to functional material, they are never sensitive to suffixes like past, near past, or remote past.[13]

As a final empirical point, consider the Kiowa agreement prefix (and those of the Tanoan languages). Although its constituents are extremely tightly interwoven, a prefix like *gyá*—used, for instance, when a first singular agent acts, for the benefit of a third singular applicative, on a third singular object—can nonetheless be decomposed into quite regular exponents for agent (*g*), applicative (´), and object (*ya*). When the full range of prefixes is analyzed

(Watkins 1984, Harbour 2007b), a consistent internal order emerges, with agent before applicative before object (as described in Sprott 1992 and Yumitani 1998 for Jemez).

On many theories of argument structure, agents are merged higher than applicatives, which are merged higher than objects (e.g., Hale and Keyser 2002, Pylkkänen 2008). Adger and Harbour (2007) and Adger, Harbour, and Watkins (2009) present several arguments that this phrase structure applies to Kiowa too (including informationally unmarked constituent order, restrictions on multiple postverbal arguments, and a derivation of the Strong Person Case Constraint). Heck and Richards (2010) successfully apply the same assumptions to various phenomena in Southern Tiwa. But all this leaves unanswered why the internal order of the agreement prefix is the same as the argument hierarchy.

An explanation of this now becomes available. Adger and Harbour argue that the applicative-introducing head comes to host agreement features of the object; the agent-introducing head, those of the applicative; and a higher head, Aspect, those of the agent, as shown in (49):

(49)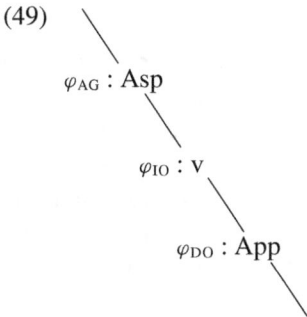

In Kiowa, the prefixes are completely invariant for anything other than phi features (and the minor variation that is found in prefixes across the family is attributable to higher functional structure—imperative force in Tewa, for instance; Speirs 1966). I take this as indicating that the functional spine is spelled out without any reference to the dependent phi structures. Consequently, as exponence proceeds up the functional sequence, creating a linear string, firstly object agreement will be placed at the left edge, then applicative agreement, then lastly agent agreement. The outcome, in abstract form, is (50), using "—" to mark the phonological juncture between prefix and verb:

(50) $\varphi_{AG} - \varphi_{IO} - \varphi_{DO}$ — VERB – APP – V – ASP – (NEG – MOD – ...)

This yields the desired internal order of agent before indirect object before direct object.

This exploration is intended to be a sketch, and I am well-aware that many questions remain. At the broadest end, one wonders how extensible this approach is to other ilks of clitic-like phenomena. At the sharper empirical end, there are a range of differences between, say, Kiowa and Yimas. For instance, in Kiowa, the agreement prefix forms a phonologically semiautonomous domain of sorts (Harbour 2003), and, at the same time, to the limited extent that Kiowa has multiple segmental exponents for single phi structures (e.g., 1S on 3D *nen* = *g-ę-d* contains both dual *ę* and nonsingular *d* exponents for the object), these do not straddle the verb. Kiowa differs from Yimas in both these properties, and so one wonders how the processes described above might interact with phonological domains and other factors. Such issues require an investigation that exceeds current confines.

6.6 Conclusion

To be viable, a theory of person must interact with a theory of number. Using the account of number in Harbour 2014a, I have shown that the current approach to person meets this criterion of viability. It captures the number distinctions that persons display in both tripartitions and quadripartitions. It makes sense of the morphological and semantic interpretation of plural and other nonatomic collections, like dual and augmented. By placing number in a projection that dominates person, the account was shown to interface cleanly with interpretation and pronunciation. And, in the latter domain, in particular, the account lends itself to the derivation of facts about precedence relations between person and number, adding further to an already substantial empirical range.

7 Spaces, Objects, Paths

7.1 Introduction

In the broad linguistic literature, there is a substantial and sustained recognition of the relationship of spatial deixis to personal deixis, beginning with Humboldt 1830 and continuing to Weissenborn and Klein 1982, Anderson and Keenan 1985, Imai 2003, and Lenz 2003, among others. In feature-based accounts of person, which are more of a generative concern, systems of spatial deixis have generally been disregarded (e.g., Noyer 1992, Halle 1997, Harley and Ritter 2002a, Cowper and Hall 2004, Sigurðsson 2004; in kindred vein, though, see Ritter and Wiltschko 2014). Yet these systems have been fundamental in my formulation of the core problem that a theory of person features should address. So, the current chapter explains why I depart from generative precedent on this score.

Section 7.2 lays out the empirical case, highlighting three broad types of evidence that underscore the relevance to person of deixis of objects (*this–that*) and of spaces (*here–there*) and of the termini or origins of paths located within those spaces (*hither–thither* and *hence–thence*, respectively). The two main strands of evidence are that person partitions correlate with spatial partitions both at a semantic and at a morphological level (sections 7.2.1–7.2.2). Reinforcing this, spatial correlates of person partitions crosscut with other means of partitioning spatial regions, like distance and elevation (section 7.2.3). This shows that person partitions are a well-defined subset of systems of spatial deixis. In consequence, these are data to which a theory of person has rights and responsibilities.

Section 7.3 shows how the syntax and semantics of person features can be embedded within an account of deixis. Given the wealth of distinctions in spatial deixis beyond person, the account is necessarily a sketch, but one to which further distinctions can plausibly be added. Section 7.3.1 proposes a syntax and semantics for a spatial head χ, and section 7.3.2 shows that the resulting system interlocks with the account of number of chapter 6 in an empirically contentful way.

7.2 Empirical Case

7.2.1 Partitional Parities

Space, object, and path deixis make many distinctions that personal pronouns and agreement almost roundly ignore. Imai (2003) presents an impressive overview of the variety of semantic shading that languages may engage in: objects may be classified as visible or invisible (in Kwak'wala/Kwakiutl; Boas 1947); as in-hand versus reachable, or in-hand versus close (for speaker and hearer, respectively, in Satawal; Yoshida 1981); as up from, down from, or level with the speaker (in Mizo; Murthy and Subbarao 2000); or as situated relative to geographic landmarks, like uphill versus downhill (in Idu; Pulu 1978) or inland versus seaward (in Manam; Lichtenberg 1983). So, any complete account of these systems must involve many features and/or projections beyond ±author and ±participant and the heads that host them.

Notwithstanding, person partitions represent a coherent subset of attested systems of space, object, and path deixis, which it makes sense for a theory of person features to rely on. These are illustrated below, beginning with monopartition and working up to quadripartition, as in chapter 4. These parities support the idea that deixis of person, space, objects, and paths shares a common semantic basis. Because several of these examples were discussed when the attested partitions were first illustrated (section 3.4), I cover the ground briskly.

7.2.1.1 Monopartition Monopartition is the hardest partition for which to demonstrate parity between person and other systems, for the reasons noted in section 3.4.5: it is hard to distinguish monopartition from absence of partition. For monopartitions of person, one has, I argued, the diagnostic of animacy. But that is not applicable to deixis of necessarily inanimate spaces, for instance. So, relaxing the condition slightly, I note that for person and various kinds of spatial deixis alike, absence of all distinctions is permissible.

Various examples of this have already been given, such as Wichita, a language without personal pronouns, and Warlpiri, a language with verbs of motion unspecified for origin or end. To these, one can add languages without distance or other distinctions among object deixis.

An example of this is Mosetén.[1] Sakel (2004, 119) states explicitly that "[w]hile place adverbs have different forms for the distance of the element involved ..., such distinctions do not exist for demonstrative pronouns."

Instead, the language has just two demonstratives, masculine *iits*, which means 'that' in (1) but 'this' in (2), and feminine *öi*, which means 'that' in (2) but 'this' in (3):

(1) *Yäe tyajke-te   iits   mintyi'.*
    1S meet- 3MO DEM.M man
    'I met that man.'

(2) *Tsin ya'-i   iits   kasko öi-   dye- tyi' nanasi'* ...
    1P buy-M DEM.M canoe DEM.F-BEN-M girl
    'We buy this canoe for that [good] girl.'

(3) *Jam yäe rai'se-'   ka-'   öi   käedäej.*
    NEG 1S want- 3FO bring-3FO DEM.F baby
    'I do not want to bring this baby.'

Considering such languages, Anderson and Keenan (1985) suggest that undifferentiated demonstratives risk being underreported because they might have the appearance of articles. Consonant with this, Sakel (2004, 119) states that "[d]emonstrative pronouns are also frequently used as determiners" (as are the third person pronouns of the language).

7.2.1.2 Author Bipartition
Author bipartition for pronouns has been exemplified with Damin, Elseng/Morwap (tentatively), and Sanapaná. Recall, for instance, that Damin *n!aa* covers 'I, we' and *n!uu*, 'you, he, she, it, they'.

The same system is found as a bipartition of spatial deixis in English. *Here* denotes spaces in the vicinity of the speaker, and *there* denotes spaces beyond (though 'beyond' is demarcated by a rather flexible boundary, as *here* can also denote the vicinity of any group containing the speaker). Similarly, *this* and *these* denote objects in the speaker's (extended) vicinity, and *that* and *those* denote objects beyond.

Somewhat archaically, the bipartition extends into English directionals, too: *hither* and *thither*, 'to here' and 'to there', and *hence* and *thence*, 'from here' and 'from there'. The morphology of these forms, and their relation to *here* and *there*, is quite transparent: the *h* forms are all +author, the *th* forms, −author.[2]

7.2.1.3 Participant Bipartition
The other bipartition is participant-based, as in the pronouns of Hocąk. Again, though rare for a person system, it has a number of instantiations in other deictic domains. Both Bulgarian and Catalan exhibit the system in spatial and object deixis alike. The distinction is the basis of Georgian directionals.[3] (For examples of how the two bipartitions are distinguished as systems of spatial deixis, see section 3.4.4 on Bulgarian and Kartvelian.)

7.2.1.4 Tripartition Tripartitions, like bipartitions, also arise in a range of deictic domains. For Korafe, Farr and Whitehead (1981) identify three deictic roots, *e*, *a*, and *o*, corresponding to the speaker, hearer, and others, respectively. These are suffixed in a variety of ways to yield deictic triples, like *emo* 'this (near speaker)', *amo* 'that (near hearer)', and *omo* 'this (removed from speaker and hearer)', and *eminda* 'here (near speaker)', *aminda* 'there (near hearer)', and *ominda* 'there (removed from speaker and hearer)' (my glossing based on Farr and Whitehead's table). Some examples of usage are given below. I distinguish first-, second-, and third-based deictics with subscripted 1, 2, and 3:

(4) *Na nene aindae setevo emo asuguseni, emo!*
 I you on.that$_2$.account said.2S this$_1$ put.on.1S this$_1$
 'You chose me, so on account of that, I have put on this (church warden's badge), this one!'

(5) *Okia amo budo fuyo!*
 pot that$_2$ getting come
 'Bring that pot near you!'

(6) *Omo nanda ghato- ra-si.*
 that$_3$ my cousin-is- certainly
 'That one over there certainly is my cousin.'

(Farr and Whitehead also describe uses of the deictic system for expressing narrative and empathic proximity or distance, a far richer version of English-style *This alien walks into a pub and the barman says ...*, used when there is no actual alien present.)

A similar system is found in Korean, for which Sohn (1999) gives the joint demonstrative and locative examples *yeki* 'here', *keki* 'there (near you)', and *ceki* 'over there', from *eki* 'place' preceded by *i* 'this', *ku* 'that (near you)', and *ce* 'that over there'.

7.2.1.5 Quadripartition Moving to the most complex systems, Waray-Waray (Wolf and Wolf 1967) exhibits quadripartition not just in its pronouns, but in its demonstratives and locatives as well (table 7.1), and its near neighbor Cebuano (Bunye and Yap 1971) extends this into its verbs of motion (a property of Waray-Waray already illustrated in section 3.4.1):[4]

(7) *Lokaw ngari.*
 come here$_{1EX}$
 'Come here.'

Table 7.1
Demonstratives and locatives in Waray-Waray

Deictic	Speaker	Speaker-hearer	Hearer	Other
'this', 'that'	*adi*	*ini*	*itu*	*adtu*
'here', 'there'	*a(a)di*	*a(a)nhi*	*a(a)da?*	*a(a)dtu*

(8) *Dadon   nganhi / nganha / ngadto ang pagkaon.*
    bring.PASS here$_{1IN}$ there$_2$ there$_3$ ART food
    'The food will be brought here / there / over there.'

7.2.1.6 Nonpartitions   Finally, I note that none of the descriptions I have read of spatial deixis, either in grammars or in surveys, present instances of the partitions that are unattested for person. For example, I have not seen described a bipartition of spaces near to hearer versus removed from hearer, hence, near either to the speaker or to a third person; nor a Zwickian tripartition where there is one special term for objects near to speaker but removed from hearer (the "exclusive"), and a second for objects close to both (the "inclusive"), and a third term for everything else (removed from speaker but near to hearer or others). This negative, which suggests that such systems are extremely rare if they exist at all, further supports the simultaneous analysis of person and spatial deixis.

In sum, the foregoing demonstrates that each of the five person partitions is also found in the deixis of objects, spaces, and the termini of paths. This parity of partitions provides initial semantic motivation for assuming that one set of features generates the partitions across all these domains and, conversely, that evidence from these domains should feed into a unified theory of all these phenomena.

7.2.2 Morphological Parities

Shared exponence presents a second strand of evidence for pursuing a joint analysis. In some languages, the sharing between person and nonperson deixis is synchronic. In others, diachronic pathways reveal the relationship between person and space.

Beginning close to home, there are dialects of English in which personal pronouns and locatives are interchangeable under certain circumstances, as in:

(9) Give it me. / Give it here.

In some Romance languages, this person–location alternation is grammatically obligatory in some multiclitic contexts. The examples below are from Catalan (Bonet, 1991), which uses locative *hi* for *li* 'to him', and the Italian dialect of Celle di Bulgheria in Campania (Manzini and Savoia, 2005), which replaces *li* 'to him' with locative *ndži*:

(10) *L' hi va recomanar.*
    3MSO LOC recommended
    'She recommended him to him.'

(11) *Ndži lu danu.*
    LOC 3MSO give.3P
    'They give it to him.'

By way of comparison, consider (10) with a full object noun phrase. Instead of the locative *ndži*, the personal, dative *li* is used:

(12) *Li danu kistu.*
    3MS.DAT give.3P this.M
    'They give this to him.'

The relationship between space and person is attested elsewhere in diachrony of Italian clitic systems. The first and second plurals, *ci* and *vi*, derive respectively from the Latin directional *hince* 'hence' and locative *ibi* 'there' (Maiden, 1995).

In a more synchronic, if still historical, vein, Medieval Japanese had a series of pronouns *konata* 'I', *sonata* 'you', *anata* 'he, she', which parallel, inter alia, the object deictics *kore* 'this', *sore* 'that (near hearer)', *are* 'that (removed from speaker and hearer)' (Martin 1988, Noriko Davidson, pers. comm.). These make the link between person and spatial deixis plain. (On the modern language and its distance-based deixis, see section 7.2.3.)

A slightly different diachronic trajectory that also shows a link between location and person is found in Armenian. What were demonstrative clitics meaning 'this', 'that (by you)', and 'that (over there)' in the classical language have come to indicate possession by the persons that define the 'this', 'that', and 'over there' spaces, namely, the speaker, the hearer, and others. Hence, *mard-s* meant 'this man (by me)' in Classical Armenian but means 'my man' in Modern Armenian. Forms for all three persons are given in table 7.2. In informal semantic terms, 'in the region of' has come to mean 'in the possession of' or 'in association with' (and, additionally, plain 'the' in the third person). Like Latin-to-Italian, then, these forms illustrate a shift from space to person.

A similar relationship is evident in the Nepalese Kiranti language, Wambule. Its demonstrative system, both nominal and adverbial, is based on five bound

Table 7.2

From deixis to personal possession: Classical versus Modern Armenian

mard 'man'	Classical Armenian	Modern Armenian
mard-s	'this man (by me)'	'my man'
mard-d	'that man (by you)'	'your man'
mard-n	'that man (over there)'	'the/his man'

Table 7.3

Possessive pronouns in Wambule

Person	Singular	Dual	Plural
1EX	a	ancuk (a-n-cu-k)	ak (a-k)
1IN		inci (i-n-ci)	ik (i-k)
2	i	inci (i-n-ci)	in (i-n)
3	aŋ	anci (aŋ-n-ci)	an (aŋ-n)

morphemes, meaning 'near', 'distant', 'distant (at the same level)', 'distant (up)', 'distant (down)'. With respect to the first two, Opgenort (2004, 208) writes:

> The morpheme ⟨a·⟩ 'near' marks a position relatively nearby or near the speaker. This morpheme seems to be related to the first person singular possessive pronoun *a* 'my'. The morpheme ⟨i·⟩ 'distant' marks a position relatively further away or nearer the hearer. This morpheme may be related to the second person singular possessive pronoun *i* '[your]'.

Some examples are: *am(e)* 'this', *im(e)* 'that'; *al(o)*, *ano* 'here', *il(o)*, *ino* 'there'; *as(e)* 'in this way, thus', *is(e)* 'in that way, thus'.[5]

The possessive pronouns that Opgenort mentions are given in table 7.3 (with his decomposition, which draws on the expression of number in verbal agreement, in parentheses). Given their distribution, one is obliged to regard spatial *a·* and *i·* as diachronically, rather than synchronically, related to possessive *a* and *i*, because the possessive morphemes are sensitive to ±participant (*i* covers +participant 1IN and 2) whereas their spatial homologues are sensitive to ±author (*a·* covers +author 1EX and 1IN).[6] Leaving aside these distortions, which may be reflexes of the divergence between quadripartition in the possessives and poorer partition in the spatial deictics, the synchronic systems nonetheless reveal the same diachronic link between person and space.

Table 7.4
Turkish deictics of persons, objects, spaces, and directions

Persons		Objects		Spaces	Directions
b-en	b-iz	b-u	b-unlar	b-urada	b-uraya
s-en	s-iz	ş-u	ş-unlar	ş-urada	ş-uraya
o	o-nlar	o	o-nlar	o-rada	o-raya

A final, more fully synchronic example arises in Turkish and is attested (with varying degrees of attenuation) across a range of related languages. As is evident from table 7.4 (Göksel and Kerslake 2005), there is an exponent, *b*, that is common to 'I' (*b-eni*), 'we' (*b-izi*), 'this' (*b-unu*), 'these' (*b-unları*), 'here' (*b-urada*), and 'hence' (*b-uraya*). Similarly, in the third person, one observes *o* in 'he, that' (*o*), 'they, those' (*o-nlar*), 'yon' (*o-rada*), and, for want of a better word, 'yonce' (*o-raya*).

It is tempting to think that another exponent alternating between *s* and *ş* is common to 'you', 'that', 'thence', and the like. However, historically, Turkish had the ±author bipartition *bu–ol*, together with emphatic forms derived by prefixation of *ş*. Of these, *şol* fell from use, leaving modern *bu*, *şu*, and *o*. So, this "medial" term does not derive from the second person pronoun. Nor has it acquired this meaning in the modern language: a speaker may refer to their own hands using *şu* (Dervillez-Bastuji 1982) and may alternate between *bu* and *şu* in referring to one and the same object, without there being any spatial rearrangement between uses (Özyürek 1998). These facts are hard to explain if *bu*-forms alone refer to spaces and objects within the speaker's vicinity.

Yet, even without a diachronic or synchronic link between pronominal *s* and spatial *ş*, Turkish still makes the point relevant here: first and third person deixis share exponents with spatial deixis.

So, a range of examples from different families, showing various diachronic and synchronic trajectories, all illustrate the same point: a morphological parity between person and space. This constitutes the first argument for the reasonableness of positing a shared featural basis for both forms of deixis.

7.2.3 Cooccurrence with Distance

A well-established distinction in the description of spatial deixis is that between person-based and distance-based systems (Anderson and Keenan 1985, Foley 1986, Wilkins 1999, Imai 2003, Meira 2003, Bhat 2004). The difference between these is most obvious in the medial term of three-term systems. If person-based, the medial term means 'close to hearer', but, if distance-based, it means 'at a distance from speaker'. These two meanings overlap but are different, as the hearer can be close to the speaker, while a place or object referred to could be at some remove even if not distant enough to be *yon*.

A potential worry is that apparent person-based deixis might be a particular conventionalization of distance-based systems. If so, their featural basis might not overlap with person at all, or else they might share features but require some means of loosening their semantics when applied to spaces. Modern Japanese seems to underline this, as, in contrast to the medieval language, it uses spatial triples *ko–so–a* on the basis of distance (Imai 2003).

However, closer examination dissolves these concerns. First, the developments specifically of Japanese fall within the natural bounds of diachronic drift. Second, and more generally, person- and distance-based deixis cooccur in a variety of languages, which strongly suggests that the distinctions and features underlying both of them are distinct. If so, this further justifies hiving off person-based deixis for special consideration in the context of a theory of person.

With regard to Japanese, other diachronic facts above are instructive. We have already seen, from the comparison between Georgian and Laz/Migrelian, that exponents may change the features to which they are sensitive. Indeed, the features to which Wambule *a·* and *i·* are sensitive as personal versus spatial deictics differ, though they persist as homologues within the same language. In this light, Japanese merely adds another shade to such degrees of difference in that the spatial deictics no longer refer to person features at all, but have become distance-based.

Supporting this, there is other evidence of reanalysis within Modern Japanese. For instance, beside wholly regular triples, like *kore* 'this', *sore* 'that', *are* 'yon', and *kochira* 'this way', *sochira* 'that way', *achira* 'yon way', one finds partial irregularities, as in the third term of *koko* 'here', *soko* 'there', *asoko* 'yon', which seems to combine the expected distal prefix *a* with the medial term *soko*. In the pronouns, too, opacities have accreted: erstwhile third person, *anata*, is now used for the second person (just as Italian and German use third person *Lei* and *Sie* for second, as vehicles of deference). In this context, the drift from person- to distance-based readings of spatial *ko–so–a* triples is not worrisome.

More importantly, however, person- and distance-based deixis may cooccur within a single language. Sámi (Nickel 1994), for instance, has speaker-based *dát* 'this (nearer me than you)' and hearer-based *diet* 'this (nearer you than me)'. Other (visible) objects are then divided between *duot* 'that (further away than *dát* and *diet*)' and *dot* 'that (far away)'. (Invisible objects are referred to with *dat* 'that'.)

A slightly different system has emerged in Brazilian Portuguese (Meira 2003). The most fundamental distinction made is between the participant and nonparticipant regions, as in Bulgarian and Catalan (section 7.2.1). For instance, the gender-neutral object deictics are *isso* 'this, that (near hearer)' and *aquilo* 'that (away from speaker and hearer)'. As in German (section 3.4.5), further distinctions can then be made using locative deictics; hence, *isso aqui* 'this here (near speaker)' and *isso aí* 'that there (near hearer)', in the participant region, and *aquilo ali* 'that near' and *aquilo lá* 'that far', in the nonparticipant region.

Slave (Rice 1989) presents an analogous crosscutting of distance with the author bipartition. Rice describes the system as comprising "a basic 'here'/'there' dichotomy, with both sets further subdivided into 'near' and 'far'"(p. 321). The four forms are author-proximal *dih*, author-distal *dúh*, nonauthor-proximal *ʔekúh*, and nonauthor-distal *yah*.

As a final example of such combinations, Fore (Foley 1986, citing Scott 1978) combines person- and distance-based deixis for space with a rather rich set of distance parameters. Horizontal distance beyond the participant region (*má·* 'this, here', *pi* 'that, there') is tripartitioned into *mí* 'that (close)', *máre* 'that (mid-distance)', and *máro* 'that (far)'. Moreover, both vertical distances exhibit bipartitions: *máe* 'that (up)' and *mayó* 'that (far up)', and *me* 'that (down)' and *mó* 'that (far down)'.[7]

Closer examination of distance-based systems makes clear that, though they may not be person-based, they are certainly person-related, in the sense that the locations of speaker and hearer play roles in determining when proximal, medial, and distal deictics are to be used. Most obviously, in both systems, the location of the speaker is crucial. Moreover, Meira (2003) (using the elicitation tool of Wilkins 1999 and departing slightly from Meira 1999) carefully shows that, in Tiriyó, speaker and hearer location are both relevant to the use of proximal–medial–distal triples, like *serë–mërë–ooni*; and Jungbluth (2003) shows that the orientation of speaker and hearer relative to each other and to deictic referents determines which of the Spanish triples, like *esto–eso–aquello*, is to be used. How the semantics of distance features should model this remains to be seen, but, with person being a nexus between person- and distance-based deixis alike, combinations of the two systems (and the development attested in Japanese) look quite natural.

Thus, if some systems of spatial deixis are not person-based and, so, should not be analyzed in terms of person features, they reassure us at the same time that person is the appropriate mode of analysis for parts or wholes of others (Brazilian Portuguese, Fore, Sámi, Slave, and the languages of section 7.2.1). These data therefore constitute a second argument for analyzing some deixis of persons and spaces in terms of a common inventory of features.

7.3 Theoretical Underpinnings

If the investigation of person requires a book, and number more or less likewise (e.g., Harbour 2007b, 2011a, 2014a), then it will be appreciated that current confines cannot accommodate full analysis of the features and phrase structure behind the rather broad sweep of semantic data above—deixis for spaces, objects, and origins and termini of paths—let alone the other dimensions that the discussion has touched on—visibility, tangibility, degrees of horizontal and vertical distance, geographic anchoring. Rather, what is relevant here is a sketch of how the account of previous chapters can be extended to the core deictic data that I have argued to be relevant to a theory of person.

To that end, section 7.3.1 posits a spatial head χ and explores its basic phrase structure, feature content, and compositional semantics. Section 7.3.2 adds the number head ω of chapter 6 to this sketched account and shows that the result immediately derives several desirable semantic and morphological properties.

7.3.1 The Deictic Core

As a locus for spatial semantics, I posit a syntactic head χ (from Greek *xōros* 'space') that dominates the person projection π:

(13) χ
$\quad\quad\diagdown$
$\quad\quad\;\pi_{[F]}$
$\quad\quad\quad\;\diagdown$
$\quad\quad\quad\;\;\varphi$

The semantic effect of χ is to take the set of individuals satisfying a particular person specification, F, and to yield, instead, the set of spaces "corresponding" to those individuals. That is, it takes a predicate P, supplies a free variable satisfying that predicate, P(x), and creates $\chi(x)$, the vicinity, or, if you like, the characteristic space, of x. Finally, it supplies a variable, y, over the domain of things, D_e, enabling one to specify particular things within the vicinity x:[8]

(14) $[\![\chi]\!] = \lambda P \,.\, \lambda y \,.\, y \in \chi(x) \land P(x)$ $\quad\quad\quad\quad\quad\quad$ x, a free variable
$\quad\;\;\langle e,t\rangle \;\;\; y \in D_e$

The definition says nothing more about y than that it is a thing. I discuss presently how y can be restricted to spaces versus objects.

It is worth noting that y is defined as something within the vicinity of x, rather than the whole vicinity itself—as would be entailed if the definition transformed the whole of P into a set of vicinities and then located y within that set, $y \in \{\chi(x) : P(x)\}$. This difference is obviously necessary for object deixis, as a book, say, referred to by *this* does not occupy all of a speaker's vicinity.

However, it is even necessary for words like *here*, which may pick out specific points or spaces within the speaker's vicinity, rather than the whole vicinity (see also Jungbluth 2003 on the effect of speaker and hearer orientation). As formulated, the definition allows this.

Given (14), compositionality is straightforward. Consider (13). For German stressed article demonstratives, F, the feature content of π, would be empty; for Laz directionals, it would contain just ±author; for Bulgarian locatives, it would contain just ±participant; and for Korafe deixis or Cebuano verbs of motion, it would contain both these features, subject to different orders of interpretation, for tripartition and quadripartition, respectively.

For this abstract F, πP has the denotation below:

(15) $[\![\pi_F - \varphi]\!] = \lambda x . x \in [\![F]\!](\mathscr{L}_\pi)$
$ {\scriptstyle x \in D_e}$

Consequently, for the whole deictic structure, we have (16). (D_e, the domain of x in (15), is passed on to the free variable x in (16); I take this to be uncontroversial.)

(16) $[\![\chi - \pi_F - \varphi]\!]$
$ = [\![\chi]\!]([\![\pi_F - \varphi]\!])$
$ = \lambda y . y \in \chi(x) \wedge x \in [\![F]\!](\mathscr{L}_\pi) \qquad x$, a free variable in D_e
$ {\scriptstyle y \in D_e}$

As already mentioned, this crude form says nothing about what y is. Languages in which spatial and object deictics are identical might be taken to suggest that some languages use this underdetermination to produce systems that are coarse-grained on this semantic plane. Examples above are Damin (section 7.2.1), Fore (section 7.2.3), and Palauan (table 3.2; Josephs (1977) translates *er* as a preposition, 'in, at, to, from, of', a sense evident in (10)–(13)). However, some further refinement of χ is required to allow for person partitions to be embedded in systems of deixis.

The simplest solution is to assume that χ itself can be endowed with all the necessary distinctions. This might include a privative feature [space], which restricts the domain, or predicates spacehood, of y. If [space] is collocated with a feature ±source, it might indicate the origin or terminus of a path. So, one could imagine that the proximal demonstrative of Catalan, *aquest* (number and gender omitted), corresponds to a bare χ, ranging over nondescript things:

(17) $[\![\chi - \pi_{+\text{participant}} - \varphi]\!]$
$ = \lambda y . y \in \chi(x) \wedge x \in [\![+\text{participant}]\!](\mathscr{L}_\pi)$
$ {\scriptstyle y \in D_e}$

Enriching slightly, the corresponding locative *aquí*, being restricted to spaces (in the vicinity of speaker and/or hearer), adds [space] to χ:

(18) $[\![\chi_{\text{space}} \text{---} \pi_{+\text{participant}} \text{---} \varphi]\!]$
$= \lambda y \,.\, y \in \chi(x) \wedge x \in [\![+\text{participant}]\!](\mathscr{L}_\pi) \wedge \text{space}(y)$
$y \in D_e$

And, enriching further, the Georgian directional *mo* specifies that the space in question is a terminus −source (of a path of motion):

(19) $[\![\chi_{\text{space −source}} \text{---} \pi_{+\text{participant}} \text{---} \varphi]\!]$
$= \lambda y \,.\, y \in \chi(x) \wedge x \in [\![+\text{participant}]\!](\mathscr{L}_\pi) \wedge \text{space}(y) \wedge \text{terminus}(y)$
$y \in D_e$

Further features, for horizontal and vertical distance and other distinctions, might be accommodated on the same head.

Of course, this is a rather lumpen solution, and typology, linear order, and semantic or morphological compositionality might be better served by projecting space and/or path as separate heads, or light nouns, of the functional sequence (see, e.g., Radkevich 2010, Svenonius 2010, Pantcheva 2011).

To see the kind of evidence that might be relevant, recall that, in Korean (section 7.2.1), 'here' and related terms are demonstratives plus the noun 'place'. Reflecting this, and the idea that place might be the honed form of more general demonstratives, I have afforded the demonstrative *aquest* just a bare χ node, but have enriched this to χ_{space} for the locative *aquí*. However, there are languages where, conversely, demonstratives seem to subsume locatives. The refinement of French adnominals by locatives provides an example. By themselves, adnominal demonstratives make no locational distinctions, allowing *cette planète* to refer to both distal Mars (20) and proximal Earth (21):[9]

(20) *Qu'irions-nous faire sur cette planète lointaine, ...?*
what would we do on DEM planet distant
'What would we do on that distant ... planet?'

(21) *"Sauvez cette planète: mode d'emploi"*
save.IMP.P DEM planet means of use
"Save This Planet: Instruction Manual"

However, postnominal locatives allow one to "import" the distality distinction: *cette planète ci* 'this planet' (lit. DEM.FS planet here) and *cette planète là* 'that planet' (lit. DEM.FS planet there). So, a full account must reconcile which, if either, of locatives and demonstratives is semantically basic. (I also leave open whether the flanking of the noun by the demonstrative, left, and locative, right, is to be analyzed as an instance of flanking of the verb by person and number.)

Pertinent evidence might come from the observation that the refining locative in French is postnominal, not fused with the demonstrative, and that the demonstrative alone bears gender and number information. English has similar structures, though they do not add any locational distinctions not present in the demonstratives themselves and are, instead, presentational. Two examples from Dickens's *Great Expectations* are *this here boy* and *these here tools*. Here, the locatives are prenominal, unlike in French, but, again, the demonstrative bears number (**this heres tools*). This may suggest that locative enhancement of demonstratives involves a more complex structure, possibly adjunction, rather than a pure segment of functional sequence. But clearly, more thorough investigation is needed.

By touching on these larger issues, I wish, again, to make clear that all I have presented here is a sketch of how a formal account of spatial deixis might be conjoined with the account of person given above. For current purposes, a sketch is all that is required to justify the use of some spatial partitions as data for a theory of person.

7.3.2 Number

Demonstratives frequently inflect for number, as in English *this–these* and *that–those*. Capturing the interaction between number and the structure for demonstratives is just as basic a requirement as capturing that between person and number. Though this is not at all challenging, laying out the approach explicitly further supports the account presented in chapter 6 in two ways. The first concerns the phrase structure in which number dominates person, and the second concerns analogues of the linear relationship between person and number.

The treatment of number for demonstratives is very straightforward. Many figures in chapter 6 show the action of number features on third person structures. For instance, figure 6.8 shows a third person with an English-style singular–plural distinction. If we assume that the object referents of demonstratives, along with other countable common nouns, are also structured as (atomic join-complete semi)lattices, then any account of number in third person pronouns automatically extends to these too.

For this to work, the number head must be in the right phrase-structural position. That is, one first forms the structure for demonstratives and then counts out the objects the demonstrative refers to. In other words, χP must be formed first and then acted on by ω:

(22)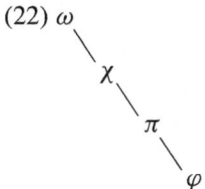

A simple derivation, for English *these*, illustrates the point. Number bears the feature −atomic, for plurality, and person bears +author, for the speaker. The first step below just expands ωP, and the second adds in the definition of −atomic and evaluates χP in the same manner as (17):

(23) $[\![\, \omega_{-\text{atomic}} — \chi — \pi_{+\text{author}} — \varphi \,]\!]$
  $= [\![\, \omega_{-\text{atomic}} \,]\!] \,(\, [\![\, \chi — \pi_{+\text{author}} — \varphi \,]\!] \,)$
  $= \lambda y. \neg \text{atom}(y) \,(\, \lambda y. y \in \chi(x) \land x \in [\![+\text{author}]\!](\mathscr{L}_\pi) \,)$
  $= \lambda y. y \in \chi(x) \land x \in [\![+\text{author}]\!](\mathscr{L}_\pi) \land \neg \text{atom}(y)$

The last step, using function modification, imposes an extra condition on *y*: its domain is no longer the whole of the demonstrative lattice, but only its upper, nonatomic portion. We therefore have plural *these* as opposed to singular *this*.

Given this phrase structure, simple transitivity provides an additional justification for placing person below number in the nondemonstrative contexts of chapter 6. If number dominates space and space dominates person (and if the functional sequence does not rearrange itself when space does not project), then number dominates person.

Moreover, the alternative, placing number lower, would be problematic for demonstratives, just as it was for person. The plural, −atomic, in *these* ought to act on the objects denoted by χ, not on the persons denoted by π. That is, a plural like *these* can pick out multiple objects in my vicinity; it is not restricted to objects in the vicinity of plural first persons. Placing ω below χ would create precisely this restriction, as the argument of −atomic would be *x*, the variable over persons, not *y*, the variable over objects.

A further consequence of this phrase structure concerns analogues of the generalization that person precedes number. Section 6.5.2 argued that this is a reflex of dominance relations and the linearization procedure. With χ dominating π, we expect to see person exponents preceding exponents of deictic category. (We also expect both to precede number, but I have not found examples where all three exponents are clearly segmentable, so I leave this aside.)

This prediction holds most obviously in languages where the deixis shares exponence with person, as in Wambule *a* 'my', *a-k* 'our', *a-m* 'this', *a-l* 'here', or Turkish *o* 'he, she, it, that', *o-nlar* 'they, those', *o-rada* 'yon'. If Wambule *a* and Turkish *o*, and the like, are always exponents of π, whether embedded in pronouns or demonstratives, then they will always linearly precede exponents of χ, like Wambule locational *l* or Turkish locational *rada*. Schematically, with exponents $x \Leftrightarrow [\chi]$ and $p \Leftrightarrow [\pi_F - \varphi]$, we obtain the order *p-x*:

(24)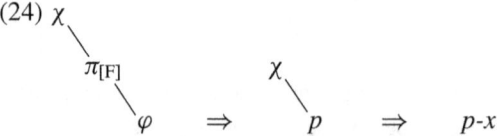

That is, person precedes place.

The generalization carries over in good measure to the languages discussed in section 7.2.1, which lack a morphologically overt connection to person. Korafe provides a clear instance, with suffixes accreting onto roots for speaker's, hearer's, and others' vicinities, as in *a-mo* 'that (near hearer)' and *a-minda* 'there (near hearer)'. These can be treated as per the previous paragraph.

An important caveat, though, is that the mechanisms of section 6.5.3 militate against an exceptionless generalization here. Imagine an exponent that spans the functional sequence from the root phi node, through the person head, and up to the spatial head. If this exponent expresses the feature content of π, then we have an undecomposable whole, like the Palauan verb *me* 'come (to speaker)':

(25) $me \Leftrightarrow [\chi_{[\text{space}, -\text{source}]} - \pi_{[+\text{author}, +\text{participant}]} - \varphi]$

However, suppose that the exponent extends to χ but does not express the feature content of π: $x' \Leftrightarrow [\chi - \pi - \varphi]$. By realizing π itself, x' anchors the exponent of [F] (like the plural *ro* of the Italian conditional *dir-ebbe-ro*; section 6.5.3). A pure person exponent, $p' \Leftrightarrow [F]$, is then linearized after the anchoring material, yielding the order x'-p':[10]

(26)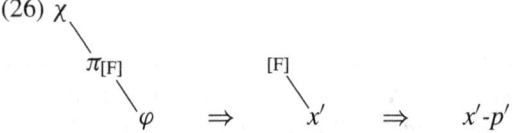

Palauan, in fact, seems to exploit precisely this option, with pure person exponents uniformly to the right of its demonstrative bases (Josephs 1975). This is apparent in the 'near hearer' forms in the snippet of the system presented in table 3.2: animate 'that' *ngilecha* and inanimate 'that' *tilecha* both end in −author +participant *lecha*.

Superficially described, (24) and (26) have person in different linear positions. However, such a description equivocates on what it calls a person exponent. These correspond to syntactically distinct entities: the whole of πP in (24), versus just the feature content of π in (26). How reliably these can be told apart in practice remains to be seen, but the worst-case scenario would be that the prediction regarding linearization would be reliably applied only to systems where there are equally reliable grounds (like person exponents shared with pronouns) for identifying an exponent as πP or as pure person features.

This complication aside, the linear correlation does indeed hold, and none of this distracts from the phrase structure for number and its desirable semantic consequences.

7.4 Conclusion

The foregoing discussion justifies the use of data from spatial deixis in formulating and solving the partition problem. Though use of these typological, synchronic, and diachronic data from semantics and morphology may be novel within a generative context, it is, in fact, a mainstreaming move, in light of other work within other linguistic frameworks. Nonetheless, the theoretical basis for this seems to be straightforward, given the ease with which one can sketch a formal account of the interaction between person deixis, spatial deixis, and number.

8 Oldfangled *and*

8.1 Introduction

Conjunction is the engine that drives traditional accounts of person and other phi features (e.g., Benveniste 1966, Hale 1973, Silverstein 1976): features denote first-order predicates, and collections of features denote conjunctions of predicates. For example, something is exclusive singular if and only if it includes the speaker *and* it does not include the hearer *and* it is singular. The current chapter compares the structure and consequences of such approaches with my fundamentally different conception of features.

The key difference between the predication-and-conjunction and lattice-and-action views of person lies, at an abstract level, in the semantics of feature values. At a more concrete level, this ramifies into the number of features each must posit. Conjunctive accounts need three (or more) as opposed to the two argued for above. (The third feature is generally, if not universally, taken to reference the hearer.) Two kinds of consideration motivate these richer systems: interlinguistic typology and intralinguistic case studies.

Section 8.2 lays out the descriptive motivation for third (and fourth and more-th) features. Focusing on Noyer 1992, Harley and Ritter 2002a, and Béjar 2003, 2008, it shows how these richer systems give rise to Zwickian problems of overgeneration and argues that the means deployed to trim the excess are unexplanatory and entrain empirical problems. The section also shows that different means of parameterizing two-feature conjunction-based systems suffer empirical difficulties (Déchaine 1999, Bobaljik 2008, Kratzer 2009, Wechsler 2010) or cannot be given compositional semantics (Halle 1997). As a result, the more parsimonious system, with two features, but eschewing conjunction as the semantic "glue," emerges as the better option.

Section 8.3 turns to language-specific studies that seem to suggest that a two-feature inventory is too tight. Focusing on Mam (Noyer 1992), Fula (Watanabe 2013), and German (Frampton 2002), section 8.3.1 shows that various arguments for a hearer feature can be transposed into my system, even though it lacks a feature that is so defined. Section 8.3.2 considers two arguments, from Menominee and Dumi (Trommer 2008), that some languages use three features at once. Although Trommer's analyses are not transposable, independently required variables over values or features can be shown to account for these more elaborate systems.

Continuing in the same vein as Trommer's arguments, section 8.4 considers the obvious challenge raised by languages that use both tri- and quadripartition in closely related domains, like subject and object agreement. When one such language (Kunwinjku; Evans 2003) splits its general first person into exclusive and inclusive, it also shares its exponents between them. The section shows, not only that analysis in terms of two features is possible, but also that such an analysis is more compact than alternatives in two three-feature systems.

The balance of evidence favors a parsimonious inventory and the move away from a conjunction-based semantics for phi features.

Throughout this chapter, I liberally rename other authors' features (eschewing "±1," "1," "speaker," and the like) and distinguish theirs from mine with prime marks. For instance, I write "±author" for my feature, "±author'" for Noyer's (Frampton's, Trommer's, and Watanabe's), and privative "author'" for Harley and Ritter's (and Béjar's).

8.2 Interlinguistic Adequacy

In past accounts, the prime drive behind third features is descriptive adequacy. As explained in section 8.2.1, this is an all but inevitable consequence of the conjunctive approach to phi features. However (section 8.2.2), if there are only two bipartitions, then third features generate unattested (bi)partitions. Concentrating on Noyer 1992, Harley and Ritter 2002a, and Béjar 2003, the section shows that various means of trimming this excess are not explanatory and do not derive actual properties of specific languages. Given these issues, section 8.2.3 turns to an alternative, Halle's (1997) suggestion for deriving all person partitions from two features via a parameter on value cooccurrence (with brief comments about three other two-feature proposals). It emerges, however, that there is no semantically compositional implementation of this idea.

8.2.1 Motivation
The easiest way to explain why conjunctive accounts traditionally assume a third feature is to reiterate why the current account does not.

Briefly put, I use monopartition to motivate an entity, π, that denotes the whole social universe, $i_o i u_o u_o o_o$. The two bipartitions motivate two features, author and participant, and the means by which they act, + and −. With this in place, I make an absence of assumptions: any choice of features, and any order of semantic composition, is legitimate. So, ±author can act on π and feed ±participant, yielding tripartition, or the reverse, yielding quadripartition. In other words, once one has the resources to generate the simplest systems, the more complex ones come for free, with no further features needed.

Matters are not so for conjunction-based accounts, because conjunction is commutative (knickers and britches are britches and knickers). So, if one has two features, ±F and ±G, denoting first-order predicates like, say, 'is (not) a plurality' and 'does (not) contain the speaker', then they are jointly interpreted by function modification and their order of application is irrelevant:

(1) $[\![-F(+G)]\!]$
 $= (\lambda x . x$ is not a plurality$)\lambda x . x$ contains the speaker
 $= \lambda x . x$ is not a plurality $\wedge$ x contains the speaker
 $= \lambda x . x$ contains the speaker $\wedge$ x is not a plurality
 $= (\lambda x . x$ contains the speaker$)\lambda x . x$ is not a plurality
 $= [\![+G(-F)]\!]$

As a result, once one has used the two features motivated by the bipartitions to jointly generate a third partition, one has exhausted their generative capacity and the only way to regain descriptive adequacy is to posit another feature (or to invoke other combinatorial considerations; section 8.2.3).

In concrete terms, the bipartition $i_o i u_o \mid u_o o_o$ motivates the first-order predicate 'does (not) contain the speaker', as i_o and $i u_o$ are elements containing the speaker, and u_o and o_o are elements excluding it. Similarly, $i_o i u_o u_o \mid o_o$ motivates 'does (not) contain the speaker, the hearer, or both'. I denote these by ±author' and ±participant'.

Jointly, as is well-known (Silverstein 1976, Noyer 1992, Kerstens 1993), these features yield tripartition. If a variable ranging over subsets of $\{i, u, o, o', o'', \ldots\}$ is specified as +author' so as to include the author, then saying that it includes a participant is redundant. So, +author' +participant' is the same as +author' alone, the general first person, $i_o i u_o$. Consequently, −author' +participant' is +participant', $i_o i u_o u_o$, with all speaker-including elements removed, hence second person, u_o. Finally, if something excludes the participants, then it excludes the author. So, +author' −participant' is empty and −author' −participant' is the same as −participant' alone, third person, o_o.

To generate the quadripartition, something must be added to the system, and that has generally been taken to be ±hearer', 'does (not) include the hearer' (Hale 1973, Silverstein 1976, Noyer 1992).[1] Exclusive includes the speaker but excludes the hearer; second person, conversely; inclusive includes both; and third person, neither. The positing of a third feature appears both simple and ineluctable.

8.2.2 Problems

The richness of this system may be forced by brute logic, but that does not mean that it is explanatorily appealing. First, the putative primitives of such theories fail a basic criterion of primitivity in that they are logically interdefinable. This problem is demonstrably insoluble. Second, a system with more than two features generates more than two bipartitions and so must be constrained in some way. Though this problem has received attention, the proposed solutions (filters and geometries) are neither theoretically nor empirically satisfactory.

8.2.2.1 Conceptual Problems The most basic issue that these accounts raise is the problem of primitivity. A reasonable expectation of primitives is that they be primitive, in the sense of not being interdefinable. However, ±participant′, ±author′, and ±hearer′ are, in that anything containing a participant contains the speaker or the hearer:

(2) $\lambda x . [\![+\text{participant}']\!](x) = \lambda x . [\![+\text{author}']\!](x) \lor [\![+\text{hearer}']\!](x)$

This makes ±participant′ logically redundant once the latter two features are specified. If ±author′ and ±hearer′ can name everything that ±participant′ does, it is unclear why language would make the last of these available if it has the first two.

This problem is not confined to the three features just given but arises in any account where a proper subset of the features generates the quadripartition. One can think of this subset as "factorizing" $[\![\pi]\!]$ into i_o, iu_o, u_o, and o_o. Any third feature, ±F, can then be redefined by listing the "factors" that +F (or −F) denotes and rewriting each in terms of the features of the quadripartition. For instance, in informal notation, +participant′ = $i_o iu_o u_o$ = +author′ −hearer′ ∨ +author′ +hearer′ ∨ −author′ +hearer′, which is equivalent to (2).[2]

The second, empirical difficulty facing three-feature theories is overgeneration. If singleton systems are admissible, then we expect to find the hearer–nonhearer bipartition $iu_o u_o \,|\, i_o o_o$, generated by ±hearer′ alone. Similarly, if features may occur pairwise, then we expect the tripartition that Zwicky originally problematized, $i_o \,|\, iu_o u_o \,|\, o_o$, generated by ±hearer′ and ±participant′ without ±author′.

In contrast to the problem of primitivity, which has received no comment in the literature, attempts have been made to staunch overgeneration. I do not find them compelling, however, as they amount to extrinsic stipulation of the explicandum, namely, that certain systems are unattested. This is clearest in Noyer 1992, where it was posited, adopting ideas from phonology (Calabrese 1988), that languages can activate, say, a clusivity contrast only if first, second, and third persons are also distinguished. This shifts the explanatory burden without diminishing it: the question becomes why language is subject to those filters and not, say, ones requiring that the clusivity contrast precede the distinction between second and third (making $i_o \mid iu_o \mid u_o o_o$ licit, but $i_o iu_o \mid u_o \mid o_o$ not).

Harley and Ritter 2002a (see also, e.g., Harley and Ritter 2002b, Béjar 2003, Cowper and Hall 2004) pursue a different tack, constraining not the semantic yield of the features, but the features themselves. Again following ideas from phonology (beginning with Sagey 1986), such constraints are called geometries. Harley and Ritter's geometry for person, using privative features, is shown in (3). (Valence is a contentful commitment and privativity, a problematic one; see below.)

(3)   participant′
        ╱   ╲
    author′   hearer′

According to this geometry, the legitimate feature inventories are:

(4) a. ∅
    b. {participant′}
    c. {participant′, author′}
    d. {participant′, hearer′}
    e. {participant′, author′, hearer′}

The illegitimate ones are:[3]

(5) a. {author′}
    b. {hearer′}
    c. {author′, hearer′}

An obvious problem with this structure is that it generates only one one-feature system and, so, only one bipartition. Harley and Ritter (2002a) consider bipartitions only in the context of pronominal systems, where they are, admittedly, rare. But, if the arguments of chapter 7 are convincing, then the geometry requires modification to make it adequate.

Harley and Ritter enrich their geometry in two ways, and these, too, might motivate a search for alternatives. First, they stipulate that a bare participant node, participant′, is interpreted as [[participant′ author′]].[4] This effectively affords author′ two distinct, context-dependent positions in the geometry, as a sister to hearer′ and as a root node. Second, Harley and Ritter posit a combinatorial parameter: languages that activate all three features must further specify whether both dependent features can cooccur, accounting for the difference between quadripartition (coccurrence permitted) and tripartition (cooccurrence barred), an idea reminiscent of Halle's (section 8.2.3). These enrichments are not obviously in harmony with the core geometric idea of a single invariant structure exhausting all cooccurrence restrictions. So, Harley and Ritter's (2002a, 2002b) proposal is best viewed as a hybrid account with geometric underlay, rather than a pure geometry.

For a purely geometric account, one can adopt the nonbranching structure introduced by Béjar (2003, 2008). She proposes a root node, π', and features equivalent to those in (6):

(6)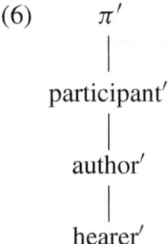

One can interpret the geometry as follows. If, in some domain, a language activates just π', then it has monopartition, assuming $[\![\pi']\!] = i_o i u_o u_o o_o$. If it activates $\{\pi', \text{participant}'\}$, then it has $[\![\pi' \text{participant}']\!] = i_o i u_o u_o$, which restricts $[\![\pi']\!]$ to o_o, by Lexical Complementarity. The result is the participant bipartition. If the top three features are activated, then we have additionally $[\![\pi' \text{participant}' \text{author}']\!] = i_o i u_o$. This restricts $[\![\pi \text{participant}']\!]$ to u_o, resulting in tripartition. Finally, use of the whole structure adds a clusivity contrast, as $[\![\pi' \text{participant}' \text{author}' \text{hearer}']\!] = i u_o$ and restricts $[\![\pi' \text{participant}' \text{author}']\!]$ to i_o.

The only deficiency in this geometry is that it derives only one bipartition: author' is too deeply embedded for the author bipartition to emerge. Two solutions (at least) are imaginable. First, one can make author' a direct dependent of π':

(7)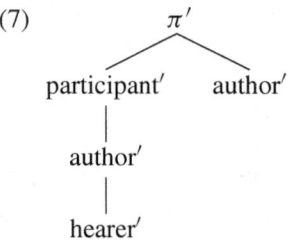

This has the unattractive consequence of repeating a feature within a single geometry. One can escape this, though, by replacing the lower occurrence with a distinct feature, not-just-you′ (see note 1). Then ⟦π′ participant′ not-just-you′⟧ removes u_o ('just you') from ⟦π′ participant′⟧ = $i_o i u_o u_o$, leaving $i_o i u_o$. This makes not-just-you′ interchangeable with the lower occurrence of author′ in (7). The following geometry (or this structure with unique-participant′ of note 1 for hearer′) then captures the correct combinatorial stipulations, free from repetition:

(8)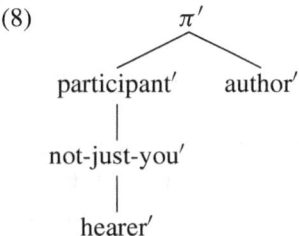

Obviously, though, the cost is an increase in the feature inventory. In contrast to my account, which uses only the two features needed for the two bipartitions, the current approach requires two more.

A more parsimonious inventory is possible if the features are assumed to be bivalent. Specifically, one can posit (9), or the same structure with ±unique-participant′ for ±hearer′:

(9)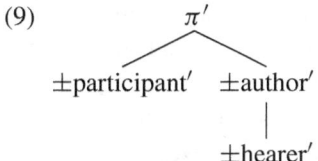

The systems that this generates are all attested: {π′}, the monopartition; {π′, ±participant′} and {π′, ±author′}, the two bipartitions; {π′, ±participant′, ±author′}, the tripartition; and {π′, (±participant′), ±author′, ±hearer′}, two different means of specifying the quadripartition. The systems ruled out involve ±hearer′ without ±author′: namely, {π′, ±hearer′}, the hearer–nonhearer bipartition; and {π′, ±hearer′, ±participant′}, Zwicky's system in which inclusive and second person are conflated to the exclusion of the other two persons, exclusive and third.

A privative version of (9) is inadmissible, as it generates the unattested system {π′, author′, hearer′}. This corresponds to the illegitimate tripartition $i_o \mid i u_o \mid u_o o_o$: ⟦π′⟧ = $i_o i u_o u_o o_o$, but is restricted to $u_o o_o$, because ⟦π′ author′⟧ = $i_o i u_o$, and this, in turn, is restricted to i_o, because ⟦π′ author′ hearer′⟧ = $i u_o$. The same consideration rules out a version of (7) that attempts to avoid repetition by making author′ a direct dependent both of the root node and of participant′:

(10)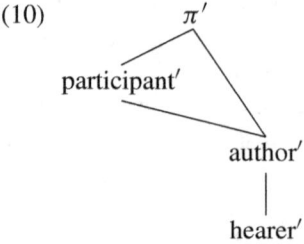

This permits a language to activate everything except participant′, generating the unattested system just described.

The foregoing shows that descriptively adequate (pure) geometries exist. Notwithstanding, I do not think that we should entertain them. First, they do not constitute explanations. Just like Noyer's filters, they shift the explanatory burden without diminishing it. In fact, this shift might put person beyond the pale of the explicable entirely. To explain, and not just generate, the inventory of possible persons, geometers must account for why their proposed geometry is the one that language uses. By Cayley's theorem, there are $(n+1)^{n-1}$ geometries for n features and a root node, excluding the "looped" structures of (10). Hence, the bivalent geometry (9) is one of 16 possibilities, and the privative (8) is one of 125.

The task here is not to show that the 15 or 124 unused arrangements generate the wrong inventory of persons, but to show that no other geometry is possible. I do not know what this kind of explanation could look like, and geometers might simply have to claim that one can only describe the structure of person systems, not offer explanations of the sort sought, traditionally, in generative grammar. The same applies to number and any other domain for which geometries might be proposed. (See Harbour and Elsholtz 2011 for more detail.)

A similar problem arises for the inventory of features. As observed several times above, one can substitute features within a given geometry without altering the empirical yield; for instance, author′ for not-just-you′ in (7) and (8), or ±unique-participant′ for ±hearer′ in (9). A proponent of (9) might legitimately be asked why language uses ±hearer′, not the alternative.

This question is made more pointed by the issue of nonprimitive primitives and its plausible corollary within geometries: ±participant′ is definable in terms of ±author′ and ±hearer′, but ±hearer′ is not definable in terms of ±author′ and ±participant′ (these last two features do not "factorize" $[\![\pi]\!]$ completely and so do not split iu_o from i_o and make it available for defining +hearer′). So, if geometries reflect entailment, ±participant′ should be the

Table 8.1

Hearer–nonhearer syncretism in Kiowa

	INTR	REFL	__:3P	__:3INV	__:3S:3P	__:3S:3INV
1EX/3	e	ét	ét*	ét	égîi*	édâw*
1IN/2	ba	bé	bát*	bét	bágîi*	báudâw*

subordinate, contrary to what is posited in (8)–(9). Alternatively, if geometries reverse entailment, placing more specific below less specific, then (8) is defensible, but (9) is still not.

None of these issues arise for the account of the previous chapters. There are no combinatorial constraints, so no issues of unexplanatoriness. And no extra features are called for beyond those that the bipartitions motivate. Moreover, the features themselves plausibly reflect natural divisions of the social ontology, solipsistic $\mathscr{L}_{au}$ and interactional $\mathscr{L}_{pt}$ (see chapter 9 for further discussion).

8.2.2.2 Empirical Problems Previous accounts (Hale 1973, Silverstein 1976, Noyer 1992, Halle 1997, Frampton 2002, Harley and Ritter 2002a, 2002b) have taken second person and inclusive to form a natural class. This is a position that I share. It is, however, one that is difficult to replicate with the correct empirical consequences within the geometries above.

Of course, in the bivalent geometry (9), second and inclusive are the natural class defined by +hearer′. The difficulty here concerns maintenance of this class, and its complement, in the face of feature deletion. Table 8.1 presents various Kiowa agreement prefixes: intransitive, reflexive, transitive with plural and inverse objects, and ditransitive with plural and inverse objects plus a third singular goal (inverse is singular for some nouns, plural for others; * denotes tone lowering of the subsequent verb, and *aw*, the long counterpart of *au*). These prefixes, and other (di)transitive ones, show the systematic syncretism between −hearer′ 1EX–3 and +hearer′ 1IN–2 that was originally illustrated in figure 2.3 for intransitive subject agreement.

The obvious way to capture this syncretism is by deletion of ±author′. If the quadripartition of person is generated by ±author′ and ±hearer′, and if ±author′ is deleted (in the relevant contexts), then ±hearer′ remains, yielding the natural classes of table 8.1.

However, since their importation into morphology (Bonet 1991), geometries have been taken to constrain operations like deletion: when a superordinate feature is deleted, all subordinate ones go with it (again, following phonological precedent, in this case, delinking). In (9), ±author′ is superordinate to ±hearer′. So, removal of ±author′ entails removal of ±hearer′ and collapses 1EX–3 and 1IN–2 into a single undifferentiated monosyncretism. Thus, deletion destroys what it is deployed to create.

If morphological manipulations do not account for the identity between 1EX and 3 and that between 1IN and 2, then the structure of the exponents or the actions of phonology must. Neither is plausible.

The structure of exponence can create identity in two ways. First, one exponent might be a default. The obvious implementation is to claim that the person that collapses with third receives default exponence. However, there is no reason to expect default exponence for exclusive, given the first person d that occurs in, say, the singular reflexive de and the nonsingular benefactives, such as the possessor-of-singular $dáu$. (Rather, deletion to bleed insertion of d looks more plausible.) Nor is b a plausible default, as it occurs only for +hearer′ (reemerging for nonsingular benefactives, like the possessor-of-singular $báu$). Specifically, it fails to emerge as a default when nothing else does (for instance, if the agent of the ditransitive prefixes in table 8.1 is changed to the third animate, then the first part vanishes, leaving, by regular phonology, just $gyâa*$ and $dâw*$, with no sign of the putative default b).[5]

The alternative, accidental homophony, is also implausible, as it would have to be very accidental, given how thoroughgoing the phenomenon in table 8.1 is in Kiowa. In fact, it leans in the direction of a metaparadigmatic effect, which, if we follow Bobaljik 2002, Frampton 2002, and Harley 2008, points again to impoverishment.

On my account, impoverishment faces no obstacle. With no dependencies between features, one can delete ±author, leaving just the −participant class 1EX/3 and the +participant class 1IN/2.

The privative geometry (8), too, can escape this dilemma. Given second person [π' participant′], exclusive [π' participant′ not-just-you′ (author′)], and inclusive [π' participant′ not-just-you′ hearer′ (author′)], one can make inclusive identical to second person by deleting not-just-you′ and hearer′ (and author′), and then make exclusive identical to third by deleting participant′ and not-just-you′ (and author′). (These would be intrinsically ordered as just given, because hearer′ is the rarest feature, making that deletion the more specific one.)

However, this geometry faces difficulties with the very first facts of chapter 5, the compositional inclusive of Bislama. Exclusive and second person are substructures of inclusive, so occurrence of exclusive mi and second yu in inclusive $yumi$ is explicable. However, second person is also a substructure of exclusive, which ought, then, to include yu as well; and any impoverishment that bleeds yu from exclusive must also mention features that make up inclusive and, so, bleed it there too.[6] As discussed in the next chapter, converse cases, where exclusive subsumes inclusive (as in Limbu and Nyawaygi; sections 5.2.2 and 9.5.2) are also problematic for privative inventories like (8).

So, in addition to the theoretical problems that geometries engender, they create empirical ones too, which an ageometric two-feature account avoids.

8.2.3 Alternative

The problems above stem from positing a third (or fourth) feature. So, it is worth revisiting two-feature proposals. The crosslinguistic adequacy of such systems has been defended in several ways. For instance, Bobaljik (2008), Kratzer (2009), and Wechsler (2010) all propose ($\pm$)author' and ($\pm$)hearer'. But this entrains three problems. First, the features generate a hearer bipartition. Second, they generate no participant bipartition. Third, the tripartition must be achieved by some extra device. For instance, Wechsler represents general first person as author' (hearer'), which necessitates an additional stipulation to rule out (author') hearer', the inclusive-cum-second person that concerned Zwicky. As a result, if two conjunction-based features are to work, they must be somewhat innovative.

The only attempt at such innovation that I am aware of is Halle's (1997): he proposes parametric deactivation of one feature combination. For this approach to not simply involve post hoc combinatorial stipulations on a par with filters and geometries, one needs to show that the deactivated feature combination is a semantically natural choice. Thus, the feature semantics of this proposal are crucial. However, Halle does not supply them, and the core idea, despite its elegance, resists compositional implementation.

Table 8.2 shows a version of Halle's proposal, that tripartition differs from quadripartition via a parameterized cooccurrence restriction (Harley and Ritter (2002a) implement the same idea in a very different way). Halle names the features, suggestively, $\pm$author-of-speech-event' and $\pm$participant-in-speech-event'. However, for the plus–minus combination to be coherent, the definitions must differ from those of $\pm$author' and $\pm$participant', for which plus–minus is empty: +author' −participant' includes the author while excluding author and hearer. Rather than seek suitable names in the absence of definitions, I dub the features simply $\pm$P' and $\pm$Q'.

For the proposal to work, something must catch the semantic slack when the plus–minus restriction is active, or else English, say, would have no way to refer to what that combination denotes (i_o in the table, but all the reasoning below applies if iu_o is chosen instead). Therefore, I have assumed that the plus–plus combination denotes both iu_o and i_o. So, if plus–minus is deactivated, we have an English-style general first person, and, otherwise, Lexical Complementarity trims plus–plus from $i_o iu_o$ to i_o.

Table 8.2

A Hallean approach to partitions

±P′	±Q′	Tripartition	Quadripartition
+P′	+Q′	$i_o iu_o$	$i_o iu_o \equiv iu_o$
+P′	−Q′	(parametrically deactivated)	i_o
−P′	+Q′	u_o	u_o
−P′	−Q′	o_o	o_o

Table 8.3

Possible implementations of Halle's idea

	−Q′ ⊂ +Q′ +Q′ = $i_o iu_o u_o o_o$ −Q′ = o_o	+Q′ ∩ −Q′ = ∅ +Q′ = $i_o iu_o u_o$ −Q′ = o_o	+Q′ ⊂ −Q′ +Q′ = $i_o iu_o u_o$ −Q′ = $i_o iu_o u_o o_o$
+P′ ⊂ −P′ +P′ = $i_o iu_o$ −P′ = $i_o iu_o u_o o_o$	}	+P′ ∩ −Q′ = ∅ $i_o iu_o \cap o_o = ∅$	+P′ ∩ +Q′ = +P′ ∩ −Q′ = $i_o iu_o$
+P′ ∩ −P′ = ∅ +P′ = $i_o iu_o$ −P′ = $u_o o_o$	}		
−P′ ⊂ +P′ +P′ = $i_o iu_o u_o o_o$ −P′ = $u_o o_o$		+P′ ∩ −Q′ = −P′ ∩ −Q′ = o_o	+P′ ∩ −Q′ ≡ −P′ ∩ −Q′ ≡ o_o

If Halle's features require Lexical Complementarity in the quadripartition, then at least one must require it in the bipartition too.[7] This means that there are three options to consider for each feature: either the denotation of the plus value subsumes that of the minus value, or vice versa, or they are disjoint. Table 8.3 lays out the possibilities.

The table, which admittedly appears complex, is best explained by considering a specific cell, say, the top right. The rightmost values for ±Q′ state that +Q′ is a subset of −Q′. This means that +Q′ has the usual denotation of +participant′, $i_o iu_o u_o$, but −Q′ denotes the superset $i_o iu_o u_o o_o$. Lexical complementarity restricts this to −Q′\+Q′ = o_o, so that the participant bipartition still results. Similarly, the topmost values for ±P′ state that +P′ denotes a subset of −P′. This sets +P′ to the usual denotation of +author′, $i_o iu_o$, and −P′ to something larger: $i_o iu_o u_o$, or $i_o iu_o o_o$, or $i_o iu_o u_o o_o$. Of these, only the last induces the full author bipartition (the first, for instance, induces the defective "partition" $i_o iu_o o_o \mid i_o iu_o \equiv o_o \mid i_o iu_o$).

By considering all 3×3 combinations of subsumption and disjointness between the values of $\pm P'$ and $\pm Q'$, the table exhausts the ways of inducing both bipartitions. The crucial question for the viability of Halle's proposal is whether any of the nine yields the quadripartition (and, if so, whether one value combination can be deactivated, in a principled fashion, to yield the tripartition).

The internal part of the table shows that no set of definitions works, as all fall foul of two criteria. First, quadripartitions require four distinct values, so no combinations of values can deliver the same persons. This criterion rules out the example two paragraphs higher, as $+P +Q' = i_o i u_o = +P -Q'$. All of the rightmost column and the bottom row fail for the same reason. Second, quadripartitions require four nonnull values, so no combination can deliver the empty set. This rules out the inner four cells, for which $+P -Q' = i_o i u_o \cap o_o = \varnothing$.

As a result, no set of values for two features is able to deliver a semantically compositional, conjunction-based implementation of Halle's person features.

8.2.4 Summary

Brute necessity has traditionally been the driving force behind positing three features, in conjunction-based accounts. Two privative or bivalent features can generate at most four feature combinations, hence, at most a quadripartition. So, to have both a tripartition and a quadripartition, one needs at least three features, two for the tripartition and two for the quadripartition; or, following Halle 1997, one needs a different means of deriving the variation. However, the foregoing has shown that all of these encounter problems: three-feature accounts overgenerate, and the means for trimming the excess (filters, geometries) are unexplanatory and empirically problematic; and Halle's parameterization resists semantically compositional implementation. I conclude that the demands of typological variation are better met within the nonconjunctive two-feature account than in alternative systems.

8.3 Intralinguistic Adequacy

If crosslinguistic considerations do not weigh in favor of three-feature accounts that conjunctive inventories precipitate, then language-specific studies might do so instead. In actuality, though, one rarely encounters cases for a hearer feature or for simultaneous use of three features. This section addresses the more compelling ones that I can find.

Two arguments for the existence of the hearer feature are Noyer's (1992) treatment of Mam and Watanabe's (2013) treatment of Fula. However, these analyses readily transpose into the current system, on substituting ±participant for ±hearer′ (section 8.3.1). A similar substitution, exploiting the alternative representation for third person, −participant(+author(π)), enables one to replicate Frampton's (2002) treatment of Germanic, which also relies on a hearer feature in its original formulation.

A greater challenge comes from languages that seem to demand reference to more natural classes than ±author and ±participant alone permit. Trommer's (2008) analysis of Menominee is a rare instance of this, as is his briefer treatment of Dumi. Nonetheless, the challenge that his work poses can be met within the current system, given the independent need for variables over values or features (section 8.3.2).

8.3.1 Transposable Arguments

Addressing quadripartition in rather different languages, Noyer (1992) and Watanabe (2013) converge on the view that the hearer feature is bivalent. If bivalent, the feature ipso facto exists. So, these studies present a challenge for the current, more minimal feature inventory.

However, this bind relents on closer inspection. As shown below, Noyer's and Watanabe's conclusion is really that the feature that joins with ±author to generate quadripartition must be bivalent. In consequence, their arguments are not about the hearer feature per se, but about valence of the nonauthor feature. Given table 8.4, which shows that ±hearer′ in conjunction-based accounts takes the same value as my ±participant feature for every person of the quadripartition, any analysis in terms of one can be directly transposed into an analysis in terms of the other.

Addressing preponderant syncretisms in the tripartite persons of Germanic, Frampton (2002) posits a slightly different feature that is, nonetheless, hearer-centered. However, Frampton's argument can be reconstrued as concerning natural classes of feature values, not feature semantics per se. When so construed, it, too, can be rephrased in terms of the features of the current proposal.

Table 8.4

Isomorphism of two two-feature quadripartitions

{±author′, ±hearer′}		{±author, ±participant}
+author′ +hearer′	1IN	+author +participant
+author′ −hearer′	1EX	+author −participant
−author′ +hearer′	2	−author +participant
−author′ −hearer′	3	−author −participant

Table 8.5

A composed exclusive in Mam possessives ('cat')

Possessor		Singular	Plural
1EX	+author′ −hearer′	n-wīxh-a	q-wīxh-a̱
1IN	+author′ +hearer′		q-wīxh
2	−author′ +hearer′	t-wīxh-a	ky-wīxh-a
3	−author′ −hearer′	t-wīxh	ky-wīxh

8.3.1.1 Mam Transposition is very straightforward for Noyer's (1992) treatment of Mam. The empirical focus here is the enclitic *a*. As evident from table 8.5, *a* occurs for exclusive, +author′ −hearer′, and second person, −author′ +hearer′, in both the singular and the plural. This is not obviously a semantically natural class. However, Noyer observes that these are the persons for which ±author′ and ±hearer′ are oppositely specified. So, he concludes that, if *a* is a single exponent, then its specification must be αauthor′ ᾱhearer′.

England (1983), on whose description of Mam Noyer relies, does not herself suppose that all these *a*'s are the same, citing data from related languages in which the four enclitics are phonologically distinct. Tacaná (Western Mam), for instance, has Ø for 1S, *o'* for 1EX.P, *a(')* for 2S, and *e'* for 2P. And Noyer, too, seems to draw his conclusion tentatively, noting that nothing rules out the existence of two homophonous *a*'s, the first for exclusive, the second for second. I share both authors' tentativity, but observe that, if it is correct, Noyer's analysis is replicable within the current approach. Given table 8.4, we can simply substitute features and write *a* ⇔ αauthor ᾱparticipant.

8.3.1.2 Fula Watanabe's (2013) argument from Fula essentially yields to the same rewrite, but Watanabe adduces some additional considerations in favor of a hearer-based approach, which I address below. The argument is based on the different patterns of linearization of Fula agreement affixes. According to Arnott (1970), these vary between prefixes and suffixes, for some person–number combinations, depending on clause type and subjunctivity. The majority pattern is prefixal, irrespective of person and number (table 8.6, left). However, in interrogatives and relative clauses, inclusive and second are suffixal (middle), and in the subjunctive, so is first singular (right).

Watanabe's purpose is to argue against accounts that posit a privative hearer feature, either as part of across-the-board privativity (Harley and Ritter 2002a, Béjar 2003, Cowper and Hall 2004, Kratzer 2006, Řezáč 2008) or in conjunction with bivalent features (Harbour 2006, Nevins 2007). Given that privative hearer′ correlates with bivalent +hearer′, Watanabe's tack is to demonstrate a sensitivity in Fula to −hearer′. To that end, he argues for a prefixation operation that creates the variable affixality in table 8.6 and that is sometimes so sensitized.

Watanabe takes the suffixal position to be the default locus of agreement in Fula, as the language is SVO but bears the morphological hallmarks of V-to-T movement in that tense, negation, and other categories are suffixes to the verb. Consequently, he takes agreement prefixes to arise in the morphology (by local dislocation; Embick and Noyer 2001). Generally, the operation affects all phi combinations (table 8.6, left), but where prefixation is phi-sensitive, Watanabe proposes that the dislocation is contextualized. The details of this contextualization lead to the conclusion that the hearer feature is bivalent.

The case is most obvious for the middle table. If prefixation is contextualized to affect just persons containing −hearer′, then it moves just exclusive and third person, as desired. In the rightmost table, where the prefixed persons (1EX.P, 3S, 3P) do not correspond to a featurally natural class, Watanabe's solution is to create one, by deletion of −hearer′ from 1S, +author′ −hearer′ +atomic. If deletion precedes dislocation, then only the three persons still specified for −hearer′ are prefixed, as desired. Thus, a commitment to feature-sensitive prefixation entrains an argument for bivalence of ±hearer′.

Readers may differ in how compelling they find this. If one rejects the claim that suffixation is the default locus and views prefixation as default, then a privative analysis is possible: in relative and subjunctive tenses, hearer′ arguments are suffixed (1IN.P, 2S, 2P); and, in the subjunctive, a second dislocation affects just first singular.[8]

But, alternatives aside, Watanabe's analysis does not present any problems for the current account. Substituting −participant for his −hearer′, we prefix all −participant persons in the middle table (1S, 1EX.P, 3S, 3P), but, in the rightmost, we delete −participant from 1S, so it remains suffixal and only 1EX.P, 3S, 3P are prefixed.

Table 8.6

Varieties of linearization in Fula paradigms

	Singular	Plural	Singular	Plural	Singular	Plural
1EX	mi-	min-	mi-	min-	-mi	min-
1IN		'en-		-en		-den
2	'a-	'on-	-aa	-on	-daa	-don
3	'o-	ɓe-	'o-	ɓe-	'o-	ɓe-

Watanabe offers a conceptual argument for his feature deletion. In the first singular, +author′ −hearer′ +atomic, the feature −hearer′ is redundant: if one knows that a singleton set contains i, then one knows that it excludes u; that is, +atomic and +author′ jointly entail −hearer′. Watanabe concludes that the feature deleted in the subjunctive is a natural one to lose. He ties this to Nevins's (2011) account of markedness-targeting and markedness-triggered impoverishment, but the connection is not obvious: entailed features could reasonably be considered the least marked of all, and so the least subject to deletion in Nevins's terms. For the naturalness rationale to be compelling, it would need to be supplemented by further crosslinguistic study of entailed features.

This question notwithstanding, one can again reconstitute a version of the argument in terms of the current account, should one wish to. Semantically, the denotation of the author feature alone is $\mathscr{L}_{au}$, or, more simply, just i, like the first person singular. (This has the appearance of a privative feature, but it is just the author lattice; whether languages use this representation requires proper study of underspecification within the current theory.) If the subjunctive triggers deletion of information that is semantically extraneous to the denotation i, then it triggers deletion of ±participant. So stripped, 1s would be overlooked by a −participant-sensitive prefixation process and would emerge as a suffix.[9]

As the cases of Mam and Fula illustrate, the current two-feature approach to person can readily accommodate arguments for a hearer feature if they are, in reality, arguments for the bivalence of the feature that joins with ±author to create quadripartitions.

8.3.1.3 Germanic A different argument for a hearer-like feature comes from second–nonsecond syncretisms in Germanic (Frampton 2002). The treatment of like syncretisms within a quadripartition was discussed for Kiowa in section 8.2.2. A $1 = 3 \neq 2$ syncretism looks particularly surprising, given the discussion under the $1 + 3 = 2$ rubric (section 5.3.2), which argued that second person forms natural classes both with first and with third. However, that discussion exploited the monotonic, minus–minus representation of third person, whereas Germanic, I will now suggest, may exploit the alternative, nonmonotonic representation for third person, −participant +author (section 4.3.4). This shifts the structure of natural classes and makes nonsecond syncretism readily available, which is the nub of Frampton's argument.

A recurrent and diachronically robust feature of the Germanic languages is the syncretism between first and third person verb inflection. In German, for instance, it affects all plurals, as well as singulars of modal verbs and of regular

Table 8.7
Hearer–nonhearer syncretism in German

Person	Present		Preterite	
	can (MOD)	walk (reg.)	walk (irreg.)	buy (reg.)
1S	kann	lauf-e	lief	kauf-te
2S	kann-st	läuf-st	lief-st	kauf-te-st
3S	kann	läuf-t	lief	kauf-te
1P	könn-en	lauf-en	lief-en	kauf-te-n
2P	könn-t	lauf-t	lief-t	kauf-te-t
3P	könn-en	lauf-en	lief-en	kauf-te-n

(suffixal) and irregular (ablauting) preterites (table 8.7). The same pattern holds for different exponents in other Germanic languages, as in the singular preterite of Anglo-Saxon 'be' (*wæs, wǣre, wæs*; Sweet 1896) and of the Gothic passive of 'call' (*háitada, háitaza, háitada*; Wright 1899).

Given this metaparadigmaticity and diachronic durability, Frampton argues that something more robust than a mere conspiracy of homophony must be at work. Like Bobaljik (2002) and Harley (2008), he takes this to be an impoverishment that renders first and third identical prior to exponence.

To achieve this, Frampton posits two features, ±author′ and the equivalent to ±just-you′.[10] As a result, he has the following person specifications (plus–plus is empty, as it stipulates both inclusion and exclusion of the author):

(11) 1 +author′ −just-you′
    2 −author′ +just-you′
    3 −author′ −just-you′

Here, first and third are the natural class defined by −just-you′. To force the syncretism, Frampton posits deletion of ±author′ in various contexts (for table 8.7, these would be modality, the preterite, and plural). The result is identity between first and third, −just-you′, both of which are distinct from second, +just-you′. So long as this impoverishment is in force, the syncretism will persist through changes in exponents.

This natural class, and the identity-forcing impoverishment, cannot be replicated in my system if first person is +author +participant, and third, −author −participant. One could posit an alpha-sensitivity, claiming that first and third form a natural class in virtue of being αauthor αparticipant. However, the idea is not overly plausible if one considers the exponents of this putative pairing

Table 8.8
Partial isomorphism of two tripartitions

Frampton	Person	Current
+author′ −just-you′	1	+participant +author
−author′ +just-you′	2	+participant −author
−author′ −just-you′	3	−participant +author

in, say, German: zero in the singular and *en* in the plural. Crosslinguistically, lack of marking often correlates with unremarkable features; and *en*, too, looks like an unmarked morpheme, as it also occurs in infinitives, like *lauf-en* 'to walk' (and, in Yiddish, in the pseudoinfinitives of predicate clefts, like *iz-n* 'is-EN'; Hoge 1998). So, these putative exponence relations would pair marked (alpha-sensitive) values with unmarked forms. Consequently, the approach is not compelling.

However, my account permits a second representation of third person in tripartitions, −participant(+author(π)). I have assumed that languages disprefer this, as it is nonmonotone: removing all participants involves removing the author, so an outer −participant is more "harmonic" with an inner −author than with +author. But this does not rule −participant +author out. It merely means that learners might need evidence for positing it. The Germanic patterns may be precisely what is needed. If so, this makes first and third the natural class of +author (table 8.8), and Frampton's analysis in terms of ±author′ deletion can now be transposed as ±participant deletion and his exponents for ±just-you′ can be rewritten as exponents for ±author.[11]

If the nonmonotonic representation of third person requires special evidence, then we expect hearer–nonhearer syncretisms to be less frequent, in tripartitions, than participant–nonparticipant and author–nonauthor syncretisms. This is consistent with typological findings (Baerman, Brown, and Corbett 2005). And the current approach is strengthened if we can find languages that exploit all the options it provides, including the subsidiary parameter of two third person representations.

8.3.2 Untransposable Arguments

More challenging arguments for a three-feature inventory are offered by Trommer's (2008) study of Menominee and its in-passing treatment of Dumi. Given that both languages have clusivity contrasts, they must use ±author′ and ±hearer′. Although ±participant′ does not add further person distinctions to the system, Trommer argues that its presence can be detected: in Menominee, in a verbal suffix that displays a third-over-nonthird preference when all arguments of the verb are animate; and, in Dumi, in a verbal prefix that registers, among other things, the presence of a nonthird person argument.

The challenge for two-feature systems, like mine (or those of Halle 1997 or Déchaine 1999, to which Trommer's paper is in part a reaction), is to characterize these sensitivities without recourse to a feature that makes a natural class of exclusive, inclusive, and second in a quadripartition. This can be met by allowing variables over values or features, devices that are independently motivated by other phenomena, such as the inverse number system of Kiowa (Harbour 2007b, 2011c), illustrated below.

8.3.2.1 Menominee

The Menominee suffix on which Trommer (2008) focuses follows the root in intransitive verbs and follows the voice marker of transitives, which shows which of two agreeing arguments acts on the other. Besides its sensitivity to (animate) third persons, its form depends on whether the verb is in the "conjunct order" or "independent order," to use Algonquianist terminology (the conjunct order, glossed C, occurs in relative clauses and like environments; Brittain 2001). In third person intransitives, and in third-on-third transitives, we find w, glossed $\exists 3$, or, in "conjunct" contexts, t, glossed $\exists 3.C$; these affixes occur for animates and inanimates, singular and nonsingular, obviative and nonobviative, and irrespective of "theme."[12] The following illustrate the key opposition for an intransitive (12) and a transitive (13):

(12) a. *po·se- w*
    embark-$\exists 3$
    'he embarks'
 b. *po·se- t*
    embark-$\exists 3$.C
    'when he embarks'

(13) a. *na·n- ɛ·- w*
    fetch-THM-$\exists 3$
    'he fetches him.OBV'
 b. *nɛ·w-a·- c- en*[13]
    see- THM-$\exists 3$.C-EN
    'when he sees him.OBV'

When these same verbs exclude third persons, we find instead m, ¬$\exists 3$, or *yan*, ¬$\exists 3$.C:

(14) a. *nelke-po·se- m*
    1/2- embark-¬$\exists 3$
    'I/you embark'

b. *po·se- yan*
   embark-¬∃3.C
   'when I/you embark'

(15) a. *ke-nɛ·w-e- m- waw*
     2- see- THM-¬∃3-2P/3P
     'you.P see me'
   b. *nɛ·w-e- yan*
     see- THM-¬∃3.C
     'when you.S see me'

The facts relevant to Trommer's argument involve transitives that mix third and nonthird arguments. If the third person is animate, *w* and *t* are used, not *m* or *yan*:[14]

(16) a. *ne-na·n- ek- w*
     1- fetch-THM-∃3
     'he fetches me'
   b. *nɛ·w-e- t*
     see- THM-∃3.C
     'when he sees me'

(17) *ne-na·n- a·- w*
     1- fetch-THM-∃3
     'I fetch him'

In other words, the suffix seems preferentially to agree with a third person over a nonthird person, which, as Trommer observes, is a strange reversal of crosslinguistic markedness tendencies.

Clearly, with a feature ±participant′, one can capture the preference for *w*/*t* over *m*/*yan* by saying that the suffix has a (syntactic or morphological) preference for −participant′ over +participant′. Equally, though, a two-feature system can treat *w* and *t* as exponents of −author −participant and *m*/*yan* as defaults. For instance, for the matrix forms, one could posit:

(18) $w \Leftrightarrow [_v -\text{author} -\text{participant}]$
     $m \Leftrightarrow [_v \ ]$

However, Trommer argues that the latter position faces a "fatal" flaw: there is another exponent, *n* (and its related conjunct form *k*) that demands to be analyzed as a default and, therefore, precludes treatment of *m* and *yan* as elsewhere items.

This *n*, the "indefinite actor" affix, occurs for unspecified subjects:

(19) a. *po·se- n*
     embark-IMPRS
     'there is embarking'

b. p⟨ay⟩o·se- h- k- en
⟨ITER⟩embark-PASS-IMPRS.C-ITER
'whenever there is embarking'

From a semantic point of view, an indefinite actor is more likely to correspond to a person-free head than a first or second person is. Moreover, *n* is nearly ubiquitous in the negative. Conjunct forms lack affixal negation, but some independent-order examples are:

(20) kan o·-po·se- n- an
NEG 3- embark-IMPRS-NEG
'he does not embark'

(21) kan ke-po·se- n- owa·w-an
NEG 2- embark-IMPRS-2P/3P- NEG
'you.P do not embark'

(22) kan ne-nɛ·w-a·- n- an
NEG 1- see- THM-IMPRS-NEG
'I do not see him'

(23) kan ke-nɛ·w-a·- n- owaw- an
NEG 2- see- THM-IMPRS-2P/3P-NEG
'you.S/P do not see them', 'you.P do not see him'

IMPRS is, possibly, not the best gloss, as these verbs are by no means impersonal. But the crucial point is that *n*, here, occurs in verbs with an animate argument, to the total exclusion of *m* and near total exclusion of *w* (which occurs only for inanimate combinations). In his own analysis of Menominee, Trommer assumes that *n* (and *k*) realize an empty v head, [$_v$]. Needless to say, this precludes *m* from having this same specification, as in (18).

Despite this lengthy exposition of the problem (Algonquian, like Yimas, demands exegetic exertion), a relatively straightforward solution is possible using just two features. The key lies in making *m* (and *yan*) default for the features ±author and ±participant, rather than for the head v. That is, leaving conjunct forms aside, one can posit:

(24) $w \Leftrightarrow$ [$_v$ −author −participant]
$m \Leftrightarrow$ [$_v$ ±author ±participant]
$n \Leftrightarrow$ [$_v$]

As per Trommer's account, *w* is strictly third person and *n* is radically underspecified; *m*, though, is of intermediate specificity. Both *w* and *m* mention the same two features, but *w* mentions specific values, where *m* simply hoovers up the rest. So *m* is less specific than *w*. Yet, because it mentions some features, as opposed to *n*, which mentions none, *m* is more specific than *n*. As represented, *m* could realize any person, but the existence of a more highly specified exponent for third restricts *m* to exclusive, inclusive, and second, as desired.[15]

Two observations about this solution are in order. First, it relies on the idea that an exponent can be sensitive to features without being concerned about particular values. This same device was argued to operate in Georgian (section 5.4.2; cf, Béjar and Hall 1999), where *t* realizes plurality for both +participant first and second and −participant (dative) third persons. Second, the specification of *m* in (24) is essentially equivalent to αauthor βparticipant, where α and β are variables over the values + and −. Early works of generative grammar posited such variables (Chomsky and Halle 1968), and arguments for them persist (see Harbour 2013 for a summary of several, focusing on phi features).

8.3.2.2 Dumi The complement to variables over values is variables over features. Trommer (2008) presents a second argument for a three-feature inventory, based on the distribution of the verbal prefix *a* of the Kiranti language Dumi. According to van Driem (1993, 123), "all scenarios involving a first or second person actant except those with a first person agent or subject" require *a*. That is, *a* appears for 2:1EX, 3:1(IN/EX), 3:2, 2:3, and for second person intransitives:[16]

(25) *a- luph- ɨ*
 A-catch-1EX.D
 'you/they caught us.EX.D'

(26) *a- phɨkhi-i*
 A-get.up-1IN.D
 'they get us.IN.D up'

(27) *a- luph- i*
 A-catch-D
 'they caught you.D', 'you.D caught them'

(28) *a- phɨkhi-i*
 A-get.up-D
 'you.D got up'

For other transitives and intransitives, there is no prefix:

(29) *luph- ɨ*
 catch-1EX.D
 'we.EX.D caught you/them'

(30) *luph- i*
    catch-1IN.D
    'we.IN.D caught you/them'

(31) *lup- si*
    catch-3D
    'they.D caught them.D'

(32) *phikhi-i*
    get.up-D
    'we.D / they.D got up'

Trommer observes that two conditions must be met for *a* to occur: the highest argument (agent of transitive or subject of intransitive) must be second or third person, and at least one argument must be nonthird. He captures the latter condition as a sensitivity to −participant′, which constitutes a potential argument for a richer person system.

An alternative is available with just two features, though. In the quadripartition, only third person has a purely negative person specification, −author −participant. All other persons contain +author or +participant. Letting F be a variable over person features, we can restate Trommer's two conditions on *a* as: the highest argument must contain −author, and some argument must contain +F.

Again, the device of variables over features has been posited before. Specifically, in Harbour 2007b, 2011c (see also Watanabe 2014), I rely on these to capture inverse number in Kiowa, that is, the phenomenon whereby one and the same suffix pluralizes some nouns (*pól* 'bug.S/D', *pów-dáu* 'bug.P'), singularizes others (*áa* 'tree.D/P', *áa-dau* 'tree.S'), and dedualizes yet others (*ául* 'hair.D', *áw-dáu* 'hair.S/P').

Following Noyer 1992, and like ideas in earlier descriptive work, the account in Harbour (2007b, 2011c) affords number features a dual role in Kiowa: they count, like normal number features on ω, but also occur, like gender features, on a classifying head, say, γ. These separate uses can lead to conflicting values, with ω bearing, say, +F and γ, −F. Such conflicts are what are pronounced as inverse number. Crucially, they can arise either for F = atomic or for F = minimal. So, an inverse suffix like *dau* is the exponent of +F −F, where F is a variable over number features.

In sum, Trommer is right that Menominee and Dumi are challenging for two-feature theories. However, positing a third feature is not the only way of meeting those challenges. Variables over values can capture the relevant facts for Menominee, as can variables over features, for Dumi. These devices have motivation independent of their use here and, unlike third features, they do not raise the problems discussed in section 8.2.2. So, the current theory picks up Trommer's gauntlet.

8.4 The Challenge of Mixed Partitions

A further test for the descriptive range of the current theory arises in languages where agreement is not uniformly tripartite or quadripartite, but varies between the two. From a Noyerian or Trommeric perspective, emergence of a tripartition from within a quadripartition is treated as a retreat from {±author', ±participant', ±hearer'} to {±author', ±participant'} alone. In consequence, this looks like another potential argument for three-feature systems. On my account, the two are featurally identical and differ only with regard to semantic parameterization of order of interpretation. To demonstrate that having two features is enough for the task, this section grasps a thorny instance a such of mixed partitioning and shows that, if anything, a more parsimonious account has an advantage over others.

Kunwinjku (Bininj Gun-wok; Evans 2003) has quadripartite subject agreement, but tripartite object agreement, together with a three-way number system. Moreover, there is no simple translation of exponents of first person object agreement to, say, exclusive subject agreement. Rather, some first person object exponents are used for exclusive, others for inclusive. The challenge is to specify these exponents broadly enough to serve both partitions, but precisely enough to license them only where appropriate. To do this, section 8.4.1 first briefly explains why, on the current approach, general first person is not appropriated by exclusive or inclusive alone. Section 8.4.2 then lays out the full transitive paradigm of Kunwinjku and isolates the person exponents. Finally, section 8.4.3 captures the sharing relationship for first person and compares the account with bivalent and privative alternatives, which, despite their greater analytic resources, are less concise.

8.4.1 Correspondence across Partitions

To set the stage for parceling out exponents to both exclusive and inclusive, I demonstrate that featural similarity and denotational similarity pull exponents in different directions when they are shared with clusives. Indeed, similar tensions characterize exponence of plurality in first persons, as a brief revisiting of facts from section 6.4.1 highlights.

Inclusive and general first are represented by the same features, composed in different orders: +author(+participant(π)) for the inclusive,

Table 8.9
Features and focal points: (mis)matches across partitions

Quadripartition	Tripartition	Features	Focal points
1IN $+\text{au}(+\text{pt}(\pi))$	1 $+\text{pt}(+\text{au}(\pi))$	match	mismatch
1EX $+\text{au}(-\text{pt}(\pi))$	1 $+\text{pt}(+\text{au}(\pi))$	mismatch	match
2 $-\text{au}(+\text{pt}(\pi))$	2 $+\text{pt}(-\text{au}(\pi))$	match	match
3 $-\text{au}(-\text{pt}(\pi))$	3 $-\text{pt}(-\text{au}(\pi))$	match	match

+participant(+author(π)) for first. Semantically, however, the two differ saliently. Let us call the minimum of each set its *focal point* (borrowing a term from anthropological linguistics). The focal point of the inclusive is the speaker–hearer dyad, *iu*; that of the general first is the speaker alone, *i*. If one matches focal points, not features, general first person is more closely connected to exclusive. We therefore have a pair of mixed (mis)matches for first persons (table 8.9): where features match, focal points do not (1IN, 1), and conversely (1EX, 1).

This tension may seem odd at first, but it sets the stage for the sharing that Kunwinjku evidences. Moreover, it has a precedent in the earlier discussion of plural marking in first persons, as follows.

Semantically, first person plurals are unlike other plurals. Whereas *we* is one *i* plus one or more non-*i*'s, *cats*, for instance, does not mean one cat plus one or more noncats. Yet, this semantic disparity contrasts with the plurals' featural parity. As shown in section 6.4.1, the same number features characterize plurals of first persons and of other (pro)nominals: *we* is −atomic applied to the first person lattice, just as *cats* is −atomic applied to the cat lattice.

Languages diverge in whether they reflect featural parity or semantic disparity in exponence of first person plurality. English *I* and *we* show total suppletion: *we* contains neither *I* nor a recognizable exponent of plurality (*s*, *en*, *ren*, ...). Elsewhere, the plural may be decomposable but still suppletive relative to the singular: in Mokilese (table 5.18), for instance, 1EX.P *kama-i* consists of 1EX.D *kama* and plural *i*, but these bear no relation to 1S *ngoah*. By contrast, some languages mark first person plurality with exponents used for common nouns: Gaamgh *ā* 'I' pluralizes as *āgg* 'we', identically to *wāā* 'lake', *wāāgg* 'lakes' (Stirtz 2011).

The conclusion that languages are free to structure their exponents purely according to featural identity, or to show sensitivity to semantic subtleties on which the features themselves are mute, parallels the tensions affecting first persons across partitions, which, as we will now see, Kunwinjku exploits.

8.4.2 Person Agreement in Kunwinjku

In Kunwinjku clauses, an agreement complex registers person and number of both subject and object (table 8.10). Subjects distinguish clusives, but objects do not; so, there are four triplets of subject rows (one for each number), but only three triplets of object columns.

Kunwinjku number distinguishes minimal (M), unit augmented (U), and augmented (A): inclusives contrast two–three–more ('you and me', 'you, me, and another', 'you, me, and others'), and other persons contrast one less than each of these, one–two–more (for exclusive, say, 'me', 'me and another', 'me and others'). For objects, where there is general first person without clusivity, all persons contrast just one–two–more. This has the appearance of a singular–dual–plural system, but that is just what minimal–unit-augmented–augmented looks like when clusivity is removed.

We isolate person exponents as follows. Subject person is identifiable from nonthird acting on third in the quadripartition, the three rightmost columns of the table.[17] The top three rows (beginning with *nga*, *nga-ne*, and *nga-rri*) identify 1EX as *nga*. The fourth row (*ngarr*, *ngarr-ben-bene*, *ngarr-ben*) identifies 1IN.M as *ngarr*, and the next two rows (beginning with *ka-ne* and *ka-rri*) identify 1IN.U/A as *ka*. Similarly, rows six to eight identify *yi* for 2M and *ngu* for 2U/A. So, for the order ±author(±participant(π)), we have exclusive *nga*, inclusive *ngarr* and *ka*, and second *yi* and *ngu*.

Object person is identifiable from 3:2, 3:1, 2:1, and, to a lesser extent, 1:2, in the tripartition. All 3:2 combinations consist of *ngun* plus number (*bene* or *di*). *Ngun* also occurs in some 1:2 combinations (obligatorily when nonminimal acts on minimal, optionally when nonminimal acts on nonminimal). This identifies *ngun* as second person. In 2:1, *kan* occurs, with the number markers of 3:2. *Kan* also occurs in 3:1, with some optionality, as does *ngan*. This identifies *kan* and *ngan* as exponents of first person. Removing the presumably case-related *n*, we have, for the order ±participant(±author(π)), *ka* and *nga* for first person and *ngu* for second.

Table 8.11 summarizes the shared exponents and shows that general first person is split between exclusive (*ka*) and inclusive (*nga*).[18]

8.4.3 Shared Exponents Across Frameworks

In explaining the shared exponence exhibited in Kunwinjku, it turns out to be helpful that both partitions are generated by the same features, as this permits exponents to transfer directly. After presenting an analysis in my own system, I present the best analyses I can devise in Noyer's (1992) bivalent and Harley and Ritter's (2002a, 202b) privative frameworks, noting that they are both slightly more verbose than mine. So, if anything, the more parsimonious inventory enjoys a slight advantage.

Table 8.10
Kunwinjku subject–object combinations (past tense)

Subject	Object							
	1M	1U	1A	2M	2U	2A	3M	3U	3A

Subject	1M	1U	1A	2M	2U	2A	3M	3U	3A
1EX.M				∅	ben-bene	∅	nga	nga-ben-bene	nga-ben
1EX.U				⎱ ngun-di			nga-ne	nga-{$_{rr}^{ne}$}-ben-bene	nga-{$_{rr}^{ne}$}-ben
1EX.A				⎰	bi		nga-rri	nga-rr-ben-bene	nga-rr-ben
1IN.M							ngarr	ngarr-ben-bene	ngarr-ben
1IN.U							ka-ne	ka-ne-ben-bene	ka-{$_{rr}^{ne}$}-ben
1IN.A							ka-rri	ka-rr-ben-bene	ka-rr-ben
2M	kan	kan-bene	kan				yi	yi-ben-bene	yi-ben
2U	⎱ kan-di						ngu-ne	ngu-{$_{rr}^{ne}$}-ben-bene	ngu-{$_{rr}^{ne}$}-ben
2A	⎰						ngu-rri	ngu-rr-ben-bene	ngu-rr-ben
3M	ngan	kan-bene	{$^{kan}_{(ngan)}$}	ngun	ngun-bene	ngun	(bi)	ben-bene	ben
3U	⎱ ngan-di	kan-di		⎱ ngun-di			bene	⎱ bin-di	
3A	⎰	(ngan-di)		⎰			bi-rri	⎰	

Table 8.11

Kunwinjku: Person exponents shared across partitions

Person	Exponent	Subject features	Object features	Match
1(IN)	ka	+auth +part	+auth +part	features
1(EX)	nga	+auth −part	+auth +part	focal point
2	ngu	−auth +part	−auth +part	both
3	bi	−auth −part	−auth −part	both

General first person and exclusive specify ±participant oppositely. So, *nga*, their shared exponent, must ignore that feature and realize +author alone (with number restrictions for 3:1, discussed shortly).

Inclusive is also +author. So, *nga* competes to realize it. That it does not succeed means that it must be outcompeted by *ka*. The obvious means of achieving this is by specifying it for both +author and +participant. (Minimal inclusive *ngarr* must further specify number to block *ka*; but I leave this straightforward exponent aside.)

The emergence of *ka* for first person objects then follows trivially, as general first person, like inclusive, is +author +participant. However, this raises the question of why object *ka*, specified for two features, does not block object *nga*, which is specified for only one. Optional contextualization of *nga* to 3:1M/A avoids this problem:

(33) *nga* ⇔ +author (/ 3: [$_\pi$___] [$_\omega$ αminimal])
    ka ⇔ +author +participant

Owing to this contextualization, +author +participant *ka* is not a simple superset of +author *nga*. Rather, when the parenthetic context obtains, *nga* is the more specific object exponent and blocks *ka*, as in 3:1M. Elsewhere, *ka* is the more specific and blocks *nga*, as in 2:1 and 3:1U. One can even capture the alternation between *ka* and *nga* for 3:1A by positing an optional rule deleting [$_\omega$ −minimal]: when the rule does not apply, *nga* is the better match, but, when it does, *ka* is.[19]

In Noyer's system and its equivalents, one can more or less use the same exponents. However, ±hearer' cannot simply substitute for ±participant, table 8.4 notwithstanding. Writing *ka* ⇔ +author' +hearer' would prevent *ka* from occurring for objects, which lack ±hearer'. Instead, ±hearer' must be loaded into a context. The neatest way of doing this is, I think, to exhaustively list contexts for the already contextualized *nga*:

(34) $nga \Leftrightarrow +\text{author}'$ / $\begin{cases} 3: [_\pi \underline{\quad}] [_\omega -\text{minimal}] \\ [_\pi \underline{\quad} -\text{hearer}'] \end{cases}$

$ka \Leftrightarrow +\text{author}'$

The reader may verify the details. With these exponents, the *nga/ka* optionality for 3:1A could be attributed to the same optional deletion of the number head as before.

For a privative account, like Harley and Ritter's, where $-\text{hearer}'$ is unavailable, *nga* must be made the default and *ka* must be contextualized, resulting, again, in slightly more verbosity (cf, Frampton 2002 on possible treatments of Kabyle Berber):

(35) $ka \Leftrightarrow \text{author}'\ \text{participant}'$ / $\begin{cases} [_\pi \underline{\quad} \text{hearer}'] \\ 2: [_\pi \underline{\quad}] \\ 3: [_\pi \underline{\quad} \text{minimal}] \end{cases}$

$nga \Leftrightarrow \text{author}'\ \text{participant}'$

(Optional deletion of minimal in (35) delivers *nga/ka* optionality.)

My main purpose in examining shared exponence in Kunwinjku has been to demonstrate the descriptive adequacy of the two-feature theory. In particular, I have wanted to show that it is plausible to view tri- and quadripartition as being built from identical features (and as differing only in order of composition). It appears, in the end, that the simplest theory offers the simplest analysis when compared with two major predecessors with larger feature inventories. Parsimony may only be persuasive, not decisive, but it is interesting that Kunwinjku should yield most parsimoniously to the most parsimonious system.

8.5 Conclusion

By eschewing a conjunctive semantics for feature bundles, the current theory of person obtains descriptive adequacy using only the features it needs for the two bipartitions. Conjunction-based accounts, by contrast, must posit one or more additional features. This leads to a problem of overgeneration, attempted solutions to which are not theoretically or empirically satisfactory. Moreover, the slimmer system can replicate analyses that purport to support larger inventories and/or hearer-based features, and, in the challenging case of Kunwinjku exponence sharing, it appears to deliver a more parsimonious analysis than major alternatives. The balance of evidence thus weighs in favor of paring person features down and abandoning oldfangled *and*.

9 The Form of the Phi Kernel

9.1 Introduction

This chapter considers the broader lessons that might be drawn from the current study of person. Primarily, I draw out core commonalities between the person and number features that I have proposed: that features are "operations" richer than first-order predicates held together by conjunction (section 9.2); that they are not subject to extrinsic constraints on order of composition (section 9.3) or cooccurrence (section 9.4); and that there are semantic and morphological grounds for representing features of both kinds bivalently (section 9.5).

It goes without saying that conclusions of this sort may well ramify on how we construct theories of other feature families in future. Additionally, though, section 9.6 tentatively suggests that the consequences of this study might ramify beyond linguistics by altering our understanding of and means of investigating the language of thought and the nature and evolution of mind. In particular, I suggest that, contrary to widespread opinion, minds do leave fossils, but these are to be sought, not by paleoanthropologists sifting through the archeological record, but by cognitive scientists, including linguists, via our theories of the structure of the mind itself.

9.2 Operations

Throughout this book, I have persistently portrayed my features as denoting operations, as in statements like "±participant *acts on* π to yield a bipartition" and "±author *acts on* that bipartition to yield the quadripartition." This choice of vocabulary is intended to contrast my theory with traditional approaches that cast phi features as first-order predicates. Of course, a first-order predicate, too, can be conceived of as an operation, because a predicate partitions its domain into elements of which it is true and elements of which it is false (assuming a two-valued logic). However, the crucial distinction to which I intend to draw attention through this choice of terms concerns the semantic glue that binds bundles of features together.

For traditional features, denoting first-order predicates, the glue is conjunction, as discussed at length in chapter 8. This entails that order of application is irrelevant (1) and that opposing values of the same feature, interpreted together, are contradictory and yield empty denotations (2).

(1) $[\![\pm F(\pm G)]\!]$
$= \lambda x.\,(\neg)[\![F]\!](x) \wedge (\neg)[\![G]\!](x)$
$= \lambda x.\,(\neg)[\![G]\!](x) \wedge (\neg)[\![F]\!](x)$
$= [\![\pm G(\pm F)]\!]$

(2) $\{x : [\![+F(-F)]\!](x) = 1\}$
$= \{x : [\![-F(+F)]\!](x) = 1\}$ by (1)
$= \{x : \neg[\![F]\!](x) \wedge [\![F]\!](x)\}$
$= \varnothing$

Neither of these consequences holds for my features. In fact, my theory of person and number crucially exploits both differential order of composition and specifications involving opposing specifications of a single feature.

Order of composition was discussed prominently in chapter 4. To recapitulate briefly, two specifications correspond to the same persons irrespective of order of composition: $-$author($+$participant(π)) is second person in the quadripartition, as is $+$participant($-$author(π)) in the tripartition; likewise, $-$author($-$participant(π)) is quadripartite third person, and $-$participant($-$author(π)) is tripartite third person.

However, the plus–plus picks out inclusive in the quadripartition, $+$author($+$participant(π)), but general first person in the tripartition, $+$participant($+$author(π)). Similarly, $+$author($-$participant(π)) is exclusive in the quadripartition but is the representation used for Germanic third person, $-$participant($+$author(π)), in section 8.3.1.

Opposing specifications, on the other hand, were seen numerous times for number in chapter 6. Unit augmented, $+$minimal($-$minimal(π)), is the most minimal of the nonminimal ways of satisfying a person specification. For instance, things that are nonminimally exclusive include not just me, but me and others. Of these, the most minimal includes me and just one other. The inclusive, by contrast, would include me, you, and just one other. So, the odd cooccurrence of plus with minus derives the correct cardinalities, two versus three, for exclusive and inclusive unit augmented.

Similarly, trial, +minimal(−minimal(−atomic(π))), is the most minimal of the nonminimal ways of satisfying both a person specification and nonatomicity. Again, for exclusive, the nonatoms include me and others. If we exclude the most minimal of these, we have things that are triadic and larger; and the most minimal of these last are the triads. Similarly, for the inclusive, the nonatoms include me, you, and others; and the nonminimal of these are triadic and larger, so the most minimal of the nonminimal are the triads. Thus, we correctly derive a trial that is cardinality-invariant for person. Chapter 6 provides greater detail, and illustrations, for these and related numbers.

Multiple approximative numbers also exploit opposing specifications. If one partitions a plural into additively incomplete and additively complete subregions, then one can interpret the first of these as a paucal, −additive (−atomic(π)), and the second, as a new plural, +additive (−atomic(π)), now slightly hemmed-in from below. One can, moreover, take this hemmed-in plural and, again, carve out an additively incomplete subregion, −additive(+additive(−atomic(π))), from its nether regions. The result is a new but cardinally larger paucal, hence greater paucal, that dovetails with the earlier one. See Harbour 2014a for further formal and factual detail.

Nonconjunctivity, then, is a property that both sets of phi features share: person exploits differential order of composition, and number, opposing value specifications.[1]

This conclusion has ramifications beyond phi theory, on what we might call the "biomathematics" of natural language semantics and of cognition more generally. Writing from a philosophico-semantic perspective, Pietroski (2006) has proposed that natural language might use nothing more than conjunction as its semantic "glue." If, as seems reasonable, we take (1) and (2) to be constitutive criteria of a purely conjunctive semantics, then phi features provide robust evidence against this position.

9.3 Order

Order of composition provides further commonality between person and number. Although it plays out differently for the two sets of features, both share the property that there is no intrinsically required or extrinsically imposed order of composition. Instead, properties of the learner's primary linguistic data are sufficient to determine the order of composition to which they should make their features subject.

For person, the trajectory of a hypothetical learner is easy to imagine. Suppose that a child tries out each singleton set of features and realizes that these provide insufficiently many distinctions for the forms observed in the target language. So, these simpler grammars are discounted, entailing that both features must be activated at once. To test the viability of this more complex grammar, the child must assign it an order of composition. One order of composition, with ±author outermost, yields four persons; the other, with ±participant outermost, yields only three (the two −participant specifications coincide). Relative to the data, either four will be too many, or three, too few. So, the data will drive the child's choice. (Similarly, if the child settles on a tripartition, then syncretic data, among others, will drive whether third person will be represented with −author or +author.)

For number, the process is similar, as laid out more fully in Harbour 2014a. Suppose that a child realizes that a single feature produces insufficiently many number distinctions. Among the feature sets they might try out is {±atomic, ±minimal}, but this can only be tested relative to an order of composition. As discussed in chapter 4, the order ±minimal(±atomic(π)) produces singular–dual–plural. The other order makes ±atomic redundant: ±minimal(π) partitions inclusive into a dyad versus things larger, $iu \mid iuo_o$, and all other persons into atoms versus nonatoms, as in $i \mid io_o$ for exclusive and $o \mid oo_o$ for third. Speaking anthropomorphically, if ±atomic applies to inclusive, it finds no work to do, as everything is −atomic; and if it applies to any other person, it finds its work already done, as the partition is +atomic versus −atomic. So, in both cases it returns the same partition. The system, then, is equivalent to {±minimal} acting alone. By hypothesis, the child only entertains two-feature grammars under the duress of data, having found that one feature was not enough. The data that drive the child to abandon one-feature grammars thus prevent the positing of the extensional equivalent of such grammars. Again, then, data drive the child's choice of order of composition.

Clearly, there is a difference between the effects of these considerations on person versus number. For person, order of composition creates extensionally distinct grammars. For number, it merely rules out redundancy. Nonetheless, the structure of the theory is the same in both cases: Universal Grammar supplies features, but not their orders of composition. That choice is driven by the data.

9.4 Combinatorics

The fewer extrinsic constraints a theory requires, the better. Freedom from constraints is crucial for the current theory: if person features were subject to a rigid constraint on order of composition, they would fail to generate either the tripartition or the quadripartition, and the theory would be inadequate. This critical absence of extrinsic constraints is a more general property of how the theory generates its typology. The freedom in question concerns what is, or is not, a licit choice of features. The answer—that all are—is, again, a common characteristic of my accounts both of person and of number.

For person, the point by now needs little discussion. As laid out in chapter 4, an inventory of two features permits 2^2 systems for person or related deictic domains. These are: (i) the null set, resulting in monopartition; (ii)–(iii) two singleton sets, resulting in bipartition; and (iv) the full set itself, resulting in tripartition or quadripartition, depending on order of composition.

For number, the principle is the same, but the possibilities are more numerous. Three features, {±atomic, ±minimal, ±additive}, afford 2^3 systems. With examples from chapter 6 and Harbour 2014a, these are: (i) the null set, resulting in numberless Jarawa (Kumar 2012); (ii)–(iii) the singletons, {±atomic} and {±minimal}, resulting in English versus Ewondo (Onambélé 2012) for tripartitions, and Min Nan (Maryknoll Language Service Center 2013) versus Timbira (de Castro Alves 2004) for quadripartitions; (v)–(vii) the two-feature systems, {±atomic, ±minimal} Sanskrit singular–dual–plural (Coulson 1992), {±atomic, ±additive} Bayso singular–paucal–plural (Corbett and Hayward 1987), and {±minimal, ±additive} Mebengokre minimal–paucal–plural (Silva 2003); and (viii) the full set, resulting in Yimas singular–dual–paucal–plural (Foley 1991).

Two points require comment here. The first is absence of (iv), the singleton system {±additive}. As noted in Harbour 2014a, +additive, applied to person, behaves oddly without other number features. If applied to a general first person, for instance, it would yield two disjoint regions: the nonpaucal plural, as in other languages where it is active, and $\{i, iu\}$, as this set, too, is closed under addition: $i \sqcup iu \in \{i, iu\}$.[2] Sandwiched between these two +additive regions would be the −additive paucal. So, this singleton would yield minimal/singular–paucal–plural for nonthird person and paucal–plural for third. If attested, the system has escaped the notice of typologists (Corbett 2000, Cysouw 2003, Siewierska 2004).

However, such sandwiching contravenes a contiguity constraint, *convexity*, that has been proposed in a number of theoretical and empirical studies, ranging from vowel systems to prepositional semantics and color terms (Liljencrants and Lindblom 1972, Zwarts 1995, Gärdenfors 2004, Regier, Paul, and Khetarpal 2007, Jäger 2008). Convexity states that, if the endpoints of a path lie within some region, then so must all intermediary points. The system just described is nonconvex because, between the +additive maximum of the whole lattice, $iuoo'o''\ldots$, and the +additive maximum of the sublattice, i or iu, lies −additive, paucal, such as $iuoo'o''$.

If convexity is a general property of the division of semantic spaces, color spaces, vowel spaces, and so on, then we can regard it as intrinsic to cognition. Consequently, absence of {±additive} and the system it would generate is not an extrinsic stipulation, but part of the underpinning logic within which the theory of person and number is embedded.

Second, the seven systems of (i)–(iii) and (v)–(viii) do not exhaust those discussed in chapter 6, which incorporated unit augmented and trial. As explained in section 9.2, these numbers, and multiple approximatives like greater paucal, arise from opposing value specifications, that is, cooccurrence of +F and −F. Such cooccurrence itself constitutes a separate parameter of variation (*value recursion*; chapter 6), and, consistent with the position laid out so far, it is constrained only by intrinsic factors.

Specifically, ±minimal may be subject to value recursion (for unit augmented or trial), as may ±additive (for greater paucal, greatest plural, or other approximative numbers). It does not occur for ±atomic on ω, but this restriction is intrinsic, arising from the logic of the system. The denotation of ±atomic is a first-order predicate, 'is (not) an atom'. So, by (2), value recursion is contradictory here. By the reasoning of section 9.3, therefore, learners do not posit this as a possible feature system. However, if +atomic and −atomic cooccur as uninterpretable features, somewhere other than on ω, then they are not interpreted semantically and, so, are not ruled out by (2). This possibility is exploited in the inverse number system of Kiowa (Harbour 2007b and section 8.3.2.2 above). In sum, then, this parameter, too, may be freely activated and is not subject to extrinsic constraints.[3]

The current approach to phi theory views freedom of association as a fundamental featural right: subsets of features may freely come together and constitute licit grammars (except where independent matters of logic rule some out). This represents a fundamentally antigeometrical conception of the feature theorist's task. Missing feature combinations are not to be reified as universal principles, but point to an imperfect understanding of the feature inventory, or its semantics, or the underlying logic. That person and number both yield to an analysis of this kind constitutes a further commonality between the two families of features.

9.5 Valence

Throughout the discussion, I have represented both person and number features as bivalent. As noted in relation to geometries (section 8.2.2), the choice between bivalence and privativity is a contentful one, and I have pointed out problematic properties of privativity in several places (especially, Harbour

2011c, 2013, 2014a). Here, however, my aim is not to argue against privativity in general, but to show that, if one accepts my features, then one must take them to be bivalent. The reasons for this are both semantic (section 9.5.1) and morphological (section 9.5.2), with analogous arguments arising for both person and number. Bivalence consequently constitutes a further commonality between these core elements of phi.

9.5.1 Semantics

Consideration of the semantics of valence must begin with the denotation of the values themselves. Given that person and number features are of different semantic types, they act on lattices in fundamentally different ways. As a result, it is inevitable that the denotations of their values also differ. Omitting lambdas, for person, $[\![+]\!] = \oplus$, disjoint addition, and $[\![-]\!] = \ominus$, joint subtraction; for number, $[\![+]\!]$ is contentless, or the identity map, and $[\![-]\!]$ is a type-flexible $\neg$. The two are not entirely unrelated, as addition of $l_1 \vee l_2 \vee \ldots \vee l_k$ versus subtraction of $l_1 \wedge l_2 \wedge \ldots \wedge l_k$ is reminiscent of De Morgan's laws, which link $\vee$, $\wedge$, and $\neg$. So, it might be possible to parcel out addition-versus-subtraction and jointness-versus-disjointness to maximize the similarity with logical assertion and negation. However, this requires greater skill with lattices and logics than I currently have. So, I confine my comments here to the semantic necessity of representing both $+$F and $-$F, irrespective of the definition of $+$ and $-$.

For number, any case for using opposing value specifications is an argument against privativity. If we rewrite $+$F as F$'$ and omit reference to $-$F, then, for instance, unit augmented, $+$minimal($-$minimal(π)), and minimal, $+$minimal(π), collapse as minimal$'$(π). The same problem arises, mutatis mutandis, for unit augmented and augmented, if we instead write $-$F as F$'$ and omit reference to $+$F. And analogous issues await the trial, which also uses opposing values of $\pm$minimal, the greater paucal, which applies the same parameter to $\pm$additive, and the Kiowa inverse, which does likewise for uninterpretable instances of both $\pm$minimal and $\pm$atomic. (On this last, see Harbour 2011c for lengthy argument against privative alternatives.)

For person, a privative rewrite is also problematic. A straightforward rewrite of $+$F as privative F$'$ and $-$F as the absence of a feature causes tripartition and quadripartition to collapse. This can be seen without recourse to new calculations. The privative rewrite of the tripartition is shown in (3) and of the quadripartition, in (4):

(3) $+$participant($+$author(π)) $\mapsto$ participant$'$(author$'$(π))
     $+$participant($-$author(π)) $\mapsto$ participant$'$(π)
     $-$participant($+$author(π)) $\mapsto$ author$'$(π)
     $-$participant($-$author(π)) $\mapsto$ π

(4) $+\text{author}(+\text{participant}(\pi)) \mapsto \text{author}'(\text{participant}'(\pi))$
   $+\text{author}(-\text{participant}(\pi)) \mapsto \text{author}'(\pi)$
   $-\text{author}(+\text{participant}(\pi)) \mapsto \text{participant}'(\pi)$
   $-\text{author}(-\text{participant}(\pi)) \mapsto \pi$

These are identical except for the (erstwhile) plus–plus combination. However, this is not enough to maintain distinct partitions, because $[\![+\text{participant}(+\text{author}(\pi))]\!] = [\![+\text{author}(+\text{participant}(\pi))]\!]$. In other words, a shift to privativity makes order of composition a parameter without semantic import. The theory undergenerates.

The same holds of the alternative rewrite of $-F$ as F' and $+F$ as absence of a feature, because, again, the only two-feature combination is unaffected by order of composition: $[\![-\text{participant}(-\text{author}(\pi))]\!] = [\![-\text{author}(-\text{participant}(\pi))]\!]$. I do not consider the other two rewrites, which map $+F$ to F' for one feature and $-G$ to G' for the other, because the denotations of the two privative features would be nonuniform to the extent that the principle underlying the featural representation of cognitive primitives (i.e., the correspondence between the object language and the metalanguage) would become too arbitrary. Without further (not very natural) stipulations, privativity cannot solve the partition problem (and, even with those stipulations, the solution produced does not interface easily with morphology; appendix B.4).[4]

9.5.2 Morphology

Just like semantics, morphology requires reference to negative values. This is best illustrated with the phenomenon of composed exclusives, discussed for Bahing, Gumbáiŋgar, Limbu, Mam, and Nyawaygi in section 5.2.2. But, in a further commonality between person and number, parallel problems arise for number. First, I lay out the general structure of the problem—*creatio ex nihilo*—by comparing Bislama and Limbu. Then I illustrate the parallel problem for number. Then, returning to the harder version of the problem, I lay out the range of possible privative solutions. However, all are cobbled-together conspiracies, meaning that, without minus values, only half the phenomena discussed here can be recaptured naturally.

9.5.2.1 Core Problem We saw above that inclusives may subsume exclusives (Bislama) and, conversely, that exclusives may subsume inclusives (Limbu). In privative systems, there is a marked disparity in the ease with which these facts are accommodated.

Consider Bislama from the point of view of Harley and Ritter 2002a, 2002b, leaving number and the participant′ feature aside:

(5) 1EX   *mi-*...   author′
     1IN   *yu-mi-*...   author′ hearer′
     2   *yu-*...   hearer′

As the underlining makes clear, it is easy to associate each feature with an exponent, and vice versa: *mi* corresponds to author′ and *yu* to hearer′. Moreover, as the quantity of features increases, so does the number of exponents: both features occur for the inclusive, and so do both exponents.

Matters are not so straightforward for the converse. In Limbu, the exclusive has fewer features but more exponents, and the inclusive, more features but fewer exponents:

(6) 1EX   *aŋ-*...*-ge*   author′
     1IN   *aŋ-*...   author′
     2   *khɛn-*...   hearer′

As the underlining shows, *ge* seems to emerge from the featural void, creating morphological somethingness from syntactic nothingness.

For accounts with negative values, such as mine or Noyer's and its kin, there is no problem: one simply regards *ge* as the exponent of a minus value (−participant for my account, −hearer′ for Noyer's). But for privative accounts, this morphological *creatio ex nihilo* is surprising. It is one thing for theme vowels to emerge from nowhere (Oltra-Massuet 2000, as they are semantically empty. Here, the syntactic nothingness that is mapped to morphological somethingness seems to have semantics: intuitively, "exclusive," theoretically, −participant.

9.5.2.2 Parallel Problems

Parallel problems arise for number, thus constituting a further similarity with person.

Consider, first, dual and plural in Bislama. For exclusive and second, plural is marked by *pela* (underlined) and dual, by superadding *tu* (double-underlined). Leaving person aside, we have:[5]

(7) S   ...-(∅)   minimal′
     D   ...*-tu-pela*   minimal′ nonatomic′
     P   ...*-pela*   nonatomic′

Turning ±atomic into privative nonatomic′, one can capture this by associating nonatomic′ with *pela* and minimal′, in the context of nonatomic′, with *tu*. The resulting system is identical to Harley and Ritter's (with group′ for nonatomic′). The same pattern is found in Kiwai (Ray 1933): its first, second, and third person plurals (*nimo, nigo, nei*) are substrings of the duals, formed by addition of *to* (*nimo-to, nigo-to, nei-to*).

However, the relationships of compositionality can be reversed, with plural subsuming dual. Several variants of such systems are discussed in Cysouw 2003, 193–197. For instance, in Damana (Amaya 1999), plural pronouns consist of the duals plus the suffix *nyina* (table 9.1). Leaving aside the number-conditioned suppletion of first person (singular *ra*, nonsingular *na*), for first and second, we have:

(8) S   ...-(∅)   minimal′
    D   ...-<u>bi</u>   minimal′ nonatomic′
    P   ...-<u>bi</u>-<u>nyina</u>   <u>   </u> nonatomic′

A more elaborate version of the pattern is found in Mokilese, which has four persons and four numbers (rather than just three and three), with the dual serving as the morphological base of both (normal) plural and greater plural (table 9.2). However, even in Damana, the problem is clear: if plural has more exponents than it does features, then it is unclear where *nyina* emerges from. Hence, the double-underlined lacuna in (8).

Table 9.1

Damana pronouns

	Singular	Dual	Plural
1	*ra*	*na-bi*	*na-bi-nyina*
2	*ma*	*ma-bi*	*ma-bi-nyina*
3	*na*	*ijkuna*	*ijkuna-nyina*

Table 9.2

Mokilese emphatic pronouns

	Singular	Dual	Plural	Greater plural
1EX	*ngoah*	*kama*	*kama-i*	*kimi* (*kama-^{i}*)
1IN		*kisa*	*kisa-i*	*kihs* (*kisa-^{i}*)
2	*koah*	*kamwa*	*kamwa-i*	*kimwi* (*kamwa-^{i}*)
3	*ih*	*ara/ira*	*ara-i/ira-i*	*ihr* (*ara/ira-^{i}*)

Again, there is no problem for bivalent accounts: *nyina* simply expresses what privativity effaces, −minimal. Cowper (2005) reverses the problem by positing a bare number node for singular, with nonatomic′ for dual, and nonatomic′ plus nonminimal′ for plural. With dual as a subset of plural, Damana becomes the easy case, and Bislama, the hard one. See Nevins 2011 for problematization of the account in relation to markedness.)

9.5.2.3 Solutions It is clear that privativized versions of the current features cannot capture Limbuesque compositionality: without minus values, exclusive consists of a single feature, which can only license a single exponent before it is consumed (Noyer 1992, Trommer 1999).[6] So, *aŋ* and *ge* demand that the exclusive contain an extra feature. However, any new person feature, like exclusive′, will be a "nonprimitive primitive" (section 8.2.2), definable in terms of author′, hearer′, and the negation available in the metalanguage. Consequently, the best solution I can envisage is to treat the category label π' as a feature on a par with person.

With π' as a feature, the persons are as laid out below, and exclusive, consisting of two features, has content enough for two exponents:

(9) 1EX π' author′   *aŋ-...-ge*
    1IN π' author′ hearer′   *aŋ-...*
    2   π' hearer′   *khɛn-...*
    3   π' *khun-..., khɛŋ-...*

A good number of analyses now become available, depending, principally, on whether author′ realizes *aŋ* and π' realizes *ge*, or vice versa (two options), and on which, if either, of author′ and π' is contextualized by the other (three choices). These six core solutions are presented in table 9.3 (leaving minor variations aside, such as, in the top left, whether *khɛn* instead realizes hearer′ in the context of π', or, in the bottom right, whether ∅ instead realizes π' and hearer′ in the context of author′).

Readers can easily verify these solutions at their leisure, but all essentially amount to the same thing. If there is an exponent purely of the feature author′ (*aŋ* or *ge*), then we expect it for exclusive and inclusive alike. So, one is forced to posit a more highly specified exponent to bleed author′ from inclusive. Similarly, if there is an exponent purely of π' (*ge* or *aŋ*), then we expect it for all persons, including third. So, one is forced to set up the list of exponents to bleed π' from inclusive, second, and third before the exponent of π' acts; in the case of third person, this sometimes involves differentiating between an exponent for the feature π' on the head, and one for a head that hosts only that feature, π'.

Table 9.3

Possible three-feature privative treatments of Limbu

π′ hearer′ ⇔ ∅ / author′	π′ hearer′ ⇔ ∅ / author′	π′ hearer′ ⇔ ∅ / author′
π′ hearer′ ⇔ khɛn	π′ hearer′ ⇔ khɛn	π′ hearer′ ⇔ khɛn
π′ ⇔ khun, khɛŋ	author′ ⇔ aŋ	π′ ⇔ khun, khɛŋ
author′ ⇔ aŋ	π′ ⇔ ge / author′	author′ ⇔ aŋ / π′
π′ ⇔ ge	π′ ⇔ khun, khɛŋ	π′ ⇔ ge
author′ hearer′ ⇔ ∅	π′ ⇔ aŋ / author′	author′ hearer′ ⇔ ∅
π′ hearer′ ⇔ khɛn	author′ hearer′ ⇔ ∅	π′ hearer′ ⇔ khɛn
π′ ⇔ khun, khɛŋ	π′ hearer′ ⇔ khɛn	π′ ⇔ khun, khɛŋ
author′ ⇔ ge	author′ ⇔ ge	author′ ⇔ ge / π′
π′ ⇔ aŋ	π′ ⇔ khun, khɛŋ	π′ ⇔ aŋ

In other words, systems like Limbu are treated as conspiracies in which a series of gags is placed on exponents. By contrast, the morphological compositionality of Bislama inclusives is treated much more straightforwardly. Thus, the issue is not one of descriptive adequacy, but one of insight. Converse containment relations are found both for person and for number, and they arise in geographically and genetically diverse parts of the world. There is no obvious reason to expect the substantial disparity of treatment that privativity forces on us. Rather, it looks like renouncing reference to negative values leaves privativity deficient and able to capture only half of the phenomenon. Bivalence simply seems to serve the facts better.[7]

9.6 Cognition and Evolution

The foregoing discussion has highlighted a variety of parallels between formal properties of features in the theory of person and the theory of number. Their status as operations rather than predicates, their freedom from extrinsic constraints on order of composition, their bivalence, and their free, rather than filtered or geometrized, combinatorics are all substantial commonalities.

Underlying these is a single point: that Universal Grammar optimally exploits the features at its disposal. This interesting result raises two further questions: whether other families of features have the same formal properties, in particular of optimal exploitation; and where the features that grammatical systems optimally exploit come from.

The first of these questions can only be answered by further investigation, perhaps using the current study as a template. Regarding the second, though, I would like to consider what lessons might be drawn from the study of phi features for the study of cognition more generally. Everything that follows is highly speculative and wanders far beyond my domain of expertise. Nonetheless, and at the risk straining the reader's indulgence, I suggest that several themes emerge that could make such formal studies of language relevant to cognitive science more broadly. These concern the notion of the programming language of the mind (section 9.6.1), the factors that might distinguish human from nonhuman cognition, at least in some domains (section 9.6.2), and the idea that, contrary to general conception, the evolution of the mind does leave fossils, but these are accessible primarily to cognitive science, not archeology or paleoanthropology (section 9.6.3).

9.6.1 Valence and the Language of Thought

Within linguistics, valence is an arcane issue, of interest only to hardcore morphologists. However, it ought, I think, to attract much more interest, and not just from linguists. From the perspective of cognitive science, valence provides a window on what we might call the programming language of the mind, or in a slight appropriation of terminology, the language of thought.

In arguing for bivalence and against privativity, or conversely, we are attempting to answer the question of whether the programming language permits reference to negation and complementation, or whether these are only accessible in the metalanguage, by which encapsulated modules speak to one another. Questions like this concern the "biomathematics" of thought by asking what its expressive capacity is.

The present very focused inquiry into the core of phi—building on the enormous effort that has gone into descriptive, typological, and previous theoretical investigation—shows that we can transform these abstract issues into concrete questions of empirical consequence. If the conclusion is that the basic language of thought consists of features and values, not features alone, then this may obviously serve as a template for theories of other feature families. Moreover, there is no reason to think that there is anything uniquely linguistic about plus and minus values of concepts. As a result, such studies might also serve as guides to the structure of theories of nonlinguistic cognition, in humans and, perhaps, in nonhumans.

9.6.2 What Might Make Humans Special

The semantic content of the features themselves is equally relevant to the wider study of cognition, and, again, this applies both to person and to number, in somewhat different ways.

A curious facet of many treatments of person, made particularly explicit in chapter 4, is that the grammar does not have direct access to the primitive persons i, u, and o, o', o'', ... Rather, access is mediated by the person lattices, a series of nested structures, consisting, first, of just the author, then of the two participants, and last, of everyone. These structures themselves are hardly very surprising. To recapitulate section 4.2.2, if one imagines the gradual stages through which one's social awareness matures, then the starting point is, very plausibly, oneself. Early interactions are one on one, between a child and a carer. One can represent the difference between these two stages as expansion from solipsistic self-awareness, just $\{i\}$, to basic social interaction, $\{i, u\}$.

In the next stage, social horizons expand to include others. The o's form a single structure with i and u because, crucially, all are interchangeable. Just as the participant lattice captures the reciprocal relation that, when you and I are talking, I interpret your u as my i and conversely, so the π lattice, consisting of i, u, and o, o', o'', ..., captures something similar. Most crucially, any o is a potential u. Moreover, this mixed structure facilitates communication using first and second person plurals (while obviating a multiplicity of u's). Regarding myself as unique, I posit a sole i and I represent first plural as ioo'. Accordingly, when I interpret your uoo', I take the u to refer to me: just as I map your u onto my i, so I map your uoo' onto my ioo'. As a result, I understand that, if I say uoo', then every o, being a potential u, will egotistically interpret the u as their i and will consider everyone else in the plurality an o. The result is second person plural communication, with everyone thinking, "That u just referred to my i."

It is, then, prima facie plausible that the author lattice, participant lattice, and π lattice reflect stages by which some of our social awareness incrementally expands.

Interestingly, these ontogenetic considerations find philogenetic resonance. In a study of wild baboons, subtitled *The Evolution of a Social Mind*, Cheney and Seyfarth (2007) observe that their subjects interact with each other almost entirely in one-on-one settings. This exclusivity recalls the participant lattice, which contains just i and u. If baboon interaction relies on a mental representation that is equivalent to, or that humans have come to represent as, $\{i, u\}$ or its unbottomed power set, then, on my theory, the participant lattice amounts to a mental fossil, one that continues to make itself manifest in the structure of pronominal systems and the like.

Musing for a moment more, the current account of person might lead to concrete conjectures concerning differences between human and baboon cognition. If humans depart from baboons in being conceptually equipped to deal with second person pluralities, then my account locates this difference in a number of possible places: either baboons lack the full phi structure, or else they lack (the capacity to apply) the operations that hone pronominal reference down to i_o, u_o, and so on, including possibly power set formation.

How we account for baboons' group behavior might be affected by the outcome. Joining a well-established philosophical and, now, experimental psychological debate about the nature of joint action or shared intentions (Tuomela and Miller 1988, Searle 1995, Bacharach 2006, Gold and Sugden 2007, Tuomela 2009, Gold 2012), Gold and Harbour (2012) argue that joint action relies on concepts like +author and −atomic. It seems unlikely that baboons lack something like these. If, however, they lack the ability to combine them as humans do (possibly because of how they are represented), then they might consequently lack the ability to form group intentions, engaging only in more loosely allied behavior. This would be a rather surprising way to judge the efficacy of a theory of pronouns, agreement, and the like in human language, but the questions seem to rise naturally on the horizons of the current theory.

My previous work on number might also be read as suggesting that, in certain domains, humans differ from other animals in virtue of combinatorial capacities, rather than our stock of concepts. In Harbour 2014a, I show that the concepts behind the number features—atomicity, minimality, additivity—are not specific to number but are, in fact, fundamental to a variety of analyses of aspect and Aktionsart, having been posited in various guises in work from Krifka 1992 to Borer 2005, among others. Furthermore, I have also shown (Harbour 2011b) that a psychologically plausible construction of the natural numbers is available from the features ±atomic and ±minimal. Grammatical numbers, like trial and greater paucal, might seem like uniquely human concerns, as might the link between verbal telicity and nominal properties, or the capacity to name numbers like 2015 or more. Yet the concepts atomicity, minimality, and additivity do not seem like such exotica that we would feel compelled to suppose that only humans possess them. If so, then, again, what is particularly human about nominal number, aspect, and integers is not the concepts themselves, but the means by which they are represented and/or combined (with nominal concepts, verbal concepts, and each other).

The idea that the combinatorial engine is one of the key properties that made human language possible is hardly novel, and its promulgation in Hauser, Chomsky, and Fitch 2002 is particularly well-known. The current study of person features and my previous work on number suggest that detailed examination of features could be a key methodology in seeking to understand the combinatorial properties of human language and similar systems.

9.6.3 Fossils in, and of, the Mind

Let us return to the observation that grammar does not access the primitives of person directly. It is commonplace to observe that minds do not leave fossils. So, the evolution of cognition is inferred from paleoanthropological artifacts, like tools and artwork, sometimes by a convoluted, and dubious, series of hypotheses about the linguistic and social prerequisites that the production of such artifacts demands. However, the foregoing discussion suggests that minds do leave fossils, and the fossil bed is the mind itself.

Social behavior is vastly more common in the animal world than language is. So, it is hardly controversial to regard human social cognition as being evolutionarily prior to language. If language consists of modules that evolved and accreted after those involved in our social cognition, then they will, metaphorically, "sit on top of" the earlier modules, depositing like sedimentation.

A plausible consequence of this is precisely the role that the socially structured ontology plays in mediating the access that grammar has to the person primitives i, u, and o, o', o'', ... The result, then, is that language deals with nested social structures of solipsism, dyadic interaction, and the full social universe—the author lattice, participant lattice, and full π lattice—and not with the primitives themselves.

Viewed in this light, the theory proposed above becomes yet more minimal. It is not an arbitrary oddity that language deals with prestructured persons, rather than the atomic persons themselves. This is forced by external factors: language came later, and accreted on top of, more basic structures. But, once given those structures, language optimally exploits them: any choice of person features is licit, as is any order of composition.

9.7 Conclusion

The purpose of this chapter has been to consider the consequences that the current investigation of person and its allied account of number might hold for how we view not just phi features, but features more generally, and the systems of thought in which they are embedded. If I am right, then the theory of phi features tells us that (at least some) features must be bivalently represented, denoting operations that are not merely conjoined, but act on their arguments in semantically nuanced ways and do so without extrinsic constraints on either order or cooccurrence. All of these may affect how we understand and investigate the language of thought, what differentiates human from animal cognition, and how we investigate the evolution of the human mind.

10 Conclusion

This investigation began with the very modest question of why, in languages like English, the meaning 'we and you' is covered by *we*, not *you*. By broadening this question to address all partitions of person and related deictic spaces, we realize that there is a substantial disparity between possible and attested systems of person and person-related deixis.

Such shortfall between the possible and the actual is a classic variety of linguistic problem, and, in responding to it, I have attempted to present a very minimal theory of person. Specifically, I have crafted a system that, once it has enough to generate monopartition (π) and the two bipartitions (±author and ±participant), immediately generates all and only what is attested: the three partitions just mentioned plus one tripartition and the quadripartition. Besides the minimality of its apparatus, the resulting system furnishes a range of desirable consequences, concerning the morphological composition of different persons, the semantic and morphological interaction of person with number, and the capacity to capture the relationship between personal and spatial deixis. This empirical coverage is achieved more easily than in traditional predication-and-conjunction accounts of person, and without any of the excess posits that these demand, such as further features and restrictions on their cooccurrence.

What emerges is a coherent, unified view of the kernel of phi, the features that make up person and number. These results may ramify beyond phi theory into the linguistic theory of other feature families and further, into broader issues in cognitive science and the evolution of mind. If so, the study of phi features brings us to a deeper understanding, not just of what *we* is as a pronoun, but of what we are as thinking creatures.

A Empirical Appendices

A.1 Preponderant Syncretism in Georgian

This appendix presents a brief case study of syncretism in Georgian (Hewitt 1995; Rusiko Amirejibi, Léa Nash, Thomas Weir, pers. comm.). It shows that the language displays a preponderant syncretism of first and second person as opposed to third, affecting at least six different parts of the verb. Despite this robustness, other morphemes prevent whole-word syncretism. As a result, phenomena like those below are excluded from the typologies in Baerman, Brown, and Corbett 2005 and Baerman and Brown 2013. This should caution proponents of morpheme-based theories against direct use of their results. The two methodologies come into concrete conflict in the current case. The cited studies found metasyncretism in the singular only between second and third person. The Georgian syncretism affects both singular and plural and, so, presents a metasyncretism between first and second singular.

Georgian neutralizes the distinction between the participants, that is, first and second person, but maintains the contrast with third. This pattern is quadruply evident in the aorist of 'give'. For recipients, participanthood is shown in the word-initial directional *mo*, in the first and third lines of (1)–(2); *mi*, shown in the second and fourth lines, is used for third person recipients. For agents, participanthood is shown in three ways: in the preroot marker *e* (underlined), used only in (1); in the (double-underlined) aorist suffixes, where number-neutral *i* is restricted to (1), as opposed to singular *a* and plural *es* in (2); and in the (bold) plural marker *t*, which is confined to (1) and contrasts with the aforementioned third person aorist-cum-plural *es* of (2).

(1) *mo-   g-   e-c-   i*   *mo-   g-   e-c-   i-   t*
    DIR$_{1/2}$-2SD-E-gave-1/2AOR   DIR$_{1/2}$-2SD-E-gave-1/2AOR-P
    'I gave it to you.s'   'we gave it to you.s'
    mi-   v-   e-c-   i   *mi-   v-   e-c-   i-   t*
    DIR$_3$-1S-E-gave-1/2AOR   DIR$_3$-1S-E-gave-1/2AOR-P
    'I gave it to him'   'we gave it to him'

mo- m- e-c- <u>i</u>   mo- m- e-c- <u>i-</u>   t
DIR₁/₂-1SD-E-gave-1/2AOR   DIR₁/₂-1SD-E-gave-1/2AOR-P
'you.S gave it to me'   'you.P gave it to me'

mi- Ø- e-c- <u>i</u>   mi- Ø- e-c- <u>i-</u>   t
DIR₃-2S-E-gave-1/2AOR   DIR₃-2S-E-gave-1/2AOR-P
'you.S gave it to him'   'you.P gave it to him'

(2) mo- g- c- <u>a</u>   mo- g- c- <u>es</u>
DIR₁/₂-2D-gave-3AOR   DIR₁/₂-2D-gave-3P.AOR
'he gave it to you'   'they gave it to you'

mi- s- c- <u>a</u>   mi- s- c- <u>es</u>
DIR₃-3D-gave-3AOR   DIR₃-3D-gave-3P.AOR
'he gave it to her'   'they gave it to her'

Experiencer predicates show the same pattern in two other ways: in the applicative head *i* for participants (3) but *u* for third (4), and (in what may count more as syntax than syncretism but is a sensitivity on either reckoning) via the auxiliary *ar* 'be', which is used only when a participant is the patient of the experience, as in the first and third lines of (3)–(4), ceding ground otherwise to plain agreement, either in the shape of third singular *s* or in the shape of plural marking of the experiencer *t* in the examples below:

(3) m- <u>i-</u> qvar-x- <u>ar</u>   gv- <u>i-</u> qvar-x- <u>ar</u>
1SD-APPL-love-2sS-be   1PD-APPL-love-2sS-be
'I love you.S'   'we love you.S'

m- <u>i-</u> qvar-s   gv- <u>i-</u> qvar-s
1SD-APPL-love-3sS   1PD-APPL-love-3sS
'I love him'   'we love him'

g- <u>i-</u> qvar-v- <u>ar</u>   g- <u>i-</u> qvar-v- <u>ar</u>-t
2D-APPL-love-1S-be   2D-APPL-love-1S-be-P
'you.S love me'   'you.P love me'

g- <u>i-</u> qvar-s   g- <u>i-</u> qvar-t
2D-APPL-love-3sS   2D-APPL-love-P
'you.S love him'   'you.P love him'

(4) <u>u-</u> qvar-x- <u>ar</u>   <u>u-</u> qvar-x- <u>ar</u>-t
APPL-love-2sS-be   APPL-love-2sS-be-P
'he loves you.S'   'they love you.S'

<u>u-</u> qvar-s   <u>u-</u> qvar-t
APPL-love-3sS   APPL-love-P
'he loves him'   'they love him'

Given how elaborately Georgian embeds first–second syncretism, one might expect a syncretic typology to count it. However, Baerman, Brown, and Corbett's (2005) criterion of absolute identity excludes these examples, because the verbs involved carry agreement and Georgian agreement never syncretizes first and second person. Whether as agents and unaccusative subjects, 1 *v* versus 2 Ø in (1) and the auxiliaries of (3)–(4), or as dative recipients and experiencers, 1S *m* and 1P *gv* versus 2 *g* in (1)–(4), they are always distinct. Furthermore, the syncretisms hold of singular and plural alike, whereas Baerman, Brown, and Corbett, using absolute identity, found metasyncretism in the singular only for second and third person.

Before leaving this data set, I point out two apparent anomalies in the distribution of plural *t* in (3)–(4), which might lead one to question the description preceding (1)–(2). First, *t* is absent from the end of *gviqvars* 'we love him', despite the first plural. Along with many others (e.g., Anderson 1992, Halle and Marantz 1993, Béjar 2003), I assume that this results from availability of the person–number portmanteau 1P *gv*, which bleeds the morphological compositionality evidenced by second person datives ($g\_\_t = 2\_\_P$) and first person agents ($v\_\_t = 1\_\_P$).

Second, *t* occurs for third person in the very last example of (4), *uqvart* 'they love him'. Lifting for a moment the veil of pretheoretic neutrality, these data are unproblematic. Various accounts (e.g., Anagnostopoulou 2003, Adger and Harbour 2007, Řezáč 2008) distinguish third persons that are unspecified for person, like direct objects, from others that have negative or categorial specification. The distribution of *t* is then stated as reflecting person in some form versus its complete absence. If the agents in (1)–(2) and the unaccusative subjects of the auxiliaries in (3)–(4) treat third person as formally personless, in contrast to first and second person and to third person datives, then the distribution of *t* in (1)–(2) still counts as a participant–nonparticipant contrast. This is discussed further in chapter 5.

A.2 Nonstandard Tripartitions?

This appendix presents case studies of the three apparent cases of nonstandard tripartitions that I have been able to find: Sanuma (section A.2.1), Teanu (section A.2.2), and Caddo (section A.2.3). The key feature that all three languages share is a paucity of paradigms, so that the method of superposition acts wholly or nearly trivially. Moreover, individual inspection of these languages gives reason to believe that they present underlying quadripartitions. This qualitative approach complements the quantitative and methodological arguments of section 5.4 defusing these apparent counterexamples.

A.2.1 Sanuma

Sanuma is a well-discussed case of seemingly nonstandard tripartition (Cysouw 2003, 2011, McGinnis 2005). According to Borgman (1990), the language exhibits a clusivity contrast, but with thoroughgoing identity between inclusive and second person. Given that he describes the language as having no verb agreement (except for a portmanteau registering number in third-on-third transitives, irrelevant here), all we have to work with are the pronouns. Shown in table A.1, these have two (all but case-invariant) forms, short and long. Looking at the plurals, the syncretism is obvious: short *makö* and long *kamakö* for inclusive and second as against exclusive *samakö* and *kamisamakö*.

Borgman's description is contested, however. Ferreira (2013) offers a comparative perspective on the agreement systems of Sanuma and its relatives Ninam, Yanomae, Yanomama, two dialects of Yanomami, and Yãroamë.

Ferreira already departs from Borgman in regarding the Sanuma short forms as agreement (on a par with related languages, many of which have much richer agreement systems, indicating dual as well as plural and displaying sensitivity to both subject and object).

More importantly, Ferreira reports clusivity only for Yanomami and not for any of the four languages on which he himself has conducted fieldwork (Sanuma, Yanomae, Yanomama, Yãroamë). For Sanuma, he finds inclusive *maki* "only ... in [a] few expressions like 'Let's go' (*maki huu*)": "the construction *samaki huu* ([with] *samaki* the 'typical' 1P) would have a reading of 'we are going (bye!)'." When he "tried to use it in a transitive clause (or even with other intransitives in non-exhortative/imperative contexts), ..."the reading was always as 2 person plural" (Helder Ferreira, pers. comm.).

Notwithstanding the doubts that Ferreira's work raises as to the reality of Sanuma as a nonstandard tripartition, it is still worth considering what one would say, should Borgman's description prove correct. In short, the morphological composition of table A.1 reveals two sets of exponents, and these show that Sanuma is subject to a conspiracy of silence from which the conflation of inclusive and second person emerges as a side effect.

Table A.1

Sanuma short and long pronouns (as in Borgman 1990)

Person	Singular	Plural[a]	Singular	Plural
1EX	sa	sa-makö	ka-mi-sa	ka-mi-sa-makö
1IN		makö		ka-makö
2	wa	makö	ka-wa	ka-makö

[a] *kö* is absent in agentive forms

Table A.2

Sanuma person exponents (shared, left; long only, right)

Person	Singular	Plural (-*makö*)	Base	Singular	Plural
1EX	*sa*	*sa*	*ka*	*-mi*	*-mi*
1IN		∅	*ka*		∅
2	*wa*	∅	*ka*	∅	∅

The short forms are composed of three exponents: *sa* for exclusive, *wa* for second singular, and *makö* for all three plurals (table A.2, left). Given that *makö* marking is insensitive to differences between these three persons, we can ignore it and concentrate on person proper. As shown in the table, the system is spartan: in the plural, inclusive and second person lack exponents at all. Consequently, there is no sense in which these actively form a single conflated person. Rather, they are excluded from singular-only *wa* and exclusive-only *sa* and, so, syncretize in the least interesting way possible: passively, by having nothing to say for themselves.

Exactly the same holds for the long forms. These consist of the short forms suffixed to a pronominal base, *kami* for exclusive, *ka* for inclusive and second (table A.1, right). Decomposing *kami* into *ka* and *mi*, we again have a part, *ka*, that does not distinguish between the three persons under discussion. Putting it aside, like *makö* above, we again find the pattern of the previous paragraph: *mi* for exclusive and silence elsewhere (table A.2, right).

Apparently, then, the identity between inclusive and second person plural, if real, is coincidental. There is no compelling evidence that they form a featurally defined natural class. Rather, they are mapped onto identical strings by dint of their person content being mapped onto nothing at all. So, if (contra Ferreira 2013) the case of Sanuma is genuine, it is not problematic for the view that clusivity always occurs within a quadripartition.

A.2.2 Teanu

The inclusion of Teanu in this section will be initially surprising, as its pronouns distinguish all four persons in both the dual and the plural, like those of Lovono and Tanema, the other two languages of Vanikoro (table A.3, leaving aside more recent colonization; François 2009). However, I argue in chapter 3 that pronouns and agreement should be considered as separate systems in robustly pro-drop languages. That is, in some cases, superposition should apply to the pronouns in all of their numbers and cases, and to the verbal affixes in all of their variety, but the results of those superpositions should not themselves be combined.

Table A.3

Pronouns in the three languages of Vanikoro

Person	Teanu	Lovono	Tanema
1s	ene	ŋane	nana
2s	eo	ago	go
3s	ini	ŋani	nini
1EX.D	keba	gema	gabe
1IN.D	kia	gita	gie
2D	kela	gamila	gamile
3D	da	dea	delalu
1IN.P	kiapa	gitu	geto
1EX.P	kupa	gamitu	gamuto
2P	kaipa	gaipa	gamito
3P	dapa	detu	dato

To judge from François's examples, all three Vanikoroan languages regularly omit subject pronouns where there is subject agreement, as illustrated in (5) for exclusive plural realis and (6) for second singular:

(5) *Pi- te ne sekele iupa, pi- wowo uo.* (Teanu)
    Nupe- lu ne amenoŋa iemitore, nupe- ŋoa upie. (Lovono)
    Tei- o   ini vasaŋola akegamuto, ti- oa   uva. (Tanema)
    1EX.P-stay in garden   1EX.P.GEN 1EX.P-plant yam
    'We were in our garden, we've been planting yams.'

(6) *A- ko u-   ka   u-   katau ene?* (Teanu)
    Nu-pu ku-   ma   ku- ki   ŋane? (Lovono)
    Go-po go- loma go- ie   nana? (Tanema)
    2S- say 2S.IRR-come 2S.IRR-follow 1S
    'Do you want to come with me?'

This makes Teanu, Lovono, and Tanema all languages in which superposition should apply to agreement separately from pronouns.

Adopting this approach yields a nonstandard tripartition for Teanu agreement (table A.4). In the singular, exclusive, second, and third are distinct, as the respective realis prefixes *ni*, *a*, *i* illustrate. However, singulars underdetermine which, if any, of these persons inclusive is conflated with. In the nonsingulars, one finds fewer distinctions than in the singulars. Here, realis and irrealis alike exhibit syncretism of exclusive with second and of inclusive with third. For

Table A.4

Syncretism in the three languages of Vanikoro

	Teanu		Lovono		Tanema	
	Realis	Irrealis	Realis	Irrealis	Realis	Irrealis
1S	*ni-*	*ne-*	*ni-*	*ka-*	*ne/i-*	*na-*
2S	*a-*	*u-*	*nu-*	*ku-*	*go/i-*	*go-*
3S	*i-*	*i-*	*i-*	*ki-*	*i-*	*i-*
1EX.D / 2D	*ba(i)-*	*ba(i)-*	*(nu)ba-*	*ba(i)-*	*ba(i)-*	*ba(i)-*
1IN.D / 3D	*la(i)-*	*la(i)-*	*la(i)-*	*sa-*	*de-*	*ja-*
1EX.P / 2P	*pi-*	*pe-*	*nupe-*	*pe-*	*te/i-*	*tu-*
1IN.P / 3P	*li-*	*le-*	*le(pe)-*	*kape-* / *se(pe)-*	*le/i-, giti-* / *le/i-*	*ba(i)-*

instance, in the realis plural, exclusive–second is *pi*, inclusive–third, *li*. As a result, in the verbal system, neither singular nor nonsingular distinguishes inclusive from third person. So, superposition converges on the nonstandard tripartition of exclusive, second, and inclusive-cum-third.

Real though this example is, relative to the assumption that pronouns and agreement are to be treated as separate partitions in some languages, it is not worrisome. The exceptionality arises from what are themselves rather exceptional factors. (See section 2.4.4 for a functionalist perspective and its problems.)

First, from comparative and historical perspectives, the Vanikoro verbal systems are remarkable. As François (2009) observes, the affixes that distinguish person are few. The languages have, for instance, lost object clitics of Proto-Oceanic and also lack, through loss or conservatism, the person-sensitive tense and aspect distinctions of their Oceanic relations (see, e.g., Lynch, Ross, and Crowley 2002). Moreover, the nonsingular syncretism of Teanu, Lovono, and Tanema, although robust within these languages, is an innovation from the particular island where they are spoken. François observes that it is not shared with neighboring Utupua (Tryon 1994) and suggests that it "may therefore constitute an important shared innovation diagnostic of a Vanikoro subgroup" (p. 117)

Second, within the island, nonstandard tripartition arises only within Teanu. For the other languages, inclusive and third person are distinguished under superposition. In Lovono, this arises solely in virtue of the plural realis, where inclusive *kape* contrasts with third person *se, sepe*. In Tanema, the distinction is even more tenuous, depending on the facultative inclusive *giti* in the plural irrealis, which exists alongside *leli*, a form common to inclusive and third. In consequence, the distinction between inclusive and third person appears to be obsolescent across the island in a process that has reached its endpoint in Teanu.

Third, though, and importantly, this casts the Teanu "tripartition" in a very particular light. The language has shed the distinction between inclusive and third by dint of implementing a metasyncretism across both dual and plural, and realis and irrealis.

In the dual, the structure of this metasyncretism involves loss of the (ir)reality contrast, with $ba(i)$ covering exclusive–second and $la(i)$, inclusive–third for both realis and irrealis. In this, Teanu is again morphologically simpler than its neighbors. In Lovono, realis and irrealis dual are distinct for both pairs of persons, and Tanema exhibits dual (ir)realis syncretism only for exclusive–second. (The syncretic exponent $ba(i)$ in Tanema is identical in Teanu and also occurs in Lovono, suggesting, again, that Teanu has generalized processes that are less developed in the other languages.)

One might, further, decompose the plural forms of Teanu, realis *pi*, *li* and irrealis *pe*, *le*, into a consonant expressing person (exclusive–second *p*, inclusive–third *l*) and a vowel for reality (realis *i*, irrealis *e*). If so, the language has lost all person sensitivity to (ir)realis nonsingular.

On this view, Teanu has a lone metaparadigm for nonsingulars. So, when it comes to inclusives, there is nothing to superpose: singulars provide nothing because there is no singular inclusive, and nonsingulars provide nothing because they are subject to thoroughgoing syncretism. The fruit of clearly contingent linguistic and geographic conditions, these are precisely the paradigmatically impoverished circumstances in which the appearance of nonstandard tripartition might arise.

A.2.3 Caddo

Caddo appears to present the same system as Teanu and not by dint of ignoring pronouns. Yet, despite a hugely rich array of affixes that accrete on the verb, the structure of this counterexample is again meager, and there are even stronger reasons than before for suspecting the tripartition is merely apparent, not the true underlying system.

Person in Caddo is indicated by one affixal position on the verb. No other categories display even allomorphic sensitivity to person, and the language lacks a detailed, let alone full, complement of pronouns. According to Wallace Chafe (pers. comm.), the language has only two to speak of, and these do not

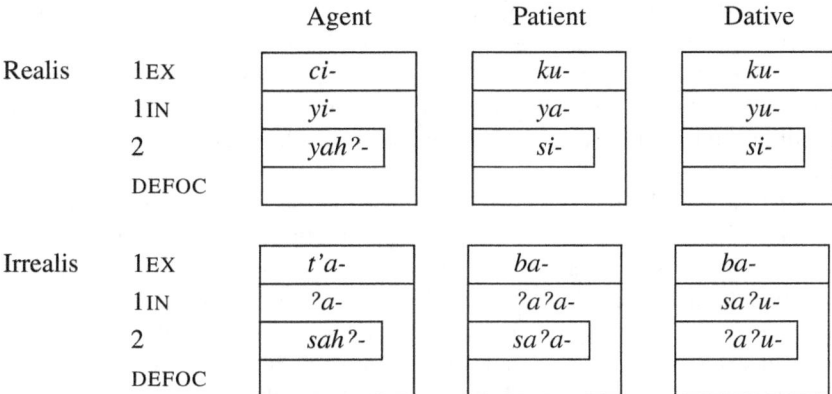

Figure A.1
Caddo person prefixes

cover the full range of meanings expressed by person and number affixes on verbs:

'I' is *kahtsi·* and 'you' is *dákah ?ya ?*. They don't belong to any coherent paradigm. 'I' is especially curious, because it looks like the nominalizing subordinator *kah-* (from *kak-*) followed by the first person realis agent prefix *tsi-* and nothing more. That isn't a normal Caddo construction, and it may have come from something longer that got eroded. 'You' begins with the locative indicative proclitic *dák=* followed by the second person realis agent prefix *ah ?* (from *yah ?-*) followed by a variety of copula ('be present') with the form *-ya ?* (from *-?i?a?*).

The second person form is reminiscent of the structures ('who am', 'who is', etc.) that stand in for pronouns in the related language Wichita (Rood 1976).

The person prefixes also encode semantic role (agent, patient, and dative) and, as on Vanikoro, indicate (ir)reality of the event. They are neutral for number, which is encoded elsewhere in the verb, without any discrimination between animate persons.

Combinations of semantic role and (ir)reality, therefore, provide for six person paradigms. However, as shown in figure A.1, all are structurally identical: there are distinct forms for exclusive and for second person, but inclusive is systematically identical with defocused third person. As the name suggests, this is a kind of third person, and so, as a result, Caddo presents a systematic syncretism between inclusive and third person. Besides defocused third person, there is "normal" third person agreement. Its dative forms are realis *(n)u-* and irrealis *?u*; all other forms are zero. However, this does not alter the fact that inclusive and some form of third person are not distinguished by any verbal morpheme.

Caddo therefore raises the question of whether it is a three-person language in which, unusually, inclusive is conflated with a person other than exclusive, or whether it is a four-person language disguised by syncretism. Several factors suggest that it does not present a compelling case for an alternative tripartition and is conducive to treatment as a quadripartition with swingeing syncretism.

First, a morphological operation is capable of mapping inclusive onto defocused third person.[1] If constrained to a particular morphosyntactic context, such as irrealis dative, the operation will produce syncretism in just one paradigm. However, the more etiolated the context, the more metasyncretic the effect. The Kiowa syncretism of exclusive with third and of inclusive with second extends to all agents and unaccusative subjects (section 2.3.2). The limiting case of metasyncretism is one in which the operation has no contextual constraint. That is, it applies across the board to produce a complete syncretism between two categories. Given that nothing rules out grammars of this kind, we are unable to exclude that some languages will emerge with all paradigms subject to such an operation—in which case, we can account for Caddo without attributing to it a nonstandard tripartition.

Closer acquaintance with the structure of the Caddo person paradigms makes this approach more appealing, showing that the morphological manipulation would not be so unconstrained as it at first appears. Instead of operating across six contexts (agentive, patientive, and dative, realis and irrealis), the inclusive–third syncretism arises in just two. Specifically, the three realis forms, yi, ya, and yu, differ with respect to their vowels. If we take agentive yi as basic, then the patientive can be derived by addition of -a and deletion of the medial vowel (a process observed when causative $\text{'}i\text{'}n(i)$ precedes perfective ah, which surface as ... $\text{'}nah$). Hence, yi-a becomes ya. Similarly, from yi-u, one can derive dative yu.

More or less the same reasoning applies to the irrealis, except that the additional vowels are preceded by glottal stops. Hence, from agentive $\text{'}a$, one derives patientive and dative by addition of $\text{'}a$ and $\text{'}u$ (not plain a, u), yielding $\text{'}a\text{'}a$ and $\text{'}a\text{'}u$, respectively.[2]

If so, there are only two cases of identity between inclusive and third person. The reason why there are six paradigms is that other persons show a richer variety of forms. From the point of view of inclusive/third, it suffices to say that there are two person morphemes, realis yi and irrealis $\text{'}a$, plus a variety of case affixes, patientive $(\text{'})a$ and dative $(\text{'})u$, where the glottal stop is conditioned by irreality. Consequently, the morphological operation one would need to induce syncretism is less free than at first appears.

Finally, an operation transforming inclusive into third person is not unreasonable when the semantics of the defocused third person is considered in crosslinguistic perspective. Chafe (1990) describes three uses for defocused person, besides the indication of inclusivity. One concerns a social taboo around the addressing and referencing of in-laws; its wider crosslinguistic character is discussed in relation to Tongan, below. The other two uses are impersonal constructions and referencing nonprotagonists.

The first of these is straightforward. Where English would use a passive in, say, 'He's been paid' or 'He's getting his hair cut', Caddo deploys defocusing to avoid specific mention of an agent:

(7) hák- yi- 'n- bih=č'ud-sa ʔ
    STAT-DEFOC.AGT-DAT-cut hair- PROG
    'he's getting his hair cut' (hákímbihčussa ʔ)

Related to this are object, agent, and action names. 'Gloves', for instance, are 'that with which one dresses the hands'; a 'courthouse' is 'where one deals with the law'; and a 'barber', 'one who cuts one's hair'. All use defocusing, as in (8):

(8) nayt- ya- 'n- bih=č'ud-hah
    one who-DEFOC.PAT-DAT-cut hair- HAB
    'barber'; lit., 'one who cuts one's hair' (naytdámbihč'utah)

The other use of defocusing is to refer, in narratives, to third persons who are not the protagonist. An example from Melnar 2004, drawing on Wallace Chafe's unpublished notes, shows this (along with plural reference, not illustrated so far). In a story in which a variety of animals go in search of water, attention falls for a while on the turtle, as he finds a big log, gets stuck, crawls over it, and then calls out, a sequence of actions that establish him as the momentary protagonist. As he calls out, he gets trampled by the other animals, who are treated as defocused agents:

(9) Nátti ʔ yi- ʔini- bi ʔ=sak- ah, ná· nabít
    then DEFOC.AGT-horizontal.surface-step.on.forcefully-PF those other
    kak hán yábah.
    sub an.pat be.P

'Then they trampled on him, those other creatures.' (Nátti ʔ di·niwsakáh, ná· nabít kahánná·bah.) (Gloss of nabít from Wallace Chafe, pers. comm.)

Given these uses, we can strengthen the case for viewing the Caddo person system as the consequence of a morphological process by now showing that use of a third person category for some first persons is not crosslinguistically isolated. In this regard, Chafe himself draws attention to French. Similar behavior is found in Brazilian Portuguese, and, more strikingly, Tongan.

In French, where impersonal *on* 'one' is regularly used for *nous* 'we', the parallels are noteworthy, even if the language lacks a clusivity contrast (and the substitution is restricted to the nominative). A passage from Proust, in search of lost cake, illustrates two Caddo-like properties (my translation):

Au moment où nous arrivions à la maison, maman s'aperçut qu'on avait oublié le saint-honoré et demanda à mon père de retourner avec moi sur nos pas dire qu'on l'apportât tout de suite. Nous croisâmes près de l'église Legrandin qui venait en sens inverse conduisant la même dame à sa voiture.

Just as we were reaching the house, mother noticed that we had forgotten the gâteau Saint-Honoré and asked my father to go back with me and tell them to have it brought at once. Near the church, we met Legrandin who was coming the other way, accompanying the same lady to her carriage.

First, the passage contains an impersonal *on* in the mother's instruction to the pâtissiers, *qu'on l'apportât* 'that one bring it'. This *on* does not specify a particular subject and, though contextually one might take it to apply to one or more of the pâtissiers, one could comply by hailing a boy on a bicycle and instructing him to deliver it. Additionally, *on* occurs in *on avait oublié* 'we had forgotten'. So, we see *on* in both its impersonal and its first plural uses. (A similar range of uses is found for *a gente* 'the people', a third person phrase used as a first person pronoun in Brazilian Portuguese. See, for instance, Zilles 2005 on southern varieties.)

The parallels to Caddo in this passage arguably extend also to defocusing. At first mention, 'we' is signaled with *nous* (*nous arrivions* 'we were arriving'). Later, however, the mother issuing instructions is the protagonist and the constituents of 'we' are dismantled, with separate mentions of both *mon père* 'my father' and the narrator, *moi* 'me'. This shift in focus is accompanied by a shift in pronoun, from *nous* to *on* (*on avait oublié* 'we had forgotten'). However, when narrative focus shifts back to father and son as a unit, with mother out of the narrative frame, *nous* returns: *nous croisâmes* 'we met'.

Of course, such defocusing does not approach the systematicity or categoricity of Caddo. Nonetheless, this discourse-level concept does seem to capture subtle shifts in emphasis in this and other passages of Proust's novel. So, it suggests that the cluster of properties associated with defocused third persons in Caddo have some semantic naturalness.

This conclusion is reinforced by Tongan (Churchward 1953). Unlike French, but like Caddo, Tongan has a clusivity contrast, as well as singular, dual, and plural number. Languages with this array of persons and numbers have an obligatory gap for the inclusive singular, as inclusives minimally reference both speaker and hearer and, so, are too big to be singular. However, in apparent analogy with the other persons, Tongan has settled into what looks, for morphological intents and purposes, like a singular of the inclusive (table A.5). To avoid confusion, I call this inclusive a "pseudosingular" (glossed ψs).[3]

The interesting point about the Tongan pseudosingulars is the meanings they have acquired, faced with the impossibility of true singular inclusive reference. Churchward describes two, both reminiscent of Caddo: generic 'one' (10), and humble or polite speech (11). These examples use both pre- and postposed forms at once (my glossing, relying on Churchward 1953 and www.tongantranslator.com):

(10) *'Oku 'ikai totonu ke te tokanga pē kiate kita.*
 PRES NEG right that 1IN.ψs attend only to 1IN.ψs
 'It is not right that one should attend only to oneself.'

Table A.5

Tongan pronouns with pseudosingular inclusives (boxed)

	Preposed			Postposed		
	Singular	Dual	Plural	Singular	Dual	Plural
1EX	ou	ma	mau	au	kimaua	kimautolu
1IN	|te|	ta	tau	|kita|	kitaua	kitautolu
2	ke	mo	mou	koe	kimoua	kimoutolu
3	ne	na	nau	ia	kinaua	kinautolu

(11) *'Okú te mā 'aupito kita 'i he'enau angafaí.*
 PRES 1IN.ΨS ashamed very 1IN.ΨS LOC their.DEF conduct
 'I for my part am very ashamed of their conduct.'

The generic reading of the inclusive pseudosingular in (10) is comparable to Caddo (8), and its honorificity-related use in (11) recalls in-law avoidance by means of defocusing, mentioned before (7). In fact, this latter point is a recurrent property of inclusives, as Cysouw (2005b) shows (see Nevins 2008 for theoretical comment).

Thus, the collapse of inclusive with defocused third person in Caddo has the hallmarks of a crosslinguistic process substituting third person forms for first or inclusive in a variety of contexts. These semantic facts bolster the plausibility of the morphological argument already given. In consequence, Caddo does not present a compelling case of a tripartition distinguishing exclusive and second person but conflating inclusive with third. Instead, it is plausible to maintain that Caddo person is, at root, quadripartite, but loses one of its distinctions owing to language-particular factors.

The three apparent examples of nonstandard tripartitions in Sanuma, Teanu, and Caddo, then, do not undermine a theory of person that is based on a categorical reading of the partition problem.

B Formal Appendices

The appendices that follow present some formal results, especially concerning alternatives to paths taken in the main text.

B.1 Zero Bottoming

Linguistic lattices generally assume the absence of zero bottom elements. That is, they are semilattices (atomic join-complete semilattices, to be precise), rather than true lattices. However, the appearance of zeroes during the action of person features is crucial in deriving the correct inventory of partitions. Moreover, the disappearance of zeroes before the action of number features is equally crucial in deriving the correct inventory of pronoun and agreement systems.

Given that zeroes do not vanish until after the action by the person features, it is natural to wonder whether they ought not to be present in the underlying structures. This appendix shows that it does not matter whether they are present or not and considers two ways in which zeroes might be added to the structures introduced in chapter 4.

In section B.1.1, zeroes are added only to semilattices. Given that $\mathscr{L}_{au}$ consists of a single point, it is trivially a lattice. Thus, zeroes are added just to $\mathscr{L}_{pt}$ and $\mathscr{L}_{\pi}$. In this system, the correct inventory of partitions still emerges, from the same feature specifications.

In section B.1.2, zeroes are added to all structures, including $\mathscr{L}_{au}$. With this thoroughgoing addition, the system fails to generate the tripartition, though the bi- and quadripartitions remain unaffected. However, if Lexical Complementarity is taken to apply cyclically—that is, not just after both features have applied, but after application, first, of ±author, and then again after application of ±participant, or vice versa—then the desired inventory of partitions reemerges, again without change to the feature specifications.

With two separate proofs of the neutrality of using zero-bottomed lattices as input structures, it is safe to conclude that the issue is irrelevant to the efficacy of the theory proposed here and that one may insert or remove them as best fits the discussion (so long as cyclicity of Lexical Complementarity itself does not come to play a crucial role, which, at present, it does not).

Zero-bottomed structures are notated below with a degree sign: $\mathscr{L}_{au}^\circ$, $\mathscr{L}_{pt}^\circ$, $\mathscr{L}_\pi^\circ$. For convenience, I repeat the statement of Lexical Complementarity:

(1) *Lexical Complementarity*
Let F, G be feature specifications such that $[\![F(\pi)]\!] \subset [\![G(\pi)]\!]$. Then $G(\pi)$ is confined to $[\![G(\pi)]\!] \setminus [\![F(\pi)]\!]$.

B.1.1 Zeroes for Semilattices

The first demonstration of the neutrality of zeroes involves adding them just to the participant and π structures. Not adding zeroes across the board may seem like an odd way of proving that their presence or absence is irrelevant. However, there are two good reasons to assume that zeroes might always be absent from the author lattice, as a matter of principle.

First, if the purpose of adding zeroes is to create lattices from semilattices, then we should not have added zero to $\mathscr{L}_{au}$, as it already has a bottom element. Obviously, the bottom element is also the top element, as i comprises the whole structure. $\mathscr{L}_{au}$ is, therefore, both meet- and join-complete. It is also, trivially, (partially) ordered by inclusion. In sum, then, $\mathscr{L}_{au}$ is already a full lattice.

Second, there is an obvious difference between the author lattice and the other two structures. The author lattice is ontologically pure. It involves no mixtures between different elements of the ontology. The participant structure mixes i with u, and the π structure further mixes these with o's. If some structures contain zeroes and others do not, it is plausible that zeroes arise as part of the combinatorial process. We therefore expect them to be absent when the sole element of a solipsistic ontology has nothing to combine with.

Calculating with plain $\mathscr{L}_{au}$ and with the zero-bottomed $\mathscr{L}_{pt}^\circ$ and $\mathscr{L}_\pi^\circ$, the correct inventory of bi-, tri-, and quadripartitions reemerges. (Monopartition, being trivial, is not considered below.)

The ±author bipartition emerges as before:

(2) $[\![-\text{author}(\pi)]\!]$
$= \mathscr{L}_\pi^\circ \ominus \mathscr{L}_{au}$
$= \{i_o, iu_o, u_o, o_o, \varnothing\} \ominus \max(\{i\})$
$= \{i_o, iu_o, u_o, o_o, \varnothing\} \ominus \{i\}$
$= \{u_o, o_o, \varnothing\}$

(3) $[\![+\text{author}(\pi)]\!]$
$= \mathscr{L}_\pi^\circ \oplus \mathscr{L}_{au}$
$= \{i_o, iu_o, u_o, o_o, \varnothing\} \oplus \{i\}$
$= \{i_o, iu_o\}$

This is the familiar author–nonauthor partition $i_o iu_o \mid u_o o_o$

The ±participant bipartition works only slightly differently:

(4) $[\![-\text{participant}(\pi)]\!]$
$= \mathscr{L}_\pi^\circ \ominus \mathscr{L}_{pt}^\circ$
$= \{i_o, iu_o, u_o, o_o, \varnothing\} \ominus \max(\{i, iu, u, \varnothing\})$
$= \{i_o, iu_o, u_o, o_o, \varnothing\} \ominus \{iu\}$
$= \{o_o, \varnothing\}$

(5) $[\![+\text{participant}(\pi)]\!]$
$= \mathscr{L}_\pi^\circ \oplus \mathscr{L}_{pt}^\circ$
$= \{i_o, iu_o, u_o, o_o, \varnothing\} \oplus \{i, iu, u, \varnothing\}$
$= (\{i_o, iu_o, u_o, o_o, \varnothing\} \oplus \{i\}) \cup (\{i_o, iu_o, u_o, o_o, \varnothing\} \oplus \{iu\})$
$\quad\quad \cup (\{i_o, iu_o, u_o, o_o, \varnothing\} \oplus \{u\}) \cup (\{i_o, iu_o, u_o, o_o, \varnothing\} \oplus \{\varnothing\})$
$= \{i_o, iu_o\} \cup \{iu_o, u_o\} \cup \{iu_o\} \cup \{i_o, iu_o, u_o, o_o, \varnothing\}$
$= \{i_o, iu_o, u_o, o_o, \varnothing\}$
$\equiv \{i_o, iu_o, u_o\}$ by (1), (4)

This is still the participant bipartition $i_o iu_o u_o \mid o_o$.

The principal difference between the calculations with $\mathscr{L}_\pi^\circ$ and $\mathscr{L}_\pi$ stems from the presence of $\varnothing$. The action of the plus value creates an exact copy of what it acts on. As a result, $+\text{participant}(\mathscr{L}_\pi^\circ) = \mathscr{L}_\pi^\circ$. So, the bipartition now requires Lexical Complementarity, which was not the case before. (In effect, $\varnothing$ makes the action of i, iu, and u redundant, as these merely create substructures of $\mathscr{L}_\pi^\circ$, which are subsumed by the full copy of $\mathscr{L}_\pi^\circ$ that $\varnothing$ creates. This redundancy vanishes in later calculations, where $+\text{participant}$ may act on structures that do not contain all of $\mathscr{L}_{pt}^\circ$.)

In the tripartition, we have two distinct representations for third person, as previously:

(6) $[\![-\text{participant}(-\text{author}(\pi))]\!]$
$= (\mathscr{L}_\pi^\circ \ominus \mathscr{L}_{au}) \ominus \mathscr{L}_{pt}^\circ$
$= \{u_o, o_o, \varnothing\} \ominus \max(\{i, iu, u, \varnothing\})$ by (2)
$= \{u_o, o_o, \varnothing\} \ominus \{iu\}$
$= \{o_o, \varnothing\}$

(7) $[\![-\text{participant}(+\text{author}(\pi))]\!]$
$= (\mathscr{L}_\pi^\circ \oplus \mathscr{L}_{au}) \ominus \mathscr{L}_{pt}^\circ$
$= \{i_o, iu_o\} \ominus \max(\{i, iu, u, \varnothing\})$ by (3)
$= \{i_o, iu_o\} \ominus \{iu\}$
$= \{o_o, \varnothing\}$

First and second person also follow more or less as before:

(8) $[\![+\text{participant}(+\text{author}(\pi))]\!]$
$= (\mathscr{L}_\pi^\circ \oplus \mathscr{L}_{au}) \oplus \mathscr{L}_{pt}^\circ$
$= \{i_o, iu_o\} \oplus \{i, iu, u, \varnothing\}$ by (3)

$$= (\{i_o, iu_o\} \oplus \{i\}) \cup (\{i_o, iu_o\} \oplus \{iu\}) \cup (\{i_o, iu_o\} \oplus \{u\}) \cup (\{i_o, iu_o\} \oplus \{\varnothing\})$$
$$= \{i_o, iu_o\} \cup \{iu_o\} \cup \{iu_o\} \cup \{i_o, iu_o\}$$
$$= \{i_o, iu_o\}$$

(9) $[\![+\text{participant}(-\text{author}(\pi))]\!]$
$$= (\mathscr{L}_\pi^\circ \ominus \mathscr{L}_{au}) \oplus \mathscr{L}_{pt}^\circ$$
$$= \{u_o, o_o, \varnothing\} \oplus \{i, iu, u, \varnothing\} \qquad \text{by (2)}$$
$$= (\{u_o, o_o, \varnothing\} \oplus \{i\}) \cup (\{u_o, o_o, \varnothing\} \oplus \{iu\}) \cup (\{u_o, o_o, \varnothing\} \oplus \{u\}) \cup$$
$$(\{u_o, o_o, \varnothing\} \oplus \{\varnothing\})$$
$$= \{iu_o, i_o\} \cup \{iu_o\} \cup \{u_o\} \cup \{u_o, o_o, \varnothing\}$$
$$= \{i_o, iu_o, u_o, o_o, \varnothing\}$$
$$\equiv \{u_o\} \qquad \text{by (1), (6), (7), (8)}$$

This yields $i_o iu_o \mid u_o \mid o_o$, as desired.

Finally, we derive quadripartition:

(10) $[\![-\text{author}(-\text{participant}(\pi))]\!]$
$$= (\mathscr{L}_\pi^\circ \ominus \mathscr{L}_{pt}^\circ) \ominus \mathscr{L}_{au}$$
$$= \{o_o, \varnothing\} \ominus \max(\{i\}) \qquad \text{by (4)}$$
$$= \{o_o, \varnothing\}$$

(11) $[\![-\text{author}(+\text{participant}(\pi))]\!]$
$$= (\mathscr{L}_\pi^\circ \oplus \mathscr{L}_{pt}^\circ) \ominus \mathscr{L}_{au}$$
$$= \{i_o, iu_o, u_o, o_o, \varnothing\} \ominus \max(\{i\}) \qquad \text{by (5)}$$
$$= \{u_o, o_o, \varnothing\}$$
$$\equiv \{u_o\} \qquad \text{by (1), (10)}$$

(12) $[\![+\text{author}(-\text{participant}(\pi))]\!]$
$$= (\mathscr{L}_\pi^\circ \ominus \mathscr{L}_{pt}^\circ) \oplus \mathscr{L}_{au}$$
$$= \{o_o, \varnothing\} \oplus \{i\} \qquad \text{by (4)}$$
$$= \{i_o\}$$

(13) $[\![+\text{author}(+\text{participant}(\pi))]\!]$
$$= (\mathscr{L}_\pi^\circ \oplus \mathscr{L}_{pt}^\circ) \oplus \mathscr{L}_{au}$$
$$= \{i_o, iu_o, u_o, o_o, \varnothing\} \oplus \{i\} \qquad \text{by (5)}$$
$$= \{i_o, iu_o\}$$
$$\equiv \{iu_o\} \qquad \text{by (1), (12)}$$

Thus, with the three full lattices $\mathscr{L}_{au}$, $\mathscr{L}_{pt}^\circ$, and $\mathscr{L}_\pi^\circ$, the feature inventory and specifications of the main text still derive exactly the attested set of partitions.

B.1.2 Zeroes for All

The opening of the previous section argued that there are good reasons for confining zeroes to $\mathscr{L}_{pt}^\circ$ and $\mathscr{L}_\pi^\circ$. In fact, if one adds zeroes to all three structures (creating $\mathscr{L}_{au}^\circ$, $\mathscr{L}_{pt}^\circ$, and $\mathscr{L}_\pi^\circ$) without, crucially, making any other changes, the system runs awry. The bipartitions and the quadripartition are still derivable, but the tripartition collapses into a bipartition. The correct inventory of partitions is retrievable if we make Lexical Complementarity a cyclic operation that applies after ±author (or ±participant) composes with $\mathscr{L}_\pi^\circ$, and then again after ±participant (or ±author) applies to the result.

B.1.2.1 Bipartitions and Tripartition The derivation of the ±participant bipartition remains as in (4)–(5). However, given the new structure $\mathscr{L}_{au}^\circ$, the ±author bipartition now requires application of Lexical Complementarity:

(14) $[\![-\text{author}(\pi)]\!]$
$= \mathscr{L}_\pi^\circ \ominus \mathscr{L}_{au}^\circ$
$= \{i_o, iu_o, u_o, o_o, \varnothing\} \ominus \max(\{i, \varnothing\})$
$= \{i_o, iu_o, u_o, o_o, \varnothing\} \ominus \{i\}$
$= \{u_o, o_o, \varnothing\}$

(15) $[\![+\text{author}(\pi)]\!]$
$= \mathscr{L}_\pi^\circ \oplus \mathscr{L}_{au}^\circ$
$= \{i_o, iu_o, u_o, o_o, \varnothing\} \oplus \{i, \varnothing\}$
$= (\{i_o, iu_o, u_o, o_o, \varnothing\} \oplus \{i\}) \cup (\{i_o, iu_o, u_o, o_o, \varnothing\} \oplus \{\varnothing\})$
$= \{i_o, iu_o\} \cup \{i_o, iu_o, u_o, o_o, \varnothing\}$
$= \{i_o, iu_o, u_o, o_o, \varnothing\}$
$\equiv \{i_o, iu_o\}$ by (1), (14)

Nonetheless, as before, ±author yields the author partition $i_o iu_o \mid u_o o_o$. (This recalls the derivation of the participant bipartition in section B.1.1. The action of i is redundant, as its output, a substructure of $\mathscr{L}_\pi^\circ$, is subsumed by the full copy of $\mathscr{L}_\pi^\circ$ that $\varnothing$ creates.)

The equivalence in generative capacity breaks down for tripartition, however. As on the previous analysis, there are two distinct ways of defining third person:

(16) $[\![-\text{participant}(-\text{author}(\pi))]\!]$
$= (\mathscr{L}_\pi^\circ \ominus \mathscr{L}_{au}^\circ) \ominus \mathscr{L}_{pt}^\circ$
$= \{u_o, o_o, \varnothing\} \ominus \max(\{i, iu, u, \varnothing\})$ by (14)
$= \{u_o, o_o, \varnothing\} \ominus \{iu\}$
$= \{o_o, \varnothing\}$

(17) $[\![-\text{participant}(+\text{author}(\pi))]\!]$
$= (\mathscr{L}_\pi^\circ \oplus \mathscr{L}_{au}^\circ) \ominus \mathscr{L}_{pt}^\circ$
$= \{i_o, iu_o, u_o, o_o, \varnothing\} \ominus \max(\{i, iu, u, \varnothing\})$ by (15)
$= \{i_o, iu_o, u_o, o_o, \varnothing\} \ominus \{iu\}$
$= \{o_o, \varnothing\}$

However, the action of +participant reconstitutes the whole of the π lattice:

(18) $[\![+\text{participant}(-\text{author}(\pi))]\!]$
$= (\mathscr{L}_\pi^\circ \ominus \mathscr{L}_{au}^\circ) \oplus \mathscr{L}_{pt}^\circ$
$= \{u_o, o_o, \varnothing\} \oplus \{i, iu, u, \varnothing\}$ by (14)
$= (\{u_o, o_o, \varnothing\} \oplus \{i\}) \cup (\{u_o, o_o, \varnothing\} \oplus \{iu\}) \cup (\{u_o, o_o, \varnothing\} \oplus \{u\}) \cup$
$\qquad\qquad\qquad\qquad\qquad\qquad\qquad\qquad (\{u_o, o_o, \varnothing\} \oplus \{\varnothing\})$
$= \{iu_o, i_o\} \cup \{iu_o\} \cup \{u_o\} \cup \{u_o, o_o, \varnothing\}$
$= \{i_o, iu_o, u_o, o_o, \varnothing\}$

(19) $[\![+\text{participant}(+\text{author}(\pi))]\!]$
$= (\mathscr{L}_\pi^\circ \oplus \mathscr{L}_{au}^\circ) \oplus \mathscr{L}_{pt}^\circ$
$= \{i_o, iu_o, u_o, o_o, \varnothing\} \oplus \{i, iu, u, \varnothing\}$ by (15)
$= \{i_o, iu_o, u_o, o_o, \varnothing\}$

The result after application of Lexical Complementarity, $i_o iu_o u_o \mid o_o$, is equivalent to bipartition by ±participant alone. Though it may be some comfort not to have produced a partition that is unattested, the more salient fact is that the tripartition has been lost, and with it, descriptive adequacy.

B.1.2.2 Quadripartition Before we proceed to a solution, in terms of cyclic application of Lexical Complementarity, it is worth noting, for completeness' sake, that only tripartition fails. Quadripartition is derivable from the same feature values and order of composition as before:

(20) $[\![-\text{author}(-\text{participant}(\pi))]\!]$
$= (\mathscr{L}_\pi^\circ \ominus \mathscr{L}_{pt}^\circ) \ominus \mathscr{L}_{au}^\circ$
$= \{o_o, \varnothing\} \ominus \max(\{i, \varnothing\})$ by (4)
$= \{o_o, \varnothing\}$

(21) $[\![-\text{author}(+\text{participant}(\pi))]\!]$
$= (\mathscr{L}_\pi^\circ \oplus \mathscr{L}_{pt}^\circ) \ominus \mathscr{L}_{au}^\circ$
$= \{i_o, iu_o, u_o, o_o, \varnothing\} \ominus \max(\{i, \varnothing\})$ by (5)
$= \{u_o, o_o, \varnothing\}$
$\equiv \{u_o\}$ by (1), (20)

(22) $[\![+\text{author}(-\text{participant}(\pi))]\!]$
$= (\mathscr{L}_\pi^\circ \ominus \mathscr{L}_{pt}^\circ) \oplus \mathscr{L}_{au}^\circ$
$= \{o_o, \varnothing\} \oplus \{i, \varnothing\}$ by (4)
$= (\{o_o, \varnothing\} \oplus \{i\}) \cup (\{o_o, \varnothing\} \oplus \{\varnothing\})$
$= \{i_o\} \cup \{o_o, \varnothing\}$
$= \{i_o, o_o, \varnothing\}$
$\equiv \{i_o\}$ by (1), (20)

(23) $[\![+\text{author}(+\text{participant}(\pi))]\!]$
$= (\mathscr{L}_\pi^\circ \oplus \mathscr{L}_{pt}^\circ) \oplus \mathscr{L}_{au}^\circ$
$= \{i_o, iu_o, u_o, o_o, \varnothing\} \oplus \{i, \varnothing\}$ by (5)
$= (\{i_o, iu_o, u_o, o_o, \varnothing\} \oplus \{i\}) \cup (\{i_o, iu_o, u_o, o_o, \varnothing\} \oplus \{\varnothing\})$

$$= \{i_o, iu_o\} \cup \{i_o, iu_o, u_o, o_o, \varnothing\}$$
$$= \{i_o, iu_o, u_o, o_o, \varnothing\}$$
$$\equiv \{iu_o\} \qquad \text{by (1), (20), (21), (22)}$$

This yields $i_o \mid iu_o \mid u_o \mid o_o$.

B.1.2.3 Cyclicity and Lexical Complementarity If we are not to alter the features, their values, or the underlying ontology, then the only other element that we might obviously target for change is Lexical Complementarity. Given that it is incorporated into many other accounts, and not only accounts of phi features, the principle itself is not the most plausible candidate for revision. Nonetheless, its timing might be.

Lexical Complementarity has so far been assumed to apply only once all features have acted. That is, first, ±author (or ±participant) acts on $\mathscr{L}_\pi^\circ$, then ±participant (or ±author) acts on the result, then Lexical Complementarity applies. An alternative is that Lexical Complementarity applies after each round of feature action: first ±author (or ±participant) acts on $\mathscr{L}_\pi^\circ$, then Lexical Complementarity applies, only then does ±participant (or ±author) apply to the result, after which Lexical Complementarity applies again. This makes Lexical Complementarity cyclic.

The reason to suspect that cyclicity of Lexical Complementarity might aid in tripartition is that ±participant would consequently act on the disjoint sets +author(π) $\equiv \{i_o, iu_o\}$ and −author(π) $= \{u_o, o_o, \varnothing\}$, rather than on the overlapping sets +author(π) $= \{i_o, iu_o, u_o, o_o, \varnothing\}$ and −author(π) $= \{u_o, o_o, \varnothing\}$. The hope would be that more differentiated inputs would lead to more differentiated outputs. Indeed, this is what happens.

Tripartition now works correctly. There are still two representations for third person, −participant(±author(π)), because removing max($\mathscr{L}_{pt}^\circ$) from any of the sets in the previous paragraph yields $\{o_o, \varnothing\} = $ (16)–(17). More interestingly, the two nonthird persons now yield distinct, and desired, results:

(24) $[\![+\text{participant}(+\text{author}(\pi))]\!]$
$$= (\mathscr{L}_\pi^\circ \oplus \mathscr{L}_{au}^\circ) \oplus \mathscr{L}_{pt}^\circ$$
$$= \{i_o, iu_o, u_o, o_o, \varnothing\} \oplus \{i, iu, u, \varnothing\} \qquad \text{by (15)}$$
$$= \{i_o, iu_o\} \oplus \{i, iu, u, \varnothing\} \qquad \text{by (1)}$$
$$= (\{i_o, iu_o\} \oplus \{i\}) \cup (\{i_o, iu_o\} \oplus \{iu\}) \cup (\{i_o, iu_o\} \oplus \{u\}) \cup$$
$$(\{i_o, iu_o\} \oplus \{\varnothing\})$$
$$= \{i_o, iu_o\} \cup \{iu_o\} \cup \{iu_o\} \cup \{i_o, iu_o\}$$
$$= \{i_o, iu_o\}$$

(25) $[\![+\text{participant}(-\text{author}(\pi))]\!]$
$$= (\mathscr{L}_\pi^\circ \ominus \mathscr{L}_{au}^\circ) \oplus \mathscr{L}_{pt}^\circ$$
$$= \{u_o, o_o, \varnothing\} \oplus \{i, iu, u, \varnothing\} \qquad \text{by (14)}$$
$$= (\{u_o, o_o, \varnothing\} \oplus \{i\}) \cup (\{u_o, o_o, \varnothing\} \oplus \{iu\}) \cup (\{u_o, o_o, \varnothing\} \oplus \{u\}) \cup$$
$$(\{u_o, o_o, \varnothing\} \oplus \{\varnothing\})$$

$$= \{iu_o, i_o\} \cup \{iu_o\} \cup \{u_o\} \cup \{u_o, o_o, \varnothing\}$$
$$= \{i_o, iu_o, u_o, o_o, \varnothing\}$$
$$\equiv \{u_o\} \qquad \text{by (1), (16), (17), (24)}$$

Thus, we have the tripartition $i_o iu_o \mid u_o \mid o_o$.

It only remains to check that quadripartition also still works. This involves rerunning (20)–(23) with +participant$(\pi) \equiv \{i_o, iu_o, u_o\}$.

Two derivations are unaffected by the change, namely, those involving −participant:

(26) $[\![-\text{author}(-\text{participant}(\pi))]\!] = \{o_o, \varnothing\}$

(27) $[\![+\text{author}(-\text{participant}(\pi))]\!] = \{i_o, o_o, \varnothing\} \equiv \{i_o\}$ by (1), (26)

The cases affected by the change are those involving +participant. However, they still yield the desired results:

(28) $[\![-\text{author}(+\text{participant}(\pi))]\!]$
$$= (\mathscr{L}_\pi^\circ \oplus \mathscr{L}_{pt}^\circ) \ominus \mathscr{L}_{au}^\circ$$
$$= \{i_o, iu_o, u_o, o_o, \varnothing\} \ominus \max(\{i, \varnothing\}) \qquad \text{by (5)}$$
$$= \{i_o, iu_o, u_o\} \ominus \max(\{i, \varnothing\}) \qquad \text{by (1)}$$
$$= \{u_o, o_o, \varnothing\}$$
$$\equiv \{u_o\} \qquad \text{by (1), (26)}$$

(29) $[\![+\text{author}(+\text{participant}(\pi))]\!]$
$$= (\mathscr{L}_\pi^\circ \oplus \mathscr{L}_{pt}^\circ) \oplus \mathscr{L}_{au}^\circ$$
$$= \{i_o, iu_o, u_o, o_o, \varnothing\} \oplus \{i, \varnothing\} \qquad \text{by (5)}$$
$$= \{i_o, iu_o, u_o\} \oplus \{i, \varnothing\} \qquad \text{by (1)}$$
$$= (\{i_o, iu_o, u_o\} \oplus \{i\}) \cup (\{i_o, iu_o, u_o\} \oplus \{\varnothing\})$$
$$= \{i_o, iu_o\} \cup \{i_o, iu_o, u_o\}$$
$$= \{i_o, iu_o, u_o\}$$
$$\equiv \{iu_o\} \qquad \text{by (1), (26), (28), (27)}$$

Thus, we have the tripartition $i_o \mid iu_o \mid u_o \mid o_o$.

B.1.3 Number above Person

The foregoing shows that the omission and addition of zeroes is immaterial under a variety of circumstances. Before leaving the topic, however, I note that, if we adopt zero-bottomed person structures, then we have yet another reason for supposing that number dominates person and not the reverse (chapters 6 and 7). With the opposite arrangement, the account of person and number given in chapter 6 breaks down in two ways, in two of the most basic and common number systems.

If +minimal applies to $\mathscr{L}_\pi^\circ$, it picks out $\varnothing$. If we then apply −participant and −author, in whichever order, for third person, we simply map $\varnothing$ onto $\varnothing$. In other words, there would be no third minimal in languages like Hocąk and Bininj Gun-wok and no third singular in languages like Ewondo, the number systems of which use only ±minimal (and feature recursion for Bininj Gun-wok).

An additional, more assumption-laden problem is that ±atomic would yield a nonconvex partition of a zero-bottomed $\mathscr{L}_\pi^\circ$. A lattice region, L, is convex if, and only if, $b \in L$ whenever $a \geq b \geq c$ and $a, c \in L$. I have argued above and, especially, in Harbour 2014a that feature systems that yield nonconvex cuts are illegitimate. Given that +atomic picks out the atomic stratum, −atomic would pick out pluralities and the empty set, which would be nonconvex because $iu \geq i \geq \varnothing$ and $iu, \varnothing \in -\text{atomic}(\mathscr{L}_\pi^\circ)$, but $i \notin -\text{atomic}(\mathscr{L}_\pi^\circ)$. So, we would lose not only minimal–augmented and minimal–unit-augmented–augmented systems, but singular–plural ones too.

Thus, again, there is a convergence of results in favor of a phrase structure in which number dominates person.

B.2 π-Internal Composition

The previous appendix is one example among many of the various possible incarnations of my proposal that I have considered while developing the ideas presented in the main text. It would try even paper's patience to lay all of these out here, but one that might be useful, arising from a question posed by Klaus Abels, concerns what happens if ±author and ±participant compose with each other before composing with π.

This will remind the reader of the mite *Acarophenax tribolii*. In a process that kills her, the pregnant female of the species gives birth to some 15 live daughters and one sole dead son. A species that delivers stillborn males ought to die out. However, before his death (and birth), the male rapes and fertilizes all of his sisters in his mother's womb.

It might seem to the genteel reader that those of Abelian bent are suggesting that my features are incestuous, matricidal, antenatal rapist mites, not the wholesome creatures they have seemed until now, one of which joins with the π lattice to generate wholesome progeny with which the other may then combine in a properly sanctioned manner. Notwithstanding, fear of descent into semantic depravity is misplaced. Nor is there danger of partitional turpitude. Tripartition and quadripartition result as before. (Bipartition is unaffected, as, in such cases, there is only one feature under π.)

As a preliminary, note the result of in utero composition between the author and participant lattices:

(30) a. $\mathscr{L}_{pt} \oplus \mathscr{L}_{au} = \{i, iu, u\} \oplus \{i\} \quad = \{i, iu\}$
b. $\mathscr{L}_{pt} \ominus \mathscr{L}_{au} = \{i, iu, u\} \ominus \max(\{i\}) = \{u, \varnothing\}$

(31) a. $\mathscr{L}_{au} \oplus \mathscr{L}_{pt} = \{i\} \oplus \{i, iu, u\} \quad = \{i, iu\}$
b. $\mathscr{L}_{au} \ominus \mathscr{L}_{pt} = \{i\} \ominus \max(\{i, iu, u\}) = \{\varnothing\}$

Quadripartition derives from the following specifications. (For the reader's convenience, they are ordered to make the application of Lexical Complementarity maximally clear.)

(32) $\mathscr{L}_\pi \ominus (\mathscr{L}_{pt} \oplus \mathscr{L}_{au})$
$= \mathscr{L}_\pi \ominus \max(\{i, iu\})$ by (30a)
$= \{i_o, iu_o, u_o, o_o\} \ominus \{iu\}$
$= \{o_o, \varnothing\}$

(33) $\mathscr{L}_\pi \ominus (\mathscr{L}_{pt} \ominus \mathscr{L}_{au})$
$= \mathscr{L}_\pi \ominus \max(\{u, \varnothing\})$ by (30b)
$= \{i_o, iu_o, u_o, o_o\} \ominus \{u\}$
$= \{i_o, o_o, \varnothing\}$
$\equiv \{i_o\}$ by (1), (32)

(34) $\mathscr{L}_\pi \oplus (\mathscr{L}_{pt} \oplus \mathscr{L}_{au})$
$= \mathscr{L}_\pi \oplus \{i, iu\}$ by (30a)
$= \{i_o, iu_o, u_o, o_o\} \oplus \{i, iu\}$
$= \{i_o, iu_o\}$
$\equiv \{iu_o\}$ by (1), (33)

(35) $\mathscr{L}_\pi \oplus (\mathscr{L}_{pt} \ominus \mathscr{L}_{au})$
$= \mathscr{L}_\pi \oplus \{u, \varnothing\}$ by (30b)
$= \{i_o, iu_o, u_o, o_o\} \oplus \{u, \varnothing\}$
$= \{i_o, iu_o, u_o, o_o\}$
$\equiv \{u_o\}$ by (1), (32), (33), (34)

Tripartition arises as follows:

(36) $\mathscr{L}_\pi \oplus (\mathscr{L}_{au} \oplus \mathscr{L}_{pt})$
$= \mathscr{L}_\pi \oplus \{i, iu\}$ by (31a)
$= \{i_o, iu_o\}$ by (34)

(37) $\mathscr{L}_\pi \ominus (\mathscr{L}_{au} \oplus \mathscr{L}_{pt})$
$= \mathscr{L}_\pi \ominus \max(\{i, iu\})$ by (31a)
$= \{o_o, \varnothing\}$ by (32)

(38) $\mathscr{L}_\pi \oplus (\mathscr{L}_{au} \ominus \mathscr{L}_{pt})$
$= \mathscr{L}_\pi \oplus \{\varnothing\}$ by (31b)
$= \{i_o, iu_o, u_o, o_o\}$
$\equiv \{u_o\}$ by (1), (37), (36)

(39) $\mathscr{L}_\pi \ominus (\mathscr{L}_{au} \ominus \mathscr{L}_{pt})$
$= \mathscr{L}_\pi \ominus \max(\{\varnothing\})$ by (31b)
$\equiv \{u_o\}$ by (38)

The only difference between this and the main text tripartition is that it gives two ways of defining second person. The main text version gives two ways of defining third. Whether this is an acceptable consequence depends on whether one accepts that it is empirically advantageous to have two representations of third person, one of which enables second person to be the morphological composition of first and third (section 5.3.2), the other of which makes a natural class of first person and third (section 8.3.1).

B.3 Larger Ontologies

I think that there are good arguments for a minimal ontology (section 4.2.1). However, I can be wrong on this score and still not need to revise my derivation of the five attested partitions, as I now show.

Let i_i stand for elements of the form $i, i', i'', \ldots, ii', ii'', i'i'', \ldots$, and similarly for u_u, iu_{iu}, and define the lattices $\mathscr{L}_{au}^* = \{i_i\}$, $\mathscr{L}_{pt}^* = \{i_i, iu_{iu}, u_u\}$, and $\mathscr{L}_{\pi}^* = \{i_{io}, iu_{iuo}, u_{uo}, o_o\}$. Then the features ±author* and ±participant* (defined by substituting $\mathscr{L}_{au}^*$ and $\mathscr{L}_{pt}^*$ for $\mathscr{L}_{au}$ and $\mathscr{L}_{pt}$ in the definitions of ±author and ±participant) yield or induce essentially the same inventory of partitions as before: ±participant* partitions $\mathscr{L}_{\pi}^*$ into o_o versus groups containing i's and/or u's, and ±author* partitions $\mathscr{L}_{\pi}^*$ into groups with no i's versus those containing at least one. Furthermore, it is easily checked that all of the calculations of sections 4.3.4–4.3.5 hold under these substitutions.

For instance, compare (40) with chapter 4 (56) = $\{i_o, iu_o\}$ and (41) with chapter 4 (64) = $\{i_o\}$:

(40) $[\![+\text{participant}^*(+\text{author}^*(\pi))]\!]$
$= (\mathscr{L}_{\pi}^* \oplus \mathscr{L}_{au}^*) \oplus \mathscr{L}_{pt}^*$
$= (\{i_{io}, iu_{iuo}, u_{uo}, o_o\} \oplus \{i_i\}) \oplus \{i_i, iu_{iu}, u_u\}$
$= \{i_{io}, iu_{iuo}\} \oplus \{i_i, iu_{iu}, u_u\}$
$= \{i_{io}, iu_{iuo}\}$

(41) $[\![+\text{author}^*(-\text{participant}^*(\pi))]\!]$
$= (\mathscr{L}_{\pi}^* \ominus \mathscr{L}_{pt}^*) \oplus \mathscr{L}_{au}^*$
$= (\{i_{io}, iu_{iuo}, u_{uo}, o_o\} \ominus \{\max(i_i, iu_{iu}, u_u)\}) \oplus \{i_i\}$
$= \{\varnothing, o_o\} \oplus \{i_i\}$
$= \{i_{io}\}$

These and similar results are unsurprising, because no calculation of chapter 4 hinged on the uniqueness of i and u.

The invariance of the account on this score is not meant to deny the importance and value of Cysouw's (2003), Simon's (2005), and Bobabljik's (2008) contributions to our understanding of choric *we*'s and mass *you*'s. If the facts had panned out differently, the current theory would have been inadequate. The pertinent observation is that, given the current theory, the facts do not militate against larger ontologies.

B.4 Privative Features

A privative rewrite of my features can be made to derive the desired partitions. However, it requires revision to Lexical Complementarity and a dubious assumption about zero-bottomed lattices, and it faces two problems at the interface with morphology. I detail these briefly after presenting the assumptions and the derivations.

To derive the partitions with privative features, we reconstitute the effect of negative values via cyclic application of Lexical Complementarity (recall section B.1.2.3): if one fails to apply F′ to G′ when one could have, then one instead calculates the complement of F′ in G′. I denote application of F′ to G′ as F′(G′) and nonapplication as (G′), the parentheses distinguishing it from absence of action on G′. Additionally, we take π to denote $\mathscr{L}_\pi^\circ$, that is, $\mathscr{L}_\pi$ with the empty set. The author and participant bipartitions (42)–(43) illustrate, with calculations translating back into bivalent features on the way for convenience:

(42) $[\![\text{author}'(\pi)]\!]$
 $= [\![+\text{author}(\pi)]\!]$
 $= \{i_o, iu_o\}$

 $[\![(\pi)]\!]$
 $= [\![\pi]\!] \setminus [\![\text{author}'(\pi)]\!]$
 $= \{i_o, iu_o, u_o, o_o, \varnothing\} \setminus \{i_o, iu_o\}$
 $= \{u_o, o_o, \varnothing\}$

(43) $[\![\text{participant}'(\pi)]\!]$
 $= \{i_o, iu_o, u_o\}$

 $[\![(\pi)]\!]$
 $= [\![\pi]\!] \setminus [\![\text{participant}'(\pi)]\!]$
 $= \{i_o, iu_o, u_o, o_o, \varnothing\} \setminus \{i_o, iu_o, u_o\}$
 $= \{o_o, \varnothing\}$

The denotation of (π) differs depending on the parameter setting: it is interpreted relative to author′ in (42) but relative to participant′ in (43). Zeroes are winnowed away as in the main text.

For the tripartition, the equivalent of plus–plus is as before:

(44) $[\![\text{participant}'(\text{author}'(\pi))]\!]$
 $= [\![+\text{participant}(+\text{author}(\pi))]\!]$
 $= \{i_o, iu_o\}$

The equivalent to −author lacks the inner author′, hence the appearance of double parentheses. It is calculated as follows:

(45) $[\![\text{participant}'((\pi))]\!]$
 $= [\![+\text{participant}]\!]([\![\pi]\!] \setminus [\![+\text{author}(\pi)]\!])$
 $= [\![+\text{participant}]\!](\{u_o, o_o, \varnothing\})$
 $= \{i_o, iu_o, u_o\}$
 $\equiv \{u_o\}$ by (1), (44)

The remaining specifications deliver the empty set and second person:

(46) $[\![(\text{author}'(\pi))]\!]$
 $= [\![(\{i_o, iu_o\})]\!]$
 $= [\![\{i_o, iu_o\}]\!] \setminus [\![+\text{participant}(\{i_o, iu_o\})]\!]$
 $= \{i_o, iu_o\} \setminus \{i_o, iu_o\}$
 $= \{\}$

(47) $[\![((\pi))]\!]$
 $= [\![([\![\pi]\!] \setminus [\![+\text{author}(\pi)]\!])]\!]$

$= [\![(\{u_o, o_o\})]\!]$
$= \{u_o, o_o\} \setminus [\![+\text{participant}(\{u_o, o_o\})]\!]$
$= \{u_o, o_o\} \setminus \{io_o, iu_o, u_o\}$
$= \{o_o\}$

Taking (45)–(47), we have tripartition, though with a slight difference that I comment on below.

The derivations of the quadripartition are:

(48) $[\![\text{author}'(\text{participant}'(\pi))]\!]$
  $= [\![+\text{author}(+\text{participant}(\pi))]\!]$
  $= \{i_o, iu_o\}$
  $\equiv \{iu_o\}$ by (1), (49)

(49) $[\![\text{author}'((\pi))]\!]$
  $= [\![+\text{author}]\!]([\![\pi]\!] \setminus [\![+\text{participant}(\pi)]\!])$
  $= [\![+\text{author}]\!](\{o_o, \varnothing\})$
  $= \{i_o\}$

(50) $[\![(\text{participant}'(\pi))]\!]$
  $= [\![(\{i_o, iu_o, u_o\})]\!]$
  $= [\![\{i_o, iu_o, u_o\}]\!] \setminus [\![+\text{author}(\{i_o, iu_o, u_o\})]\!]$
  $= \{i_o, iu_o, u_o\} \setminus \{i_o, iu_o\}$
  $= \{u_o\}$

(51) $[\![((\pi))]\!]$
  $= [\![([\![\pi]\!] \setminus [\![+\text{participant}(\pi)]\!])]\!]$
  $= [\![(\{o_o, \varnothing\})]\!]$
  $= \{o_o, \varnothing\} \setminus [\![+\text{author}(\{o_o, \varnothing\})]\!]$
  $= \{o_o, \varnothing\} \setminus \{i_o\}$
  $= \{o_o, \varnothing\}$

Winnowing removes the empty set, and quadripartition results.

So, privativized, my features can still solve the partition problem. But parity of partitions notwithstanding, I believe this alternative is to be deprecated, for four reasons, two semantic, two morphological.

First, the cyclic implementation of Lexical Complementarity suggests that privativity masks the semantic truth, which is that something denotationally contentful needs to be posited exactly where the bivalent account places negative values. Second, the distribution of zeroes that the privative account requires is stipulative. As explained in appendix B.1, it makes sense to posit zeroes for all semilattices, or for none. But to mix $\mathscr{L}_\pi^\circ$ with $\mathscr{L}_{pt}$ is ad hoc (and one can check that privativity with $\mathscr{L}_\pi$ and $\mathscr{L}_{pt}$ fails to deliver quadripartition, and, with $\mathscr{L}_\pi^{(\circ)}$ and $\mathscr{L}_{pt}^\circ$, fails to deliver the participant bipartition).

Third, with a single representation of the tripartition, privativity does not lend itself to direct representation of the morphological differences between the Gahuku and German tripartitions (sections 5.3.2, 8.3.1). Fourth, a range of parallel phenomena in person and number point to the inadequacy of treating only one value of a feature, be it plus or minus, as visible for exponence. These are laid out in section 9.5.2, following on from the discussion to which this aside is appended.

B.5 Number: Formal Details

Formal definitions of the three number features of chapter 6 are given below. Bracketed negation is present for minus values.

The feature ±atomic assumes atomicity as a basic concept:

(52) $[\![\pm\text{atomic}]\!] = \lambda x.(\neg)\text{atom}(x)$

Being of type $\langle e, t \rangle$, this combines with $\pi_{(F)}$, or with common nouns, by function modification, returning an output of the same type. For instance, first singular is:

(53) $[\![+\text{atomic}(+\text{participant}(+\text{author}(\pi(\varphi))))]\!]$
$= [\lambda x . \text{atom}(x)] \, (\lambda x . x \in \{i_o, iu_o\})$
$= \lambda x . x \in \{i_o, iu_o\} \wedge \text{atom}(x)$
$= \lambda x . x \in \{i\}$

The feature ±minimal takes a property and, of the elements satisfying it, characterizes the subset that (for plus) have or (for minus) lack a proper subelement that satisfies it. (It is, therefore, of type $\langle\langle e, t\rangle, \langle e, t\rangle\rangle$. So, it composes by function application with an argument of type $\langle e, t \rangle$ to return a value of the same type.) In other words, it is concerned with downward percolation of properties, minimal elements being the point at which the property of being within a lattice region peters out.

(54) $[\![\pm\text{minimal}]\!] = \lambda P \lambda x . (\neg) \neg \exists y \dfrac{P(y) \wedge y \sqsubset x}{P(x)}$

The notation here represents proposition and presupposition as the numerator and denominator of a fraction (so that, just like an arithmetic fraction, the whole expression is undefined if the presupposition has the truth value 0 and equals the numerator when the presupposition has the truth value 1). By making $P(x)$ a presupposition, we ensure that ±minimal partitions the elements x that satisfy P, and, by making $P(y) \wedge y \sqsubset x$ the nucleus, we partition the x according to whether they have or lack a proper subelement y within P.

Using this feature, we can express inclusive augmented as follows:

(55) $[\![-\text{minimal}(+\text{author}(+\text{participant}(\pi(\varphi))))]\!]$
$= \left[\lambda P \lambda x . \neg \neg \exists y \dfrac{P(y) \wedge y \sqsubset x}{P(x)} \right] (\lambda x . x \in \{iu_o\})$

$$= \lambda x . \exists y \frac{y \in \{iu_o\} \wedge y \sqsubset x}{x \in \{iu_o\}}$$

$$= \lambda x . x \in \{iuo_o\}$$

The last step in the calculation is achieved by noting that iu is in $\{iu_o\}$, that anything of the form iuo or larger has $y = iu$ as a subelement, but that iu itself lacks a subelement within $\{iu_o\}$. This restricts x to $\{iu_o\}\setminus\{iu\} = \{iuo_o\}$.

Last, approximative numbers, like paucal and greater plural, are defined by a feature concerned with additive closure. It takes a lattice region (or, if you prefer, property), P, supplies a subregion, Q, and characterizes the elements of Q. These are all presuppositions (denominators below). The nucleus of the feature asserts or denies whether Q is additively complete (like a full plural), or additively incomplete (like a paucal). As with ±minimal, this feature is of type $\langle\langle e, t\rangle, \langle e, t\rangle\rangle$ and the same observations about input and output apply; thus, no matter which of the features acts first on a noun or pronoun, the next is able to take the output as its argument.

(56) $[\![\pm\text{additive}]\!] = \lambda P \lambda x (\neg) \dfrac{\forall y (Q(y) \to Q(x \sqcup y))}{Q(x) \wedge Q \sqsubseteq P}$

For a third person paucal, for instance, we have:

(57) $[\![-\text{additive}(-\text{participant}(-\text{author}(\pi(\varphi))))]\!]$

$$= \left[\lambda P \lambda x . \neg \frac{\forall y (Q(y) \to Q(x \sqcup y))}{Q(x) \wedge Q \sqsubseteq P}\right] (\lambda x . x \in \{o_o\})$$

$$= \lambda x . \neg \frac{\forall y (Q(y) \to Q(x \sqcup y))}{Q(x) \wedge Q \sqsubseteq \{o_o\}}$$

$$= \lambda x . x \in \{o^* \in \{o_o\} : |o^*| \leq n\}$$

where n is a culturally determined, contextually relevant upper bound (e.g., generally five to seven for Yimas, less for Koasati, but potentially more for Boumaa Fijian; Foley 1991, Kimball 1991, Dixon 1988, respectively). The last step follows because, first, $Q = \{o^* \in \{o_o\} : |o^*| < n\}$ is a proper subset of $P = \{o_o\}$. Moreover, Q is not closed under addition: if $n = 3$, then Q contains $oo'o''$ and $oo'o'''$, but not their join $oo'o''o'''$, which contains more than three elements. Of course, there is much more to be said about Q, in particular, why this kind of subset of P, rather than any other, is available (e.g., the set of dyads, which is also additively open). These details are discussed at length in Harbour 2014a.

Notes

Chapter 2

1. All features other than my own are tagged with prime marks.
2. These tallies are given by the Stirling numbers of the second kind. $S(n,k)$, the number of ways of partitioning a set of size n into k partition elements, satisfies the recursion relation $S(n,k) = k \times S(n-1,k) + S(n-1,k-1)$ with initial conditions $S(0,0) = 1$ and $S(n,0) = S(0,n) = 0$. Therefore, $S(4,3) = 6$ and $S(4,2) = 7$ are, respectively, the numbers of three-way and two-way syncretisms of the four-element person space.
3. Sources for figure 2.3 are (Bilua) Obata 2003, (Buma) Tryon 2002, (Halia) Allen 1978, (Kiowa) Watkins 1984, (Lenakel) Lynch 1983, (Southern Efate) Thieberger 2006, (Wai Wai) Hawkins 1998, (Zia) Wilson 1980. As a matter of interest, readers may like to know that the data displayed in figures 2.2–2.3 were not overly onerous to amass. Most could be found (on a rainy Christmas afternoon near the Schulenberger Forest) in the grammars I happened to have on my laptop, and the gaps were filled once I could return to various online sources. Only the Buma syncretism of exclusive-cum-second as against inclusive-cum-third took a few hours' needless rootling—because I had not read Allen 1978 closely enough to notice the two instances there.
4. Like many other three-person languages, English has a hortative (*let's* ...) with solely inclusive force. However, this lone inclusive does not form part of a tense, mood, or other category that systematically contrasts inclusive with exclusive and the other persons. Rather, hortative inclusives, like imperatives, are a stand-alone category. In fact, one might view their inclusivity as arising from addition of the author to the second person category of imperatives. By contrast, when forms with hortative force are part of larger paradigms, such as jussives, optatives, or subjunctives, they apparently cover all first persons, whether clusive or not. For instance, in Hungarian (Kenesei, Vago, and Fenyvesi 1988, de Groot 2010), subjunctives serve as imperatives and hortatives. Thus, of the (definite object) subjunctives *öl-j-em* 'I kill', *öl-j-ed* 'you kill', *öl-j-e* 'he/she/it kills', *öl-j-ük* 'we kill', *öl-j-étek* 'you kill', *öl-j-ék* 'they kill', the second person forms also function as imperatives (*öljed* 'kill.S', *öljétek* 'kill.P'), the third persons, as polite imperatives (*ölje* 'kill.S.HON', *öljék* 'kill.P.HON'), and the first plural, as a hortative (*öljünk* 'let's kill'). However, this last form can also have exclusive force, being amenable to use in an invocation

prior to battle with a monster, for instance (preferably with the additional particle *hadd*, which is also usable with other persons; Sylvia Blaho, Dániel Szeredi, pers.comm.). This makes it parallel to other first person plurals in Hungarian. In sum, then, neither in languages like English, nor in those like Hungarian, do hortatives constitute grounds for positing an underlying quadripartition.

5. A further problem arising from Algonquian is the treatment of the so-called obviative third person. Although I offer some suggestions below as to how the obviative might be distinguished from the proximal at the featural level (note 12, chapter 8; note 1, chapter 9), a full analysis is not possible within current confines. The Algonquian obviative is deeply embedded within a range of very intricate morphological systems, which would require proper survey (possibly in conjunction with those of other languages of North America, Sudan, and further regions). Moreover, the Algonquian obviative is, on the one hand, implicated in person-case-like effects (Branigan 2006) and, on the other, bound up with the choice of "theme" or "direction" markers (the who-is-acting-on-who suffix) of the verb. Both of these phenomena are themselves analytically contentious. As a result, it would be injudicious to attempt analysis of obviatives without a survey of the variation and in isolation from other phenomena. This survey might well be at home in a wider survey of ilks of third person.

6. There are three two-cell paradigms because these are derived by picking two cells and merging them together, and $^3C_2 = 3$. More specifically, the row of two-cell paradigms in figure 2.3 (or the row of bipartitions in figure 3.1) consists of four that distinguish one person and collapse three, $^4C_1 = 4$, and three that collapse two pairs, $\frac{1}{2}{^4C_3} = 3$. Each three-cell paradigm has two subparadigms of the first type— the number of ways of picking two two-cell paradigms from four equals the number of three-cell paradigms on four distinctions, $^4C_2 = 6 = S(4,3)$—and one of the second type—each $(ab|cd)$ is a subparadigm of two different three-cell paradigms, one that distinguishes one of its paired cells $(a|b|cd)$, and one that distinguishes the other $(ab|c|d)$.

7. Tiwi has minimal–augmented number. This differs from singular–plural with regard to the inclusive. Singular is undefined for inclusive, as no singleton set of referents can contain both speaker and hearer. Minimal, by contrast, is defined for all persons (which may in part explain why Tiwi is so rich in syncretisms: inclusive occurs in twice as many paradigms as in languages with singular). For exclusive, second, and third, minimal is identical to singular, as the minimal exclusive is the speaker alone, the minimal second person, the hearer alone, and so on. The minimal inclusive is the speaker and hearer alone, hence a dyad, not a singleton. (Augmented is minimal with one or more third persons added; so triadic or larger for inclusive, dyadic or larger for other persons. For more detail, see chapter 6.)

8. "Inverse" is a Kiowa-Tanoan amalgam of number and noun class, referring to combinations of singular, dual, and plural, on a noun-by-noun basis. There is a certain risk in asserting syncretism for the agreement prefixes, as Rosen (1990) and her sources do not mark tone, with only very sporadic exceptions. However, if Kiowa is a guide, then the first two sets of examples used here are likely to avoid this, coming from parts of the agreement system where tone is uniform. For the third example, *bi–i–i*, certainty is lower. Nonetheless, first–nonfirst syncretism is seen for some

singular agents. For instance, a second singular agent acting for a third singular applicative on a third plural object (though object number is not crucial here) is *am* 2S:3S:3P. The same prefix is used when the second singular agent is absent (*am* also encodes a third singular applicative possessing a third plural object, ∅:3S:3P). However, a first singular agent causes *t* to be added: *t-am* 1S:3S:3P. The zero agreement of second person singular is shared with third person singular in a number of circumstances, most obviously, in third-singular-on-third-singular transitives, for which the entire agreement prefix is ∅. Thus, we again have a first–nonfirst pattern for singular agent agreement, t–∅–∅. (Kiowa has the same pattern with cognate morphemes; for instance, *n-en* is 1S:3S:3D, but ∅-*en* covers both 2S:3S:3D and 3S:3S:3D.)

Chapter 3

1. It goes without saying that the *i–u–o* notation is not Anglocentric, but is based on the tripartite spatial deictics of Comanche (Charney 1993), in which *i-* is local to the speaker, *u-* covers the hearer's space, and *o-* is removed from both.
2. The partition elements are io_o (sets containing *i* and at least one *o*), iu_oi (that is, iu_o with *i*: sets containing *i* alone, or *i* and *u* alone, or *i*, *u*, and at least one *o*), and u_o and o_o as before. In the partition notation presented immediately below in the main text, the novel systems are the quadripartition (i) $io_o | iu_oi | u_o | o_o$; the five tripartitions (ii) $io_ou_o | iu_oi | o_o$, (iii) $io_oo_o | iu_oi | u_o$, (iv) $io_o | iu_oiu_o | o_o$, (v) $io_o | iu_oio_o | u_o$, and (vi) $io_o | iu_oi | u_oo_o$; and the four bipartitions (vii) $io_ou_o | iu_oo_oi$, (viii) $io_oo_o | iu_ou_oi$, (ix) $io_o | iu_ou_oo_oi$, and (x) $iu_oi | io_ou_oo_o$.
3. Number exponents (leaving allomorphy and the like aside) pare these down to smaller sets of referents. For instance, in *mitupela*, the exclusive dual, *tupela* confines reference to elements of the form $\{i, o\}$, that is, the author plus one other. See chapter 6 for full discussion of number.
4. This approach requires a mechanism of suppressing the interpretation of adjectival *e* as biologically feminine when agreement is purely formal, as in *la meringue française* 'French meringue'. Such mechanisms are required independently of the current approach, for noun phrases like feminine *chaque personne* 'every person' and masculine *chaque ouvrier* 'every worker', both of which permit reference to males and females alike. See Percus 2011 for a proposal.
5. Vicinities are extremely flexible notions and, under the right circumstances, can be practically infinitely large, allowing Douglas Adams to wonder, for instance, "what the Universe is for and why it is *here*" (my emphasis). I do not offer a theory of how vicinities are constrained and negotiated during actual usage but note merely that exactly the same infinite extensibility affects pronouns too: Adams could equally have asked "why *we* have a universe at all," allowing *we* to encompass everyone from "Far out in the uncharted backwaters of the unfashionable end of the western spiral arm of the Galaxy" to the "Restaurant at the End of the Universe."
6. Kawi, Classical Chinese, and Qawasqar/Kawésqar are at times cited as languages without pronominal number, following, respectively, Becker and Oka 1974, Norman 1988, and Clairis 1985. However, other studies contradict these reports:

Uhlenbeck 1968 on Kawi; Unger 1987, Pulleyblank 1995, and Meisterernst 2012 on Classical Chinese; and Aguilera 2011 on Kawésqar. All are discussed in Harbour 2014b.

7. Following official Palauan orthography, reflected in Josephs's later work, *e* replaces the *ę* of Josephs 1975; *ch* is glottal stop.

   Josephs glosses the three categories as 'near speaker and hearer', 'near hearer but far from speaker', and 'far from speaker and hearer'. My tripartition affords speaker-related forms both an inclusive meaning ('near speaker and hearer') and an exclusive meaning ('near speaker but not near hearer'). If 'this place' meant only 'near speaker and hearer', it would be impossible to use *er tia* in a letter, to say, for instance, 'It's cold here'. I doubt this is the case, and so I take Josephs's label 'near speaker and hearer', not as precluding an exclusive reading, but as reflecting the fact that hearers are normally near speakers. Justin Nuger (pers. comm.) suspects that this interpretation is correct; it is not contradicted by Josephs's later descriptive work.

8. Correcting *le-ntep* to *len-tep* 'P-leave', on the basis of (18) and similar cases.

9. Hocąk verbs display minimal–augmented number agreement (where *minimal* means dual for inclusive but singular for other persons, and *augmented* means triplural for inclusive but diplural for other persons; for fuller discussion, see chapter 6). Only augmented is overt. So, verbs showing person agreement alone are to be interpreted as minimal.

   Examples (23), (26), (27) are from Helmbrecht and Lehmann 2010, (24) from Hartmann and Marschke 2010, and (25) is from Lipkind 1945 (with slight change in orthography). Examples (23), (25), and (27) show my glossing, as the originals are glossed incompletely or not at all.

10. The notion of animacy is somewhat loose, extending to entities that have the human likeness (like dolls) or human-like autonomy (like gods, winds, the sun). It is not so loose, however, as to match up with the so-called animate gender of Algonquian languages, which, in Menominee (Bloomfield 1962), for instance, includes 'raspberry' and 'kettle'.

11. The examples in (35)–(38) and in Harbour 2013 come from the bilingual texts collected in *Téwa Pehtsiye: Tewa Tales, San Juan Dialect* (San Juan Pueblo Bilingual Program 1982), which Kyle Helke, a former MA student, and I glossed and analyzed using a variety of Tewa resources, especially Martinez 1983.

12. When used to refer to masculine inanimates, like *stol* 'table', *on* still collapses accusative with genitive. In these cases, the animacy marking is formal, not semantic. See Percus 2011 for a proposal about how to switch semantic content off so as to give rise to marking in form only.

13. In chapter 4, I posit a principle of Lexical Complementarity, which states (in abbreviated form) that, if the denotation of G subsumes that of F, then F is used whenever possible, and G is used only where F is inappropriate; that is, if $[\![F]\!] \subset [\![G]\!]$, then G is restricted to $[\![G]\!]\setminus[\![F]\!]$. In the current case, one might then wonder why the proximal *dies* forms do not restrict *der/die/das* to distal uses. However, it is plausible that Lexical Complementarity is triggered only when F and G have different values of the same features (chapter 4, note 6). In terms of the theory developed below,

the requisite trigger is then absent here, as *dies* is +author but *der/die/das* lack any feature specification. The absence of lexical complementation thus reinforces the view of the main text that the emphatic definite articles constitute monopartition of π.

Chapter 4

1. Influenced in part by an earlier version of the current proposals, Ackema and Neeleman (2013) too propose an action-based semantics, but with privative features. I defer comparison of our accounts until a later date, in part because Ackema and Neeleman's ideas are enjoying further development under a project that is to last several years. More substantially, though, I am interested here in accomplishing a reframing of the core questions and in establishing the broad principles of the solution. It is, therefore, sensible to undertake elsewhere a comparison of two accounts that agree on the fundamental rejection of predicative features in favor of action-based ones.
2. The significant point is the failure of the argument: if it fails, then support for multi-*i* ontology is weakened. However, this is a one-way implication. Consider *You have made hollandaise and you have eaten it*, where each *you* refers to a different individual. I do not interpret this as an argument for an ontology with multiple *u*'s; rather, I interpret it as showing that a speaker can reassign the referent of *u* mid-utterance.
3. Heim and Kratzer (1998) would write $[\![\varphi]\!] = \lambda S . \lambda x \in S : x$, using the colon to indicate that the expression only returns a value if a presupposition is met. I leave this convention aside.
4. Under different assumptions, the semantic parameter affecting order of composition (29c) might be made syntactic. Specifically, if one projects each feature-cum-value as an autonomous head, then parameterization of order of composition could be recast as parameterization of the functional sequence. I have not examined the consequences of such an approach, preferring a syntax in which the functional sequence concerns itself only with categorial heads like π and φ, which are the loci of features like ±author and ±participant.
5. Sometimes this variation affects order of composition. When it does, I assume that the parameter is set for each deictic domain. That is, I assume that languages cannot switch orders of composition within a domain, having, say, author-first composition for some values and participant-first composition for others—+participant(−author) versus +author(−participant), for instance. I have not calculated what systems this microvariation would permit.
6. If active across the board, Lexical Complementarity would entail the absence of pronominal systems with members that have overlapping denotations. Such systems do exist, though. In the four-member system of Kawi (Uhlenbeck 1968), for instance, first singular *aku* exists alongside number-neutral *kami*, without $\{i\} = [\![aku]\!] \subset [\![kami]\!] = \{i_o, iu_o\}$ triggering restriction of *kami* to 'we'. For a more elaborate series of overlaps within a similarly exiguous system, see Irwin 1974 on Salt-Yui. A plausible means to constrain Lexical Complementarity while

permitting these cases is to require that F and G in (31) be different specifications of the same features (making them part of the same "scale," so to speak). Hence, Lexical Complementarity will act in cases where, say, $F = +$author $-$participant and $G = +$author $+$participant. However, it will not act on the pair *aku–kami* if *aku* is $+$atomic but *kami* lacks number features (relatedly, see note 13 of chapter 3). This yields the correct distribution of action and inaction for the cases examined here.

7. For readability, I write just $[\![F]\!]$ and $[\![G]\!]$ in this paragraph, rather than $[\![F(\pi)]\!]$ and $[\![G(\pi)]\!]$, as in (31). For $[\![F]\!] \cap [\![G]\!] = \{i_o, iu_o\}$ to count as smaller than $[\![G]\!] = \{i_o, iu_o, u_o\}$, the number of o's must be taken to be finite, which is not a troubling commitment.

Chapter 5

1. My understanding of this system was aided by Itamar Kastner's very able work as a research assistant.

2. One might posit the underlying concatenation *aŋ-ge-a*, in which the last two vowels coalesce into surface *a*; but the motivation for this view is not evident. Presumably, this morpheme *a* would be the singular, but its position, after *ge*, contrasts with the pre-*ge* placement of dual *chi* and plural *i*; and *a* as an exponent of singular does not enjoy support from the apparent marker of singular in second and third person, ε?

3. There is, however, a different and intriguing parallel between Gumbáiŋgar *gei* and Limbu *ge*, namely, final affinity. Just as *ge* is final in both pronouns and verbs, so, for the most part, is *gei*. In Gumbáiŋgar, this is to be observed in case-marked pronouns, where *gei* attaches after the case morphemes and not immediately after the other person and number morphemes. For instance, the exclusive dual accusative and possessive are *ŋali-nja-gei* and *ŋali-mbandi-gei*, respectively. Similarly, the inclusive plural dative and locative are *ŋīā-njamba* and *ŋīā-njamba-la*, and the corresponding exclusives, *ŋīɛ-njamba-gei* and *ŋīɛ-njamba-la-gei* (with a minor change in the final vowel of the root). Adding to the interest, the allative has a further complication, in that *gei* occurs in the midst of the case morphology: compare the inclusive and exclusive plurals *ŋīā-njambeigu* and *ŋīā-njambageigu*. (These forms should, perhaps, be decomposed into dative *njamba* and a locative *eigu*, which accretes onto the dative and deletes any preceding vowel. We then have inclusive *ŋīā-njamb[a]-eigu* and *ŋīā-njamba-g[ei]-eigu*, which is at least phonologically systematic, even if the placement of locative *eigu* remains at odds with that of other case exponents.) One might well wonder if this shared final affinity of the exclusive morpheme is principled.

4. This is possible because, in the quadripartition, second and third share $-$author, which *t* realizes in the singular and *ky* realizes in the plural. Nonetheless, features that give rise to these persons are distinct and *a* is evidently sensitive to this difference, realizing the $+$participant that distinguishes second from third. (Again, I leave

aside the question of whether exclusive and second person use the same, or merely homophonous, enclitics; see section 8.3.1.)

5. When considering tripartitions, I assume the "harmonic" representation of third person, −participant −author. On the alternative, see section 8.3.1.

6. A different decomposition of the French clitics might be considered desirable, treating *s* as a plural shared among all three persons. If so, one might then worry that first and second decompose into *nou-s* and *vou-s*, which would mean that there is nothing shared between first and second to the exclusion of third *le-s*. However, even with a plural morpheme, I think a better-justified decomposition would be *n-ou-s* and *v-ou-s*, as this allows for carryover of *n* and *v* into the genitive *n-o-s* and *v-o-s* (cf, third plural *leur*). Thus, in both pairs of forms, there is an element (*ou*∼*o*) shared between first and second to the exclusion of third.

7. I use the term *agreement* loosely in relation to Yimas. As Foley's description makes clear, "agreement" is omissible, optionally in some information-structural configurations, obligatorily in some Ā-dependencies (see also section 3.3.2).

8. Nothing in Yimas verb morphology is straightforward, as anyone who has ever delved into Foley's description will be aware. As a result, various addenda must be made to the discussion in the main text.

First, readers may have noticed that, in (21)–(23), the paucal is always second person (and, in fact, Foley treats *paŋ* here as an exponent of second person). However, its nonoccurrence for first person does not reflect a second-person-only specification of the exponent; rather it arises from more general facts about the treatment of first-on-second argument combinations. When first acts on second, the language forbids separate exponence of both arguments. If the second person is singular, then a portmanteau is used (i), or, if the second person is nonsingular, the first person is not registered on the verb at all, as in (23) and (ii).

(i) *paŋkt k-   mpan- tkam- r- ŋkt*　　　　*ipa ta- mpan- tpul*
　　1PC 3sO-1A.2s-show-PF-PC　　　　　　1P NEG-1A.2s-hit
　　'we few showed you it'　　　　　　　　'we did not hit you'

(ii) *ta- ŋkul- cpul-c- rm*　　　　　　　　*paŋkt kul- cpul*
　　NEG-2DO-hit- PF-D　　　　　　　　　1PC 2PO-hit
　　'I did not hit you two'　　　　　　　　'we few hit you all'

Thus, *paŋ* occurs when second paucal acts on first, as expected, but is absent when first paucal acts on second for independent reasons.

A further restriction on *paŋ* is partly phonological. In first-on-second scenarios, *paŋ* occurs only if the first person begins with *ŋ*, as in (21)–(22). For first person plural (and the excrescent paucal), *paŋ* is absent:

(iii) *paŋkt kra- tpul*　　　　　　　　　　*paŋkt kra- tpul-ŋkt*
　　 2PC 1PO-hit　　　　　　　　　　　2PC 1PO-hit- PC
　　 'you few hit us'　　　　　　　　　　 'you few hit us few'

Given that *paŋ* occurs before *k* in (23) and (19), this restriction is unexpected. However, it is not unprecedented in Yimas. Within negative (di)transitive verbs, third person *pu* occurs only before *n*-initial agreement markers and is zero otherwise (Harbour 2008, remarshaling Foley's description):

(iv)   ta-   pu-nan- tpul-c- um   ta-   ∅-kul- cpul-c- um
       NEG-3- 2PA-hit- PF-P   NEG-3-2PO-hit- PF-P
       'you all did not hit them'   'they did not hit you all'

However, just as for *paŋ*, there are argument combinations for which this phonological restriction is relaxed. It occurs, for instance, in any negated third person intransitive, as exemplified by the dual:

(v)   ta-   pu-wa-na-   rm
      NEG-3- go- NRPST-D
      'they two did not go'

So, varying phonotactic-cum-syntactic constraints on *paŋ* have precedent.

Finally, in all of its occurrences, *paŋ* is word-initial. It never occurs if there is another word-initial morpheme, as in the negated version of (19):

(vi)   ta-   kay- wa-r- ŋkt
       NEG-1PS-go- PF-PC
       'we few did not go'

In consequence, *paŋ* cannot occur in clauses containing third persons, as third person always precedes both first and second:

(vii)   na-   nan- tay   na-   n-   tay
        3SA-2SO-see   3SO-2SA-see
        'he saw you'   'you saw him'

In sum, the restrictions on *paŋ* in transitive verbs are coincidental. Although they may seem to detract from the interest of the example that Yimas presents of second person compositionality and of +participant exponents, none of this is particularly worrisome once one is acquainted with Yimas more generally, and, certainly, it does not affect in any way the cleanness of the initial example of compositionality in Yimas pronouns, involving ^{w}.

One final comment is due regarding linearization of verbal *paŋ*. The procedure discussed in chapter 6 for discontiguous linearization of single phi structures can return a single prefix and multiple suffixes (as occurs in Classical Arabic), but not multiple prefixes. The latter appears to occur in Yimas, however, as in (19) *paŋ-kra-wa-t* 'we/you few went', where the prefixes 1/2 *paŋ* and paucal intransitive *kra* both track the same argument, and likewise for 1/2 *paŋ* and 2PO *kul*, which track the object in (23) *paŋ-kul-cpul-c-ŋkt* 'I hit you few'. Accordingly, in Harbour 2008, I did not regard these prefixes as synchronically decomposable. If one rejects that view and accepts instead a more decompositional approach, then one possible reconciliation is to treat *paŋ* as agreement on a higher head and to regard *kra* and *kul-... -ŋkt* as the phi structure itself. I have not worked out such a proposal, but my starting point would be to tie this to the syntactic analysis of Yimas word-initial case alternations given by Phillips (1993).

9. In one small corner, Japanese too presents an apparently composed third person, in the domain of spaces. Japanese has a triple of spatial deictics, designating proximity to speaker (*ko*), proximity to hearer (*so*), and distance from both (*a*). Most formations from these are entirely morphologically transparent, as in the bare demonstratives *kore, sore, are* 'this one', 'that one (near you)', 'that one (not near you)', the adnominal demonstratives *kono, sono, ano* 'this', 'that (near you)', 'that (not near you)', and the directionals *kochira, sochira, achira* 'over to me', 'over to you', 'over there (away from you)'. For spatial locations, there is a slight wrinkle in the third person form. It is *asoko* 'there (not near you)', not *ako. By contrast, the adnominal demonstratives *koko* 'here' and *soko* 'there (near you)' are regular.

   The irregular *asoko* looks like third person *a* prefixed to the second person form *so*, prefixed to the root *ko*. This is certainly featurally possible. If first, second, and third person are +participant(+author), +participant(−author), and −participant(−author), then *so* must realize just −author, the feature common to second and third, and *a*, −participant. (I assume, here, the double negative representation of third person. The alternative, −participant(+author), would require a more complex rejigging of *so*, involving an alpha rule to realize αauthor in the context of −αparticipant.) To block the compositional forms elsewhere, we could posit a homophone, either *so* +participant(−author) or *a* −participant(−author).

   However, little, if anything, commends this analysis over simple allomorphy: third person features, though generally pronounced as *a*, are pronounced as *aso* in the context of locative *ko*. (These data, and an apparent irregularity in its extension to person deixis, are discussed further in section 7.2.3.)

10. *Chúng* occurs in the third person plural *chúng nó* 'they', which has the singular *nó*. There is no second person correspondent for this form, as there is no *ấy* to remove, and *nó* is not a kin term. Ngô (1999) says that *nó* and *chúng nó* are used in referring to children, animals, and, sometimes, inanimates, and that they may cause offense if used to refer to adults. (There is, in addition, *họ* 'they', for which Ngô gives no corresponding singular.)

11. The feature −participant also differentiates exclusive from inclusive. However, *ấy* would, in any event, be blocked from first person if *tôi/mình* express the full feature specification of exclusive +author −participant.

12. *Anh* can have third person reference without *ấy* (Tuệ Trinh, pers. comm.). This shows that *anh* cannot be second person, but it does not argue against the pronominal view, unless additional assumptions are made. Advocates of the pronominal view could claim that third person is optionally underspecified for ±participant. When underspecified, it consists solely of −author and so would be pronounced precisely as plain *anh*. Third person use of plain *anh* is unproblematic for the epithet view. It shows merely that *ấy* is not the only possible third person binder.

13. I take the absence of a stress mark on 2S *čiti* to be a misprint, for *číti*. For completeness, the third person forms are singular *iméri* and plural *c'əméri*. Presumably, the possessive suffix is *ri*, becoming *ti* after *i*.

14. One could, in principle, regard *d* and *i* as being sensitive to the presence of any +F on π. In previous work on noun class and inverse number in Kiowa-Tanoan (Harbour 2007b, 2011c), I have exploited such variables over features.

15. Adger and Harbour (2007) claim that direct object third persons lack ±participant but receive −participant as indirect objects. Treating third person as −participant(φ), and hence, syntactically, as π_{-pt}—φ, is incompatible with this position. One could reassign to ±author the role that Adger and Harbour attribute to ±participant. Or one might pursue the more radical underspecification presented next in the main text.

16. Not all third person datives encode their plurality through t. If the dative is not the highest argument, then t is absent, as in *mi-s-c-a* 'he gave it to them(/him/her)' and *da-u-mal-a* 'he hid it from them(/him/her)'. A similar restriction applies to plural -*x* in Svan, even though it is not cognate with Georgian *t*. In *x-o-k'wš-e* 'he breaks it for them(/him/her)' and *x-o-k'wīš-a-x* 'they have (he/she has) broken it', both third person plurals share the dative prefix *x*-. However, only the latter also marks plurality of the dative with suffixal -*x*. Just as in Georgian, the presence of a higher argument blocks the third person dative plural marking.

    A natural explanation for these facts is to suppose that these plural markers are sensitive to the existence of an Agree relation between T (or some similar head) and the plural argument (at least for third person). Presence of an agent blocks Agree between T and the dative and, hence, exponence of plurality by *t*/*x* (for third person). Consistent with this, third plural imperfectives in Svan, where the third person is the highest argument, do take plural -*x* (though, naturally, without any dative or applicative): *amara-x* 'they were preparing it'.

Chapter 6

1. I leave aside systems in which some numbers are confined to particular persons, as in the singular–plural contrast of Kwakiutl (Boas 1911), or the Chocktaw paucal (Broadwell 2006), which occur in the first person only. A simple way to model this is by assuming that feature content on number, or the ability of the head to project at all, may be sensitive to the content of π. (Alternatively, one can posit an impoverished set of exponents that fail to express number distinctions present in the syntax, or morphological operations that efface these before exponence occurs.)

2. Naturally, this should not be taken to imply that a minimal–augmented contrast is less natural than singular–plural. The lattices are so aligned that elements of the same cardinality are on the same line. If, instead, all bottom elements were on the same line, then the inclusive lattice, in the middle, would be one row lower, so ±minimal would cast a straight cut and ±atomic would have to kink down to exclude the speaker–hearer dyad.

3. There is a degree of optionality to the use of number in Mussau. This is not reflected in figure 6.14. When used, both the trial and the paucal trigger confinement of the plural to its higher ranges, a process that can be captured by Lexical Complementarity (chapter 4).

4. The unsuffixed forms are numberless, not minimal. This can be captured by supposing that the number head is optional and that, when present, only −minimal is pronounced, leading to identity between numberless and minimal forms.

Notes 275

5. A plausible contributory factor is the rampancy of allomorphy. Agreement is taken, in many frameworks, to involve feature sharing. Yet, as Bonet and Harbour (2012) observe, shared features are seldom pronounced identically. Languages like Biak (i) (my notes, working with Suriel Mofu), in which nominal number triggers homophonous agreement, are in an apparent minority. I am not aware of any quantitative studies of the phenomenon (though see Corbett 2006 on "alliterative agreement"), but my strong impression is that a majority of languages display either mere likeness, as in Classical Arabic (compare tables 6.4 and 6.6), or no likeness at all, as in Sanskrit (ii) (Coulson 1992):

(i) a. *mansuari- sko-ya   sko- yom   snon mamuni*
       cassowary-PC- the 3PC-chased the hunter
       'The few cassowaries chased the hunter.'
    b. *mansuari- s-ya   s- yom   snon mamuni*
       cassowary-P-the   3P-chased   the hunter
       'The cassowaries chased the hunter.'

(ii) a. *rājā   nayati*   *rājānau nayataḥ*   *rājānaḥ nayanti*
        king.S   lead.3S   king.D   lead.3D   king.P   lead.3P
        'The king / Two kings / Kings lead.'
     b. *tvam nayasi*   *yuvām   nayathaḥ*   *yūyam   nayatha*
        2S   lead.2S   2D   lead.2D   2P   lead.2P
        'You (two/all) lead.'

If syntactically shared features are not pronounced identically, then it suggests that features are generally pronounced differently when in distinct morphosyntactic contexts. Presence of the π/φ projection in pronouns, versus its absence from common nouns, plausibly makes these distinct contexts. So, the relative rarity of languages like Gaahmg, Mandarin, and Pipil, which share plural marking between pronouns and common nouns, is less surprising, but affording a role to π/φ leads us to expect, apparently rightly, that number exponents shared just between third and nonthird pronouns should be relatively more common.

6. Extralinguistic context (in the form of real-world knowledge, for instance) also plays a role in how readily available a singular reading of a morphological plural is. For instance, in my judgment, *Do you have dogs (at your place)?* is a strange question to ask a city dweller because few would own more than one and so at most an answer in the singular is expected. In the countryside, though, where ownership of multiple dogs is more common, the same question is felicitous (and permits the answer *Yes, one*; cf, *Do you have children? Yes, one*). Dogs contrast with cats, for which multiple ownership is more common even in cities, and the question *Do you have cats (at your place)?* is less odd, or fully acceptable. Reversing matters, absence of the plural is marked for pets that are generally owned in multiples: if I know you have a pond, then asking *Do you have a fish?* is notably odd as compared to *Do you have fish?*

7. Jonathan Bobaljik (pers. comm.) points out that mass nouns have the same property. *If they find the drugs, they'll arrest us* would normally be understood to mean that finding of any part of the drugs will result in arrest. I take this as showing that not only atoms, but any constituent part, can be restituted. In a related vein, (15)–(16)

do not require sighting of a whole atomic person, but would normally be satisfied synecdochically, by noticing a face, or even a funny hat or suspicious scar.

8. A further but more technical problem concerns how number features are meant to work. As explained in appendix B.5, number features need arguments of type $\langle e, t \rangle$, which is not the type of φ. One might get around this by taking $[\![\varphi]\!]$ to be $\lambda x . x \subseteq D_e$, that is, as ranging over the power set of its domain. Alternatively, more contentfully, one could swap the denotations of φ and π, setting $[\![\varphi]\!]$ as the power set of $\{i, u, o, \ldots\}$ and having π introduce the variable that ranges over it (as I did in an earlier version of the current proposals).

9. The chief difference between my previous work and the current implementation of the same core idea is phrase structure. Previously, I had placed φ at the top, dominating π, which dominated ω, the exact opposite of what I have argued for here. At that time, I was just beginning to transition into a Mirror-Theoretic mode of thinking, with syntactic trees consisting, potentially, of nothing but functional spine, and I had not yet assimilated the full consequences. Hopefully, those kinks are now ironed out.

   The account of linearization that follows and the data it is intended to capture concern only phi structures, the functional spine $\omega - \pi - \varphi$. If a language has independent loci for person versus number agreement, say, then these will be linearized in tandem with the heads that host them, not with respect to each other. (Béjar 2008) provides a framework for and analysis of some quite challenging cases.

   A more modest example of what I do not intend my account to cover comes from, for instance, Bantu languages in which number-cum-class markers are the initial morphological constituents of DP. Treating Swahili, Carstens (1991) proposes that D copies number (and class) information from within its complement and is the locus for its pronunciation. Adopting this, we can derive the order *number–person* by pronouncing person in situ and number on a higher D.

10. Saying that linearization is not about disestablishing adjacency is not to deny the reality of morphological and phonological metathesis. (My own treatment of Walmatjari relies on metathesis; see note 11.) Rather, it is to claim that they are independent processes that require special mechanisms (see, e.g., Raimy 2000, Harris and Halle 2004, Frampton 2008, Arregi and Nevins 2012).

11. To avoid the sequence *n-rna* in (35), Walmatjari uses metathesis, resulting in the order *pa-rna-n-panya-(pila)*. In terms of person-left–number-right, this is unproblematic. It does, though, superficially violate the flanking restriction, in that one agreement split intercalates with the other, instead of straddling it. However, if this violation results from phonologically driven surface repair of the underlying straddling structure (35), then there is no issue, just a curiosity. See Harbour 2008 on the full variety of phonological repair strategies that the language deploys.

12. The difference in vocalism between the cleft form *bārōk* of (44) and *bārēk* of (45) is immaterial: *bārōk* is the root of *bārēk* with binyan (conjugation class) omitted. See Harbour 1999 for discussion of the full range of patterns.

13. Rather, the sensitivities are to prefixal material, like modality and negation, and to Ā-configurations like relativization and *wh*-questions. They affect, particularly, the

highest/leftmost set of agreement features. Consequently, a T–C relationship may be operative. These sensitivities of the agreement prefixes do not affect the main point.

Chapter 7

1. I leave the Damin and German examples of section 3.4.5 aside here, as both are bound up with more differentiated systems of deixis, as previously discussed.
2. Other speaker-based directional systems exist. Some, focusing on source versus goal of motion, contrast not *hither* and *thither*, but *hither* and *hence*. An extremely elaborate system of this kind arises in Kemtuk (van der Wilden 1976), where the motions *hither* and *hence* are divided into horizontal, upward, and downward motions (*san, ban, kan*) for *hither*, with *hence* enriching these divisions still further with a distinction between proximal (∅, *bi, si*) and distal (*sa, ba, na*). These are not objects of analysis here, because they contrast directionality relative to a fixed person; as person systems, they are defective, representing only first (recalling the defective pronoun systems of Caddo and Kawésqar).
3. Paralleling the previous note, there are also participant-based *hither–hence* systems, as in the Mohawk trans- and cislocative. Bonvillain (1981, 61) writes that the translocative *y* "depicts the occurrence of an event in a location (of space or time) distant from the speaker/hearer or in a direction of movement (in space) away from the speaker/hearer" and that, if the agent is first person, then "the location or direction occurs away from the hearer." The same holds for events near or motion toward the participants, using the cislocative *t*. Moreover, Bonvillain gives the example of the cislocative *t-asatáweya?t* 'Come in!', which implies that, if the agent (or subject) is second person, then proximity to the speaker is implied. Again, these are not objects of analysis here, but I include this example to demonstrate the parallelism between author- and participant-based systems of this kind.
4. In both these languages, locatives fuse with tense markers, yielding a quite intricate set of spatiotemporal coordinates for events. I abstract away from this splendid device, with regret.
5. These two roots can also be used anaphorically and temporally. The other three roots, pertaining to degrees of distance and elevation, cannot and form a morphological family of their own: for example, *hwam(e)* 'that at the same level', *twam(e)* 'that up', *ywam(e)* 'that down'.
6. It may be that this is the only contrast for which person features are responsible. Alternatively, it may be that proximal, distal, and elevational constitute a tripartition—in which case, *a·* is +participant +author, *i·* is +participant −author, and *Cwa*—that is, *hwa, twa,* and *ywa* of the previous note—is −participant −author together with some elevational specification.
7. There is an interesting difference between how the four languages just discussed crosscut distance with person. In Sámi and Fore, distance distinctions are confined to third person, whereas Brazilian Portuguese and Slave permit them for nonthird persons. A full analysis should account for this difference, but a more thorough

description of the crosslinguistic terrain is needed first. For instance, we need to know whether it is coincidence or not that Brazilian Portuguese and Slave use bipartitions in this domain, where Sámi and Fore have richer systems.

8. Slightly sloppily, I use χ to represent both a syntactic entity and a semantic relation, but context should make clear which is which: the syntactic version occurs between semantic brackets $[\![\ldots]\!]$ or in a tree, and the semantic version generally takes an argument. Readers who so choose could treat P(x), and indeed $y \in \chi(x)$, presuppositionally.

   If one assumes that distance-based deictic systems differ from person-based ones in lacking a π projection, then one encounters a type problem: $[\![\chi]\!] = \lambda P . \lambda y . y \in \chi(x) \wedge P(x)$ cannot compose with $[\![\varphi]\!] = \lambda P . \lambda x . x \in S$ by function application. One might type-shift to yield $\lambda y . y \in \chi(x) \wedge x \in S$, but it is unclear what S is in this context. I leave open how this should be solved, but one option is obviously to claim that π is an obligatory projection, even if featureless and morphologically invisible. A possible advantage of obligatory projection of π is that it allows for the interaction of persons with distance distinctions: 'near' and 'far' are often anchored to the speaker—and sensitive to hearer location (Jungbluth 2003, Meira 2003)—even in systems that are not person-based in the strict sense. If one did pursue this approach, then apparent nonpartitions of spatial deixis, as in Mosetén, would, in fact, be monopartitions.

9. Example (21) is the title of an environmentalist book. Example (20) comes from a comment on an online article about Martian exploration—in full:

   Franchement, qu'irions-nous faire sur cette planète lointaine, poussiéreuse, sèche et stérile? On ne connaît pas encore la nôtre (suffit de voir les prévisions météorologiques ⟨emoticon⟩) et on veut fouler le sol d'une planète à 56 millions de kms. Absurde ⟨emoticon⟩.

   Frankly, what would we do on that distant, dusty, dry, and sterile planet? We still don't know our own (just look at our weather forecasts . . .) and we want to set foot on a planet 56,000,000 km away. Absurd . . .

   Just as much as the physical distance, the writer's psychological distance from supporting the mooted mission (and the contrastive topic 'our own [planet]', which, if referred to by a demonstrative, would demand 'this') forces one to translate the opening sentence with the distal 'that'. The psychological factors recall the distinctions of Korafe (section 7.2.1).

10. The middle structure of (26) is not a specifier configuration, which forces linearization at the left edge: that applies only to parts of complex heads, like those that host agreement. Here π is a pure person head, and its opening up to exponence anchors its content to the right.

Chapter 8

1. Presumably, parity with 'does (not) include the speaker' has made this feature the posit of choice. One could, though, posit 'does (not) include a unique participant',

that is, 'does (not) include the speaker or the hearer, but not both'. More generally, one can generate the quadripartition from any two of the following features:

(i)   a.   ±author′ ($i_o i u_o \mid u_o o_o$)
       b.   ±hearer′ ($i u_o u_o \mid i_o o_o$)
       c.   ±unique-participant′ ($i_o u_o \mid i u_o o_o$)

Similarly, one can generate the tripartition from any two of the following (the last of which is equivalent to the ±2 feature of Frampton 2002):

(ii)   a.   ±author′ ($i_o i u_o \mid u_o o_o$)
        b.   ±participant′ ($i_o i u_o u_o \mid o_o$)
        c.   ±just-you′ ($u_o \mid i_o i u_o o_o$)

Consideration of bipartitions excludes ±just-you′ as a choice in the latter case: (iia) and (iib) correspond to bipartitions and so are independently motivated, unlike (iic). And parsimony dictates that one recycle (iia) for the quadripartition (ia), using just one other feature. But generative capacity alone does not decide between (ib) ±hearer′ and (ic) ±unique-participant′.

2. The equivalence can be observed by noting that $P = (P \wedge Q) \vee (P \wedge \neg Q)$. So, omitting lambdas and variables:

(i)   (+au ∨ +hr) = ((+au ∧ +hr) ∨ (+au ∧ −hr)) ∨ (+hr ∧ +au) ∨(+hr ∧ −au)
                    = (+au ∧ −hr) ∨ (+hr ∧ +au) ∨ (−au ∧ +hr).

3. Harley and Ritter (2002a, 2002b) do not formulate an explicit semantics for their person (or number) features, but the right results follow given Lexical Complementarity and setting ⟦F′⟧ in Harley and Ritter's system to ⟦+F′⟧ in Noyer's (e.g., ⟦author′⟧$_{HR}$ = ⟦+author′⟧$_N$)—with two exceptions. First, Harley and Ritter have a special rule of interpretation for the bare participant node; see the main text. Second, they suggest the following identities for tripartition with a singular–plural distinction in first person and no number elsewhere: 1S participant′, 1P participant′ author′ hearer′, 2 participant′ hearer′, 3 ∅. I cannot devise a compositional semantics for these representations. So, I suggest that this, in my opinion, peripheral aspect of their proposal is best ignored, if we wish to maintain semantic compositionality at the level of features.

4. To simplify the discussion, I leave aside that Harley and Ritter actually argue for a parameter here: that bare participant′ is interpreted either as ⟦participant′ author′⟧ or as ⟦participant′ hearer′⟧, with the first as the default setting. They motivate this with facts from Algonquian (Zwicky 1977, Déchaine 1999), but McGinnis (2005), examining the data more fully, argues convincingly against the idea of a second person default.

5. For benefactive prefixes, one does, superficially, see *b* for some third persons, as in third inverse possessor-of-singular, *bé*, or third inverse possessor-of-dual/plural/inverse, *bét*. However, comparing these with the corresponding second person forms, *báu*, *bét*, *bát*, and *báut*, one sees that the third person forms contain an *e* that is absent from second person and overwrites the vowel corresponding to object agreement. This makes the exponent of third person look like *be*, distinct from second person *b*.

6. One might think to confine the putative impoverishment to exclusive by mentioning the features it excludes, but mentioning the absence of features simply brings into question the viability of privativity.

7. Informally, $[+P' +Q']$ holds of x if and only if $x \in P \cap Q$, which holds if and only if $x \in P$ and $x \in Q$. So, $[+P' +Q']$ and $[+P' -Q']$ both hold of x only if $x \in Q$ and $x \in \bar{Q}$, the complement of Q. By definition, partitions require that every x be contained in exactly one partition element. So, $\{Q, \bar{Q}\}$ is not a partition.

8. A second alternative approach to Fula is the treatment of variable affixality given in section 6.5.3 for Classical Hebrew, according to which suffixal exponents are anchored in place if they are of the form $\epsilon \Leftrightarrow [(\omega - \pi -)\varphi\ T]$, where T is linearized suffixally, but are linearized to the left, as a prefix, if of the form $\epsilon \Leftrightarrow [(\omega - \pi -)\varphi]$. Fula offers marginal support for this approach: prefixal agreement is invariant for tense, and 2S varies between prefixal '*a* and suffixal *aa*. Table 8.6 also implies fusion of tense with agreement in +participant subjunctives, like 2P *don*, which supports the idea of suffixal anchoring through coexponence with tense (if finer decompositions, like *d-on*, are not posited). This approach would tie variable affixality to the exponents themselves: 3S, say, would be '*o* $\Leftrightarrow [\omega_S - \pi_3 - \varphi]$, but 1S would be *mi* $\Leftrightarrow [\omega_S - \pi_1 - \varphi\ (T_{SUBJ})]$, so that it is anchored suffixally by T in the subjunctive, but is unanchored, and so prefixal, otherwise. This is a very language-specific analysis, which is a good thing, if, as one suspects, the phi- and tense-specifics of the phenomenon are parochial to Fula.

9. Watanabe notes that his conclusion, that ±hearer' is bivalent, contradicts an earlier attempt of mine (Harbour 2006) to address Zwicky's problem of overgeneration by taking the hearer feature to be privative, in contrast to the other two person features. Nevins (2007), too, exploits the idea to derive the correct range of crosslinguistic variation in person case effects (again, the unfettered feature overgenerates). To address both problems, Watanabe proposes instead that ±author' must be activated before any other person feature. This in essence feature-geometric solution raises the same questions of explanatory adequacy as other such accounts (section 8.2.2), and, more gravely, it rules out the possibility of activating ±participant' in the absence of ±author', preventing derivation of the participant bipartition. So, I do not endorse this aspect of Watanabe's account.

10. Frampton, like Trommer (2008), calls the feature ±2, but defines x as satisfying +2 if and only if $u \in x$ but $i \notin x$. The second condition is not part of +hearer' as usually defined. (Frampton discusses quadripartition as well as tripartition, and does so using only two feature names. However, his is, in reality, a three-feature account, as the definition of ±2 changes between partitions. For the quadripartition, it is equivalent to ±hearer' as usually defined.)

11. My account and Frampton's differ regarding the remaining natural class in this partition: his ±author' lends itself to first–nonfirst syncretism, my ±participant, to third–nonthird. German may seem to favor Frampton's account, in that present tense ablaut is restricted to nonfirst singular (witness the distribution of *läuf* versus *lauf* in present tense 'walk'; table 8.7). I have to attribute this to the exponents themselves, positing, say, 2S (')*st*, 3S (')*t*. Recall, though, that a language can display all possible syncretisms within the tripartition (Girawa; figure 2.1). Not

all of these can be accounted for through natural classes of two features. So, all two-feature theories must capture some syncretisms through defaults, homophones, or devices like those just suggested.

12. Valentine (2001) characterizes obviation in terms of narrative backgrounding, reminiscent of defocused third person in Caddo (section A.2.3). He explains that "within a given clause, only one third person animate referent can be in the foreground at a time; all other third person referents are backgrounded by making them obviative, which is marked by suffixes on animate nouns and by inflection on verbs" (p. 623). This suggests that obviation requires features beyond person, such as distality or topicality (but see note 1 of chapter 9 for a suggestion concerning a pure person treatment).

    The theme suffix occurs in transitive animate verbs and has four nonnull forms, depending on the argument combination present in the clause: $a\cdot$ for 3:OBV; ek for OBV:3, inanimate actors, and 1/2 passives; e for 3:1EX, 2S:1S; and en for 3:1IN/2, 1S:2S. Otherwise, it is null.

13. Bloomfield describes *en*, ordinarily a plural marker, as "anomalous" here.

14. One would expect the conjunct form corresponding to (17) to exhibit t, but it does not (*na·nak* 'when I fetch him'). One might attribute this to suppression by k, as it is morphophonologically systematic: t is also absent form 2P:3S *na·nɛ·k* and from the corresponding object plurals, 1S:3P *na·nak-uaq* and 2P:3P *na·nɛ·k-uaq*; but it is present in, for instance, 2S:3S *na·nat* and 3P passive *na·neht-uaq*. Thus, these t-free examples would be orthogonal, rather than exceptional, to Trommer's case. Similarly, k suppresses w if word-final, as in (16a); but I follow Trommer in representing it.

15. Trommer's analysis is couched in a combination of Distributed Morphology and Optimality Theory, which defies compact presentation here. An interesting aspect of his framework is that an exponent $\epsilon \Leftrightarrow$ [F G] can realize both larger feature bundles, like [F G H], and smaller ones, like [F], provided the constraints and competing exponents are configured correctly. Trommer does not comment on this aspect of his account, but it means that he departs both from the Subset Principle (Halle 1997) and from the Superset Principle (Caha 2009). If this corresponds to empirical reality, it would be an intriguing result.

16. Translations of the Dumi examples do not always exhaust the agent–patient pairings they encode. The examples are confined to dual number to avoid the orthogonal complication of vowel lowering in the root.

17. The discussion here focuses on 1/2:3 combinations because subject person is suppressed when the object is nonthird. In general, for these combinations, person agreement tracks the object and number agreement tracks the subject (with some exceptions for unit augmented objects). I leave the mechanisms behind this aside.

18. Third person *bi* in table 8.11 is evident, with some subtlety, in 3:3 combinations (the bottom right-hand corner of table 8.10).

    One exponent of third person object agreement, *bin*, is identifiable from combinations of third nonminimal arguments (3U/A:3U/A): *bin-di* is clearly comparable to *ngun-di* (3U/A:2, 1EX.U/A:2), *kan-di* (3U/A:1, 2:1), and *ngan-di* (3M/A:1). In other 3:3 combinations, object agreement is zero. Subtracting *n*, the object marker, from *bin*, leads us to posit *bi* as the (nonzero) exponent of third person.

Confirming this, *bi* is identifiable for third person subjects from 3M:3M, given that other minimal-on-third-minimal (M:3M) prefixes express only subject person (1EX.M:3M, 1IN.M:3M, and 2M:3M consist only of the subject exponents, *nga*, *ngarr*, and *yi*, respectively). Similarly, 3M:3A *bi-rri* consists of 3M:3M plus *rri*, in parallel to 1EX.M:3A *nga-rri*, 1IN.M:3A *ka-rri*, and 2M:3A *ngu-rri*.

There are some complications here, but nothing disquieting. Given other persons, one would expect *bi* in 3M:3A and 3M:3U (2M:3A *yi-ben* and 2M:3U *yi-benbene* obviously both include *yi*). But we find 3M:3A *ben* and 3M:3U *ben-bene*, not *bi-ben and *bi-ben-bene. This may be a phonological quirk, avoiding *bi* followed by *b*.

3U:3M is also surprising in lacking *bi*. Given 1EX.U:3M *nga-ne*, 1IN.U:3A *ka-ne*, and 2U:3A *ngu-ne*, one expects 3U:3M *bi-ne*, but finds *bene*. Two hypotheses are:

Analysis I 3U:3M *bene* is indeed *bi-ne*, but the *i* is subject to a lowering process.

Analysis II 3U:3M is in fact *bi-bene*, that is, the regular person exponent with the exponent of unit augmented, *bene*, that normally occurs for objects. (Object *bene* is identifiable in, for instance, the rightmost column of table 8.10, where *ben* realizes −minimal, hence A/U, and *bene* realizes +minimal in the context of −minimal, hence, U alone.) Deletion of *bi* before *b* yields surface *bene*.

If Analysis I is correct, then we might regard object *ben* as third person *bi* plus object case *n*, subject to lowering. This would increase the amount of evidence in favor of both exponents and for the sharing of person exponents across partitions. It would, however, make 3U/A:3U/A *bin-di* slightly irregular in not undergoing lowering (to become *ben-di*), though, clearly, one could attribute this to a vowel harmony effect (cf, 3A:3M *birri*). Either way, there is sufficient evidence for regarding *n* as object case and *bi* as third person shared across partitions, which is the main point.

19. Phrased in terms of the whole head, rather than a single feature, neither (33) nor the deletion rule targets unit augmented [$_\omega$ +minimal −minimal], making *ka* obligatory for 3:1U. Clearly, the deletion does not apply everywhere, but several other nonthird objects are syncretic for minimal and augmented: 1EX.M:2M/A ∅, 2M:1M/A *kan*, and 3M:2M/A *ngun*. So, the rule is a plausible posit. The best analyses I can devise within three-feature frameworks require a similar rule (see the main text).

Chapter 9

1. It is natural to ask whether person exploits opposing values, or number, order of composition. Section 9.3 addresses the latter. Concerning the former, it is easily, if tediously, shown that opposing specifications yield no new persons, no matter what their order of composition. However, I have said nothing about the proximal/obviative distinction that is prominent in so many Algonquian languages. It is possible that these involve a feature that is distinct from the person features

Notes 283

discussed above, one more akin, perhaps, to a distality or topicality distinction. However, we have seen that person features can measure proximity (chapter 7), and so one can imagine that a proximal third person in, say, a quadripartition, is −author(−participant(+participant(π))) or −author(+author(−participant(π))), whereas an obviative has the more regular minus–minus representation, −author (−participant(π)). Whether such a move offers insight remains to be seen.

2. Of course, sets like {io} are also closed under addition. However, these fail another condition discussed in Harbour 2014a: permutation invariance (fungibility). A specific io, as opposed to io', can only be picked out if the o's are distinguishable. The feature ±additive delivers desired dividends only if lattices are taken to be equivalence classes that lack such information.

3. Some logically possible grammars involving value recursion on number features are unattested. The most complex grammar, involving all features and two occurrences of value recursion, singular–dual–trial–paucal–greater-paucal–plural, is absent, as are systems eschewing ±atomic but with both ±minimal and ±additive, and at least one instance of value recursion: minimal–unit augmented–paucal–plural, minimal–paucal–greater-paucal–plural, or the union of these two. Value-recursed numbers are, however, relatively confined, both statistically and geographically. So, lacunae of cooccurrence do not seem overly worrisome. See Harbour 2014a for further discussion.

4. In Harbour 2013, I used epistemic alignment to argue for variables over values, and ipso facto for values, of person features. I can now conceive of a potential analysis that would be neutral with regard to valence, if the details could be successfully worked out. For completeness, I briefly lay the matter out here.

In epistemic alignment, a single exponent marks first person in statements and second in questions, and another marks the reverse configuration (as well as third persons). Illustrating for singulars in Akhvakh (Creissels 2008), we find *ada* for statements with a first person agent (i) and questions with a second person agent (ii):

(i) *Eλ- ada,* "*Di-λa q'abuλ-ere goλa.*"
   say-PF.1Q̄/2Q̄ 1S-DAT agree- IMPF COP.NEG
   'I said, "I don't agree."'

(ii) *Me-de čugu eλ- ada habe?*
    2S- ERG why say-PF.1Q̄/2Q̄ that
    'Why did you say that?'

By contrast, we find *ari* when the persons of the statement and question are reversed:

(iii) *Me-de- la eλ- ari,* "*Di-λa- la.*"
     2S- ERG-and say-PF.1Q̄/2Q̄/3 1S-DAT-and
     'And you said, "Me neither."'

(iv) *De-de čūda eλ- ari habe?*
    1S-ERG when say-PF.1Q̄/2Q̄/3 that
    'When did I say that?'

Third persons use *ari* uniformly, in questions and statements alike:

(v) *Huswe čūda b- eχ- ari hu mašina?*
he.ERG when 3ɦS-buy-PF.1Q/2Q̄/3 DEM car
'When did he buy this car?'

(vi) *Šuni b- eχ- ari.*
yesterday 3ɦS-buy-PF.1Q/2Q̄/3
'He bought it yesterday.'

The phenomenon may be relatively confined (to perfectives of transitives and unergatives) in its Akhvakh incarnation, but it is robust enough not to be fobbed away with homophony, having evolved convergently at genetic and geographic distance in Barbacoan, Nakh-Dagestanian, and Tibeto-Burman (see Curnow 2002, Creissels 2008, and references therein).

Bivalence can capture this in ways that privativity cannot (Harbour 2013). Positing +Q for questions and −Q for assertions, one can describe *ada* as a +participant (first or second) exponent used either when −Q and agentive +author cooccur (first person statements) or when +Q and agentive −author do (second person questions). More compactly, *ada* occurs for +participant αauthor ᾱQ, and *ari* elsewhere—which is statable only in virtue of (variables over) values of a person feature.

Valence-neutrally, though, one might seek to characterize epistemic alignment, and evidentiary source more generally, in terms of "epistemic paths." Like the other paths of chapter 7, these might indicate their sources using person features. If (some) statements involve epistemic paths with first person sources, and (some) questions, epistemic paths with second person sources, then *ada* might be described as occurring when agent and epistemic source have identical person features. The viability of this approach might depend on the behavior of questions asked without expecting the hearer to know the answer, or statements made with a degree of speaker uncertainty—for which further research is required. However, the approach is equally open to privative and bivalent features, leaving epistemic alignment ambivalent about valence.

5. The inclusive and third person duals are regular in terms of composition, respectively *yumitupela* and *emtupela* (compare with third singular, *em*). The plurals, however, are irregular. Third person is expressed by *ol(geta)*, and the inclusive, *yumi*, has no overt number. As a person–number portmanteau, the third person needs no further analysis: it simply outranks the would-be compositional form **empela*. For *yumi*, I have nothing more insightful to say than that the number features are irregularly pronounced as zero or are deleted. Krifka (2007) attempts a more principled explanation. His rather ingenious account predicts, however, that inclusive plurals could not be built off duals. This is contradicted, though, by languages like Mokilese, in which, for instance, the inclusive dual is *kisa* and the inclusive plural *kisai* (Harrison 1976).

6. For a person morpheme, the linear position of *ge* is surprising; though, as noted in chapter 7, individual morphemes can linearize idiosyncratically. Nonetheless, if one did consider *ge* a number morpheme, the problem of more exponents than features would persist. van Driem (1987) analyzes the nonsingular exclusives as consisting, diachronically at least, of *aŋ* and *ga* for person, and plural *i* or dual *chi*, together with nonsingular *y*, for number (*y* infixes into *ga* to give *gya* in some

dialects; in most, it fuses, or has fused, into *ge*). If there is only a single feature to either plural (Harley and Ritter 2002a) or dual (Cowper 2005), then there are insufficient features for past or present varieties of Limbu in which there are two exponents.

7. The same criticisms hold of the solutions available to privative number systems incorporating the number head ω' (or #, in the notation of Harley and Ritter 2002a, 2002b and other works) as a feature.

For instance, given Damana ∅ for singular ω' minimal', *bi* for dual ω' minimal' nonatomic', and *bi-nyina* for plural ω' nonatomic', a Harley-Ritter-style analysis could posit either of the following (the order of the first two exponents in the left-hand solution is crucial but stipulative):

(i) $\omega' \Leftrightarrow bi$ / nonatomic' ω' nonatomic' $\Leftrightarrow$ ∅
     nonatomic' $\Leftrightarrow$ ∅ / minimal' $\omega' \Leftrightarrow nyina$ / minimal'
     nonatomic' $\Leftrightarrow nyina$ minimal' $\Leftrightarrow bi$

Similarly, given Bislama ∅ for singular ω', *tu-pela* for dual ω' nonatomic', and *pela* for plural ω' nonminimal' nonatomic', a Cowperian analysis could posit either of the following (again, the stipulative order in the left-hand solution is crucial):

(ii) $\omega' \Leftrightarrow pela$ / nonatomic' ω' nonminimal' $\Leftrightarrow$ ∅
     nonatomic' nonminimal' $\Leftrightarrow$ ∅ $\omega' \Leftrightarrow tu$ / nonatomic'
     nonatomic' $\Leftrightarrow tu$ nonatomic' $\Leftrightarrow pela$

This does not exhaust the solution space but is illustrative of the range of choices. Matters are more straightforward, here, because one of the numbers, the singular, is null. When one of the persons in a quadripartition is null, simpler solutions also become available. Consider, for instance, Upper Necaxa Totonac (Beck 2004; McFarland (2009) presents similar data from Filomeno Mata Totonac), where inclusive (iiib) is clearly a substring of the exclusive (iiic):

(iii) a. *ik- tuks-a*
         1EX-hit- IMPF
         'I hit him'
      b. *tuks-yaa- w*
         hit- IMPF-1̄P
         'we.IN hit him'
      c. *ik- tuks-yaa- w*
         1EX-hit- IMPF-1̄P
         'we.EX hit him'

This permits the simple solution in which *w* realizes person-sensitive number and *ik* realizes author', and ∅ $\Leftrightarrow$ author' hearer' blocks *ik* in the inclusive (with ample features remaining for second and third).

But, fortuitous factors aside, the same conspiracy characterizes the treatments of Damana and Bislama number: zeroes and contexts bleed features that would otherwise permit exponents to occur where they are unwelcome. This creates solutions very different from what a Harley-Ritter-style treatment of Bislama number, or a Cowperian account of Damana, would look like, reinforcing the conclusion of the main text, that the entirety of a natural phenomenon has not been grasped.

Appendix A

1. Without having yet introduced person features, it is hard to specify details, but readers familiar with such operations might think of impoverishment (Bonet 1991, Noyer 1992) or value-changing operations (Noyer 1998, Harbour 2003).
2. Supporting this, the patientive/dative suffixes *ʔa* and *ʔu* are apparent in the irrealis forms of second person too, *saʔa* and *ʔaʔu*. If so analyzed, these concatenations are concomitant with changes in the expression of second person, from agentive *sahʔ* to patientive *sa* and dative *ʔa*—a reasonable move, as other persons also vary according to case, though without discernible suffixes (e.g., second person realis agentive *yahʔ* versus nonagentive *si*).
3. Two notes are in order here. First, existence of an apparently singular inclusive might lead seasoned readers to wonder whether Tongan has minimal, unit augmented, and augmented number. However, Churchward (1953) is clear that what he terms "dual" forms refer to exactly two both for inclusive and for other persons, and that, similarly, "plural" refers to groups of three or more. The language thus lacks the hallmark of minimal-augmented systems, whereby one and the same morphological class refers to n people for exclusive, second, and third person, but to $n + 1$ people for inclusives.

   Second, the morphological relationships are clearest for the "prepose" pronominals, in which there are three forms of the inclusive, *te-ta-tau*, closely paralleling the singular-dual-plural triplets of other persons. This is transparent for third person, *ne-na-nau*, but partially obscured for exclusive, *ou-ma-mau*, by suppletion in the singular, and for second person, *ke-mo-mou*, by a consonant change, *k* for *m*, in the singular, and a vowel change, *o* for *a*, in the nonsingular.

   Suppletion makes matters opaque in the "postposed" forms too. One readily sees that all nonsingular forms can be described as consisting of *ki* plus the preposed dual plus *ua* for dual and *utolu* for plural—hence, for instance, exclusive and inclusive dual *ki-ma-ua and ki-ta-ua*, and inclusive and second person plural *ki-ta-utolu and ki-mo-utolu* (though I do not suggest that these are the actual morpheme boundaries). The singular forms for exclusive, second, and third person are all suppletive, relative to this pattern. However, removal of the number markers correctly derives the inclusive pseudosingular *kita* from *kitaua, kitautolu*.

   Table A.5 omits variants for first singular preposed forms. CV forms are enclitic, as reflected in the different accentuation of *'oku* in (10) and *'okú* in (11).

References

Abbott, Clifford. 2006. Oneida teaching grammar. Ms., University of Wisconsin, Green Bay. http://www.uwgb.edu/oneida/filesToDownload/teaching%20grammar%20revised4.pdf.

Ackema, Peter, and Ad Neeleman. 2013. Person features and syncretism. *Natural Language and Linguistic Theory* 31:901–950.

Adelaar, Willem with Pieter Muysken. 2014. *The Languages of the Andes*. Cambridge: Cambridge University Press.

Adger, David. 2012. *A Syntax of Substance*. Cambridge, MA: MIT Press.

Adger, David, and Daniel Harbour. 2007. Syntax and syncretisms of the Person Case Constraint. *Syntax* 10:2–37.

Adger, David, Daniel Harbour, and Laurel J. Watkins. 2009. *Mirrors and Microparameters: Phrase Structure beyond Free Word Order*. Cambridge: Cambridge University Press.

Aguilera, Oscar. 2011. Los relatos de viaje kawésqar, su estructura y referencia de personas. *Magallania* 39:119–145. http://www.scielo.cl/pdf/magallania/v39n1/art08.pdf.

Aikhenvald, Alexandra. 1998. Warekena. In Desmond C. Derbyshire and Geoffrey K. Pullum, eds., *Handbook of Amazonian Languages, Vol. 4*, 225–439. Berlin: Mouton de Gruyter.

Allen, Gerald Norman. 1978. Halia verb morphology: From morpheme to discourse. Master's thesis, University of Texas at Arlington.

Amaya, María. 1999. *Damana*. Munich: Lincom Europa.

Anagnostopoulou, Elena. 2003. *The Syntax of Ditransitives: Evidence from Clitics*. Berlin: Mouton de Gruyter.

Anceaux, J. C. 1965. *The Nimboran Language: Phonology and Morphology*. The Hague: M. Nijhoff.

Anderson, Stephen. 1992. *A-Morphous Morphology*. Cambridge: Cambridge University Press.

Anderson, Stephen. 2015. The morpheme: Its nature and use. In Matthew Baerman, ed., *The Oxford Handbook of Inflection*, 11–34. Oxford: Oxford University Press.

Anderson, Stephen, and Edward Keenan. 1985. Deixis. In Timothy Shopen, ed., *Language Typology and Syntactic Description*. Vol. 3, *Grammatical Categories and the Lexicon*, 259–308. Cambridge: Cambridge University Press.

Arnott, D. W., ed. 1970. *The Nominal and Verbal Systems of Fula*. Oxford: Oxford University Press.

Arregi, Karlos, and Andrew Nevins. 2012. *Morphotactics: Basque Auxiliaries and the Structure of Spellout*. Dordrecht: Springer.

Bacharach, Michael. 2006. In Natalie Gold and Robert Sugden, eds., *Beyond Individual Choice*. Princeton, NJ: Princeton University Press.

Baerman, Matthew, and Dunstan Brown. 2013. Syncretism in verbal person/number marking. In Matthew S. Dryer and Martin Haspelmath, eds., *The World Atlas of Language Structures Online*, Leipzig: Max Planck Institute for Evolutionary Anthropology. http://wals.info/chapter/29.

Baerman, Matthew, Dunstan Brown, and Greville Corbett. 2005. *The Syntax-Morphology Interface: A Study of Syncretism*. Cambridge: Cambridge University Press.

Baker, Mark. 1996. *The Polysynthesis Parameter*. Oxford: Oxford University Press.

Banksira, Degif Petros. 2000. *Sound Mutations: The Morphophonology of Chaha*. Amsterdam: John Benjamins.

Beck, David. 2004. A grammatical sketch of Upper Necaxa Totonac. http://www.arts.ualberta.ca/totonaco/PDF/UNT.pdf.

Becker, A. L., and I Gusti Ngurah Oka. 1974. Person in Kawi: Exploration of an elementary semantic dimension. *Oceanic Linguistics* 13:229–255.

Béjar, Susana. 2003. Phi-syntax: A theory of agreement. Ph.D. thesis, University of Toronto.

Béjar, Susana. 2008. Conditions on Phi-Agree. In Daniel Harbour, David Adger, and Susana Béjar, eds., *Phi-Theory: Phi-Features across Modules and Interfaces*, 130–154. Oxford: Oxford University Press.

Béjar, Susana, and Daniel Hall. 1999. Marking markedness: The underlying order of diagonal syncretisms. Paper presented at the Eastern States Conference on Linguistics (ESCOL).

Béjar, Susana, and Milan Řezáč. 2003. Person licensing and the derivation of PCC effects. In Ana Teresa Pérez-Leroux and Yves Roberge, eds., *Romance Linguistics*, 49–62, Amsterdam: John Benjamins.

Benincà, Paola, and Cecilia Poletto. 2005. The third dimension of person features. In Leonie Cornips and Karen P. Corrigan, eds., *Syntax and Variation*, 265–299. Amsterdam: John Benjamins.

Benveniste, Emile. 1966. *Problèmes de linguistique générale*. Paris: Gallimard.

Bhat, D. N. S. 2004. *Pronouns: A Cross-Linguistic Study*. Oxford: Oxford University Press.

Bickel, Balthasar, and Johanna Nichols. 2005. Inclusive–exclusive as person vs. number categories worldwide. In Elena Filimonova, ed., *Clusivity: Typology and Case Studies of the Inclusive–Exclusive Distinction*, 29–72. Amsterdam: John Benjamins.

Bloomfield, Leonard. 1933. *Language*. New York: Holt.

Bloomfield, Leonard. 1962. *The Menomini Language*. New Haven, CT: Yale University Press.

References

Boas, Franz. 1911. *Handbook of American Indian Languages*. Washington, DC: U.S. Government Printing Office.

Boas, Franz. 1947. Grammar of Kwakiutl (with a glossary of the suffixes). *Transactions of the American Philosophical Society* 37:201–377. Edited by Helene Boas Yampolsky and with contributions from Zellig S. Harris.

Bobaljik, Jonathan. 2002. Syncretism without paradigms: Remarks on Williams 1981, 1984. In Geert Booij and Jaap van Marle, eds., *Yearbook of Morphology 2001*, 53–86. Dordrecht: Kluwer.

Bobaljik, Jonathan. 2008. Missing persons: A case study in morphological universals. *The Linguistic Review* 25:203–230.

Bobaljik, Jonathan, and Uli Sauerland. 2013. Syncretism distribution modeling: Accidental homophony as a random event. In Nobu Goto, Koichi Otaki, Atsushi Sato, and Kensuke Takita, eds., *Proceedings of GLOW in Asia IX 2012: The Main Session*, 31–53. http://faculty.human.mie-u.ac.jp/~glow_mie/IX_Proceedings_Oral/GLOWIXProceedings_Final.pdf.

Bonet, Eulàlia. 1991. Morphology after syntax: Pronominal clitics in Romance. Ph.D. thesis, MIT.

Bonet, Eulàlia, and Daniel Harbour. 2012. Contextual allomorphy. In Jochen Trommer, ed., *The Morphology and Phonology of Exponence*, 195–235. Oxford: Oxford University Press.

Bonvillain, Nancy. 1981. Locative semantics in Mohawk: Time and space. *International Journal of American Linguistics* 47:58–65.

Booij, Geert. 2010. *Construction Morphology*. Oxford: Oxford University Press.

Borer, Hagit. 1983. *Parametric Syntax: Case Studies in Semitic and Romance Languages*. Dordrecht: Foris.

Borer, Hagit. 2005. *Structuring Sense*. Vol. 2, *The Normal Course of Events*. Oxford: Oxford University Press.

Borgman, Donald M. 1990. Sanuma. In Desmond C. Derbyshire and Geoffrey K. Pullum, eds., *Handbook of Amazonian Languages, Vol. 2*. 15–248. Berlin: Mouton de Gruyter.

Branigan, Phil. 2006. Feature values in intervention effects in a polysynthetic language. Paper presented at GLOW XXIX, Barcelona.

Brittain, Julie. 2001. *The Morphosyntax of the Algonquian Conjunct Verb*. New York: Garland.

Broadwell, George Aaron. 2006. *A Choctaw Reference Grammar*. Lincoln: University of Nebraska Press.

Brody, Michael. 2000. Mirror Theory: Syntactic representation in perfect syntax. *Linguistic Inquiry* 31:29–56.

Brody, Michael, and Anna Szabolcsi. 2003. Overt scope in Hungarian. *Syntax* 6:19–51.

Brown, Bob. 1990. Waris grammar sketch. http://www-01.sil.org/pacific/png/abstract.asp?id=928474543835.

Brownie, John, and Marjo Brownie. 2007. *Mussau Grammar Essentials*. Ukarumpa, Papua New Guinea: SIL-PNG Academic Publications. http://www.sil.org/pacific/png/pubs/48552/MussauGrammarEssentials.pdf.

Buccellati, Giorgio. 1997. Akkadian. In Robert Hetzron, ed., *The Semitic Languages*, 69–99, New York: Routledge.

Bunye, Maria, and Elsa Yap. 1971. *Cebuano Grammar Notes*. Honolulu: University Press of Hawai'i.

Burung, Wiem. 2000. A brief note on Elseng. SIL International Electronic Survey Reports 2000-001. http://www-01.sil.org/silesr/2000/2000-001/SILESR2000-001.pdf.

Caha, Pavel. 2009. The nanosyntax of case. Ph.D. thesis, Universtitetet i Tromsø.

Calabrese, Andrea. 1988. Towards a theory of phonological alphabets. Ph.D. thesis, MIT.

Calabrese, Andrea. 2008. On absolute and contextual syncretism: Remarks on the structure of paradigms and on how to derive it. In Asaf Bachrach and Andrew Nevins, eds., *Inflectional Identity*, 156–205. Oxford: Oxford University Press.

Campbell, Lyle. 1985. *The Pipil Language of El Salvador*. Berlin: Mouton.

Caplice, Richard. 2002. *Introduction to Akkadian*. Rome: Editrice Pontificio Instituto Biblico.

Carstens, Vicki May. 1991. The morphology and syntax of determiner phrases in Kiswahili. Ph.D. thesis, University of California, Los Angeles.

Chafe, Wallace. 1990. Uses of the defocusing pronominal prefixes in Caddo. *Anthropological Linguistics* 32:57–68.

Chapman, Shirley, and Desmond C. Derbyshire. 1991. Paumarí. In Desmond C. Derbyshire and Geoffrey K. Pullum, eds., *Handbook of Amazonian Languages Vol. 3*, 161–352, Berlin: Mouton de Gruyter.

Chappell, Hilary. 1996. Inalienability and the personal domain in Mandarin Chinese discourse. In Hilary Chappell and William McGregor, eds., *The Grammar of Inalienability: A Typological Perspective on Body Parts and the Part–Whole Relation*, 465–527. Berlin: Mouton de Gruyter.

Charney, Jean Ormsbee. 1993. *A Grammar of Comanche*. Lincoln: University of Nebraska Press.

Cheney, Dorothy, and Robert Seyfarth. 2007. *Baboon Metaphysics: The Evolution of a Social Mind*. Chicago: University of Chicago Press.

Chierchia, Gennaro. 1998. Plurality of mass nouns and the notion of 'semantic parameter'. In Susan Rothstein, ed., *Events and Grammar*, 53–103. Dordrecht: Kluwer.

Chomsky, Noam. 1966. *Cartesian Linguistics: A Chapter in the History of Rationalist Thought*. New York: Harper and Row.

Chomsky, Noam. 1977. On *wh*-movement. In Peter Culicover, Thomas Wasow, and Adrain Akmajian, eds., *Formal Syntax*, 71–132. New York: Academic Press.

Chomsky, Noam. 1980. On binding. *Linguistic Inquiry* 11:1–46.

Chomsky, Noam. 1981. *Lectures on Government and Binding*. Dordrecht: Foris.

References

Chomsky, Noam. 1986. *Knowledge of language: Its nature, origin, and use*. New York: praeger.

Chomsky, Noam. 1995. Bare Phrase Structure. In Gert Webelhuth, ed., *Government and Binding Theory and the Minimalist Program*, 383–439. Cambridge, MA: Blackwell.

Chomsky, Noam, and Morris Halle. 1968. *The Sound Pattern of English*. New York: Harper and Fwd.

Churchward, C. Maxwell. 1953. *Tongan Grammar*. Tonga: Vavaʻu Press.

Clairis, Cristos. 1985. *El Qawasqar: Lingüística fueguina, teoria y descripción*. Valdivia, Chile: Universidad Austral de Chile.

Clark, Ross. 1975. Mele notes. Auckland University Working Papers in Anthropology, Archaeology, Linguistics, and Maori Studies, 40. http://paradisec.org.au/fieldnotes/image_viewer.htm?VMELE102,29.

Cooke, Joseph. 1968. *Pronominal Reference in Thai, Burmese, and Vietnamese*. Berkeley: University of California Press.

Cooper, Robin. 1983. *Quantification and Syntactic Theory*. Dordrecht: Reidel.

Corbett, Greville. 2000. *Number*. Cambridge: Cambridge University Press.

Corbett, Greville. 2006. *Agreement*. Cambridge: Cambridge University Press.

Corbett, Greville. 2007. Canonical typology, suppletion, and possible words. *Language* 83:8–42.

Corbett, Greville, and Richard Hayward. 1987. Gender and number in Bayso. *Lingua* 73:1–28.

Coulson, Michael. 1992. *Sanskrit: An Introduction to the Classical Language*. 2nd ed., revised by Richard Gombrich and James Benson. London: Hodder and Stoughton.

Cowper, Elizabeth. 2005. A note on number. *Linguistic Inquiry* 36:441–455.

Cowper, Elizabeth, and Daniel Currie Hall. 2004. The pieces of π. paper presented at the Canadian Linguistic Association, University of Manitoba, Winnipeg.

Creissels, Denis. 2008. Person variations in Akhvakh verb morphology: Functional motivation and origin of an uncommon pattern. *Sprachtypologie und Universalienforschung* 61:309–325.

Crowley, Terry. 2004. *Bislama Reference Grammar*. Honolulu: University of Hawaiʻi Press.

Curnow, Timothy. 2002. Conjunct/Disjunct marking in Awa Pit. *Linguistics* 40:611–627.

Cysouw, Michael. 2003. *The Paradigmatic Structure of Person Marking*. Oxford: Oxford University Press.

Cysouw, Michael. 2005a. Syncretisms involving clusivity. In Elena Filimonova, ed., *Clusivity: Typology and Case Studies of the Inclusive–Exclusive Distinction*, 73–111. Amsterdam: John Benjamins.

Cysouw, Michael. 2005b. A typology of honorific uses of clusivity. In Elena Filimonova, ed., *Clusivity: Typology and Case Studies of the Inclusive–Exclusive Distinction*, 213–230. Amsterdam: John Benjamins.

Cysouw, Michael. 2011. The expression of person and number: A typologist's perspective. *Morphology* 21:419–443.

Cysouw, Michael. 2013. Inclusive/Exclusive distinction in independent pronouns. In Matthew S. Dryer and Martin Haspelmath, eds., *The World Atlas of Language Structures Online*. Leipzig: Max Planck Institute for Evolutionary Anthropology. http://wals.info/chapter/39.

Daniel, Michael. 2013. Plurality in independent personal pronouns. In Matthew S. Dryer and Martin Haspelmath, eds., *The World Atlas of Language Structures Online*. Leipzig: Max Planck Institute for Evolutionary Anthropology. http://wals.info/chapter/35.

de Castro Alves, Flávia. 2004. O Timbira falado pelos Canela Apãniekrá: Uma contribuição aos estudos da morfossintaxe de uma língua Jê. Ph.D. thesis, Universidade Estadual de Campinas.

Déchaine, Rose-Marie. 1999. What Algonquian morphology is really like: Hockett revisited. In Leora Bar-El, Rose-Marie Déchaine, and Charlotte Reinholtz, eds., *Papers from the Workshop on Structure and Constituency in Native American Languages, 25–72*. MIT Occasional Papers in Linguistics 17. Cambridge, MA: MIT, MIT Working Papers in Linguistics.

Dedrick, John, and Eugene Casad, eds. 1999. *Sonora Yaqui Language Structures*. Tucson: University of Arizona Press.

de Groot, Casper. 2010. Mood in Hungarian. In Björn Rothstein and Rolf Thieroff, eds., *Mood in the Languages of Europe*, 551–568. Amsterdam: John Benjamins.

Deibler, Ellis W. 1976a. A Gahuku-Yaweyuha comparative grammar. Ms., SIL Pacific. http://www-01.sil.org/pacific/png/abstract.asp?id=50164.

Deibler, Ellis W. 1976b. *Semantic Relationships of Gahuku Verbs*. Norman, OK: Summer Institute of Linguistics.

Dempwolff, Otto. 1939 [2005]. *Grammar of the Jabêm Language of New Guinea*. Translated and edited by Joel Bradshaw and Francisc Czobor. Honolulu: University of Hawai'i Press.

Dervillez-Bastuji, Jacqueline. 1982. *Structures des relations spatiales dans quelques langues naturelles: Introduction à une théorie sémantique*. Geneva: Librairie Droz.

Dixon, R. M. W. 1988. *A Grammar of Boumaa Fijian*. Chicago: University of Chicago Press.

Dixon, R. M. W. 1994. *Ergativity*. Cambridge: Cambridge University Press.

Donohue, Mark. 1999. *A Grammar of Tukang Besi*. Berlin: Mouton de Gruyter.

Donohue, Mark. 2004. A grammar of the Skou language of New Guinea. Ms., National University of Singapore.

Downing, Laura, and Barbara Stiebels. 2012. Iconicity. In Jochen Trommer, ed., *The Morphology and Phonology of Exponence*, 379–426. Oxford: Oxford University Press.

Dresher, Elan. 2009. *The Contrastive Hierarchy in Phonology*. Cambridge: Cambridge University Press.

Dryer, Matthew. 1989. Plural words. *Linguistics* 27:865–895.

Duarte, Eugênia. 1995. A perda do principio "Evite pronome" no português brasileiro. Ph.D. thesis, Universidate Estadual de campinas.

Eaton, Helen. 2010. *A Sandawe Grammar*. SIL. http://www-01.sil.org/silepubs/Pubs/52718/52718_EatonH_Sandawe_Grammar.pdf.

Einarsson, Stefán. 1945. *Icelandic: Grammar, Texts, Glossary*. Baltimore: Johns Hopkins University Press.

Elbert, Samuel H., and Mary Kawena Pukui. 1979. *Hawaiian Grammar*. Honolulu: University Press of Hawai'i.

Embick, David, and Rolf Noyer. 2001. Movement operations after syntax. *Linguistic Inquiry* 32:555–595.

England, Nora. 1983. *A Grammar of Mam, a Mayan Language*. Austin: University of Texas Press.

Evans, Nicholas. 2003. *Bininj Gun-Wok: A Pan-Dialectal Grammar of Mayali, Kunwinjku and Kune*. Canberra: Pacific Linguistics.

Evans, Nicholas, and Stephen Levinson. 2009. The myth of language universals: Language diversity and its importance for cognitive science. *Behavioral and Brain Sciences* 32:429–492.

Everett, Daniel. 1986. Pirahã. In Desmond C. Derbyshire and Geoffrey K. Pullum, eds., *Handbook of Amazonian Languages, Vol. 1*, 200–325. Berlin: Mouton de Gruyter.

Farr, Cynthia, and Carl Whitehead. 1981. This, that, and the other: A study of Korafe demonstratives. *Languages and Linguistics in Melanesia* 13:64–80.

Ferreira, Helder Perri. 2013. Patrones de marcación argumental en lenguas yanomami. Paper presented at Congreso de Idiomas Indígenas de Latinoamérica VI, Conference on Indigenous Languages of Latin America VI, University of Texas at Austin.

Foley, William. 1986. *The Papuan Languages of New Guinea*. Cambridge: Cambridge University Press.

Foley, William. 1991. *The Yimas Language of New Guinea*. Stanford, CA: CSLI Publications.

Forman, Michael L. 1971. *Kapampangan Grammar Notes*. Honolulu: University of Hawai'i Press.

Frampton, John. 2002. Syncretism, impoverishment, and the structure of person features. In Mary Andronis, Erin Debenport, Anne Pycha, and Keiko Yoshimori, eds., *Papers from the 38th regional Meeting, Chicago Linguistic Society*, 207–222. Chicago: University of Chicago, Chicago Linguistic Society.

Frampton, John. 2008. *Distributed Reduplication*. Cambridge, MA: MIT Press.

François, Alexandre. 2009. The languages of Vanikoro: Three lexicons and one grammar. In Bethwyn Evans, ed., *Discovering History through Language: Papers in Honour of Malcolm Ross*, 103–126. Canberra: Australian National University.

Gärdenfors, Peter. 2004. *Conceptual Spaces: The Geometry of Thought*. Cambridge, MA: MIT Press.

Gasaway, Eileen, Pat Lillie, and Heather Sims. 1977. Girawa grammar. SIL. http://www-01.sil.org/pacific/png/abstract.asp?id=928474543865.

Göksel, Asli, and Celia Kerslake. 2005. *Turkish: A Comprehensive Grammar*. London: Routledge.

Gold, Natalie. 2012. Team reasoning, framing and cooperation. In Samir Okasha and Ken Binmore, eds., *Evolution and Rationality: Decisions, Cooperation and Strategic Behaviour*, 185–212. Cambridge: Cambridge University Press.

Gold, Natalie, and Daniel Harbour. 2012. Cognitive primitives of collective intentions: Linguistic evidence of our mental ontology. *Mind and Language* 24:109–134.

Gold, Natalie, and Robert Sugden. 2007. Collective intentions and team agency. *Journal of Philosophy* 104:109–137.

Goldberg, Adele E. 1995. *Constructions: A Construction Grammar Approach to Argument Structure*. Chicago: University of Chicago Press.

Goldberg, Adele E. 2009. The nature of generalization in language. *Cognitive Linguistics* 20:93–127.

Gomes, Antonio Almir Silva. 2013. Sanapaná, uma língua maskoy: Aspectos gramaticais. Ph.D. thesis, Universidade Estadual de Campinas.

Güldemann, Tom. 2002. Die Entlehnung pronominaler Elemente des Khoekhoe aus dem !Ui-Taa. In Theda Schumann, Mechthild Reh, Roland Kießling, and Ludwig Gerhardt, eds., *Aktuelle Forschungen zu afrikanischen Sprachen: Sprachwissenschaftliche Beiträge zum 14. Afrikanistentag, Hamburg, 11–14. Oktober 2000*, 43–61. Cologne: Rüdiger Köppe.

Hale, Kenneth, with appendix by Albert Albarez. 1972. A new perspective on American Indian linguistics. In Alfonso Ortiz, ed., *New Perspectives on the Pueblos*, 87–133. Albuquerque: University of New Mexico Press.

Hale, Kenneth. 1973. Person marking in Walbiri. In Stephen R. Anderson, and Paul Kiparsky, eds., *A Festschrift for Morris Halle*, 308–344. New York: Holt, Rinehart and Winston.

Hale, Kenneth. 1997. Some observations on the contribution of local languages to linguistic science. *Lingua* 100:71–89.

Hale, Kenneth. 1998. On endangered languages and the importance of linguistic diversity. In Lenore Grenoble and J. Whaley Lindsey, eds., *Endangered Languages: Current Issues and Future Prospects*, 192–216. Cambridge: Cambridge University Press.

Hale, Kenneth, and Samuel Jay Keyser. 2002. *Prolegomenon to a Theory of Argument Structure*. Cambridge, MA: MIT Press.

Hale, Kenneth, LaVerne, Jeanne, and Paula Pranka. 1990. On suppletion, selection and agreement. In Carol Georgopoulos and Roberta Ishihara, eds., *Interdisciplinary Approaches to Languages*, 255–270. Dordrecht: Kluwer.

Hale, Kenneth, and David Nash. 1997. Damin and Lardil phonotactics. In Darrell Tryon and Michael Walsh, eds., *Boundary Rider: Essays in Honour of Geoffrey O'Grady*, 247–259. Canberra: Pacific Linguistics.

Halle, Morris. 1997. Distributed Morphology: Impoverishment and Fission. In Benjamin Bruening, Yoonjung Kang, and Martha McGinnis, eds., *PF: Papers at the Interface*, 425–449. MIT Working Papers in Linguistics 30. Cambridge, MA: MIT, MIT Working Papers in Linguistics. Reprinted in Jacqueline Lecarme, Jean

Lowenstamm, and Ur Shlonsky, eds., *Research in Afroasiatic Grammar: Papers from the Third Conference on Afroasiatic Languages, Sophia Antipolis, France 1996*, 125–150. Amsterdam: John Benjamins (2003).

Halle, Morris, and Alec Marantz. 1993. Distributed Morphology and the pieces of inflection. In Kenneth Hale and Samuel Jay Keyser, eds., *The View from Building 20*, 111–176. Cambridge, MA: MIT Press.

Harbour, Daniel. 1999. The two types of predicate clefts: Classical Hebrew and beyond. In Vivian Lin, Cornelia Krause, Benjamin Bruening, and Karlos Arregi, eds., *Papers on Morphology and Syntax, Cycle Two*, 159–176. MIT Working Papers in Linguistics 34. Cambridge, MA: MIT, MIT Working Papers in Linguistics.

Harbour, Daniel. 2003. The Kiowa case for feature insertion. *Natural Language and Linguistic Theory* 21:543–578.

Harbour, Daniel. 2006. Person hierarchies and geometries without hierarchies or geometries. Presentation at Leipzig Morphology Colloquium. Queen Mary's OPAL #6. http://webspace.qmul.ac.uk/dharbour/Queen-Mary's-OPALs.html.

Harbour, Daniel. 2007a. Against PersonP. *Syntax* 10:223–243.

Harbour, Daniel. 2007b. *Morphosemantic Number: From Kiowa Noun Classes to UG Number Features*. Dordrecht: Springer.

Harbour, Daniel. 2008. Discontinuous agreement and the syntax–morphology interface. In Daniel Harbour, David Adger, and Susana Béjar, eds., *Phi-Theory: Phi-Features across Modules and Interfaces*, 185–220. Oxford: Oxford University Press.

Harbour, Daniel. 2011a. Descriptive and explanatory markedness. *Morphology* 21: 223–240.

Harbour, Daniel. 2011b. The generative syntax of the natural numbers. Ms., Queen Mary University of London.

Harbour, Daniel. 2011c. Valence and atomic number. *Linguistic Inquiry* 42:561–594.

Harbour, Daniel. 2013. "Not plus" isn't "not there": Bivalence in person, number, and gender. In Ora Matushansky and Alec Marantz, eds., *Distributed Morphology Today*, 135–150; references, 223–249. Cambridge, MA: MIT Press.

Harbour, Daniel. 2014a. Paucity, abundance, and the theory of number. *Language* 90:185–229.

Harbour, Daniel. 2014b. Small pronoun systems and what they teach us. *Nordlyd* 41:125–143.

Harbour, Daniel. 2016. Parameters of poor pronoun systems. *Linguistic Inquiry* 47.4.

Harbour, Daniel, and Christian Elsholtz. 2011. Feature geometry: Self-destructed. Ms., Queen Mary University of London and Technische Universität Graz.

Hardman, M. J. 2001. *Aymara*. Munich: Lincom Europa.

Harley, Heidi. 2008. When is a syncretism more than a syncretism? Impoverishment, metasyncretism, and underspecification. In Daniel Harbour, David Adger, and Susana Béjar, eds., *Phi-Theory: Phi-Features across Modules and Interfaces*, 251–294, Oxford: Oxford University Press.

Harley, Heidi, and Elizabeth Ritter. 2002a. Person and number in pronouns: A feature-geometric analysis. *Language* 78:482–526.

Harley, Heidi, and Elizabeth Ritter. 2002b. Structuring the bundle: A universal morphosyntactic feature geometry. In Horst J. Simon and Heike Wiese, eds., *Pronouns: Grammar and Representation*, 23–40. Amsterdam: John Benjamins.

Harris, James, and Morris Halle. 2005. Unexpected plural inflections in Spanish: Reduplication and metathesis. *Linguistic Inquiry* 36: 195–222.

Harrison, Sheldon. 1976. *Mokilese Reference Grammar*. Honolulu: University Press of Hawai'i.

Hartmann, Iren, and Christian Marschke, eds. 2010. *Hocąk Teaching Materials*. Vol. 2, *Texts with Analysis and Translation and an Audio-CD of Original Hocąk Texts*. Albany: State University of New York Press.

Haspelmath, Martin. 2002. Explaining the ditransitive person-role constraint: A usage-based approach. http://journals.linguisticsociety.org/elanguage/constructions/article/download/3073/3073-6093-1-PB.pdf

Hauser, Marc D., Noam Chomsky, and W. Tecumseh Fitch. 2002. The faculty of language: What is it, who has it, and how did it evolve? *Science* 298:1569–1579.

Hawkins, Robert. 1998. Wai Wai. In Desmond C. Derbyshire and Geoffrey K. Pullum, eds., *Handbook of Amazonian Languages, Vol. 4*. 25–224. Berlin: Mouton de Gruyter.

Heck, Fabian, and Marc Richards. 2010. A probe-goal approach to agreement and incorporation restrictions in Southern Tiwa. *Natural Language and Linguistic Theory* 28:681–721.

Heim, Irene, and Angelika Kratzer. 1998. *Semantics in Generative Grammar*. Oxford: Blackwell.

Helmbrecht, Johannes, and Christian Lehmann, eds. 2010. *Hocąk Teaching Materials*, Vol. 1, *Elements of Grammar/Learner's Dictionary*. Albany: State University of New York Press.

Hewitt, George. 1995. *Georgian: A Structural Reference Grammar*. Amsterdam: Philadelphia John Benjamins.

Higginbotham, James. 1993. Interrogatives. In Kenneth Hale and Samuel Jay Keyser, eds., *The View from Building 20*, 195–227. Cambridge, MA: MIT Press.

Higginbotham, James. 1997. A plea for implicit anaphora. In Hans Bennis, Pierre Pica, and Johann Rooryck, eds., *Atomism and Binding*, 183–203. Dordrecht: Foris.

Hockett, Charles. 1947. Problems of morphemic analysis. *Language* 23:321–343.

Hoeksema, Jack. 1983. Plurality and conjunction. In Alice ter Meulen, ed., *Studies in Model-Theoretic Semantics*, 63–83. Dordrecht: Foris.

Hoge, Kirstin. 1998. The predicate cleft construction in Yiddish. In David Willis, ed., *Oxford Working Papers in Linguistics 2*. 85–98. Oxford: Clarendon Press.

Hudson, Joyce. 1978. *The Core of Walmatjari Grammar*. Atlantic Highlands, NJ: Humanities Press.

Humboldt, Wilhelm von. 1830. *Über die Verwandtschaft der Ortsadverbien mit dem Pronomen in einigen Sprachen*. Berlin: Königlichen Akademie der Wissenschaften, https://archive.org/details/berdieverwandts00humbgoog.

Humboldt, Wilhelm von. 1836 [1999]. *On Language: The Diversity of Human Language Construction and its influence on the Mental Development of the Human Species*. Edited by Michael Losonky and translated by Peter Heath. Cambridge: Cambridge University Press.

Hutchisson, Don. 1986. Sursurunga pronouns and the special uses of quadral number. In Ursula Wiesemann, ed., *Pronominal Systems*, 217–255. Tübingen: Narr.

Imai, Shingo. 2003. Spatial deixis. Ph.D. thesis, State University of New York, Buffalo.

Irwin, Barry. 1974. *Salt-Yui Grammar*. Canberra: Linguistic Circle of Canberra.

Jäger, Gerhard. 2008. Applications of Game Theory in linguistics. *Language and Linguistics Compass* 2:406–421.

Jakobson, Roman. 1958 [1971]. Морфологические наблюдения над славянским склонением: Состав русских падежных форм [Morphological observations on Slavic declensions: The structure of Russian case forms]. In Roman Jakobson, ed., *Selected Writings*. Vol. 2, *Word and Language*, 154–183. The Hague: Mouton.

Jakobson, Roman, Sergei Karcevsky, and Nikolai S. Trubetzkoy, 1958 [1971]. Quelles sont les méthodes les mieux appropriées à un exposé complet et pratique de la grammaire d'une langue quelconque? In Roman Jakobson, ed., *Selected Writings*. Vol 2, *Word and Language*. 3–6. The Hague: Mouton.

Jelinek, Eloise. 1993. Ergative splits and argument type. In Jonathan D. Bobaljik and Colin Phillips, eds., *Papers on Case and Agreement I*, 15–42. MIT Working Papers in Linguistics 18. Cambridge. MA: MIT, MIT Working Papers in Linguistics.

Josephs, Lewis S. 1975. *Palauan Reference Grammar*. Honolulu: University of Hawai'i Press.

Josephs, Lewis S. 1977. *New Palauan-English Dictionary: Based on the Palauan-English Dictionary by Fr. Edwin G. McManus*. Honolulu: University of Hawai'i Press.

Jungbluth, Konstanze. 2003. Deictics in the conversational dyad: Findings in Spanish and some cross-linguistic outlines. In Friedrich Lenz, ed., *Deictic Conceptualisation of Space, Time and Person*, 13–40. Amsterdam: John Benjamins.

Kautzsch, Emil. 1910. *Genesius' Hebrew Grammar*. 2nd ed. Translated and edited by A. E. Cowley. Oxford: Clarendon Press.

Kenesei, István, Robert Vago, and Anna Fenyvesi. 1998. *Hungarian*. London: Routledge.

Kerstens, Johan. 1993. *The Syntax of Person, Number and Gender: A Theory of Phi-Features*. Berlin: Mouton de Gruyter.

Kimball, Geoffrey D. 1991. *Koasati Grammar*. Lincoln: University of Nebraska Press.

Koch, Harold. 2004. A methodological history of Australian linguistic classification. In Claire Bowern and Harold Koch, eds., *Australian Languages: Classification and the Comparative Method*, 17–60. Amsterdam: John Benjamins.

Kratzer, Angelika. 2006. Minimal pronouns: Fake indexicals as windows into the properties of bound variables. Ms., University of Massachusetts at Amherst. Available at http://semanticsarchive.net.

Kratzer, Angelika. 2009. Making a pronoun: Fake indexicals as windows into the properties of pronouns. *Linguistic Inquiry* 40:187–237.

Krifka, Manfred. 1992. Thematic relations as links between nominal reference and temporal constitution. In Ivan Sag and Anna Szabolcsi, eds., *Lexical Matters*, 29–53. Stanford, CA: CSLI publications.

Krifka, Manfred. 2007. A note on the pronoun system and the predicate marker in Tok Pisin. In Patrick Brandt and Eric Fuss, eds., *Form, Structure, and Grammar: A Festschrift Presented to Günther Grewendorf on the Occasion of His 60th Birthday*, 79–92. Berlin: Akademie Verlag.

Kroeber, Alfred. 1907. The Washo language of east central California and Nevada. *University of California Publications in American Archaeology and Ethnology* 4:251–317.

Kumar, Pramod. 2012. Descriptive and typological study of Jarawa. Ph.D. thesis, Jawaharlal Nehru University, New Delhi.

Laidig, Wyn D., and Carol J. Laidig. 1990. Larike pronouns: Dual and trials in a Central Moluccan language. *Oceanic Linguistics* 29:87–109.

Laycock, Don. 1977. Me and you versus the rest. *Irian* 6:33–41.

Lenz, Friedrich, ed. 2003. *Deictic Conceptualisation of Space, Time and Person*. Amsterdam: John Benjamins.

Lewis, Paul, Gary Simons, and Charles Fennig. eds. 2014. *Ethnologue: Languages of the World*. 17th ed. Dallas, TX: SIL International. Online version: http://www.ethnologue.com.

Lichtenberg, Frantisek. 1983. *A Grammar of Manam*. Honolulu: University of Hawai'i Press.

Lieber, Rochelle. 1980. On the organization of the lexicon. Ph.D. thesis, MIT.

Liljencrants, Johan, and Björn Lindblom, 1972. Numerical simulation of vowel quality systems: The role of perceptual contrast. *Language* 48:839–862.

Link, Godehard. 1983. The logical analysis of plurals and mass terms: A lattice-theoretical approach. In Rainer Bäuerle, Christoph Schwarze, and Arnim von Stechow, eds., *Meaning, Use and Interpretation of Language*, 302–323. Berlin: Walter de Gruyter.

Lipkind, William. 1945. *Winnebago Grammar*. New York: NY King's Crown Press.

List, Christian. 2014. Three kinds of collective attitudes. *Erkenntis* 79:1601–1622.

Lynch, John. 1983. Switch-reference in Lenakel. In John Haiman and Pamela Munro, eds., *Switch Reference and Universal Grammar: Proceedings of a Symposium on Switch Reference and Universal Grammar, Winnipeg, May 1981*, 209–222. Amsterdam: Jhon Benjamins.

Lynch, John. 2002. Anejom̃. In John Lynch, Malcolm Ross, and Terry Crowley, eds., *The Oceanic Languages*, 723–752. Surrey: Curzon Press.

Lynch, John, Malcolm Ross, and Terry Crowley. eds. 2002. *The Oceanic Languages*. Surrey: Curzon Press.

Maiden, Martin. 1995. *A Linguistic History of Italian*. New York: Longman.

Manzini, Maria Rita, and Leonardo Maria Savoia. 2005. *I dialetti italiani e romanci: Morfosintassi generativa*. 3 Vols. Alessandria: Edizioni dell'Orso.

Martin, Samuel E. 1988. *A Reference Grammar of Japanese*. Rutland, VT: Charles E. Tuttle. Originally published New Haven, CT: Yale University Press (1975).

Martinez, Esther, ed. 1983. *San Juan Pueblo Téwa Dictionary*. Portales, NM: Bishop Publishing Co., a production of the San Juan Pueblo Bilingual Program.

Maryknoll Language Service Center. 2013. *The Maryknoll Taiwanese-English Dictionary and English-Taiwanese Dictionary*. Taichung, Taiwan: Maryknoll. http://www.taiwanesedictionary.org/.

Matthews, Peter. 1972. *Inflectional Morphology: A Theoretical Study Based on Aspects of Latin Verb Conjugation*. Cambridge: Cambridge University Press.

Matthews, R. H. 1904. The Wiradyuri and other languages of New South Wales. *Journal of the Anthropological Institute of Great Britain and Ireland* 34:284–305.

McFarland, Teresa Ann. 2009. The phonology and morphology of Filomeno Mata Totonac. Ph.D. thesis, University of California, Berkeley.

McGinnis, Martha. 2005. On markedness asymmetries in person and number. *Language* 81:699–718.

Meinhof, Carl. 1930. *Die Koranadialekt des Hottentottischen*. Zeitschrift für Eingeborenen-Sprachen: Beiheft 12. Hamburg: Eckhart & Messtorff.

Meira, Sérgio. 1999. A grammar of Tiriyó. Ph.D. thesis, Rice University.

Meira, Sérgio. 2003. 'Addressee effects' in demonstrative systems: The cases of Tiriyó and Brazilian Portuguese. In Friedrich Lenz, ed., *Deictic Conceptualisation of Space, Time and Person*, 3–12. Amsterdam: John Benjamins.

Meisterernst, Barbara. 2012. Number in Chinese: A diachronic study of *zhū* from Han to Wei Jin Nanbeichao Chinese. In Dan Xu, ed., *Plurality and Classifiers across Languages in China*, 143–182. Berlin: Mouton de Gruyter.

Melnar, Lynette. 2004. *Caddo Verb Morphology*. Lincoln: University of Nebraska Press.

Milne, William Stanley. 1913 [1993]. *A Practical Bengali Grammar*. New Delhi: J. Jetley.

Mirikitani, Leatrice T. 1972. *Kapampangan Syntax*. Honolulu: University of Hawai'i Press.

Mühlhäusler, Peter. 1987. Tracing predicate markers in Pacific Pidgin English. *English World Wide* 2:97–121.

Murthy, B. Laliyha, and K. V. Subbarao. 2000. Lexical anaphors and pronouns in Mizo. In Barbara Lust, James W. Gair, K. V. Subbarao, and Kashi Wali, eds., *Language Typology and Syntactic Description*. Vol. 3, *Grammatical Categories and the Lexicon*, 777–840. Berlin: Mouton de Gruyter.

Næss, Åshild, and Brenda Boerger. 2008. Reefs–Santa Cruz as Oceanic: Evidence from the verb complex. *Oceanic Linguistics* 47:185–212.

Nevins, Andrew. 2007. The representation of third person and its consequences for Person-Case effects. *Natural Language and Linguistic Theory* 25:273–313.

Nevins, Andrew. 2008. Cross-modular parallels in the study of phon and phi. In Daniel Harbour, David Adger, and Susana Béjar, eds., *Phi Theory: Phi-Features across Interfaces and Modules*, 329–367. Oxford: Oxford University Press.

Nevins, Andrew. 2011. Marked targets versus marked triggers and impoverishment of the dual. *Linguistic Inquiry* 42:413–444.

Nevskaya, Irina. 2005. Inclusive and exclusive in Turkic languages. In Elena Filimonova, ed., *Clusivity: Typology and Case Studies of the Inclusive–Exclusive Distinction*, 341–358. Amsterdam: John Benjamins.

Ngô, Như Bình. 1999. *Elementary Vietnamese*. Boston, MA: Tuttle Publishing.

Nickel, Klaus. 1994. *Samisk Grammatikk*. Karasjok: Davii Girji.

Norman, Jerry. 1988. *Chinese*. Cambridge: Cambridge University Press.

Noyer, Rolf. 1992. Features, positions and affixes in autonomous morphological structure. Ph.D. thesis, MIT.

Noyer, Rolf. 1998. Impoverishment theory and morphosyntactic markedness. In Steven Lapointe, Diane Brentari, and Patrick Farrell, eds., *Morphology and Its Relation to Phonology and Syntax*, 264–285. Stanford, CA: CSLI Publications.

Oatridge, Des, and Jennifer Oatridge. 1965. *Sentence Final Verbs in Binumarien*. Ukarumpa: Summer Institute of Linguistics. (Language name misspelled as *Binumarein* in original title.).

Obata, Kazuko. 2003. *A Grammar of Bilua: A Papuan Language of the Solomon Islands*. Canberra: Australian National University, Research school of Pacific and Asian Studies.

Oltra-Massuet, Isabel. 2000. On the notion of theme vowel: A new approach to catalan verbal morphology. MIT Occasional Papers in Linguistics 19. Cambridge, MA: MIT, MIT Working Papers in Linguistics.

Onambélé, Christophe. 2012. Vers une grammaire minimaliste de certains aspects syntaxiques de la langue ewondo. Ph.D. thesis, Université Paris 8.

Opgenort, Jean Robert. 2004. *A Grammar of Wambule: Grammar, Lexicon, Texts, and Cultural Survey of a Kiranti Tribe of Eastern Nepal*. Leiden: Brill.

Osborne, C. R. 1974. *The Tiwi Language*. Canberra: Australian Institute of Aboriginal Studies.

Özyürek, Asli. 1998. An analysis of the basic meaning of Turkish demonstratives in face-to-face conversational interaction. In Serge Santi, Isabelle Guaïtella, Christian Cavé, and Gabrielle Konopczynsk, eds., *Oralité et gestualité: Communication multimodale, interaction*, 609–614. Paris: L'Harmattan.

Pantcheva, Marina. 2011. Decomposing Path: The nanosyntax of directional expressions. Ph.D. thesis, Universitetet i Tromsø.

Percus, Orin. 2011. Gender features and interpretation: A case study. *Morphology* 21:167–196.

Pertsova, Katya. 2011. Grounding systematic syncretism in learning. *Linguistic Inquiry* 42:225–266.

Phillips, Colin. 1993. Conditions on agreement in Yimas. In Jonathan D. Bobaljik and Colin Phillips, eds., *Papers on Case and Agreement I*, 173–213. MIT Working Papers in Linguistics 18. Cambridge, MA: MIT, MIT Working Papers in Linguistics.

Pietroski, Paul. 2006. *Events and Semantic Architecture*. Oxford: Oxford University Press.

Popjes, Jack, and Jo Popjes. 1986. Canela-Krahô. In Desmond C. Derbyshire and Geoffrey K. Pullum, eds., *Handbook of Amazonian Languages, Vol. 1*. 128–199. Berlin: Mouton de Gruyter.

Pulleyblank, Edwin. 1995. *Outline of Classical Chinese Grammar*. Vancouver: UBC Press.

Pulu, Jatan. 1978. *Idu Phrase Book*. Shillong: The Director of Information and Public Relations.

Pylkkänen, Liina. 2008. *Introducing Arguments*. Cambridge, MA: MIT Press.

Radkevich, Nina. 2010. On location: The structure of case and adpositions. Ph.D. thesis, University of Connecticut.

Raimy, Eric. 2000. *The Phonology and Morphology of Reduplication*. Berlin: Mouton de Gruyter.

Ray, Sidney. 1933. *A Grammar of the Kiwai Language, Fly Delta, Papua. With a Kiwai Vocabulary by Rev. E. Baxter Riley*. Port Moresby: Edward George Baker, Government Printer.

Redden, James. 1966. Walapai II: Morphology. *International Journal of American Linguistics* 23:141–163.

Regier, Terry, Paul Kay, and Naveen Khetarpal. 2007. Color naming reflects optimal partitions of color space. *Proceedings of the National Academy of Sciences* 104:1436–1441.

Renck, G. L. 1975. *A Grammar of Yagaria*. Canberra: Australian National University.

Řezáč, Milan. 2008. Phi-Agree and theta-related case. In Daniel Harbour, David Adger, and Susna Béjar, eds., *Phi Theory: Phi-Features across Modules and Interfaces*. 83–129. Oxford: Oxford University Press.

Rice, Keren. 1989. *A Grammar of Slave*. Berlin: Mouton de Gruyter.

Riley, Carrol. 1952. Trade Spanish of the Piñaguero Panaré. *Studies in Linguistics* 10:6–11.

Ritter, Elizabeth, and Martina Wiltschko. 2014. The composition of INFL. *Natural Language and Linguistic Theory* 32:1331–1386.

Rodrigues, Aryon. 1990. You and I = neither you nor I: The person system of Tupinambá (Tupí-Guaraní). In Doris Payne, ed., *Amazonian Linguistics: Studies in Lowland South American Languages*, 393–407. Austin: University of Texas Press.

Rood, David. 1976. *Wichita Grammar*. New York: Garland.

Rosen, Carol. 1990. Rethinking Southern Tiwa: The geometry of a triple agreement language. *Language* 66:669–713.

Ross, Malcolm. 2002. Jabêm. In John Lynch, Malcolm Ross, and Terry Crowley, eds., *The Oceanic Languages*, 270–296. Surrey: Curzon Press.

Rostovtsev-Popiel, Alexander. 2012. Grammaticalized affirmativity in Kartvelian. Ph.D. thesis, Goethe University Frankfurt.

Sadler, Louisa. 2011. Indeterminacy, complex features and underspecification. *Morphology* 21:379–417.

Sagey, Elizabeth. 1986. The representation of features and relations in non-linear phonology. Ph.D. thesis, MIT.

Sakel, Jeanette. 2004. *A Grammar of Mosetén*. Berlin: de Gruyter.

San Juan Pueblo Bilingual Program. 1982. *Téwa pehtsiye: Tewa tales, San Juan dialect*.

Sauerland, Uli. 2005. Don't interpret focus! Why a presuppositional account of focus fails and how a presuppositional account of givenness works. In Emar Maier, Corien Bary, and Janneke Huitink, eds., *Proceedings of SuB9*, 370–384. Nijmegen: NCS. http://ncs.ruhosting.nl/sub9/proceedings.html.

Sauerland, Uli, Jan Anderssen, and Kazuko Yatsuhiro. 2008. The plural is semantically unmarked. In Stephan Kepser and Marga Reis, eds., *Linguistic Evidence: Empirical, Theoretical and Computational Perspectives*, 413–433. Berlin: Mouton de Gruyter.

Schadeberg, Thilo. 1977. Der Kohortativ «Dual» und Plural in den Bantusprachen. In Wolfgang Voigt, ed., *XIX. Deutscher Orientalistentag von 28. September bis 4. Oktober 1975 in Freiburg im Breisgau, Vorträge*, 1502–1507. Wiesbaden: Franz Steiner.

Schmidt, Wilhelm. 1919. *Die Personalpronomina in den australischen Sprachen. Mit einem Anhang: Die Interrogativpronomina in den australischen Sprachen*. Vienna: A. Hölder.

Schwarzschild, Roger. 1996. *Pluralities*. Dordrecht: Kluwer.

Scott, Graham. 1978. *The Fore Language of Papua New Guinea*. Canberra: Australian National University.

Searle, John. 1995. *The Construction of Social Reality*. New York: Free Press.

Seiler, Walter. 1985. *Imonda, a Papuan Language*. Canberra: Australian National University, Research School of Pacific Studies.

Siewierska, Anna. 2004. *Person*. Cambridge: Cambridge University Press.

Siewierska, Anna, and Dik Bakker. 2005. Inclusive/Exclusive in free and bound person forms. In Elena Filimonova, ed., *Clusivity: Typology and case studies of the Inclusive–Exclusive Distinction*, 151–178. Amsterdam: John Benjamins.

Sigurðsson, Halldór Ármann. 2004. The syntax of person, tense, and speech features. *Rivista di Linguistica* 16:219–251.

Silva, Amélia Reis. 2003. Pronomes, ordem e ergatividade em Mebengokre (Kayapó). Master's thesis, Universidade Estadual de Campinas. http://aix1.uottawa.ca/asalanov/Docs/tese-reis-silva.pdf.

Silverstein, Michael. 1976. Hierarchy of features and ergativity. In R. M. W. Dixon, ed., *Grammatical Categories in Australian Languages*, 112–171. Canberra: Australian Institutes of Aboriginal Studies.

Simon, Horst. 2005. Only *you*? Philological investigations into the alleged inclusive–exclusive distinction the second person plural. In Elena Filimonova, ed., *Clusivity:*

Typology and Case Studies of the Inclusive–Exclusive Distinction, 113–150. Amsterdam: John Benjamins.

Simpson, Jane. 2002. From common ground to syntactic construction: Associated path in Warlpiri. In N. J. Enfield, ed., *Ethnosyntax: Explorations in Grammar and Culture*, 287–309. Oxford: Oxford University Press.

Sivan, Reuven, and Edward Levenston. 1975. *The New Bantam-Megiddo Hebrew and English Dictionary*. New York: Bantam Books.

Smythe, W. E. 1948–49. *Elementary Grammar of the Gumbáiŋgar Language (North Coast, N.S.W.)*. Monographs Sydney: Australian National Research Council.

Sohn, Ho-Min. 1999. *The Korean Language*. Cambridge: Cambridge University Press.

Spector, Benjamin. 2007. Aspects of the pragmatics of plural morphology: On higher order implicatures. In Uli Sauerland and Penka Stateva, eds., *Presupposition and Implicature in Compositional Semantics*, 243–281. Basingstoke: Palgrave Macmillan.

Speirs, Randall H. 1966. Some aspects of the structure of Rio Grande Tewa. Ph.D. thesis, State University of New York, Buffalo.

Sprott, Robert W. 1992. Jemez syntax. Ph.D. thesis, University of Chicago.

Stirtz, Timothy. 2011. A grammar of Gaahmg: A Nilo-Saharan language of Sudan. Ph.D. thesis, LOT.

Sušnik, Branislava. 1977. *Lengua Maskoy: Su hablar – su pensar – su vivencia*. Asunción del Paraguay: Muséo Etnográfico "Andrés Barbero."

Svenonius, Peter. 2010. Spatial P in English. In Guglielmo Cinque and Luigi Rizzi, eds., *Mapping Spatial PPs: The Cartography of Syntactic Structures, Vol. 6*, 127–160. Oxford: Oxford University Press.

Sweet, Henry. 1896. *The Student's Dictionary of Anglo-Saxon*. Oxford: Clarendon Press.

Thieberger, Nicholas. 2006. *A Grammar of South Efate: An Oceanic Language of Vanuatu*. Honolulu: University of Hawai'i Press.

Thomas, David. 1955. Three analyses of the Ilocano pronoun system. *Word* 11:204–208.

Topuria, Varlam. 1965. Gardamavali dialekt'is sak'itxisatvis svanurši k'iloebis monacemta mixedvit [On the question of transitional dialects according to data from Svan dialects]. *Tbilisis Saxelmc'ipo Universit'et'is Šromebi* 114:61–72.

Trommer, Jochen. 1999. Morphology consuming syntax' resources: Generation and parsing in a Minimalist version of Distributed Morphology. In *Proceedings of the ESSLI Workshop on Resource Logic and Minimalist Grammars, Utrecht*. http://home.uni-leipzig.de/jtrommer/papers/ma.pdf.

Trommer, Jochen. 2002. The interaction of morphology and syntax in affix order. In Geert Booij and Jaap van Marle, eds., *Yearbook of Morphology 2002*, 283–324. Dordrecht: Kluwer.

Trommer, Jochen. 2008. Direction marking and case in Menominee. In Daniel Harbour, David Adger, and Susana Béjar, eds., *Phi Theory: Phi-Features across Modules and Interfaces*, 221–250. Oxford: Oxford University Press.

Tryon, Darrell. 1976. *New Hebrides Languages: An Internal Classification*. Canberra: Australian National University.

Tryon, Darrell. 1994. Language contact and contact-induced language change in the Eastern Outer Islands, Solomon Islands. In Tom Dutton and Darrell Tryon, eds., *Language Contact and Change in the Austronesian World*, 611–648. Berlin: Mouton de Gruyter.

Tryon, Darrell. 2002. Buma. In John Lynch, Malcolm Ross, and Terry Crowley, eds., *The Oceanic Languages*, 573–586. Surrey: Curzon Press.

Tuite, Kevin. 1998. A short descriptive grammar of the Svan language. Ms., Université de Montréal. www.uni-jena.de/unijenamedia/Downloads/faculties/phil/kaukasiologie/Svan%5Bslightlyrevised%5D.pdf.

Tuomela, Raimo. 2009. Collective intentions and Game Theory. *Journal of Philosophy* 106:292–300.

Tuomela, Raimo, and Kaarlo Miller. 1988. We-intentions. *Philosophical Studies* 53:367–389.

Uhlenbeck, E. M. 1968. Personal pronouns and pronominal suffixes in Old Javanese. *Lingua* 21:466–482.

Unger, Ulrich. 1987. Grammatik des Klassischen Chinesisch (volume I). Ms., Münster.

Unruh, Ernesto, and Hannes Kalisch. 2003. Enlhet-Enenlhet: Una familia lingüística chaqueña. *Thule, Rivista italiana di studi americanistici* 14/15:207–231. http://www.enlhet.net/pdf/nne28-enlhet-enenlhet.pdf.

Valentine, J. Randolph. 2001. *Nishnaabemwin Reference Grammar*. Toronto: University of Toronto Press.

van der Wilden, Jaap. 1976. Simplicity and detail in Kemtuk predication. *Irian: Bulletin of Irian Jaya Development* 2:59–84.

van Driem, George. 1987. *A Grammar of Limbu*. Berlin: Mouton de Gruyter.

van Driem, George. 1993. *A Grammar of Dumi*. Berlin: Mouton de Gruyter.

Verratti, Vittore. 1968. *Fonologia e morfologia del volgare abruzzese*. Lanciano: Editrice Itinerari.

Wares, Alan. 1956. Suffixation in Tarascan. Master's thesis, Indiana University.

Watanabe, Akira. 2013. Person–number interaction: Impoverishment and natural classes. *Linguistic Inquiry* 44:469–492.

Watanabe, Akira. 2014. Valuation as deletion: Inverse in Jemez and Kiowa. *Natural Language and Linguistic Theory* 33:1387–1420.

Watkins, Laurel J. 1984. *A Grammar of Kiowa*. With the assistance of Parker McKenzie. Lincoln: University of Nebraska Press.

Wechsler, Stephen. 2010. What 'you' and 'I' mean to each other: Person marking, self-ascription, and theory of mind. *Language* 86:332–365.

Weissenborn, Jürgen, and Wolfgang Klein, eds. 1982. *Here and There: Cross-Linguistic Studies on Deixis and Demonstration*. Amsterdam: John Benjamins.

Wilkins, David. 1999. The 1999 demonstrative questionnaire: 'This' and 'that' in comparative perspective. In David Wilkins, ed., *Manual for the 1999 Field Season*, 1–24. Nijmegen: Max Planck Institute for Psycholinguistics.

Wilkins, David, and Deborah Hill. 1995. When "go" means "come": Questioning the basicness of basic motion verbs. *Cognitive Linguistics* 6:209–259.

Williams, Edwin. 1994. Remarks on lexical knowledge. *Lingua* 92:7–34.

Wilson, Darryl. 1974. Suena grammar. SIL. http://www-01.sil.org/mean to each other-pacific/png/abstract.asp?id=12746.

Wilson, Darryl. 1980. A brief comparative grammar of Zia and Suena (Papua New Guinea). SIL. http://www-01.sil.org/pacific/png/abstract.asp?id=50265.

Wolf, John, and Ida Wolf. 1967. *Beginning Waray-Waray, Vol. 1*. Ithaca, NY: Cornell University Press.

Wright, Joseph. 1899. *A Primer of the Gothic Language: With Grammar, Notes, and Glossary*. Oxford: Clarendon Press.

Yoshida, Shuji. 1981. Kūkan ninshiki no ruikeika ni tsuite [On typology of spatial recognition]. *Kikan Jinruigaku* 12–13:80–129.

Yumitani, Yukihiro. 1998. A phonology and morphology of Jemez Towa. Ph.D. thesis, University of Kansas.

Zilles, Ana. 2005. The development of a new pronoun: The linguistic and social embedding of *a gente* in Brazilian Portuguese. *Language Variation and Change* 17:19–53.

Zwarts, Joost. 1995. The semantics of relative location. Ms., OTS, Utrecht University.

Zwicky, Arnold. 1977. Hierarchies of person. In Woodford A. Beach and Samuel E. Fox, eds., *Papers from the Thirteenth Regional Meeting of the Chicago Linguistic Society*, 714–733. Chicago: University of Chicago, Chicago Linguistic Society.

Zwicky, Arnold. 1985. How to describe inflection. In *Mary Niepokuj et al., eds., Proceedings of the Eleventh Annual Meeting of the Berkeley Linguistics Society*, 372–386. Berkeley: University of California, Berkeley Linguistics Society.

Index

Abruzzese, 54
acquisition. *See* learnability and learners
Afrikaans, 119
Afroasiatic, 115–118, 123, 158, 161, 162, 166
agreement, 2, 4, 10–11, 23–25, 28–29, 37, 39–40, 44–50, 52–54, 60–62, 86, 93, 96–97, 104–105, 109, 114–118, 120, 127, 129–130, 141, 154, 158–164, 166–168, 170, 185, 188, 195, 201–202, 211, 213, 231, 236–243, 249. *See also* base position, flanking, linearization, splitting, straddling
Äiwoo, 144, 148, 155
Akhvakh, 283n4
Akkadian, 116–117
Algonquian, 18, 102, 105, 266n5, 268n10
allomorphy, 107, 109–111, 122, 242, 273n9, 275n5
alpha rules, 204, 273n9
Anejoṁ, 24–25, 33
Anglo-Saxon, 204
animacy, 37, 60–64, 67, 68, 78, 170, 184, 196, 206–208, 243, 268n10, 268n12, 273n10, 281n12
approximative, 142, 144, 219, 222, 263
Arabic, 156–161, 162, 272n8, 275n5
Armenian, 174
augmented, 57–58, 141, 144, 148, 151–152, 155, 213–216, 223, 257, 262, 266n7, 268n9, 286n3
axiom of extension, 82–84, 87–88
Aymara, 138, 148

baboons, 230–231
Baerman, M., 15–17, 235–237
Bahing, 111–113, 224
base position (for agreement), 160–163
Basque, 123
Bayso, 221
Béjar, S., 50, 192–195
Bengali, 53
Biak, 275n5
Bickel, B., 34–35
Bilua, 14, 18, 26, 111–113
Binumarien, 11
Bislama, 103–106, 196, 224–228
bivalence. *See* valence
Bobaljik, J., 17–18, 147, 197, 259
bottom elements. *See* zero elements
Brazilian Portuguese, 48–49, 62, 93, 178, 246
Brown, D., 15–17, 235–237
Bulgarian, 58, 171, 178, 180
Buma, 14, 265n3

Caddo, 29, 36, 47, 242–247, 277n2, 281n12
Canela-Krahô, 52, 96
Catalan, 58, 171, 174, 178, 180–181
Cayley's theorem, 194
Cebuano, 52, 56, 96, 172–173, 180
Celle di Bulgheria, 174
Chinese, Classical, 267n6
Choctaw, 136, 274n1
choric *we,* 68–70, 259
combinatorics, 4–5, 65, 189, 192, 193, 195, 197, 220–222, 228, 231, 250. *See also* filters, geometry

Comanche, 141, 267n1
composition
  morphological, 9, 16, 101–121, 164, 166, 175, 196, 212, 224, 226–228, 237–239, 242
  semantic, 3, 5, 65–66, 78, 81, 86, 89, 93, 130, 147–148, 155, 179–181, 188–189, 197, 199, 211, 216–221, 224, 228, 232, 249–258, 262
commutativity, 5, 66, 75, 78, 189
Construction Grammar, 39
conjunction, 1, 5, 66, 187–189, 197, 200–201, 217–219, 233
convexity, 221–222, 257
Corbett, G., 15–17, 68, 235–237
Cowper, E., 227, 285n7
Cysouw, M., 16–17, 33, 36–37, 259

Damana, 226–227, 285n7
Damin, 32, 55, 62–63, 171, 180
Daonda, 52
decomposition. *See* composition, morphological
deletion, 15, 118, 195–196, 202–205, 216, 244, 282n18, 282n19
diachrony, 4, 8, 19, 29, 33–35, 38, 110, 114–116, 120, 173–176, 185, 203–204, 241, 284n6
differential object marking, 60–62
directionals, 2, 45, 52–54, 56, 58, 60, 96, 171, 174, 180–181, 235, 273n9
discontiguous. *See* linearization
distance (physical, social, empathetic), 54, 69, 169–170, 172, 175–179, 181, 273n9, 277n5, 277n7, 278n8, 278n9
Djanggu, 55
domain
  partitional, 2, 40, 44–47, 49–50, 52, 54, 56, 60, 79, 81, 102, 109, 115, 117–118, 172–173, 192, 194, 221
  semantic, 73, 78, 80, 86, 88, 93, 97, 100, 155, 171, 179–180, 183, 188, 217–218
dominance, 105, 183
Dresher, E.,100
Dumi, 205–206, 209–211
Dutch, 46
Dyirringany, 110

egocentricity, 67, 71, 74
Elseng, 55, 171
empty set, 66, 72–73, 80, 84–86, 88, 91, 95–97, 199, 257, 260–261
English, 10, 18, 23, 32, 35, 45–47, 49, 56, 58, 68, 70, 79, 104, 124, 133, 141, 148, 151–152, 155, 171, 173, 182–183, 212, 221, 233
Enlhet-Enenhlet, 37, 50, 55
epistemic alignment, 283n4
evolution, 5, 218, 228–232
Ewondo, 141, 155, 221, 256

factorization, 190, 194
Fijian, 263
filters, 1, 3, 65, 78, 190–191, 194, 197, 228
flanking, 159–162, 166, 181–182, 276n11
focal point, 212, 215
Fore, 178, 180, 277n7
fossils, 231–232
Frampton, J., 200, 203–205
French, 11–12, 46, 48, 69, 114, 181–182, 245–246
Fula, 199, 201–203
functionalism, 8, 29, 31, 35–38, 45, 50, 69, 103, 123, 241
functional hierarchy, 46, 64, 47, 71, 74, 76–77, 127, 153–168, 181–184, 269n4, 276n9
functional pressures. *See* functionalism

Gaahmg, 148, 212, 275n5
Gahuku, 120, 262
gaps, lexical, 47
gender, 23, 62, 48, 106, 114, 116–117, 122, 157–158, 182, 210, 267n4, 268n10
geometry, 1, 3, 65, 78, 191–197, 222, 228, 280
Georgian, 16, 58–59, 69, 125–127, 171, 177, 181, 209, 235–237, 274n16
German, 46, 47, 63–64, 93, 177, 178, 180, 200, 203–205, 262, 280n11
Germanic, 200, 203–205, 218
Girawa, 10–11, 280n11

Gothic, 204
Gumbáiŋgar, 108–11, 224
Gundungaurra, 110

Halia, 14, 265n3
Halle, M., 197–199
Harley, H., 68, 191–192, 213–216, 225–228, 285n6, 285n7
Hasse diagrams, explanation, 130–133
Hawaiian, 141, 150–152, 155
Hebrew, 116–117, 123, 157, 162–163, 166, 280n8
Hiaki, 59–60
history. *See* diachrony
Hocąk, 49, 57–58, 144, 171, 256
honorificity, 69, 115, 177, 244–247, 265n4
Hopi, 101–102, 105, 124, 156
hortative, 141, 238, 265n4
Humboldt, W. von, 45–46
Hungarian, 265n4

i, definition, 41
Icelandic, 115
iconicity, 106
Idu, 170
Imonda, 50–52, 96
impoverishment. *See* deletion
integers, 5, 231
intentions, joint, 68–69, 231
Italian, 11, 47, 114, 164–166, 174, 177, 184. *See also* Abruzzese and Celle di Bulgheria

Jabêm, 27–28
Janggu, 55
Japanese, 174, 177–178, 273n9
Jarawa, 52, 54, 76, 133, 221
join, 75, 82, 131–133, 250, 263

Kapampangan, 151–152
Kartvelian, 58, 171
Kawésqar, 47, 267n6, 277n2
Kawi, 267n6, 269n6
Kemtuk, 277n2
kin terms, 47, 122, 244, 247, 273n10
Kiowa, 14, 18–19, 27–29, 49, 56, 104–106, 166–168, 195–197, 203, 206, 210, 222, 223, 244, 267n8

Kiowa-Tanoan, 142, 166, 266n8, 273n14
Kiwai, 136, 226
Koasati, 263
Korafe, 172, 180, 184, 278n10
Korean, 172, 181
Kratzer, A., 197
Kunwinjku, 188, 211–216
Kwak'wala/Kwakiutl, 170, 274n1

Lardil, 55
lattices, 1–5, 40, 65–67, 72–76, 80–82, 84–98, 126, 129–155, 182–183, 187, 203, 212, 221, 223, 229–230, 232, 249, 263§
Latin, 174
Laz, 56, 58–59, 125, 177, 180
learnability and learners, 13, 15, 39, 55, 92–93, 126, 205, 219–220
Lenakel, 14, 265n3
Lengua-Maskoy, 55
Lexical Complementarity, 80, 90–91, 94–95, 96–97, 142, 268n13, 269n6
Limbu, 107–109, 111–113, 197, 224–228, 285n6
linearization, 77, 130, 153–154, 156–162, 165–167, 181–185, 201–202, 272n8, 276n9, 276n10, 278n10, 280n8, 284n6. *See also* prefixes and suffixes
Lovono, 239–242

Mam, 102, 110–111, 113, 118–119, 199, 201, 224
Manam, 170
Mandarin, 134, 138, 147, 275n5
Maskelynes, 148
mass *you*, 70, 259
Mebengokre, 221
Melanesian Pidgin. *See* Bislama and Tok Pisin
Mele-Fila, 142
Menominee, 205–209, 210, 268n10
metaparadigm, 21–23, 31, 33, 196, 204, 242
metasyncretism, 6, 15–16, 93, 235, 237, 242, 244
Migrelian, 59, 125, 177

Min Nan, 138, 155, 221
minimal, 58, 151, 155, 213–216, 221, 266n7, 268n9
minus. *See* valence
Mirror Theory, 77, 130, 153–154, 157, 159, 162, 276n9
Mizo, 170
Mohawk, 277n3
Mokilese, 124, 148, 212, 226, 284n5
monopartition, 49, 59–64, 81, 170–171, 180
Morwap, 55, 171
Mosetén, 170–171, 278n8
Mussau, 142, 148, 274n3

natural classes, 7–9, 17, 38, 64, 92, 103, 111, 121, 125–128, 195, 200–206, 239, 258, 280n11
negative. *See* valence
Ngunawal, 110
Nichols, J., 34–35
Nimboran, 52, 138
Nishnaabemwin, 18, 105–106, 108
noncommutativity. *See* commutativity
Noyer, R., 9–10, 161, 194, 200–201, 210, 213–216
Nubian, 33

o, definition 41
obviation, 206, 266n5, 281n12, 282n1
Oneida, 115, 119, 123
'only inclusive' pattern, 96
ontogeny, 70, 230
ontology, 3, 41–42, 65–72, 74, 97, 130, 132, 147, 155, 195, 232, 250, 255, 259
operations
  lattice-theoretic, 3, 5, 66–67, 72, 75, 81, 87, 217–220, 228, 230
  morphological and phonological, 13, 15, 17, 29, 31, 46, 49, 195
!Ora, 106, 108
order of composition. *See* composition
overgeneration, 1, 5, 103, 121, 128, 188, 190, 199, 280n9

Palauan, 53–54, 180, 184
Panaré pidgin Spanish, 52

paradigms, 2, 7, 10, 15–35, 38, 39, 42, 44, 49, 63, 125, 130, 162–163, 196, 204, 211, 237, 242–244
parameters, 3, 17, 65–66, 70, 78–79, 81, 86, 89, 92, 93, 98, 129, 142, 154, 178, 187–188, 192, 197, 199, 205, 211, 222–224, 260, 279n4
Partition Element Problem, 42, 97–100
Partition Problem, 3, 40, 43, 65, 73, 78–95, 98, 185, 224, 247, 261
Paumarí, 120–121
Person Case Constraint, 37, 125–127, 167
Pietroski, P., 219
Pipil, 147, 148, 275n5
Pirahã, 52, 133
Polish, 115
polyploidy, 45, 79
Portuguese. *See* Brazilian Portuguese
poverty of the stimulus, 15
power sets, 3, 65–67, 71–73, 80, 131, 155, 230
presuppositions, 77, 262–263, 278n8
primitivity, problem of, 190, 194, 227
privativity. *See* valence
prefixes, 4, 61–62, 104–105, 110, 113, 117, 120–121, 123–125, 130, 158–168, 176–177, 195–196, 201–203, 209, 240, 243
probable grammars, 19, 50
Punda, 52

Qawasqar. *See* Kawéskar

recursion. *See* value recursion
redundancy, 1, 10, 75, 82–83, 87, 89, 126, 189–190, 203, 220, 251, 253
restitution
  of atoms, 150–151
  of partitions, 7, 21, 38
Ritter, E., 68, 191–192, 213–216, 225–228, 285n6, 285n7
robustness, 6, 30, 34, 38–40, 48, 101–102, 108, 110, 119, 124, 156, 203–204, 235, 241, 284n4
Romanian, 114
Russian, 9, 62, 69

Index 311

Salt-Yui, 269n6
Sámi, 177–178
Samoan Plantation pidgin English, 52
Sanapaná, 44, 55–56, 144, 171
Sandawe, 54
Sanskrit, 136, 221, 275n5
Sanuma, 29, 238–239
Satawal, 170
Sauerland, U., 17–18
Sawa, 55
Scots, 54
Silverstein, M., 8–9
Simog, 52
Skou, 55
Slave, 178
social cognition/ontology, 35–36, 70, 188, 195, 230–232
Solomon Islands' Pijin, 103
South Efate, 14, 265n3
South Australian, 110
Southeast Asian languages, 47
Southern Tiwa, 28–29, 167
Sowanda, 52
Spanish, 11–12, 16, 47, 60, 114, 164, 166, 178
splitting (of agreement), 159–162, 276n11
straddling, 158–162, 168, 276n11
subparadigm, 21–22, 30–31, 33, 35, 44
subpartition, 39, 44, 64
subsumption, 3–4, 10, 18, 23, 80, 110, 113, 115, 122–125, 128, 133, 142, 156, 181, 197–199, 224, 226, 251, 253, 268n13
Successive Division Algorithm, 100
Suena, 26–27, 33
suffixes, 4, 21, 57, 61, 105, 108, 115–117, 119, 121–123, 125, 130, 147–148, 156–164, 166, 172, 184, 201–208, 210, 226, 235, 239, 272n8, 273n13, 274n16, 286n1
superposition, 7–8, 18–32, 35, 38, 39, 237, 239–242
suppletion, 11, 16, 101–102, 212, 226, 286n4

surfeit of the stimulus, 15
Sursurunga, 124, 142, 148
Svan, 123, 125–127
Swahili, 276n9
syncretisms, 2, 6–7, 9–19, 23–30, 36–38, 39–40, 45–46, 62, 93, 104–105, 115, 156, 195–196, 200, 203–205, 220, 235–239, 241–244

Tabu, 55
Tacaná, 201
Tanema, 239–242
Tarascan, 115, 124
Teanu, 29, 36–37, 239–242
Tewa, 60–62, 167
Thurawal, 110
Tigrinya, 116–117
Timbira, 138, 144, 148, 155, 221
Tiriyó, 54, 178
Tiwa. *See* Southern Tiwa
Tiwi, 18, 23–25
Tok Pisin, 8–9, 52, 80, 103, 111–113, 138
Tongan, 245–247
Totonac, 285n7
Trommer, J., 205–211
Tukang Besi, 136
Tupinambá, 36–37
Turkic, 141
Turkish, 176, 183–184
typology, 6, 9, 15–16, 34, 36, 45, 70–71, 86, 96, 102, 123–124, 156, 181, 199, 205, 221, 229, 235, 237

u, definition, 41
uninterpretable features, 44, 142, 154, 222–223
union, 75, 82–83, 97, 132, 152
Utupua, 241

valence, 4–6, 10, 66–67, 80–81, 102, 107, 126, 180, 188, 191, 193–197, 199, 200–211, 209, 211, 213–217, 220, 222–229, 259–262, 269n1, 283n3. *See also* value recursion
value recursion, 129–130, 142–144, 155, 218–219, 222–223, 256, 283n3

variables
  over features/values, 200, 206, 209–210, 273n14, 283n4
  semantic, 60, 65–66, 73, 76–78, 80, 86, 88, 97, 100, 123, 133–134, 138, 179–180, 183, 188–189, 276n8
Vietnamese, 122–123

Wai Wai, 14, 265n3
Walapai, 136
Walmatjari, 25–26, 130, 156–161, 276n10
Wambule, 174–175, 177, 183–184
Waray-Waray, 52, 53, 59, 172–173
Warekena, 144
Waris, 52
Warlpiri, 59–60, 170
Washo, 53–54
Watanabe, A., 201–203
Wechsler, S., 197

Wichita, 47, 60, 170, 243
Winnebago. *See* Hocąk
winnowing, 80, 86, 93, 97, 100, 260–261

Y-model, 13, 101
Yagaria, 119–120, 122
Yaweyuha, 120
Yiddish, 205
Yimas, 46–48, 117–118, 123, 136, 159–161, 166, 168, 221, 263

zero elements (of lattices), 73, 80, 91, 96–98, 132–133, 138, 230, 249–257, 259–261
zero morphemes, 112–113, 121, 205, 225–228, 243, 267n8, 282n18, 284n5, 285n7
Zia, 14, 265n3
Zwicky's problem, 1–3, 17–18, 36, 40, 49, 67, 74, 105, 190, 193, 197, 280n9

Linguistic Inquiry Monographs

Samuel Jay Keyser, general editor

1. *Word Formation in Generative Grammar*, Mark Aronoff
2. *Syntax: A Study of Phrase Structure*, Ray Jackendoff
3. *Recent Transformational Studies in European Languages*, Samuel Jay Keyser, editor
4. *Studies in Abstract Phonology*, Edmund Gussmann
5. *An Encyclopedia of AUX: A Study of Cross-Linguistic Equivalence*, Susan Steele
6. *Some Concepts and Consequences of the Theory of Government and Binding*, Noam Chomsky
7. *The Syntax of Words*, Elisabeth O. Selkirk
8. *Syllable Structure and Stress in Spanish: A Nonlinear Analysis*, James W. Harris
9. *CV Phonology: A Generative Theory of the Syllable*, George N. Clements and Samuel Jay Keyser
10. *On the Nature of Grammatical Relations*, Alec P. Marantz
11. *A Grammar of Anaphora*, Joseph Aoun
12. *Logical Form: Its Structure and Derivation*, Robert May
13. *Barriers*, Noam Chomsky
14. *On the Definition of Word*, Anna-Maria Di Sciullo and Edwin Williams
15. *Japanese Tone Structure*, Janet Pierrehumbert and Mary E. Beckman
16. *Relativized Minimality*, Luigi Rizzi
17. *Types of Ā-Dependencies*, Guglielmo Cinque
18. *Argument Structure*, Jane Grimshaw
19. *Locality: A Theory and Some of Its Empirical Consequences*, Maria Rita Manzini
20. *Indefinites*, Molly Diesing
21. *Syntax of Scope*, Joseph Aoun and Yen-hui Audrey Li
22. *Morphology by Itself: Stems and Inflectional Classes*, Mark Aronoff
23. *Thematic Structure in Syntax*, Edwin Williams
24. *Indices and Identity*, Robert Fiengo and Robert May
25. *The Antisymmetry of Syntax*, Richard S. Kayne

26. *Unaccusativity: At the Syntax–Lexical Semantics Interface*, Beth Levin and Malka Rappaport Hovav
27. *Lexico-Logical Form: A Radically Minimalist Theory*, Michael Brody
28. *The Architecture of the Language Faculty*, Ray Jackendoff
29. *Local Economy*, Chris Collins
30. *Surface Structure and Interpretation*, Mark Steedman
31. *Elementary Operations and Optimal Derivations*, Hisatsugu Kitahara
32. *The Syntax of Nonfinite Complementation: An Economy Approach*, Željko Bošković
33. *Prosody, Focus, and Word Order*, Maria Luisa Zubizarreta
34. *The Dependencies of Objects*, Esther Torrego
35. *Economy and Semantic Interpretation*, Danny Fox
36. *What Counts: Focus and Quantification*, Elena Herburger
37. *Phrasal Movement and Its Kin*, David Pesetsky
38. *Dynamic Antisymmetry*, Andrea Moro
39. *Prolegomenon to a Theory of Argument Structure*, Ken Hale and Samuel Jay Keyser
40. *Essays on the Representational and Derivational Nature of Grammar: The Diversity of Wh-Constructions*, Joseph Aoun and Yen-hui Audrey Li
41. *Japanese Morphophonemics: Markedness and Word Structure*, Junko Ito and Armin Mester
42. *Restriction and Saturation*, Sandra Chung and William A. Ladusaw
43. *Linearization of Chains and Sideward Movement*, Jairo Nunes
44. *The Syntax of (In)dependence*, Ken Safir
45. *Interface Strategies: Optimal and Costly Computations*, Tanya Reinhart
46. *Asymmetry in Morphology*, Anna Maria Di Sciullo
47. *Relators and Linkers: The Syntax of Predication, Predicate Inversion, and Copulas*, Marcel den Dikken
48. *On the Syntactic Composition of Manner and Motion*, Maria Luisa Zubizarreta and Eunjeong Oh
49. *Introducing Arguments*, Liina Pylkkänen
50. *Where Does Binding Theory Apply?*, David Lebeaux
51. *Locality in Minimalist Syntax*, Thomas S. Stroik
52. *Distributed Reduplication*, John Frampton
53. *The Locative Syntax of Experiencers*, Idan Landau
54. *Why Agree? Why Move?: Unifying Agreement-Based and Discourse-Configurational Languages*, Shigeru Miyagawa
55. *Locality in Vowel Harmony*, Andrew Nevins
56. *Uttering Trees*, Norvin Richards
57. *The Syntax of Adjectives*, Guglielmo Cinque
58. *Arguments as Relations*, John Bowers

59. *Agreement and Head Movement*, Ian Roberts
60. *Localism versus Globalism in Morphology and Phonology*, David Embick
61. *Provocative Syntax*, Phil Branigan
62. *Anaphora and Language Design*, Eric J. Reuland
63. *Indefinite Objects: Scrambling, Choice Functions, and Differential Marking*, Luis López
64. *A Syntax of Substance*, David Adger
65. *Subjunctive Conditionals*, Michela Ippolito
66. *Russian Case Morphology and the Syntactic Categories*, David Pesetsky
67. *Classical NEG Raising: An Essay on the Syntax of Negation*, Chris Collins and Paul M. Postal
68. *Agreement and Its Failures*, Omer Preminger
69. *Voice and v: Lessons from Acehnese*, Julie Anne Legate
70. *(Re)labeling*, Carlo Cecchetto and Caterina Donati
71. *A Two-Tiered Theory of Control*, Idan Landau
72. *Concepts, Syntax, and Their Interface: Tanya Reinhart's Theta System*, Martin Everaert, Marijana Marelj, and Eric Reuland, editors
73. *Contiguity Theory*, Norvin Richards
74. *Impossible Persons*, Daniel Harbour